PRAISE FOR *JAILCARE*

"There were pregnant women in every prison and jail I have been held in
or have visited. Carolyn Sufrin holds the fates of these women and their
children up to the light and reveals the complexity of motherhood and
reproductive justice in the most difficult circumstances—behind bars.
Jailcare is a moving and galvanizing story of pregnant women in jail and
those responsible for their health. It is essential reading for anyone who
cares about women, children, and justice."

Piper Kerman, author of *Orange Is the New Black: My Year in a
Women's Prison*

"*Jailcare* delves deep into the complex and tragic realities of mass
incarceration in a large city jail for women. We follow the author, an
anthropologist and jail physician, hard at work as a caring and critically
reflexive 'double agent.' Sufrin's clients are revolving-door jail inmates—
women with multiple medical, social, psychological, and addiction
problems—for whom a few nights or weeks in jail is about as stable a home
place as it gets. Jails, like most other penal institutions, produce both
violence and care. Sufrin's captivating, beautifully told, but extremely
disturbing stories of pregnant women and mothers in jail and the people
charged with caring for them indict a cruel society that all but coerces
women living on the extreme margins of urban life to commit a crime in
exchange for transient but necessary medical and reproductive care. This
stunning book is a must-read not only for professionals in the field, but for
every citizen who does not understand the consequences of mass
incarceration for women, their children, their caretakers, and the society
that allows it. Sufrin makes clear that we cannot ignore our own complicity
in the Kafkaesque system."

Nancy Scheper-Hughes, author of *Death without Weeping: The Violence
of Everyday Life in Brazil*

"Carolyn Sufrin's unique positionality as a physician/anthropologist delivering healthcare to pregnant women in the San Francisco County Jail renders visible the coercive and bureaucratically litigious contortions of caregiving for 'unworthy' mothers. Her ethnography of the judgmentally triaged, hypermedicalized practices of a clinical oasis within the carceral services documents genuine expressions of solitary care by guards wielding arbitrarily discretionary punitive power. It serves as a condemnation of our society, in which indigent, addicted mothers too often access prenatal care only behind bars."

Philippe Bourgois, author of *In Search of Respect: Selling Crack in El Barrio* and coauthor of *Righteous Dopefiend*

"In this remarkable and vividly descriptive ethnography, Carolyn Sufrin has given us a fresh and sophisticated exploration of the contemporary intersection between custody and treatment, punishment and 'care.' Disturbing and unforgettable, *Jailcare* is a must-read for anyone concerned with the fate of women in the U.S. criminal justice system."

Lorna A. Rhodes, author of *Total Confinement: Madness and Reason in the Maximum Security Prison*

"The art of mass incarceration has been finely tuned in the United States, such that more women are incarcerated there than in any other nation in the world—more than Russia, China, and India combined. The devastating conditions that some women experience behind bars, including medical neglect, are rarely seen or documented. Sufrin opens Pandora's box and provides an absorbing, accessible, and stunning view of women's reproductive health within the criminal justice system. *Jailcare* offers a rare, substantive engagement on the intersections of sex, race, and class behind bars and exposes the strange and troubling paradoxes that attend pregnancy and reproductive health behind bars."

Michele Bratcher Goodwin, Director of the Center for Biotechnology and Global Health Policy, University of California, Irvine School of Law

Jailcare

Jailcare

FINDING THE SAFETY NET
FOR WOMEN BEHIND BARS

Carolyn Sufrin

UNIVERSITY OF CALIFORNIA PRESS

University of California Press, one of the most distinguished university presses in the United States, enriches lives around the world by advancing scholarship in the humanities, social sciences, and natural sciences. Its activities are supported by the UC Press Foundation and by philanthropic contributions from individuals and institutions. For more information, visit www.ucpress.edu.

University of California Press
Oakland, California

Library of Congress Cataloging-in-Publication Data

Names: Sufrin, Carolyn, 1975– author.
Title: Jailcare : finding the safety net for women behind bars / Carolyn Sufrin.
Description: Oakland, California : University of California Press, [2017] | Includes bibliographical references and index.
Identifiers: LCCN 2016054036 (print) | LCCN 2016058048 (ebook) | ISBN 9780520288669 (cloth : alk. paper) | ISBN 9780520288683 (pbk. : alk. paper) | ISBN 9780520963559 (Epub)
Subjects: LCSH: Women prisoners—Medical care—California—San Francisco. | Pregnant women—Medical care—California—San Francisco. | Reproductive health services—California—San Francisco.
Classification: LCC HV8738 .S84 2017 (print) | LCC HV8738 (ebook) | DDC 365/.6670820979461—dc23
LC record available at https://lccn.loc.gov/2016054036

Manufactured in the United States of America

25 24 23 22 21 20
10 9 8 7 6 5 4 3 2

For Shirley

Contents

Acknowledgments

When I first heard the steel door at the entry to the San Francisco jail click open nine years ago, I could never have imagined that it would lead to such a profound professional and personal transformation. I certainly could not have predicted that I, recently finished with my Ob / Gyn training, would return to school and someday write a book about this jail. But the people I met in jail compelled me to do so. It took only a few clinic sessions of my providing care to women in the San Francisco jail to realize there was something unsettlingly larger going on in that clinic than just an Ob / Gyn seeing patients. To the many incarcerated women who let me into their lives beyond the terms of a doctor-patient relationship, I offer my deepest thanks. With their tenacity, their resilience, their sense of humor, and their self-reflection, these women have left a mark on my spirit. The woman I call Evelyn remains in my thoughts daily. These women continue to inspire me to work for reproductive justice and criminal justice system reform.

To maintain anonymity, I cannot name the many people working at the San Francisco jail who allowed me to cross the lines of professional, personal, and research relationships. I wish to thank Sheriff's Department administrators and deputies for welcoming my research presence as an ethnographer. The jail clinic staff, in particular, were such important presences in my life for the seven years I lived in San Francisco. They were colleagues, mentors, and friends before they were informants. Conducting ethnographic fieldwork in this setting brought me even closer to them, and I remain inspired by their dedication. Only one day a week of doctoring at the jail emotionally exhausted me, whereas they do this work full time. To Joe Goldenson and to the clinician I call Vivian, I am particularly indebted. I have learned so much from the two of them about how to be a better physician, about how to be an unwavering advocate for the most marginalized people in society, while still maintaining a sense of humor in the face of the tragedy and complexity we encounter.

I have been fortunate to receive generous financial support for this research and for other projects with incarcerated women, all of which have cultivated my deep commitment to them and illuminated this analysis. I wish to thank the following organizations: the Mount Zion Women's Health Fund and the Hellman Fellows Fund, both through the University of California, San Francisco; the Wenner-Gren Foundation for Anthropological Research; an anonymous foundation; and the Society of Family Planning.

This book comes from the research I conducted for my PhD dissertation in the joint program in medical anthropology at the University of California, San Francisco, and the University of California, Berkeley. My intellectual guides there provided more stimulation and support than I could have imagined. Vincanne Adams has been a rock throughout the research and writing phases. She has helped me immeasurably to clarify my arguments as I sorted through the troubling complexities of clinical and ethnographic experiences I encountered in the jail. I have a deep appreciation for Ian Whitmarsh for pushing me to think in more nuanced ways about the jail, for encouraging me from the start that the coexistence of violence and care in a jail is worth exploring. I have always been able to rely on him for a challenging, engaging conversation.

I hit the dissertation committee jackpot by having Lorna Rhodes on my committee. As a fellow ethnographer of carceral institutions, she provided me with critical guidance to navigate and analyze the relationships inside. I have benefited enormously from conversations over my years at UCSF and UC Berkeley with Lawrence Cohen, Sharon Kaufman, Cori Hayden, Donald Moore, Paul Rabinow, Nancy Scheper-Hughes, and Jonathan Simon. Kelly

Knight has challenged my thinking with immeasurably useful insights, especially given the overlap in our respective work. I am grateful to Angela Garcia for a long-nurtured friendship as well as strategic and thoughtful advice on this work at critical moments. Megan Comfort, Michele Goodwin, and Danielle Bessett also provided illuminating advice. Participants in workshops at the Vera Institute of Justice and the UC Berkeley Radical Medicine Group were generous in helping me refine key arguments of the book. I am indebted to the anonymous reviewers with the University of California Press for their invaluable comments and, along with Naomi Schneider, for their confidence in this work; Naomi's astute input has helped me focus my writing. Christine Marshall provided expert editorial guidance and reassurance to keep me going when my writing felt unmoored.

There is a rapidly enlarging cohort of physician-anthropologists who have inspired and supported me along the way. I am grateful to Rachel Niehuus, Na'amah Razon, Dana Greenfield, Jeremy Greene, Seth Holmes, and Scott Stonington for their shared commitments and advising. Emily Ng, Francesca Nicosia, Maryani Rasidjan, Marlee Tichenor, Raphaelle Rabanes, and my other cohort-mates in the UCSF/UCB medical anthropology program have also been tremendous friends and teachers.

Since my days as an undergraduate, I have long been compelled by anthropological thought. It was ongoing encouragement from my early anthropological mentors that reinforced my desire to return to anthropology after my medical training. Arthur Kleinman helped me believe that it was still possible for me, entrenched as I was in clinical practice, to be an engaged anthropologist; I am grateful to him for his continued support. Without Deborah Gewertz, who first exposed me to the world of critical anthropological inquiry during college, I would not have gone down this path. Her comment on my first paper, "You should write more than prescriptions," has been a mantra of support for the last twenty years. I continue to grow because of her scholarship and heartfelt mentorship.

It is an unusual trajectory for a practicing physician to pursue a PhD. My co-workers, whom I am lucky to call friends, in the San Francisco General Hospital Division of the Department of Obstetrics, Gynecology, and Reproductive Sciences at the University of California, San Francisco, provided profound support and encouragement, from their innate understanding of why medical anthropology and this project matter to our shared mission of serving the underserved, to their flexibility with my constrained schedule in covering clinical work. Thanks to Rebecca Jackson, Phil Darney, Linda Guidice, and Uta Landy, who enthusiastically helped make it possible for me to get a PhD and still be an Ob/Gyn. Dr. Darney in particular was the first to help me recognize that working with incarcerated women could be "my niche." Tracy Weitz remains an invaluable mentor and friend whose example of incorporating rigorous social science perspectives into reproductive health research and policy has propelled me; her warm encouragement has sustained me. I am also grateful to my colleagues in the Gyn/Ob Department at Johns Hopkins, particularly Anne Burke, Vicky Handa, Jenny Robinson, Torri Ross, Andy Satin, and Katrina Thaler.

For friendship, diversions, and reminders of why it all matters throughout the writing process, I am thankful for Colin Carter, Christine Dehlendorf, Eleanor Drey, Ian Gary, Rachel Farbiarz, Amy Fettig, Rachel Harold, Meredith Heller, Ilyse Hogue, Jen Kerns, Alex Laskey, Thellea Leveque, Molly Lyons, Sara Newmann, Amy Park, Suzanne Peterson, Rachel Roisman, Jody Steinauer, and Peter Sufrin. I am also grateful for the unexpected friendship of Geneva Kyles, and the humble grace with which she cares for the world.

After all these years I am still amazed that my parents, Janice and Jerry Sufrin, were right. As an undergraduate, I pondered going to graduate school instead of medical school as my academic version of post-adolescent rebellion. My parents gently redirected me to the pragmatic benefits of becoming a physician—advising me that I could always find a job in medicine and that I could later return to anthropology. Not only was their practical insight true for me, but taking care of patients has kept me grounded and has inspired my anthropological inquiry. My gratitude for their pride and unwavering support is deep.

To my husband, Jacob Harold, I am beside myself with appreciation for his patience and engagement with my work. His insistence on the value of anthropological perspectives in advancing social justice has been a constant reminder for me of why I am doing this work. I feel fortunate to have a partner who can spar with me on critical theory, and keep me honest about the bigger picture of it all. Our son, Cyrus Nelson, has deepened my personal understanding of care. His joy and enthusiasm for life have reaffirmed my commitments to help build a more just world for him to grow up in.

Introduction

"Everyone says I got arrested, but I got rescued." Evelyn was 34 weeks pregnant, although you could not tell that a baby was gestating beneath the baggy, extra-large, standard-issue orange sweatshirt she wore. She had just arrived at the San Francisco County Jail five days earlier, for the third time this pregnancy. On an outstanding warrants charge, Evelyn had turned herself into the cops who were patrolling the corner where she regularly sold, bought, and used crack cocaine. "I was so sick," she explained to me in jail, "I didn't want to get high no more. I just wanted to be in jail where I knew that I could eat, I could sleep, and that even if it's not the best of medical care, I was going to get some type of care."

This was Evelyn's self-proclaimed rock bottom. She had been addicted to drugs and in and out of jail more than twenty times since she was 18. She was now 29. Before this current incarceration, she had spent six weeks on San Francisco's streets, "rippin' and runnin'"—staying up for days at a time, smoking crack cocaine, getting into fistfights, selling any drug she could to make some money. The violence of this drug- and poverty-induced insomnia was familiar to her. But what was new, what made her feel more desperate than ever, was that she had no place to lay her head, not even a dingy room in a daily rent hotel. When she tried sleeping on the hard tile floor in the subway station, she felt rats running over her feet. Before now, she had never had to eat out of garbage cans, had never been eager when people left half-eaten food on top.

Before she came back to jail, I had run into Evelyn one day when I exited the subway station that was the closest thing she had to home; she was about 32 weeks pregnant at the time. She sat alone on a concrete ledge on the perimeter of the subway plaza, a cool area shaded from the midday sun. She wore a purple and black–striped shirt, a black hoodie, jeans, and a jacket draped over her legs. If I had not known her, I would not have been able to tell that she was pregnant under all those layers. Evelyn knew me as her doctor from a stint in jail earlier in her pregnancy; I was the only obstetrician she had seen for prenatal care. "Is it OK if I sit down?" I asked. "Yeah," she said. As we spoke, she kept her head concealed in her hoodie, and her scratched face turned to the ground. She tried, not so subtly, to hide a crack pipe behind her ear. "How are you?" seemed too trite to ask, so instead I offered, "It's good to see you." And it was. I remembered Evelyn from her clinic visits in jail, and had been worried that after her jail release she had not shown up to prenatal appointments at the county hospital, where I also worked. It was a relief to see her in person. We sat quietly amid the strange recognition of interacting with each other outside of jail for the first time. After a few minutes, Evelyn broke our silence with, "I need some more prenatal vitamins. I ran out. Do you know how I can get some?"

Evelyn's question illustrates a poignant contradiction about women who are poor, pregnant, and dependent on the state for their survival. On the one hand, she was using drugs she knew to be harmful to her growing baby. Evelyn struggled with addiction and was overwhelmed with cravings. As she described, "I wasn't making my prenatal appointments because I didn't care about anything but getting high." On the other hand, the night she got into a fight that left her with scratches on her face and bruises on her belly, she got herself to the county hospital a mile away, because she was worried something had happened to the baby. She cared about the baby.

Two weeks after our subway plaza meeting, I saw Evelyn in jail. This was not the first pregnancy during which she had spent time in jail; in fact, she had been incarcerated at this jail during her other two pregnancies, and had given birth to her second son while in custody. She was not raising either of them. And here she was again, a belly full of baby in a place that had come to be familiar to her: jail. Jail: a place of punishment and deprivation; a place where guards watch constantly and order their charges into submission. The story behind a pregnant woman like Evelyn desiring to enter a punitive institution like jail is more complicated than her assessment—that at least in jail she would get access to prenatal care—might make it seem. In truth, this complex reality of finding care behind bars is about the interconnected forces of racial inequality, poverty, societal dependence on incarceration, imperatives of medical care, and the state's obligation to care. The version of care that pregnant Evelyn sought in jail is part of the everyday reality of mass incarceration.

MATERNAL BLISS

"Doctor, I just want to know, is it OK if I dance to Beyoncé?" Kima sat in front of me in the clinic exam room, 34 weeks pregnant, tilting her head and looking intently at me as she waited for my professional opinion. I had not been prepared for pop music to be part of my prescription strategy at a prenatal checkup, but Kima wanted to know. Tomorrow was the talent show in the D-pod housing unit at the San Francisco County Jail, and Kima was used to being the life of the party. Now that she had gotten sober in jail, she did not want to do anything to harm the baby growing inside her. I smiled, told her it was safe, and watched the next day as she took the makeshift stage in the common area of her jail dorm. She shimmied her shoulders vigorously to Beyoncé's "Get Me Bodied," issuing from an old boom box. Her orange T-shirt was loose, but still showed her protruding belly, which she rubbed with pride during the performance.

Four weeks later, still in jail, Kima began having painful contractions— familiar to her, since, like Evelyn, she had given birth two times before; also like Evelyn, the births occurred during incarceration. Due to her struggles with addiction and a variety of other factors, Kima too had not been given custody of her children. That night, a jail nurse decided Kima needed to go to the hospital. Deputies escorted her to a car and drove her to the nearby county hospital. Kima arrived at the labor and delivery unit with the conspicuous fanfare of a jail inmate—bright orange clothes and a uniformed officer at her side. After a nurse checked her in, Kima exchanged her orange garb for a drab blue-and-white-checkered hospital gown. The sartorial shift transformed her from prisoner to patient, albeit with a guard sitting outside her room to ensure she would not escape between contractions.

Aside from the orange clothes discreetly balled up in a corner, the birthing room was like any other: filled with excitement and anticipation, and even a few family members, who came between 2 and 3 p.m., the jail's designated visiting hours for hospitalized inmates. To a cheering crowd of doctors (including myself), nurses, and a doula, Kima pushed her baby out. And then, "freed" from the incarceration of the womb, baby Koia was placed in her mother's arms. We joyfully congratulated her. Even the guard outside, hearing the unmistakable cries of new life, popped his head into the delivery room. Respectfully, he said, "I just want to wish you congratulations, Kima." A quick glance at the babe in arms, and then he returned to his post. Kima basked in the attention, a blissful look on her face as she held her newborn against her chest.

Kima was optimistic for a new start. She was eager to stay clean, to finally be able to be a mother. She had only two more weeks in jail, during which time her sister would take care of the baby, and then she was going to a residential treatment program for moms and babies. Kima dreamed that the connection she felt to her daughter at childbirth could be sustained well into the future. She hoped childbirth could be an escape route from her present life of drugs and petty crime.

These portraits of Kima and Evelyn—pregnant and incarcerated—are startling for those unfamiliar with the world of jails and prisons, yet strangely normal for those who directly encounter this world. Their portraits, furthermore, suggest that in our contemporary moment, jail accomplishes more than discipline and punishment. Indeed, the cultivation of maternal identity and pregnancy in the carceral environment urges us to think about the presence of care in a space presumed to be devoid of it.

JAILCARE

Jail and the broader system of incarceration, which I refer to as the carceral system, have become an integral part of our society's social and medical safety net.[1] Evelyn and Kima have both been affected by this uneasy convergence. Their lives, including their pregnancies, have been shaped by a historical trajectory that is peculiar to the United States and that represents one of its greatest tragedies. This tragedy is defined by the whittling away of public services for the poor, coupled with an escalation in the number of jails and prisons serving as sites for the care of that same population. Indeed, a disproportionate number of those suspended in the criminal justice system are not only poor and addicted to drugs, but are people of color; they can expect to cycle through the system for years. Thus, poverty, drug addiction, racism, and recidivism are inextricably linked, in a complex carceral system in which prisoners know that they will not only be subjected to a regimented, disciplinary environment, but that they will receive certain services, many of which they do not receive outside of jail. Jail is the new safety net.

Carceral institutions are commonly and rightly understood as sites of various forms of violence. In them, both physical and sexual violence between guards and inmates and among inmates has been widely documented. There is additional violence in the daily degradation by which inmates' bodies and psyches are controlled, devalued, and limited, so that even decisions such as when inmates may go to the bathroom are made by others. The more subtle violence of this kind of disciplinary power entails constant surveillance and a detailed, systematic organization of human activity.[2] Finally, there is structural violence in the disproportionate confinement of the poor and people of color, and in the reproduction of inequalities within the carceral system, which disrupts communities and families in profound ways.[3] When I refer to the violence of carceral systems throughout this book, I am indexing these multiple forms of physical, psychic, relational, and structural violence. These violent realities within jails and prisons lead to a tacit assumption that relations of care are impossible.

And yet, the emerging equivalence between the carceral net and the safety net has created opportunities for care and discipline not only to coexist, but to shape each other in unexpected ways. "*Jailcare*" suggests the disturbing entanglement of carcerality and care. Connections between these two domains are, of course, not new. The welfare state is founded upon a belief that the state bears some responsibility—the nature of which has been deeply contested throughout history—to care for its citizens. It is also simultaneously understood as inscribing certain groups of people into regimes of power, mirroring the controlling aspects of incarceration.[4] Medical apparatuses, too, integrate care into disciplinary regimes, by imposing expected norms of behavior in order to produce ideal, healthy citizens.[5]

But jailcare indexes different links between care and the disciplinarity of incarceration. Jailcare tends to the intimate, affective dimensions of care foreclosed by a strictly regulatory reading of relations inside punitive institutions.[6] In examining jailcare, I am concerned with care "as the way someone comes to matter and as the corresponding ethics of attending to that other who matters."[7] Pregnancy is a particularly revealing domain through which to examine care in jail—for the pregnant woman and her fetus raise a variety of questions about how specific subjects come to matter behind bars.

The expansive and generative nature of pregnancy poses problems for a carceral environment designed to confine, and challenges a simple understanding of carceral regimes as punitive. Accordingly, as poor, pregnant women of color, Kima and Evelyn encountered profound ambivalence within the jail medical system, its custody apparatus, the hospital, Child Protective Services (CPS), and drug treatment programs about how they and their offspring mattered. At the same time, their pregnancies in jail revealed that care is actually central to incarceration. This is the crux of jailcare: a form of care in which the state's impulses to govern and tend its citizens are knotted into each other not merely as a controlling strategy, but as everyday, affective relationships. This form of care that emerges behind bars is a symptom of broader social and economic failures to care for society's most marginalized people.

Certainly, the presence of a fetus in jail raises thorny questions for a punitive institution. Is the fetus incarcerated? Does the fetus mark pregnant inmates' bodies as worthy of special protection, or of excess punishment? What aspects of motherhood does incarceration foreclose and what does it enable? These questions signal tensions between various risk-management approaches to the pregnant inmate and the fetus. Prisoners are seen as dangerous, and thus must be confined and controlled.[8] Pregnant women and their fetuses are seen as at-risk, which thus justifies medical and political interventions on their bodies and behaviors, in the name of fetal protectionism.[9] When a carceral institution so pervaded by risk management discourses is faced with a woman whose body has come to be an exemplary site for managing risk, relationships of care are elaborated in ways that differentially value and devalue such woman's reproduction and motherhood.

Jailcare is also evocative of "health care," one of the services the public safety net struggles to provide amid the ongoing national debate about who deserves health care and who should pay for it. In terms of health care in carceral institutions, the landmark 1976 Supreme Court case *Estelle v. Gamble* is critical to the debate. *Estelle* determined that not to provide prisoners with medical care was cruel and unusual punishment, and therefore a violation of the Eighth Amendment of the U.S. Constitution.

Since *Estelle*, prisoners have been the only segment of the U.S. population with a constitutional right to health care. This fact raises two important contradictions. First, incarceration is a deliberate technique for suspending most rights of prisoners as part of their punishment.[10] And yet, a prisoner's constitutional right to health care is something that nonincarcerated U.S. citizens cannot claim. Ironically, more than half the people in jail were among the more than thirty million Americans without health insurance prior to jail.[11] Indeed, for many, including Evelyn and Kima, jail is the only place where they access health care. A second contradiction is the presence of healing medicine in an institutional state setting designed to administer dehumanizing, repressive punishment.[12] Medical care has the potential to nourish people in this environment of deprivation; but it can also, when inadequate, inflict further harm. Amid these contradictions, a therapeutic discourse pervades the criminal justice system: from notions of rehabilitating the criminal (limited as these commitments might be in the age of mass incarceration) to diversion programs like drug courts, the therapeutic rationality of transformation and cure is partially embedded in state approaches to confinement.[13]

The existence of care within jails should, then, be expected. But jailcare emerges from the everyday activities of providing care to people who are also prisoners. This book examines how the contradictions of prisoners' right to health care take shape in the everyday lives—specifically the reproductive lives—of women like Kima and Evelyn, as well as the people charged with caring for them while they cycle through jail.

A SNAPSHOT OF MASS INCARCERATION

The conditions surrounding Evelyn and Kima's pregnancies arise from a perfect storm of two deeply entrenched crises in U. S. society:[14] mass incarceration[15] and health care inequalities. Since the 1980s' escalation of "the war on drugs," the United States has seen an exponential rise in the number of people behind bars, from 501,886 in 1980 to 2,173,800 in 2015.[16] The U. S. holds only 5 percent of the world's population, but more than 20 percent of the world's prisoners.[17] We incarcerate more women than Russia, China, Thailand, and India combined.[18] Blacks have been disproportionately targeted, imprisoned at a rate that is more than five times that of whites,[19] a statistical fact which reflects the continuities between racist criminal justice system policies and plantation slavery and Jim Crow segregation.[20] Amid this expansion, women are the fastest-growing segment of the prison population.[21] And yet incarcerated women and their health needs remain consistently excluded from public discussions of mass incarceration.[22]

Numerous scholars have chronicled the rise of mass imprisonment, arguing that the phenomenon reflects not a response to a rise in violent crime, but the "penal treatment of poverty."[23] Put simply, where the state once had a strong moral and financial investment in robust public services for the poor, it now invests in an increasingly large and punitive penal system to manage them. The public safety net has failed to help millions of people stabilize lives made precarious by inequality and trauma.

The health status of incarcerated persons is a case study in structural violence. Marginalized by poverty, limited in their access to health care, and abandoned through the siphoning of public resources from their communities, the incarcerated also suffer from higher rates of HIV, hepatitis C, sexually transmitted infections, tuberculosis, chronic illness, drug addiction, and mental illness.[24] Yet while mass incarceration has generated innumerable problems, it has also, paradoxically, remediated the problem of health care access for millions of Americans. As Loïc Wacquant has astutely noted, "the U. S. carceral system has become a perverse agency for the delivery of human services."[25] What has yet to be examined is how, inside a jail, this delivery of human services actually works.

THE CURIOUS ECLIPSE OF WOMEN[26]

Women have been particularly affected by both the war on drugs and shifting welfare policies;[27] between 1977 and 2007, there was an 832% increase in the number of women in prison, a rate twice that of men.[28] At year-end 2015, there were 210,595 women behind bars: 111,495 in prisons and 99,100 in jails.[29] The majority of women are incarcerated for nonviolent crimes, and 59% of women in federal prison are serving time for drug offenses.[30] As with men, the racial disproportionality is notable among incarcerated women: black women are imprisoned at twice the rate of white women.[31] The majority of incarcerated women are younger than 50.[32] Nearly two thirds of these women are mothers, and leave behind the children they were caring for when they become incarcerated.[33] If a woman has no one to care for her children, then most commonly they will be placed into foster care. By federal law, parental rights are terminated after children have lived in foster care for fifteen months, a time period shorter than many prison sentences.[34] Despite the relatively small number of women behind bars, the impact on families and communities runs deep.[35]

Logically, as our country incarcerates more women in their 20s and 30s (prime fertile years), the carceral system is forced to confront women's reproductive capacities. Some of those women are going to enter jail and prison pregnant; a few will become pregnant while in custody, either from rape or conjugal visits from male partners. Pregnancy in jail or prison distinguishes the prisoner through a highly gendered state—pregnancy—which biologically male prisoners cannot experience. The facets of gender that I explore in this book are thus largely focused on women's reproduction and motherhood. There are many other gendered dimensions of carcerality, such as the cultivation of masculinities, and the experiences of transgendered persons. It follows, too, that given assumptions of maternal caregiving and statistical evidence of incarcerated mothers, we cannot ignore the myriad effects of parental incarceration on children. Over 5 million children in the United States have experienced a parent who is incarcerated.[36] From feelings of abandonment to shuffling between caregivers and foster care, to increased likelihood of intergenerational incarceration, there are deep collateral consequences for a generation of children.[37] Concentrating on gendered domains of reproduction and motherhood enables an understanding of how carceral institutions play a role in actively making mothers and families.

More than half of incarcerated women have experienced physical or sexual abuse as children or adults, a phenomenon recently being examined as the "sexual abuse to prison pipeline."[38] Many women begin their time in the criminal justice system as girls in juvenile detention. Incarceration can be re-traumatizing for many of them, through strip searches, gynecologic exams, and verbal and other abuse they might experience from some guards. Symptoms of a mental illness are present in close to three quarters of women who are incarcerated, and as many as 60 percent struggle with addiction.[39] Incarcerated women have high rates of sexually transmitted infections, higher than incarcerated men.[40]

Because they comprise only 9 percent of the incarcerated population, women have been neglected both in terms of understanding the specific paths they have taken to incarceration and their gender-specific health needs.[41] Research and public narratives document a systematic lack of reproductive health care for incarcerated women on a national scale, from absent or substandard prenatal care, to forced withdrawal from opiates in pregnancy (despite the known pregnancy risks), to lack of access to abortion and contraception.[42] This disregard for providing adequate reproductive health care is a subtle way of devaluing incarcerated women's reproduction, suggesting that their reproductive health does not warrant adequate medical care.

Inattention to the different ways women are engaged in the criminal justice system and their different health needs rests on an illusion of gender neutrality. However, our institutions of incarceration have always been implicitly gendered, in accordance with the assumption that males are the default prisoners, and are designed with men in mind.[43] The rapid rise of women behind bars and the problems in providing adequate services to them have revealed masculinist assumptions about physical space, medical services, and attempts at prisoner rehabilitation. Even providing tampons and pads for menstruating women becomes problematic: concern that incarcerated women can fashion weapons from them or will clog toilets has led many prisons and jails to limit the number of menstrual products women can use.[44]

One recent response to the recognition of the deficiencies in women-specific services has been to implement "gender-responsive strategies": prisons built with more open layouts to facilitate community among women; programs acknowledging that the trauma experienced by incarcerated women often results in different pathways to crime than men, and that incarceration can be re-traumatizing.[45] The irony of such approaches is that prisons have always been "gender responsive" in their heavy orientation toward men.[46] Moreover, gender-responsive strategies have been criticized for encouraging the further expansion of incarceration, even if that expansion addresses women's unique needs.[47]

The argument that women's needs are neglected in institutions of incarceration rests on an essentialist understanding of differences between men and women. While such renderings of difference have been productive in making certain advances, it is important to recognize that gender essentialism simplifies the diversity of women and their needs. I acknowledge that my focus on women's reproduction reinforces essentialist notions that associate women with their capacity to procreate. Certainly, not all women in jail are pregnant, and not all have children. Yet pregnancy and motherhood are complex states that do exist in jail. And without a doubt, these states lend themselves to my inquiry into forms of care.[48]

The gender dynamics of prisons and jails, especially in the age of mass incarceration, must be understood alongside trends in policing the reproduction and motherhood of poor women of color.[49] The child welfare system, for instance, inserts itself more broadly and aggressively in the lives of poor black families than those of white middle-class families, making assumptions about maternal behavior based on race and class.[50] The policing of reproduction is also evident in the panic that emerged in the 1980s over a perceived epidemic of "crack babies," a condition now discounted by medical evidence, which led to the incarceration of a disproportionate number of black mothers for fetal or child endangerment.[51]

These women were depicted as "monster mothers" rather than as women adversely affected by structural circumstances and struggling with addiction.[52] This weight of criminal judgment continues today, as some states have recently passed punitive measures to incarcerate women for using drugs in pregnancy, rather than providing addiction treatment.[53] Even as drug addiction becomes increasingly medicalized—a move that neutralizes addiction into a neurochemical process—judgments of moral failure continue to be ascribed to individuals who struggle with it.[54]

Another instance of the trend to police the reproduction of specific populations can be seen in laws passed in the 1990s by several counties that mandated that women on welfare use contraception, or in financial incentives for women on welfare to use the long-acting Norplant birth control implants.[55] These policies disproportionately targeted women of color, who were stereotyped as "welfare queens": poor black mothers procreating irresponsibly in order to live off entitlement programs.[56] Our country has created a hostile environment for these women, with relentless images of them as lazy and drug addicted. Such denigration from cultural narratives is impossible for women like Kima and Evelyn to escape. The increasing vilification of black mothers is connected to trends of racialized mass incarceration, partially through the incarceration of women viewed as bad mothers. This connection extends to jailcare.

Evelyn and Kima's experiences contribute to a larger story about the process by which jail workers, medical providers, and inmates work through structures of inequality and their repercussions. That story presents care emerging within the compromised milieu of a jail enmeshed in various forces of political, economic, racial, and medical marginality. In this context, pregnancy is an exemplary moment. The management and experiences of reproduction in jail can elucidate what it means to care—and be cared for—when the fundamental conditions of generating new life and restricting life are brought into contact. Incarcerated reproduction means thinking about what forms of life are sustained—and in what ways—by carceral institutions. It also means thinking about the possibilities—troubling as they might seem—for cultivating a sense of maternal identity behind bars.

This book attends to the granular aspects of everyday relations surrounding reproduction in a jail, and reveals that these experiences are not simply about structural violence, or the oppressive nature of the carceral state. Rather, these experiences tell us that jail can be a normative and unsettlingly caring institution amid precariously lived lives.

RACE AND JAILCARE

That prisons and jails disproportionately house African Americans is a social and statistical fact: blacks comprise 13% of the overall U. S. population, but 38% of the prison population;[57] 54% of jail inmates are people of color.[58] While blacks are no more likely to sell or use drugs than whites, they are eleven times more likely to be arrested for drug-related offenses.[59] Such statistics represent a number of complex underlying forces, among them: the historical continuity between targeted black imprisonment, Jim Crow, and slavery;[60] the production of symbolic imagery that equates criminality with blackness;[61] the crumbling urban ghetto as the intersection of race and class control.[62]

It is impossible to overlook the racialized dimensions of mass incarceration in the United States. Too many studies to cite comprehensively critique mass incarceration, and explore racialization from various political, historical, economic, and social perspectives. Increasingly, in the wake of several highly publicized murders of black citizens by police officers, the Black Lives Matter movement has also drawn critical attention to the racialized violence that marks our entire criminal justice system.[63] Even inside prison and jail walls, there is evidence that black individuals are treated more harshly and arbitrarily than others by staff.[64] The ways that race and incarceration are entangled to negatively impact black lives are aptly captured by Ruth Wilson Gilmore's definition of racism: "Racism is the state-sanctioned and / or extralegal production of group-differentiated vulnerability to premature death."[65]

To be sure, racial dynamics infuse every aspect of this ethnography. These defining, racialized features of policing and incarceration in the United States are at the core of the processes and relations of jailcare. Most of the women incarcerated in the San Francisco jail are black, though according to the city's 2012 census, the population of the city of San Francisco at the time was only 6 percent black. Their lives have been shaped by racism. Black children are overrepresented in foster care, with half of children younger than five entering foster care in San Francisco being black.[66] This disproportionality reflects and propagates numerous intersections with the criminal justice system, from the placement of children of incarcerated parents into the system to the increased risk of foster children being incarcerated as adults.[67] Race also informs patterns of interactions among those living and working inside the jail. Deputies and medical staff I worked with came from diverse backgrounds; they identified as white, black, Latino, Filipino American, Chinese American, Korean American, Indian American. Race affected negotiations of power and intimacy among the incarcerated women and jail workers in complex and fluid ways. From the identities of those most likely to be incarcerated in the first place, to racially charged maternal stereotypes, the phenomena that create jailcare are part of larger dialogues in this country about racial bias in the criminal justice system. However, the racial dynamics of daily care in jail were not a primary ethnographic focus of this project, and race was not the singular determinant of how people cared for and related to each other inside jail.

This is not to say that race was irrelevant to the jail experiences of black women like Kima and Evelyn, nor is it to say that it was categorically sidelined in the project. Rather, it is an acknowledgment that other forces, ones that often intersect with race, also shape how care emerges in the day-to-day workings of the carceral environment. As legal scholar Marie Gottschalk has argued, focusing excessively on the racial disparities of the carceral state elides other processes and overlooks other marginalized groups that are part of the problematic reality of mass incarceration.[68]

The contours of race in jail undoubtedly affected my relationships with informants, especially since I am white. Indeed, after working at the San Francisco jail's clinic for three years, nurses told me that inmates were initially skeptical of me, asking "Who does this white lady think she is?" It took some time, the nurses added, but eventually these women began conveying trust. My whiteness was an inescapable part of my positionality as doctor and ethnographer. While those dynamics were certainly pervasive, and will come up in discussing the formation of relationships of care, I have chosen to center on other aspects of relationality in this analysis. These relations of jailcare, however, are indisputably made possible because of broader racial injustices.

IN AND OUT OF JAIL

I worked as a doctor at the San Francisco jail. This status tremendously facilitated my ethnographic access to a space typically closed to scrutiny by researchers. Likewise, being a physician providing care to incarcerated pregnant women led me to broader questions about care and carcerality. I first encountered an incarcerated patient in 2004, when I was a first-year Ob/Gyn resident in Pennsylvania. A woman from the local jail was in labor, and I was the doctor delivering her baby—as she remained shackled to the hospital bed.

I was deeply troubled by this moment, and horrified at my own complicity in the act. A scripted authority figure in the birth room, I did not demand that the guard unshackle the mother. Among many disbelieving thoughts, the simplest was this: there were women—pregnant women—behind bars. Like many Americans, I had not given much thought, other than what the news media and popular culture had fed me, to institutions of incarceration and the people inside them. Having come to medicine with a strong sense of social justice, I committed myself to learning about and improving reproductive health services available to incarcerated women.

When I moved to San Francisco, I sought the opportunity to work with women in San Francisco's jail, volunteering intermittently as the jail's only on-site Ob/Gyn (a skilled women's health nurse practitioner already provided routine services). After a few months of doctoring in this setting, I was overwhelmed by the complexities of providing medical care in this charged environment that was both constraining—*it was a jail*—and beneficial—*I provided clinical services that most of these women did not access outside.* The relationships I had with other medical staff, with deputies, and with patients at the San Francisco jail were, I sensed, telling a larger story about care and inequality in America, one that differed from standard narratives of mass incarceration. I turned to anthropological tools to try to make sense of the discordance. The material in this book, then, is drawn from my experiences at the San Francisco jail from 2007 to 2013 as both a doctor and an ethnographer, creating methodological complexities that are evident throughout the book.

I had worked at the San Francisco women's jail for over four years when I officially began ethnographic research there and in San Francisco's surrounding community. For ten months, I inserted myself into spaces and routines of the jail that I had previously not entered as a physician.[69] This involved spending time observing the clinical area that I already knew from a doctor's perspective, but whose dynamics I had not had time to observe. I accompanied nurses as they carried out their tasks, and took note of interactions among my fellow clinicians, nurses, and patients in the open areas of the clinic. I observed the nurses in the intake jail assess the medical stability of new arrestees.[70]

These clinically oriented experiences were the foundation of how I saw care as part of the fabric of the entire jail. Because I started my experience in the jail's clinic, where medical care was the focus, I began to see other processes throughout the jail through an analytic of care. While I focus heavily on the voices of providers, I do not discount that care is a collaborative endeavor that includes patients' experiences, which necessarily differ from caregivers'. Indeed, patients appear throughout, for through interactions with patients we see what constitutes care in the eyes of providers. But seeing the practices and preoccupations of those who, by professional definition, inhabit the clinical space helps us understand the contours of institutionalized care—and how care in the jail confronts critical issues around the broader safety net and deservingness of care. My clinical expertise made some ethnographic moments intelligible to me in specific ways (e.g., immediately recognizing the symptoms of a miscarriage in jail). It also cast me in a position of authority that I could never fully escape.

Beyond the jail clinic, I chatted with deputies as they watched over their charges, day and night. I was present with incarcerated women in the housing units during their day-to-day activities. I spent time with nurses and deputies outside the jail, sharing meals or other social activities. I followed some women into the community when they were released, tracking them down on street corners, at drug treatment programs, or at the county hospital. I chauffeured them to court appearances and supervised visits with their babies. And I spent time with them when they returned to jail. I also continued to work as an ob-gyn at the county hospital, where many of these women were patients, either still incarcerated or released in the community.

Narrative and ethnographic accounts of carceral institutions frequently begin with an entry story: a heavy metal door clanging shut, irrationally long wait times, storing belongings in a locker, going through a metal detector. Indeed, every time I entered the San Francisco jail, I walked through a metal door that an all-seeing guard clicked open, and my bag was cursorily searched. But my entry was usually unremarkable, and my cell phone was never confiscated. I exchanged small talk with the deputy who looked at my "permanent clearance" jail identification badge. The ease with which I entered (and exited) the jail was largely due to the fact that I worked there. It also speaks to the familiarity that can be engendered in jail, and to a flow of bodies between jail and the community.

This methodological continuity between the jail and the community is in part an intervention on existing ethnographic approaches to the prison, where fieldwork takes place only in the institution, and where the focus has been on prisons, not jails. The majority of these accounts focus on the social worlds inmates create inside;[71] they understand the social control of prisons to be the primary force of life, where the task has been to find examples of inmate agency and resistance. A notable exception to this tradition is Lorna Rhodes's ethnography of a maximum-security prison, in which prisoners, mental health workers, and guards probe existential questions of what it means to be human in their daily interactions.[72] In general, though, the current body of prison ethnography reinforces the myth that the prison is a site detached from mainstream society. Even ethnographies that offer insight into the connections between inside and outside do so through prisoners' narrative reflection on their lives outside of prison.[73] In my fieldwork approach, I was privy to parts of women's lives in the community, and how those lives maintained fluidity with the jail in which they were periodically incarcerated.

I had intended, during those ten months of dedicated fieldwork, to compartmentalize my roles at the jail: Mondays would remain my doctor days, when I would run the reproductive health clinic I had built over the previous four-and-a-half years; the other days would be my anthropologist days, when I would observe daily life. This sounded easier, less messy, and with less risk of violating HIPAA.[74]

But in truth, I never served as just an anthropologist or just a doctor. Mondays, while I worked in the care system that is the subject of this book, I adjudicated decisions about how best to help people in this environment. But I also listened as an ethnographer to women's heart-wrenching stories of violence, manipulation by boyfriends, addiction, and dreams of transformation, with an intimate degree of detail enabled by the privacy of the doctor-patient relationship. Some patients who knew about my research would tell me relevant stories during their clinic visits.

Likewise, Tuesdays through Sundays, while inserting myself in situations outside the clinic exam room, I answered medical questions from nurses, inmates, and even deputies. When Evelyn had painful contractions one Sunday afternoon, instead of transporting her to the hospital, I examined her cervix at the jail, and determined that it was false labor. I should note that once women's pregnancies ended, while in some cases our research relationships expanded, I no longer provided them medical care.

My status as a doctor gave me access to sites and situations that would have been off-limits if I were "just an anthropologist"—and had I not had history there, for the staff had come to trust me. I also knew how to navigate the rules and spaces of the institution. This insider status enabled me to eschew, to a large degree, the surveillance of the researcher that other prison ethnographers have experienced from prison workers.[75] My position as an insider and, some might argue, as a part of the carceral system allowed me to see the daily rhythms of the jail as more than surveillance and degradation, qualities visible at first glance in any jail. This perspective provided a specific lens of care through which to understand aspects of life in jail. It is necessarily partial. As feminist scholars have long argued, all knowledge is partial and situated; all views come from somewhere.[76] The ethical task is to recognize that somewhere.

In my dual roles as physician and anthropologist, I became involved in some of these women's lives at very intimate and vulnerable moments. When Kima pushed her baby out, I was there to catch Koia in my own gloved hands. As an anthropologist, I spent extended time with Kima in the hospital after the birth, time I would not have spent were I just her doctor. Because I wore scrubs and a hospital ID badge, I could be in the hospital late the next night, after official visiting hours, when a CPS worker unexpectedly put a "police hold" on Koia. This designation meant that for the two days in the hospital, before she returned to jail, Kima could no longer have her newborn in her room but could only visit her in the nursery, accompanied by a guard and walking in shackles. These limits shattered Kima's maternal bliss. Though it was prohibited contact with an inmate, I hugged Kima as she wailed, safely out of sight of the guard outside her hospital room.

The night Evelyn was transported from jail to the hospital because she thought her water had broken, I was on call at the county hospital. While she was in the triage area of labor and delivery, she had a seizure. It was not her first seizure (she had been diagnosed with a seizure disorder ten years prior), not even in this pregnancy, but it was concerning. I had already come to know her well, both as an anthropologist and a doctor at the jail. We had become close. A few weeks later, when Evelyn gave birth, she named her baby Carolyn, partly after her deceased mother and partly, she said, after me.

Eventually, it was evident that it was impossible to distinguish my roles and insights gained from being a doctor and an ethnographer. My patients and co-workers were not concerned with compartmentalizing my roles. They absorbed me as a practitioner and researcher. I began to see my work at the jail more as "observant participation" than as participant observation.[77] I was already enmeshed as an integral actor in the phenomenon I was studying, making direct contributions in real time.[78] And so, the data in this book reflect an entanglement of my perspectives as a practicing physician and an engaged ethnographer. The material comes not only from my ten months of focused fieldwork, but from the cumulative six years in which I practiced as a physician at the jail; indeed, as I cared for patients I was often struck by the anthropological implications of what I heard, saw, or did. When I share stories that include medical information, I have either been given permission to do so by the individuals involved, or have changed identifying details. In some cases, I have merged information about people to further make them unidentifiable. In all cases, I have changed names of incarcerated women and jail workers to pseudonyms; I have also done so with various jail and social service agencies in San Francisco.

Observant participation at the San Francisco jail and its surrounding community comprised the bulk of my methodological approach. I also conducted interviews with incarcerated women, jail medical staff, deputies, and administrators. With some women, I could only hold conversations in a semi-private room in the housing units. Additionally, a few months into my research, word got out about my study, and a few women came to me with the idea that they wanted to share, in writing, their experiences accessing medical care in jail. Their writings are used as data in this book. Finally, I attended national meetings of correctional organizations, where I met administrators and clinicians from other prisons and jails; this helped me gain insight into the national conversations about health care for incarcerated populations.

While overlapping data from being a doctor and an anthropologist in the same place may seem messy and risky—for the potential confusion in roles and trust—I see analytic richness and feel an ethical imperative to using overlapping data.[79] After all, anthropologists and doctors both deal in messiness. It is essential to the human experience we seek to understand and to heal. To write myself out of an ethnographic narrative in which I delivered Kima's baby and tried to prevent a CPS worker from putting a police hold on the baby would be a misleading elision, not unlike ways anthropologists omitted their colonially enabled positions and surrounding revolutions in describing "other cultures" throughout the twentieth century.[80] In addition, the interweaving of information gleaned from my dual roles as clinician and anthropologist reflects a major argument of this book: that we are all implicated in this reality in which the disenfranchised must turn to jail to receive care. The jarring failure of the safety net is inextricably tied to, among other things, government policies, underfunded public education and mental health care, and tremendous income inequality—especially pronounced in San Francisco, where the latest technology boom has furthered the gap between rich and poor. These processes implicate everyone in the conditions that sustain the inequalities behind mass incarceration. Whether we are struggling to make ends meet without a safety net, or whether we ourselves benefit from the scales of racial and economic inequality, we are all connected to jail; we are all part of the system that benefits those with socioeconomic and racial privilege and punishes those without. Witnessing and being part of this complex and flawed system also compelled me to act. I became involved in national efforts to improve health care conditions for incarcerated women, to pass laws prohibiting the shackling of incarcerated pregnant women, and to advance criminal justice system reform.

SCRUTINIZING THE ASSUMPTIONS OF CARE

"Care" is an elusive word. It is frequently invoked to describe what health professionals provide, but its meaning is rarely specified. In its most basic use, it may conjure compassion, intimacy, and affective qualities of human connection. Care may also signify services rendered, especially in biomedical institutions. Relationships of care are often marked by dependency and unequal power relations between the one providing and the one receiving care, sometimes authorized as expertise and professional designation. Or, care may signal moral responsibility to others: children, family members, citizens.

Care cannot be distilled to a singular definition or practice, nor should it be. Neither should it be deployed casually, taking for granted that its ephemeral and practical qualities speak for themselves. Care must be understood as an ongoing process people work through in everyday lives, not as a distinct category of activity.[81] This book argues that care, through a variety of relations and practices, is central to everyday life in jail. In this context, care is best understood in an expansive sense as "the way that someone comes to matter."[82] This understanding is premised on the recognition that one's own existence is always oriented toward and entangled with another;[83] care thus emerges in the delicate labors of paying attention to that other. From this formulation, and while describing the mundane intimacies of care in the jail, I expand on three particular dimensions of care: as concern, as relationship, and as practice.

This book will explore how care in the jail clinic where I worked involved constant, daily attention to inmates who came to matter in myriad ways. Jail workers questioned how to best tend inmates—what kind of services, gestures, and concern did these people deserve? Care among jail staff also attended to certainties prescribed by the carceral institution—namely, the presumption that the inmates were criminals, staff were not, and consequently, the relationships between them were oppositional. Yet the standard perception that jail relationships can only be understood through power dynamics between jail worker and inmate has cracks in it; it is in these cracks, and in the ways people in jail confront them, that jail-care emerges as a source of both violence and care.

Care is also relational. Relationships may be institutionally prescribed, such as that between a healer and a patient, or structured by sentiment or social obligation, such as that between a parent and a child.[84] The relational qualities of care are existential, and premised on our shared vulnerability, since all humans suffer and will die.[85] We rely on institutions to help address certain needs, mitigate vulnerabilities, and protect from harm. Because of this, we are open to controlling regimes of care.[86] Indeed, humans' vulnerability to suffering is the reasoning behind the legal responsibility of jails and prisons to care for and protect those inside. This responsibility also, then, sets up the potential for litigation against the jail as an impetus to care. Jail guards and jail medical workers enact this state obligation on a daily basis.

At the same time, one's vulnerability is materially dependent on certain economic and social relationships.[87] Suffering, certainly, is unequally distributed, as it is shaped in part by structural forces.[88] Outside of jail, the lives of women like Kima and Evelyn were characterized by tremendous structural vulnerability, in which their position as poor, black women manifested in forms of physical and psychic suffering.[89] This reality challenged the jail to confront the inequalities and precarity of inmates' lives on the streets as it cared for them inside jail.

Relations of care are deeply intersubjective. As Judith Butler has written, our "precariousness implies living socially, that is, the fact that one's life is always in some sense in the hands of others."[90] Intersubjective relationships of care unfold in many ways—through touch, practices, words, gestures, concern about another's suffering, or simply the close presence of another.[91] These engagements create the potential for intimacy and emotion, even in the jail, where sentiment may be notable by its presence or its absence.

Care, especially when attached to "medical care," is also a technical practice. The increasingly technological kinds of care that characterize contemporary biomedicine have displaced the romanticized relational aspects of care.[92] This displacement also indexes another distinction in conventional understandings of the professional domains of care: historically, doctors have been understood as emotionally distant technocrats, with nurses as the agents of tender caregiving.[93] "Care" is often invoked as central to nursing philosophy. While this simplified caring dichotomy is perhaps more attenuated now, the professional identity of nurses—the majority of whom are women—as caring remains strong. In fact, one of the nurses in the San Francisco jail, bemoaning what she perceived to be the laziness and detachment of her colleagues, vented to me on several occasions, "Whatever happened to the 'care' in nursing care?"

As Foucault has famously argued, techniques of care in the clinic are fundamentally disciplinary practices that serve to normalize people into healthy bodies that can be more productive and ideal citizens.[94] Of course Foucault also argued that such disciplinarity was characteristic of modern incarceration.[95] He also elucidated the ways in which care is sutured to power and violence through pastoral care, the ways the ancient shepherd cared for and controlled his flock of sheep with nurturance and control.[96] This intersection of the technical practices of the clinic and the prison make medical care in a carceral setting a particularly intriguing site to study care, by formalizing and accentuating power dynamics that exist more casually in nonpunitive settings.[97] But a central premise of this book is that care inside must be understood through its everyday intersubjective processes of how someone comes to matter, rather than through pregiven disciplinary power relationships and institutional subordination. Care can involve affective attachments, which can slip through and around formal boundaries prescribed by the carceral and clinical environments.

Feminist theories of care have expanded on these coercive dimensions of caregiving. Traditional understandings have viewed care as a gendered domain, associating femininity with fulfilling the needs of others, disproportionately burdening women with the labors of care.[98] This distribution of the responsibility to care, the expectation that women should be caregivers, is itself a coercive aspect of care.[99] This comes to bear on mothers and pregnant women in jail, who are not only receiving care from the jail, but who are also forced into expectations of how they should care as mothers.

Annmarie Mol has argued for an understanding of the practice of care as a collaborative relationship between clinicians and patients who, together, navigate the uncertainty of disease and treatments to resolve their disarray.[100] In contrast to this perspective, the jail clinic began with the certainties of its surrounding jail architecture: regimentation of time and space and housing alleged criminals. Medical providers in the jail did not resolve biomedicine's messiness; rather, they tapped into it. In this way, care emerges through practice, through attentiveness, and through relationships that arise within the ambiguous engagement of tending people—including pregnant women who are carrying a fetus—in a punitive space. The ambiguity of this engagement is important; ambiguity, where no single certain path exists, is central to jailcare. Ambiguity is the indeterminate space where, through intimate, individual encounters, jail workers compare the scale of health care inside and outside the jail and reflect on the political implications of the differences. This view acknowledges that care does not putatively hold a positive valence of pure kindness nor a negative valence of controlling another's behavior.

Jailcare, relatedly, entails the conflicting emotions of ambivalence. That is, it may be uncomfortable to acknowledge the potential for compassionate care in a violent space. Embracing the potential of jailcare, such as Evelyn's desire for that care while she was pregnant, may lead to arguments about symbolic violence.[101] This insidious form entails the "misrecognition" of violence as natural, so that even its sufferers do not perceive their experiences to be based in violence.[102] Evelyn's desire to be in jail could certainly be read through this lens—a form of violence she misrecognizes as care. In this schema, desire for care from jail would manifest her oppression. But labeling Evelyn's desire to be cared for in jail as violence yields a limited understanding of the relationships between her and jail workers—and with the institution itself—as predictable, hierarchical, punitive relationships of power. Jailcare, instead, emphasizes that there can be tender, affective dimensions to care, and that these dimensions arise from the very forms of violence that characterize incarceration.[103]

JAIL VS. PRISON

The jail of jailcare is not a casual colloquialism, the way "jailhouse" sometimes refers to any institution of incarceration. The specific characteristics of jail as a local, short-term space of confinement matter for understanding how care is cultivated inside and how this reflects the deficiencies of the safety net outside. Jail is different than prison. Yet the majority of a vast critical literature on institutions of incarceration focuses on prisons. When jails are considered, both in scholarly works and in popular consciousness, they are usually conflated with prisons as interchangeable institutions of confinement; or jails are dismissed as a way station along the path to prison.

Whereas prisons are under state or federal jurisdiction, jails are local, at the county level. When people are arrested, they come to jail first (where they remain until they pay bail, are released for dropped charges, are convicted of a felony and go to prison, or, if they are convicted of a minor offense, where they serve a short sentence). Similar to national trends, roughly half of the people in the San Francisco jail were pretrial. Over 450,000 people in the United States are in jail are because they cannot pay bail.[104] As such, jail is often thought of as an entry or reentry point into the criminal justice system, a holding place before prison, a chaotic, people-processing site.[105] Millions of people interface with the criminal justice system through jail—in 2008, there were over 2.5 million arrests of women—and many never spend any time in prison.[106]

In contrast, prison is relatively static. Prisons house people convicted of crimes, mostly felonies. People stay in prison for multiple years, even their entire lives, whereas people spend as little as four hours in jail, or up to a year (occasionally longer). Recidivism rates are high for both jail and prison, but the temporal interval for returning to jail is much shorter than prison, since jail is the first stop. Some people never go to prison, but cycle frequently through the local jail. I saw people in San Francisco get released from jail one day to return the next. Kima and Evelyn did not have a pre-jail life and a jail life, for they were constantly cycling between the two.[107] The comparatively short intervals between jail stays and the frequency with which jail stays occur create tremendous opportunities for familiarity between staff and inmates. Recidivism is thus much more than a statistic; it is a substrate for the care that emerges in jail.[108]

This frequent cycling also points to the porosity between jail and the larger community, which also exists because of the geographic proximity of jails to the community. Whereas prisons are usually far away from people's homes, jails are located within the communities where people live— or at least where they commit their alleged crimes.[109]

Despite these differences between jail and prison, analyses of jails are notably absent from the literature on carceral systems. John Irwin's short ethnography from 1985 of processing into and social life within the San Francisco jail remains one of the few.[110] This book, then, aims to understand jail as a distinct, though related, phenomenon from prison, connected to the community in ways that make it hard to ignore the relationship between the community safety net and the carceral net.

Given the paucity of ethnographies of jail, my work is in conversation with several recent ethnographies that explore the political economy and its racial and gendered dimensions of urban marginality in the United States, specifically in San Francisco. Philippe Bourgois and Jeff Schonberg's *Righteous Dopefiend* describes the lives of men and women struggling with drug addiction as they live in homeless encampments in San Francisco.[111] The authors show the intimate, everyday violence of neoliberal economic shifts in the labor market, racial hierarchies, public health interventions, and draconian drug laws. Kelly Ray Knight offers a rich account of pregnant, poor women addicted to drugs in San Francisco's daily rent hotels in *addicted.pregnant.poor.*[112] Knight situates their struggles to stay clean in pregnancy in housing policies and medical treatment that make social failures appear as these women's personal failures. As they navigate the demands of addiction and housing instability, pregnancy and the likely removal of their babies by CPS fit into the overall uncertainty of their daily lives. Knight's analysis of the intersection of pregnancy, addiction, and institutional entrapment resonates strongly with my observations of pregnant women's struggles in jail. While *Jailcare* engages directly with the themes of Knight's book, it takes the management of these women's pregnancies in a different direction, exploring the nuances of intimacy within one of the institutions setting the terms of their motherhood.

The women I came to know in the San Francisco jail lived in the very streets, hotels, and encampments these authors describe, and most of them spent time in the San Francisco jail.[113] But Knight and Bourgois and Schonberg did not enter jail, and their analyses cannot elaborate on the nuances of jail, the porousness of its walls, and the role that it plays in the disenfranchisement of people's lives on the streets.

THE SAN FRANCISCO JAIL

During my time at the San Francisco jail, there were seven jail units across the county, managed by the San Francisco Sheriff's Department; this

Figure 1. The San Francisco County Jail, in the midst of the city. (Photo by author)

included a locked jail ward in the county hospital. Before 2006, women were housed at jails throughout the county. Subsequently, they were all moved to be housed in one location, County Jail 2 (CJ2), so that it would be easier to staff the female housing units only with female deputies. The aim of this gender pairing was to eliminate the potential for sexual assault of inmates by guards. I spent most of my time in CJ2, the only jail that houses women. The nearby intake or "booking jail," County Jail 1 (CJ1), where I also conducted fieldwork, was the reception unit where police officers would bring in newly arrested men and women to be processed into the jail. CJ1 and CJ2 were located in the same five-story building in downtown San Francisco, which stood adjacent to a major highway. Thousands of San Francisco area residents passed the jail every day. Yet few could identify the rounded-walled, concrete building with art-deco frosted glass window panes (see figure 1).

The building was rounded to the contours of "pod style" housing units, circular dorms in which the guard tower of each housing unit was located panoptically in the middle and the "cells" were arrayed around the periphery. There were six pods in CJ2, A through F; F pod was for men, and A pod was a transitional unit for men from the prison system released to San

Francisco. C pod was the medical pod: nurses were stationed there all the time, and this pod housed men and women with high-level medical needs; when pregnant women were close to their due date, they were sent to C pod so nurses could quickly respond to possible labor symptoms.

These pods, built in San Francisco in the early 2000s with the hope that open architecture would facilitate a more positive, rehabilitative environment, were not the long hallways of cubic cells with iron bars vividly represented in popular media.[114] A single metal door at the entrance to the pod provided security and was opened and closed by an unseen deputy at the central control tower. Most of the cells in the pods did not have doors; they were open to the common area where inmates ate, exercised, socialized, and attended classes, among other activities. Each cell had two bunk beds and a narrow space between them. Shared toilets and showers were located in individual stalls on each level of each pod. The upper-level cells in the pods had locked glass doors for people classified as needing higher security; these cells were euphemistically called "ad seg," for "administrative segregation."[115]

The midyear count at the San Francisco jail in 2013 (the last year of my fieldwork) was 1,445 inmates, with 137, or 9%, women.[116] Reflecting national trends in racial disparities, 58% of these women were black. The majority (76%) were arrested for nonviolent crimes, with drug-related offenses being the most common. The median length of stay in 2012 was 82 days, and the recidivism rate hovered around 70%. The total jail population in 2013 represented a 29% drop from when I began working there in 2007. This decline was even more dramatic for women, whose population dropped by 45%—from 251 in 2007 to 137 in 2013. One of the pods in CJ2 even closed in early 2013, because the jail census was so low. One reason jail workers explicitly identified for the low numbers was a 2010 scandal in a crime lab in the city, in which an employee took drug evidence from a criminal case for her own personal use; hundreds of cases had to be discarded and many people released.[117] Another reason for this decline is that the city expanded its commitment to alternative, community-based sentencing for low-level offenders, as well as probation and drug treatment programs that help people convicted of nonviolent crimes and those struggling with addiction stay out of jail. Nonetheless, some evidence suggests that the overall decline may be differentially benefiting nonblack

San Franciscans, with racial disparities in arrests and convictions still apparent.[118]

San Francisco's declining jail population is notable compared to the rest of California. In fact, most jails in the state have seen an increase in their population since the 2011 "Public Safety and Realignment Law," known as "Realignment," was passed in response to the Supreme Court case *Brown v. Plata.* In *Brown v. Plata,* after decades of litigation surrounding the abysmal medical care in California prisons, the court mandated the depopulation of state prisons to reduce the ill effects of overcrowding.[119] Those convicted of nonviolent, nonserious, nonsexual crimes are now managed under local jurisdictions. Most counties in the state have responded to this mandate by incarcerating more people in jails (and even building more jails).[120]

San Francisco's Jail Medical Care (JMC) operated inside the jails as a branch of the city's public health department, rather than the Sheriff's Department that ran the jails.[121] As such, JMC was oriented toward a broader vision of health care than at jails where services are contracted out to a profit-driven private corporation. JMC employed doctors, nurse practitioners (NPs), registered nurses (RNs), licensed vocational nurses (LVNs), pharmacists, clerks, and administrators. NPs receive training that enables them to evaluate, diagnose, and treat patients. Though a physician supervises, NPs function with relative independence; such was the case at the San Francisco jail clinic, where NPs outnumbered physicians. Nurses, including RNs and LVNs, comprised the bulk of the JMC clinical workforce, both in number and in their 24/7 presence at the jail. During weekdays, 5–10 RNs and LVNs staffed clinical duties in CJ2, as well as 2–5 NPs and doctors for routine and urgent clinic visits. When I describe events involving a registered nurse (RN) or licensed vocational nurse (LVN), I refer to that person generally as a nurse in order to veil the person's identity. For the same reason, when describing an NP or a physician, I call that person a "clinician," which is how these care providers were collectively referred to in the daily and administrative workings of the jail. When I speak generally about medical providers, I write in third person for grammatical ease, but I use that pronoun understanding that I too was one of those medical providers.

Medical care was free for inmates at the San Francisco jail. However, at many jails and prisons across the country, inmates must pay a fee—usually around five dollars—to see a physician. This fee intends to deter inmates from overusing the medical system, but erects an unnecessary barrier to services for people with limited means and for whom the jail or prison is required to provide health care.

A parallel organization provided mental health care, including psychiatric care, group and individual therapy, case management, and some addiction treatment for people in the San Francisco jail.[122] Among incarcerated populations, the burden of mental illness is tremendous.[123] The jail mental health providers I worked with were compassionate, dedicated, and very, very busy. Most of the women I cared for had at least one psychiatric diagnosis, some of which was related to their histories of trauma and abuse. While these experiences were integral to the lives of the women I describe, the carceral management of mental illness is not the subject of this book.

The Sheriff's Department's primary responsibility was to run the city's jails and to oversee the daily lives of inmates, a task often referred to as "custody." The daily tasks of custody provided a structure for caregiving relationships that exceeded the predictions of disciplinarity. Sheriff's Department employees did not generally arrest people—police officers did—nor did they determine whether or how long someone would be in jail—that was the purview of the courts.[124] At the same time, the Sheriff's Department worked closely with the probation department and community agencies to try to ease reentry and curb recidivism. Those who took turns staffing the pods, twenty-four hours a day, seven days a week, were typically the lowest rank officers, called deputies. The chain of command continued with senior deputies, lieutenants, sergeants, watch commanders, captains, and chiefs at the jail. At the top of the hierarchy was the sheriff, an elected official who spent most of his time in city hall. Unless distinction in rank is necessary, I refer to all Sheriff's Department professionals as deputies (in other settings, they might be called guards or correctional officers).

SAN FRANCISCO'S PROGRESSIVE POLITICS AND ANTHROPOLOGICAL LESSONS

This jail field site and its surrounding urban community are, on the one hand, exceptional. San Francisco is known for investing in social services, enacted through a variety of innovative programs for the poor, marginally housed, sick, unemployed, malnourished, and drug addicted, the majority of whom are racial and ethnic minorities. While the broader political narrative in the United States and in the state of California is one of reduction in social services for the poor, and while San Francisco's services remain at once underfunded and underutilized by those who need them most, San Francisco finds ways to fill in gaps created by depleted state and federal funds. Moreover, partially due to the most recent technology boom, San Francisco has also been at the center of scrutiny of the widening gap between the rich and the poor in urban centers in the United States.[125] These progressive and economic specificities of San Francisco factor in to the reality that makes jailcare possible. This is why I have chosen to name the city in this book rather than giving it a pseudonym.[126]

This citywide commitment to helping the poor was also found in the philosophy of San Francisco's Sheriff's Department. Despite an overall arc in U.S. prisons and jails away from rehabilitation and toward mass incarceration, leadership at the San Francisco's jail was interested in helping people with successful reentry.[127]

While life inside the San Francisco jail was not as desolate as monolithic representations of "warehouse prisons" would indicate, there is tremendous variability of jails and prisons throughout the United States. Some jails have activities similar to those of the San Francisco jail; many do not. Every jail, and every prison, though it may share a certain modus operandi or similar architecture with other jails and prisons, is its own ecosystem. I have visited several other jails and prisons in different geographical regions, and have spoken with people who work at facilities across the United States. As one prison nurse at a conference told me, "we are all in our own silos."

In my capacity as an obstetrician, I have served as an expert witness in lawsuits involving jails in other states where pregnant women are so categorically mistreated with substandard medical care that I have doubted whether my case study of reproduction and health care at the San Francisco jail—where basic standards of medical care were generally met and sometimes exceeded—are worth telling. In the records I reviewed from these legal cases, pregnant women were rarely seen by a qualified health care provider, even when reporting concerning symptoms like bleeding or contractions. These women delivered babies in toilets and experienced the trauma of miscarrying five-month pregnancies, despite pleas to be transported to the hospital where their physical and emotional pain, not to mention their safety, might be addressed. I have heard similar stories from activists and other incarcerated women at jails across the country, such as a woman withdrawing from drugs who was assigned to a top bunk; she had a seizure, fell off her bunk, and died. Or the Kentucky jail that did not have enough pants or menstrual products for all the women they confined, including making them appear in court without pants.[128] Many incarcerated women, as written narratives and conversations I have had with women at this and other jails indicate, do not trust medical providers in jails and prisons.[129] These appalling accounts remind me how much work there is to do in addressing the unnecessary reproductive and medical suffering that still occurs during incarceration.

The fact that such fundamental departures from standard medical care and from basic safety standards were not systematically present in the San Francisco jail does not preclude us from learning about care and carcerality in this setting. We would hear a different story from jails where substandard medical care is the norm, and where the documenting of overt cruelty demands immediate work to improve basic conditions. What this points to is the fact that reform requires a more nuanced approach than to say simply that we need a more humane carceral system with better health care. In fact, gross deficiencies at other jails make it more necessary to understand the nexus of violence and care as they occurred at the San Francisco jail.

Certainly, the variability among jails and prisons does not mean that what happens in San Francisco can only tell us about San Francisco. Indeed, one of anthropology's central tenets is that we can look to the particular to learn about the general.[130] And so San Francisco's notable progressive politics and innovative spirit, which seep into the jail and the jail clinic, serve as a particular backdrop to the story I tell of the equivalence of the carceral net and safety net in our society, and how they are both suspended by interwoven threads of discipline and care.

ETHNOGRAPHY OF THE OBVIOUS

A goal of ethnography is often summarized as follows: "to make the strange familiar and the familiar strange, all the better to understand them both."[131] In a sense, prisons and jails in the United States occupy the "strange" category: although 2.2 million Americans are incarcerated on any given day, hundreds of millions more will never set foot in one of these institutions and can only imagine them through media and political representations.[132] I hope this book will make these strange institutions seem a little more familiar, and thereby will make readers more aware of our collective complicity with mass incarceration. At the same time, I seek to make the familiar strange, by destabilizing monolithic representations of prisons (and the limited depictions of jails) as sites where only discipline and punishment occur, where individuals are churned through regulatory structures that at once dehumanize them and at the same time make them properly governable subjects. These representations of prisons in critical scholarly and activist literature have become predictable. Such an interpretation of the medical care in a jail would be easy, and not altogether inaccurate on some days. But it would be dangerously incomplete.

Accordingly, I see this project as "an ethnography of the obvious," not merely of the familiar.[133] An ethnography of the obvious signals an intervention on the obvious and fetishized representations of "The Prison." It also means looking to obvious phenomena—including jail itself—that have been eclipsed by dominant narratives. In the jail clinic, doctors and nurses practice healing arts with patients. This type of caregiving leads us to see anew the rest of the jail, where deputies manage the intimate activities of women's daily lives—eating, sleeping, bathing, socializing—in ways that are a complex of care mixed with discipline. Overlooking one obvious phenomenon—the intimacy of jail—for another—its repressive violence—may yield a coherent story, but would not capture the complexity of everyday realities.

The lives of many people in jail are shaped by the failure of the safety net to protect them from violence, hunger, homelessness, and ill health. This abjection makes jailcare possible. There are times that my descriptions make jail seem like a safe, nurturing, fun place to be. These descriptions should not be interpreted as suggesting that jail is an ideal place to care for marginalized women; rather, the comforts and affective ties that can flourish in jail reflect the tragically precarious conditions outside jail. This book elucidates the carceral experiences of women who have been failed by the safety net. If it unsettles you to read an account of a carceral institution that focuses on the nurturance that can happen inside, then you share my anxieties. I am critical of the war on drugs, the abandonment of the mentally ill, and other racially directed policies that have led to the imprisonment of millions of people, most of whom I believe should not be there in the first place. Writing about seemingly positive elements of jail risks undermining a larger agenda of criminal justice system reform. It also risks perpetuating a "culture of poverty" argument, which blames recidivism on individuals' complacent reliance on jail.[134] Finally, revealing desirable aspects of jail risks triggering a backlash against providing quality services for people inside, and risks arguments that we should make jails less "comfortable." I would be devastated if my work were taken as an endorsement of mass incarceration. Yet real tension exists between criticism of unjust practices and recognition of the contingent good that jail can do. This contradiction is something many jail workers, including myself, and many of the incarcerated women I met, grappled with on a daily basis. I hope you, the reader, will feel similar ambivalence, for this reflects the complicated and thorny reality of many contemporary jails.

I should add another note on ambivalence. The majority of the pregnant women I cared for and came to know in my time at the San Francisco jail struggled with drug addiction; they injected, snorted, or smoked heroin, crack cocaine, or methamphetamines—or combinations of them all—during their pregnancies. Structural violence and abandonment created the conditions of possibility for their addiction. As a doctor and an ethnographer, I cared for these women through that understanding, rather than one of individual behavioral attribution. But there were times when their actions frustrated me and made them seem to me ill-equipped to care for a baby. Holding the structural recognition against the consequences that their constrained choices had for their babies is disquieting, to say the least.

A NOTE ON TERMINOLOGY

There are many words used to signify a person who is incarcerated: inmate, prisoner, offender, criminal, convict, felon, or, as used in corporate-speak, client. Each of these has an array of connotations, a linguistic history, and political signification. Choosing one term in a book that features these people so prominently is a tricky task. I would prefer to use the term "incarcerated person." Incarceration would thus remain an adjective, a descriptor of a current state, rather than an identity category in itself; person would convey that there are transgendered people in a women's jail—although all of the females I describe in these pages did identify as women. However, this terminology is cumbersome, and has led me to choose the term most frequently used for themselves by the people who animate these pages: inmate.[135] Sometimes I substitute it with prisoner, for stylistic variation and to suggest the instability of these categories.

Additionally, there are times when I refer to prisons and jails as "correctional facilities." This is how people who work inside, professional organizations, court cases, and many other sources refer to all institutions of incarceration. I recognize the implications and shortcomings of the word "correctional"—that incarceration should correct a flaw—and the benign sound of the word facility. When I refer generally to institutions of incarceration, it would be less weighty to name them as such, but that too would be cumbersome. And so at times I use "correctional facility," understanding the limits of that choice.

JAIL AS AN INTIMATE AND INSTITUTIONAL SAFETY NET

Each chapter of this book considers how, for certain people whose street lives are characterized by social and economic marginality, jail acts as a safety net, providing medical and other supportive services generally lacking from their lives outside jail, where the safety net has failed them. Within this unsettling reality, care emerges in multiple and often contradictory ways that are inextricable from the structures of carcerality that paradoxically enable caregiving. Part I describes the medical apparatus within jail—its broader historical and legal context alongside the historical and governmental structure of the safety net, as well as the specific workings of the San Francisco jail's clinic. These chapters focus on the routines of providing clinical services, as animated by clinic staff, and how staff grapple with people's deservingness of health care along with the jail's obligation to provide health care. These chapters highlight the work of care from the clinical providers' perspectives, less so from the patients' position; these chapters are less explicit in addressing motherhood and reproduction at the medical-carceral nexus, but establish the mechanics of care that adapt in specific ways to the figure of the pregnant inmate. Part II, then, harnesses these interlocked notions of care and violence to the context of pregnancy in jail—how custody and medical staff manage pregnant women and how women experience motherhood in jail and in relation to its constitutive outside. The forms of motherhood that become available to women in jail can cultivate a cruel optimism, where women are enticed into idealized versions of mothering that are generally not available to them outside of jail. Here again, the idea that certain kinds of motherhood can be cultivated and repressed in jail is depicted more broadly as a failure of our larger social systems to care for these women outside of jail, and a failure of our social imagination to value poor, black women's reproduction.

This book is about the way in which the nuanced interactions around care in jail work through broader social, economic, racial, and health inequalities that comprise the conditions of possibility for contemporary incarceration in the United States. The disarray of the safety net directly contributes to the poverty and marginality experienced by people who also find themselves behind bars, and enables jail to then fill in for those deficiencies. Throughout this work, it is my aim to show how jail is a safety net not only because of its services, but also for the tragic ways that its care, even amid carceral violence, can exceed the safety and care available outside its walls.

This book comes at a time when public discourse about our overcrowded institutions of incarceration is beginning to shift. The far-reaching consequences of draconian drug laws, of criminalizing poverty, and of practices that disproportionately target communities of color are being questioned by more than just critical scholars and activists. San Francisco, where this book takes place, is at the forefront of innovative restructuring of its local criminal justice policies and social services. The Supreme Court in 2011 ordered the state of California to depopulate its overcapacity and under-resourced prisons. Former President Obama and other politicians have castigated our current system of incarceration as a moral and economic failure for its destructive, racialized effects on our society.[136] Conservative and liberal lawmakers are pushing for comprehensive reform in drug laws and sentencing practices.[137] It is my hope that this book will provide useful insights into how people on the ground work through the everyday complexities of mass incarceration that all too often get simplified in broader policy debates.

PART I

1 Institutional Burden to Care

What's wrong with our society that so many people are
ending up in jail who are really sick?

Health administrator at the San Francisco jail

The correctional system should not be held to account for
the weaknesses of the community system.

Kevin, medical administrator at a private correctional
health corporation

DESERVINGNESS AND THE CARCERAL BURDEN

In 1975, prisoner J. W. Gamble injured his back while doing labor on a
prison farm in Texas.[1] He alleged that the medical care he then received
was inadequate and that he was further punished for not working due to
back pain. The Supreme Court, which considered his claims in the landmark 1976 case *Estelle v. Gamble,* disagreed, and Gamble lost the case.
However, the court used his case to establish health care as a right for
prisoners. Justice Thurgood Marshall declared "that deliberate indifference to serious medical needs of prisoners constitutes the 'unnecessary
and wanton infliction of pain,' *Gregg v. Georgia, supra,* at 173 (joint opinion), proscribed by the Eighth Amendment."[2] This legal mandate for
health care that *Estelle* created is foundational for jailcare, for it acknowledges that incarcerated people deserve some degree of care. This recognition opens the possibility that people might seek jail for the promise
of care.

Since *Estelle,* administrators, accrediting organizations, private health
care corporations, lawyers and judges, advocacy groups, correctional

health workers, and inmates have actively translated the meaning of "serious medical needs" and "deliberate indifference" into facility policies, contracts, lawsuits, activism, and everyday health care relationships.[3] The vagueness of these phrases has nurtured a central tension in thinking about care for prisoners, one that is at the core of jailcare. One aspect of this tension appears in questions about the prison or jail's responsibility to care for those whom it confines, which legal scholar Sharon Dolovich calls "the state's carceral burden": its obligation to fulfill prisoners' basic human needs, since prison deprives them of their ability to sustain themselves and places them in potentially dangerous situations.[4] This line of questions parallels larger questions about the state's role in ensuring citizens' well-being through a safety net for the most vulnerable. Another aspect of this tension appears in questions about for whom the state is obligated to care. Here, notions of "health-related deservingness" are useful. Deservingness, Sarah Willen has argued, is the "flip side of rights."[5] Rather than being understood in universal claims of truth or legal assurances, deservingness is negotiated relationally. Certain groups are constructed as worthy of public support. Others are unworthy.[6]

This chapter describes the institutional and historical contours of this tension between the obligation to care and prisoners' deservingness of care. These contours determine the existence of the San Francisco jail clinic, Evelyn's desire to use its services, and the flourishing of its daily intimacies of care. The context this chapter provides involves four domains. The first is the twinned rise of mass incarceration and retreat of the public safety net. These interrelated processes have deep economic and racialized roots, and are unified by the argument that the state has, over the last forty years, managed poverty by incarcerating the poor rather than investing in robust and effective services.[7] The second of these domains is judicial. The courts have played a major role in establishing prisoners' rights to health care and delineating what it should look like. The third domain is the emergence of "correctional health care" as a professional field and source of profit. Finally, organized social justice advocacy has shaped the terms of prisoners' rights to health care. Together, these institutional and historically located forces situate the unfolding of care inside the jail.

RETREAT OF THE SAFETY NET AND RISE
OF MASS INCARCERATION

Evelyn was born in 1983, during a radical shift in the state's approach to managing poverty that accompanied rising concerns about crime.[8] Her parents were poor, black, held no steady employment, and struggled with addiction. Her mom used drugs while she was pregnant with Evelyn. When Evelyn was five years old, her mother was murdered. Evelyn was alternately cared for by her father and a cousin, whom she referred to as Aunt Vera. When Evelyn was nine years old, the state discovered that Evelyn's father and uncle had been molesting her, so she was removed from Aunt Vera's custody, nurturing though it was, and funneled into a series of group homes and foster care families. She never received mental health care for the sexual abuse or her mother's murder. Not surprisingly, this unaddressed trauma manifested in anger and drug use, and eventually led to juvenile detention and an early entry into adult correctional facilities.[9]

Evelyn is one of millions whose involvement in the criminal justice system is a product of the twinned rise of mass incarceration and the waning public safety net. These phenomena emerge from a racially biased historical arc in the management of poverty, one end of which is rooted in social services and the other in the "penal treatment of poverty."[10] This historical convergence is important in contextualizing the experiences of pregnant women like Kima and Evelyn.

In exploring these paired historical trajectories, I understand the safety net to be a complicated and multidimensional phenomenon, one explored by many scholars. In common usage, "safety net" denotes the provision of services for disenfranchised people who need help meeting their basic needs and who would otherwise "slip through the cracks." As a social institution, the safety net represents a contested moral and ethical stance toward society's most vulnerable. From an operational standpoint, the safety net includes a set of government-sponsored programs, medical clinics and publicly funded health insurance, and tens of thousands of nonprofit service organizations. Perennial debates about the nature of the safety net overlap debates about prisoners' right to health care, involving obligation and deservingness: what is the state's responsibility to care for its citizens, and which subjects are constructed as worthy of that care?

A brief historical sketch clarifies the connections between the safety net and mass incarceration. The first institutional threads of the public safety net were spun in the 1930s by New Deal programs designed to mitigate the effects of the Great Depression, and grounded in the notion that it was the government's responsibility to help struggling citizens.[11] From its inception, this safety net excluded African Americans from accessing federal benefits.[12] Unsurprisingly, racially encoded language like "deserving" and "undeserving" poor followed this exclusion. Several decades later, President Lyndon Johnson's Great Society programs endeavored to equalize access to the safety net for black citizens; his "war on poverty" expanded government services, including food stamps and federally funded medical care for the poor (Medicaid) and elderly (Medicare).[13]

The growing safety net, however, left behind the mentally ill. The 1960s and 1970s saw the closing of state-run mental institutions, considered inhumane and coercive, while the expansion of community-based mental health treatment services never materialized.[14] Without adequate support, many suffering from mental illness found themselves incarcerated for petty and nonpetty crimes, or for being "nuisances" to the public. By default, jails and prisons became the largest provider of mental health services in the country.[15]

Johnson's war on poverty coincided with civil rights activism over the effects of racial segregation—including the unequal availability of safety net services for African Americans. By the 1970s, protest in urban centers spilled into civil unrest, which in turn generated unprecedented fear of crime.[16] Incarceration became an anxiolytic for these fears, isolating and removing groups perceived to threaten the dominant moral order.[17] Not coincidentally, the imagined "dangerous underclass" was poor, black, and located in now-abandoned urban ghettos.[18]

Simultaneously, shifts in the industrial labor market and the deregulation of the market economy generated a surplus of unemployable laborers. The already disenfranchised, particularly in urban ghettos, were further undermined by neoliberal economic policies that shifted the responsibility for economic insecurity from the state to the free-market individual.[19]

These transformations disproportionately affected urban communities of color and deepened racial economic inequality.[20]

Under the leadership of President Ronald Reagan, the 1980s witnessed the dismantling of publicly funded social welfare programs, through privatization, decentralization, and elimination of many programs. The poor were left to precarious wage opportunities and illicit markets, including the drug economy. As many women at the San Francisco jail told me, selling drugs remained the only reliable way they could make money, and they made more than at a minimum-wage job.[21]

Formalizing the neoliberal restructuring of the public safety net, President Bill Clinton's 1996 welfare reform act shortened the duration in which one could receive public assistance and applied more stringent criteria, emphasizing individual responsibility to join the workforce while refusing to provide a living minimum wage or universal childcare.[22] The law allowed states to cap the number of children for whom mothers and families could receive Temporary Assistance for Needy Families (TANF) benefits.[23] Moreover, welfare policy changes focused on poor women, single mothers, and black women, blaming their reproductive patterns for the cycle of poverty and directing their children into child welfare programs.[24] These changes accompanied social narratives stereotyping poor black mothers as drug addicts and "welfare queens" who ostensibly produced children to get subsidies from the state.[25]

The rise of mass incarceration is inseparable from these racially grounded reformulations of public welfare.[26] Even as the Reagan administration rolled back government financing of the safety net, it expanded the prison system. In addition to neoliberal reformulations of welfare, Clinton, too, passed harsher sentencing laws and increased funding to prisons and policing,[27] investing an astounding amount of money in prisons, jails, and their management, disproportionately punishing African Americans and profiting private corporations.[28] This financial trend has continued for decades: in 1982, approximately $16 billion was spent on state prisons; in 2010, that number was $40 billion (adjusted for inflation).[29] The war on poverty morphed into the "war on drugs" and the "war on crime."[30] Tellingly, a senior advisor to former president Richard Nixon has admitted that the Nixon administration invented the war on drugs as a political tool, criminalizing drugs and associating drug use with antiwar activists and blacks.[31] Although drug crime was declining, states ramped up incarceration through increased policing and draconian sentencing laws, such as mandatory minimum sentences and California's notorious "Three Strikes" law.[32] Changes to drug sentencing laws also reflexively increased sentencing for violent crimes, leading to overall longer imprisonments for all convicted felons.

While it posed as a response to increasing crime rates, mass imprisonment actually resulted from "a politics of resentment toward categories deemed undeserving and unruly, chief among them the public aid recipients and street criminals [who] came to dominate the . . . debate on the plight of America's urban poor."[33] Increased policing in and of black communities has become a central feature of the urban landscape, with the criminal justice system playing a key role in inner-city governance and reinstantiating processes of racial dispossession.[34] Overcrowded "warehouse prisons" and jails are now characterized by harsher and more punishing conditions, in which the imprisoned—a disproportionate number of whom are African American—linger idly, increasingly unprepared for reentry and doomed to both recidivism and marginality.[35] These qualities reflect a shift in prisons, which focus less on regulating and transforming individuals for reentry into society and more on maximizing security, and a parallel social shift in emphasis from discipline to risk management.[36] Even post-release, prisoners remain under the control of the carceral state via probation and parole and restrictions imposed by criminal records. Exorbitant bails and fines, even for minor offenses, keep the poor in jail.[37] In many poor urban neighborhoods, especially those inhabited by African Americans, the threat of impending arrest, increased policing, and the relational impact of imprisonment of family members become part of the fabric of the community, a process Megan Comfort calls "secondary prisonization."[38]

A significant proportion of incarcerated adults likely receives some form of public assistance when not confined, though that number has not been documented. Being jailed or imprisoned results in the suspension or discontinuance of these benefits.[39] To reinstate benefits upon release from prison or jail, individuals must complete stacks of paperwork, provide documentation of eligibility, and submit these forms in person at government offices. Some states preclude convicted felons from receiving food stamps or subsidized housing; in most states, employers can legally refuse to hire a convicted felon.[40] Incarceration thus disrupts safety net services people previously received, and furthers their economic marginality upon release. What's more, some law enforcement agencies use food stamp and other public benefit rosters to locate and arrest people with outstanding warrants.[41]

The entwined histories of the public safety net and mass incarceration are crucial for understanding the relationships of care between jail workers and inmates.[42] A safety net catches people when they fall. Certainly for some, jail is part of that fall. But for many, jail is a normalized part of life. Its shelter and other material resources routinely provides them respite from the danger of the streets, in ways public assistance, free clinics, and nonprofit social service agencies have failed to do.

SAN FRANCISCO'S EXPANSIVE SAFETY NET

Most of the women I knew in the San Francisco jail received services from myriad government agencies, publicly funded clinics, and community organizations. San Francisco is known as a progressive city committed to helping marginalized people. As a San Francisco resident working with marginalized groups, I was astounded by the number of community programs serving the poor, homeless, addicted, and transgender communities.[43] One public official told me the city provided grants to over eight hundred nonprofit organizations, most of which serve poor and vulnerable residents.

One group visited daily rent hotels to provide health care and harm-reduction interventions; one nonprofit clinic hosted a "Ladies Night" where women could drop in for food, HIV testing, toiletries, entertainment, manicures, Narcan kits to prevent opiate overdoses, and meetings with case managers. I helped at several of these events, and usually saw at least one woman I knew from jail.[44] The city's county hospital was known for its clear mission, and provided care for anyone who walked through its doors.[45]

Another example of San Francisco's commitment is the "Healthy San Francisco" program implemented in 2007—years before the Affordable Care Act—to provide coordinated health care coverage to approximately sixty thousand residents who lacked health insurance.[46] In addition to a network of health department clinics, more than a dozen nonprofit community clinics provided free care.[47]

City government and nonprofit agencies administered safety net services specifically for pregnant women. For instance, one organization has been helping homeless pregnant women and families find housing, employment, and other services for twenty-five years, and has worked inside the jail to establish connections with women before release. Several residential drug treatment centers allowed pregnant and parenting women to live with their children, though many did not.

Alisha, a pregnant woman I met in jail during her third trimester, lived at many such programs, one while she was pregnant, and others after her baby was born. At one program she was permitted to live with her son, Deijan, but she relapsed, and he was placed in foster care. Alisha's circulation among programs specifically designed for women like her raises questions about the "success" and "failure" of the safety net, specifically in terms of programs to help mothers.

Some services delivered to individuals in San Francisco were channeled through the city's criminal justice system; they included basic safety net services as well as "rehabilitation programs," which city agencies hoped would prevent reincarceration.[48] During my fieldwork, for example, the Adult Probation Department opened a "One Stop" center for San Franciscans on probation, where they could get social work and case management services, mental health care, job training, housing assistance, education, and referrals for medical care. The Sheriff's Department has received national recognition for innovative programs in and out of the jail: the 5 Keys Charter High School where people can study upon release;[49] art and music therapy workshops; an antiviolence initiative, "Resolve to Stop the Violence"; drug treatment programs; a "Women's Re-Entry Center," offering a variety of social services and support groups; work alternatives to incarceration programs; and an array of classes about computer skills, parenting, harm reduction, trauma support, anger management, and more.[50] In addition to programs directly administered by the Sheriff's Department, dozens of community organizations sent volunteers into the jail to provide everything from health education to music and art workshops.

In my observations of the nature of jailcare in the San Francisco jail, I struggled with a core question: how, in a progressive city like San Francisco, which expresses an explicit commitment to help its vulnerable residents, are so many people slipping through the cracks to the extent that jail becomes their safety net? Over time, I have found many possible explanations. One, offered by several jail and public health administrators, was that there were not enough safety net services, particularly supportive housing units, mental health services, and drug treatment programs. In 2016, the city was developing a multisector initiative for police officers to take people using drugs on the streets to a treatment program instead of jail, but it was not clear that there would be enough treatment spots.[51] Furthermore, the city is experiencing a deepening income inequality, in part due to a recent tech boom; many activists claim that the mayor's pro-business policies have further marginalized and displaced people in desperate need of safety net services.

Another explanation is an extension of critiques of welfare reform and the individualizing ethos it propagated, alongside implicit racial bias. Craig Willse offers a related argument, that government and nonprofit agencies dedicated to the poor depend upon and perpetuate the continued marginality of those they serve; rather than ameliorating root causes, the goal has become to manage insecurity.[52] In this view, the robust safety net in San Francisco depends on people continuing to slip through the cracks.

While the Sheriff's Department provided social services in and out of jail, it also inserted law enforcement activities into safety net sites. I frequently heard from women in the jail that they sometimes avoided seeking medical care at the county hospital, because deputies stationed in the emergency room would run their names for outstanding warrants—and could arrest them there.[53]

Another answer to my question about San Francisco's extensive social services involves bureaucratic hoops, duplication, and lack of coordination among services. When I accompanied Evelyn to reinstate her general assistance benefits after a release from jail, we were sent on a wild goose chase to offices throughout the Bay Area to obtain an official copy of her birth certificate. I was astounded by the array of rules, acronyms, and numerical details Evelyn and other women could rattle off to me— information I could never keep straight. Receiving safety net support services required resourcefulness and tremendous time. Moreover, the bureaucratic demands were such that the services did not always arrive— government checks sent to the wrong place, signatures missed here, boxes unchecked there, appointments cancelled because of court appearances. Even after enrolling in programs, utilizing those programs' services requires a challenging degree of surveillance.[54] This is compounded by the fact that many people receiving benefits are on probation or parole, with a variety of reporting requirements and restrictions.

Knight's ethnography of pregnant, drug-addicted women in San Francisco paints a vivid picture of medical and social programs that failed to improve lives but used their enrollees as subjects for ongoing legal and social interventions. For example, Knight notes that a pregnant woman in a methadone program would be considered too stable for a residential drug-treatment program; as a pregnant woman, though, she would be excluded from the city's supportive housing units and would have to add her name to a long waitlist for low-income housing.[55]

I asked an administrator in the health department who has worked for decades with homeless people why, amid a seemingly robust public safety net in San Francisco, so many people still struggle with basic survival. He pithily replied, "Access does not mean quality." Just because free services for, say, health care exist does not mean people's needs are met. He added, "It's all about relationships, and how interactions make someone feel" while that person is accessing safety net services. The connection between feelings and quality of care surfaces, he posited, through a number of interactions, what he called "touches," with people working at these sites. For example, a patient's first human contact at one of San Francisco's public health clinics is with an armed guard. This introduction to the clinic means patients are more likely to feel judged, unsafe, and alienated from the services they seek. Five more "touches" with staff occur before patients receive their service; each touch can potentially make patients "bristle" and increase their unease. This administrator's diagnosis of public safety net problems suggests that shortcomings are not due simply to lack of funding or material services, or even the neoliberal need to manage marginalized bodies. Rather, the quality of these services hinges on their ability to convincingly demonstrate care. If people using the services feel cared for, they are more invested in the outcome.

There is no single answer to the question about the discrepancy between San Francisco's robust safety net and its failures. Clearly, though, the relationships and structures of the social safety net are entangled in jailcare and the services and care that jailcare provides.[56]

"JUDICIALISATION OF THE RIGHT TO HEALTH" FOR PRISONERS

These features of the safety net and mass incarceration have forced the carceral system to confront the reality that it must tend the basic needs of the bodies it confines—Dolovich's carceral burden. The courts have been deeply involved in delineating the nature and scope of this health care. Juridical claims surrounding prisoner health care grapple with the unresolved tension between obligation to care and an individual's deservingness.

In the 1920s, several state-level court cases recognized the state's carceral burden to provide medical care within jails and prisons.[57] Fifty years later, in the wake of civil rights activism that resulted in the jailing of many activists, the 1970s saw a surge in prisoners' rights lawsuits.[58] Lower court cases in the early part of the decade revealed atrocious medical conditions. Instances of prisoners' death by neglect and their conscription to perform procedures on fellow inmates prompted prisons and jails to establish formal health care systems.[59] This was true in San Francisco, where a 1970s lawsuit against the city for abysmal jail conditions forced the creation of health care services; a 1982 case created a "consent decree," allowing for expansion of services, and a 1991 class action lawsuit further mandated the jail improve medical conditions.[60] As one longtime jail health administrator told me, "All of this [health care in the San Francisco Jail] has developed through lawsuits. It wasn't because someone said, 'Wow, we really need to do right by these people.'" While the response to this surge in litigation across the nation in the 1970s and 1980s established systems of health care in jails and prisons, many facilities improved services just to the point of avoiding more lawsuits.

The most influential case was undoubtedly *Estelle v. Gamble,* notable for invoking the Eighth Amendment's proscription of cruel and unusual punishment.[61] The majority opinion of the Supreme Court came to this conclusion by appealing to "standards of decency." It is worth citing at length:

> These elementary principles establish the government's obligation to provide medical care for those whom it is punishing by incarceration. An inmate must rely on prison authorities to treat his medical needs; if the authorities fail to do so, those needs will not be met. In the worst cases, such a failure may actually produce physical "torture or a lingering death," (*In re Kemmler, supra*), the evils of most immediate concern to the drafters of the Amendment. In less serious cases, denial of medical care may result in pain and suffering which no one suggests would serve any penological purpose. (*Cf. Gregg v. Georgia, supra,* at 182–183 [joint opinion]). The infliction of such unnecessary suffering is inconsistent with contemporary standards of decency as manifested in modern legislation codifying the common law view that "it is but just that the public be required to care for the prisoner, who cannot, by reason of the deprivation of his liberty, care for himself." We therefore conclude that deliberate indifference to serious medical needs of prisoners constitutes the "unnecessary and wanton infliction of pain," *Gregg v. Georgia, supra,* at 173 (joint opinion), proscribed by the Eighth Amendment.

The Court's use of pathos appeals to the reader's sympathy and sense of justice, as its diction—"torture or a lingering death," "evils," "decency," "suffering"—imbues prisoners' right to health care with moral weight.

Likewise, Justice Marshall's phrase "deliberate indifference" suggests that lack of sentiment in prisoner health care is a problem.[62] This lack of sentiment, or indifference, is the classic attitude of modern bureaucracy, and the "moral alibi for inaction."[63] But indifference can also be seen as an active "rejection of common humanity."[64] It takes effort not to care. The courts have, subsequent to *Estelle,* codified deliberate indifference as "action or inaction taken in conscious disregard of a substantial risk of serious harm."[65] That is, if a prison guard were not aware that his actions (or inactions) would lead to injury, his (in)actions would not qualify as deliberate indifference. Ignorance cannot be prosecuted.[66] In order to be in violation of the Constitution, concern must be consciously withheld. Furthermore, deliberate indifference can be prosecuted only if it is directed toward a "serious medical need."

Because the phrases are difficult to pin down, there have been tens of thousands of lawsuits[67] since *Estelle* to challenge and define the meaning of both "serious medical needs" and "deliberate indifference."[68] Such extensive litigation of prisoner health care has contributed to the "judicialisation of the right to health,"[69] as well as the medicalization of the prisoner, whose body becomes terrain for demonstrating the presence or absence of the state's deliberate indifference.[70]

Identifying "serious medical needs" has largely been retroactive, defined through lawsuits that then designate certain neglected health issues as "serious."[71] Examples include: untimely or absent distribution of critical medications; incompetent health care providers who neglected symptoms; suicides that could have been prevented; the shackling of pregnant women in labor; the prevention of women from getting abortions; and the ignoring of a pregnant woman's labor pains, resulting in the jail-cell birth of a baby who died.[72] As individual cases, each seeks to specify serious medical need and deliberate indifference. Each, too, grapples with moral questions about the state's carceral burden to care, the kind of care incarcerated people deserve, and the way sentiments of concern or indifference figure into care.

The judicialization of prisoners' right to health care has set the stage for a spectacular intersection of juridical power, human rights, health, and imprisonment. In the 2011 case *Brown v. Plata*, the Supreme Court ordered California to depopulate its prisons by forty-six thousand people in three years, because health conditions in its overcrowded prisons were abysmal and previous court-mandated attempts to overhaul the prison's medical system were inadequate. In *Brown*, the Supreme Court reaffirmed the moral stakes of prisoner health care, arguing that suffering due to inadequate medical and mental health care in California prisons was "incompatible with the concept of human dignity and has no place in a civilized society."[73]

Nurses at the San Francisco jail did not speak the judicial language of "serious medical needs" and "deliberate indifference." In fact, many of the medical staff were not aware of the *Estelle* mandate that made their work a matter of constitutional rights. Once, I heard a patient in the waiting area of the jail clinic threaten to sue the jail because she had to wait two weeks for a gynecologic exam. The medical staff hardly gave her notice, and those who did mocked her. Perhaps they, like I, assumed that the patient was unlikely to pursue legal action, and that even if she did, she was unlikely to win. What is clear in these caregivers' derisive responses is that health care rights for prisoners are not only adjudicated in courtrooms, but through everyday human relationships and practices of care. After all, rights are not pre-political entitlements but are configurations of social, political, and institutional arrangements, made meaningful through human interaction.[74]

PROFESSIONALIZING AND PRIVATIZING CORRECTIONAL HEALTH CARE

While the courts have retroactively attempted to create a taxonomy for serious medical needs and criteria for identifying the absence of appropriate concern, a burgeoning professional health care community has attempted to prospectively delineate such medical conditions and obligations. A field of practice catalyzed by the *Estelle* mandate and known as "correctional health care" has emerged around the problem of the carceral burden to care.[75]

The professional organization of carceral health care is relatively recent—since the 1970s—though doctors and nurses have long served prisons and jails in varyingly limited capacities.[76] The National Prison Association (now the American Correctional Association) formed in the reformist era of 1870, and asserted in its foundational document, "Declaration of Principles," that the prison has a role in caring for its inmates: "The hospital accommodations, medical stores and surgical instruments should be all that humanity requires and science can supply; and all needed means for personal cleanliness should be without stint."[77]

Literature on medical care in prisons in the days before it was legally mandated is sparse, but there are accounts of inmates being made to act as nurses to other inmates and doctors participating in the overall management of prisons and presiding over electric chair executions.[78] One exposé of Arkansas prison farms suggested that sections of the on-site prison hospital served as a torture chamber, with assistance from prison doctors.[79] Alongside medical atrocities, the post–World War II era of penology aspired to rehabilitate prisoners using a curative, medical model of criminality and confinement.[80] Yet many jails and prisons had no official on-site medical staff until *Estelle* came along. According to several former San Francisco health administrators I interviewed, this was the case in the San Francisco jail until lawsuits in the 1970s and 1980s. If someone got sick, deputies called paramedics. The jail stocked a few medications distributed by custody staff or other nonmedical professionals. In 1983, "Forensic Services" (the name was later changed) was established as a division of the San Francisco health department to provide health care services inside the jail, although there was minimal interest from the health department. As one jail health administrator who had worked in the jail since the 1970s told me:

> It was seen as a necessity, but leaders in the health department did not have much concern for health care services inside the jail. [People at the health department] absolutely did not see that . . . the people we were treating [in jail] were also [getting care] in the rest of the health department when they weren't in custody. And so we had to do a lot of work to persuade people to fund and integrate our system of care with the rest of the department. . . . We were really sort of trying to push the idea that the person next to you on the bus, your next-door neighbor, your nephew, were all people who had been in and out of jail, and they were going to be back out on the streets and therefore we needed to do better.

This attitude was corroborated by another early Forensic Services administrator, who reminisced that the agency's offices were located in the jail's plumbing chase, and operated on a shoestring budget. The only way the administrator could get anything done, like hiring nurses and doctors, was by using "the heavy hammer or hand of the court." Forensic Services leaders built their division from scratch, hiring health care staff, developing protocols, building relationships with custody staff, creating innovative programs for HIV patients in the early days of the epidemic, and cultivating a mission to help the inmate who was also "the person next to you on the bus."

The first national-scale effort of the medical community to address health care for incarcerated people was a 1973 American Medical Association (AMA) report. The AMA surveyed 1,159 sheriff's jurisdictions and found a systematic and egregious absence of adequate medical care.[81] This prompted the AMA, in 1975, to undertake a pilot program at thirty jails to systematize health care provision.

In 1983, this pilot program formalized into the nonprofit organization the National Commission on Correctional Healthcare (NCCHC).[82]

According to NCCHC's website, its "early mission was to evaluate, formulate policy, and develop programs for a floundering area clearly in need of assistance."[83] The NCCHC now accredits hundreds of jails, prisons, and juvenile facilities across the United States that have chosen to meet its nationally accepted standards of health care.[84] The American Correctional Association also offers an accreditation program. Interestingly, the San Francisco jail clinic was not accredited by the NCCHC. A health department official explained to me that accreditation was an expensive logistical hassle; since the services provided at San Francisco exceeded the standards, the leadership did not see a need for accreditation.

Although the NCCHC is not a legal organization, the juridical framework established by *Estelle* nonetheless gets played out through the organization's regulatory guidance for prison and jail clinics. Standardizing clinical care provides jails and prisons with a road map for what the NCCHC deems a "constitutionally acceptable level of care,"[85] or avoiding deliberate indifference to serious medical needs. The NCCHC's two-hundred-page book of standards translates these phrases into specific logistics and services, from personnel and administration to medical diets and health care services.[86] Most standards are "required" for an accredited facility, but a few are optional. Such a dichotomy parallels the central tension between the minimum care to which prisoners are entitled—rights and constitutional requirements—and the moral vernacular of their deservingness.

One jail nursing administrator whom I met at a conference told me that her facility's NCCHC accreditation saved them from several lawsuits. "It's an assurance," she told me, "that you're not showing 'deliberate indifference.'" She rolled her eyes disdainfully. The legal mandate of *Estelle* was imbricated into her sense of professional obligation, which was to avoid being perceived as indifferent. Her reliance on accreditation for its legal protections suggests a risk-management approach to health care for prisoners.

Over the past three decades, NCCHC has grown into a vibrant professional society for nurses, doctors, administrators, and mental health workers in prisons and jails. The NCCHC holds educational conferences, publishes an academic journal and textbooks, and confirms individuals with the title "Certified Correctional Health Professional."[87] The majority of the correctional health care workforce is composed of nurses, followed by mental health workers. These forces of professionalism try to normalize the work of health care providers in an area that continues to be marginalized by mainstream professional circles. In some cases, correctional health care gives rise to what some bioethicists have called a "dual loyalty problem," where doctors and nurses experience tension between their obligations to care and the regimented, punishing space of prison.[88] This tension sets these providers apart from doctors and nurses who work in hospitals or community clinics.

Correctional health care has also become a revenue-generating business. Total health care spending in correctional institutions in 2010 was nearly $8 billion.[89] Privatized prison health care emerged in the years immediately following *Estelle*, with classic neoliberal reasoning that the private sector could more efficiently and cheaply manage prison medical services in prisons than the government. Private prison health contracts now account for 40% of all inmate care in the United States.[90] Corizon, the largest private prison health company, earns an estimated $1.5 billion in profits annually.[91] A 2012 article in the trade journal *Corrections Forum* asserts that the predominant concern for a facility choosing to privatize health care is cost savings: "With corrections agencies facing deficits and projected deficits in their budgets they are looking for privatization to close gaps in coverage. . . . [L]awmakers [in Florida] are hoping to achieve $30 million in annual savings through privatization."[92] Nowhere does the article mention quality of health care for patients or inmates.

I visited several of these corporate headquarters, all located in pleasant, generic suburban office parks, which made privatized prison services seem a normal, unobtrusive part of the economy. The sleek office architecture and granite outdoor fountains were a stark contrast to the prisons and jails these corporations managed across the country. People at headquarters spoke of "vendors" and "clients," referring to jails and prisons that contracted for their services. Their relationship was with paying customers, not inmates or patients.

Sleek corporate headquarters and high profit margins contribute to a stark reality at many privatized correctional health care sites, where media and courtroom accounts have documented neglectful care and avoidable deaths.[93] Understaffing, unqualified doctors, missed diagnoses, and withheld drugs are evidence cited by journalists and attorneys to link "cost-effectiveness" strategies to harmful, unconstitutional care. Corizon alone was sued 660 times for unconstitutional care from 2008–2013.[94] After Arizona privately contracted its health care services, medical spending in prisons dropped while the number of inmate deaths increased.[95]

Pressure to keep health care costs below what the prison pays the company can influence decisions health care providers make about what constitutes serious need, and how to actively avoid indifference in decision making. When I asked Kevin, a physician-administrator at a private company, the ways in which the profit needs of the company influence medical decisions, he replied: "We're interested in cost-effectiveness everywhere."

The calculus of care for Kevin had an implied moral argument. He claimed that the state's carceral burden should not unburden the constitutive outside of its responsibility to provide care. He used hepatitis C, prevalent in incarcerated populations and expensive to treat, as the example: "I mean, we're not going to screen them [for hepatitis C] at short-stay facilities. That's the community's responsibility. If the community doesn't do it, then . . . why should you expect the county jail to?" For Kevin, the solutions to problems affecting both the jail and the community were not part of the carceral burden. Kevin added, "The correctional system should not be held to account for the weaknesses of the community system. That's my belief." Yet Kevin's beliefs are in contrast to the everyday realities of jailcare, in which the jail occupies the default position of redressing the deficiencies of the safety net.

This is not to say that care at all private sites is putatively worse, or that correctional medical care delivered by public entities is immune to cost concerns or incompetent care; the San Francisco jail's medical services were administered through the city's health department, and budgetary constraints and clinical incompetencies were perennial issues. Nor is it to disregard the nuanced compassion in the everyday experiences of nurses, doctors, and patients at private sites. Rather, this attention to privatized prison health care illuminates the prominent role of market forces in adjudicating the state's carceral burden.

PUBLIC HEALTH JUSTICE AND PRISONER HEALTH CARE

The overlapping dimensions of public health and social justice represent another domain central to prisoner health care in the United States.

Academic researchers, administrators, jail providers, public health workers, and prisoner activist groups alike have emphasized the broader implications of care (and its absence) inside jails and prisons, for incarcerated individuals and the larger community. For one, prisons house large numbers of people in common space, creating a reservoir for the transmission of infectious diseases. Public health advocates argue that health care infrastructure within prisons should work to prevent disease.

A second public health perspective is opportunistic, premised on an understanding that most incarcerated people have poor indices of health and limited pre-incarceration access to health care. Incarceration becomes an opportunity, albeit an unfortunate one, to work with populations with an already-high prevalence of mental illness, addiction, chronic disease, sexually transmitted infections, hepatitis, HIV, and other conditions. Incarceration may exacerbate those conditions or, when care and reentry services are provided, ameliorate them. It is no surprise, then, that jail has become a primary health care provider to women like Evelyn and Kima. The opportunistic approach, however well intentioned, is nonetheless problematic, for it reflects the deficiencies of health care outside of jail or prison. Moreover, correctional facilities are not designed to treat illness but to punish and confine.

A third public health perspective on prisoner health care builds on the reality that, ultimately, most incarcerated people are released back into mainstream society. This was the message that San Francisco jail health administrators used in the 1980s to procure funding from the health department.[96] Stephanie, a nurse in San Francisco's intake jail, told me on many occasions that she loved her job because she felt like she was "on the frontlines of public health." In this view, tending inmates' health benefits the health of the communities to which people return; it envisions a body of productive citizens whose health has been improved by incarceration.[97] Through this lens, mass incarceration is understood as both a problem and a disturbing solution to absent health care.

These public health approaches coexist with a social justice imperative present among certain circles of activists and medical academic researchers.[98] That is, many researchers and people who provide care to prisoners—myself included—are motivated by a humanistic desire to help individuals they see as marginalized by broader structures of poverty, racism, and inequality. Many of these activists liken mass incarceration to a public health epidemic, a scourge as destructive as any infectious disease.[99] Human Rights Watch, Justice Now, Legal Services for Prisoners with Children, and California Coalition for Women Prisoners are but some of the hundred or so nonprofit groups in the United States who advocate for health care improvements in prisons.[100] Indeed, there is much to improve.

Both the social justice and public health perspective were part of the ethos of San Francisco's Jail Medical Care (JMC). Although these views did not resonate with all staff, they were explicit driving forces for some clinical staff and JMC leaders who set the tone and policies of the agency. Many of these leaders had been involved in grassroots social activism in the 1960s and 1970s, and were on the front lines of AIDS activism in the 1980s. One leader who held the position for over twenty-five years worked to expand JMC services beyond the minimum required by law, beyond the "deliberate indifference" standard. He fought for budget increases so that preventive health care services could be provided, and patients could access the same quality and standard of care in jail that existed in the community. When the city government threatened to privatize medical services in the jail, he spoke passionately of society's responsibility to the city's most vulnerable citizens:

> What is wrong with our society that so many people are ending up in jail who are really sick? You know, of course there's always going to be people who commit crimes and need to go to jail for whatever reason or, you know, but an overwhelming majority of people are not there because they're bad people; they're just in bad situations. . . . There isn't housing, there isn't food, there, you know, there isn't substance abuse treatment except for very small numbers of people.

He and other JMC leaders had a mission, one infused with justice, to care for people in jail whom they saw as marginalized by broader forces in society.

CARE AND CUSTODY, DESERVINGNESS AND OBLIGATION

Once a month, a joint meeting was held among San Francisco Sheriff's Department leadership—usually the chief custody officer at each jail—and

JMC and jail psychiatric services administrators. These meetings addressed the tricky intersection between overall management of a jail and health care services. One example of an agenda item: what to do with an inmate who needed a cane or walker for mobility, given that these devices could be used as weapons. For the most part, these meetings were collegial; medical and custody staff exchanged pleasantries over coffee and doughnuts before the meetings started. But amid the snacks, formal agendas, and polite exchanges, people discussed fundamental issues at the interface of confinement and medical care: what kind of care did inmates deserve and what was the jail's responsibility to ensure that care? JMC's public health and social justice orientation, the position of the jail in the city's safety net, legal requirements to care, and the health care providers' professional integrity provided the critical backdrop to these meetings.

As I delve into the everyday realities of care within an institution of confinement in San Francisco, these four macro level forces—the safety net intertwined with mass incarceration; legal; professional; and public health—must be kept in mind. These forces take form in the unique circumstances of carcerality: punishment, normalizing regimes, restricted liberty, inequality, violence, and, ultimately, human relations. If the analysis were left to an exploration of these four intersecting spheres of prisoner health care, we would have an interesting narrative of the convergence of policies, ideologies, and calls for change in defining who and under what circumstances people deserve health care. Instead, we must look to the ways that health and care are made meaningful on the ground as individuals contemplate in action the complex moral terrain of obligation and deservingness of health care, and the sentiments that get worked through those assessments. The remaining chapters of *Jailcare* pursue the everyday instantiations of these structural forces in the routine unfolding of care in the jail, and how the inequalities surrounding the jail make it possible for intimate care to flourish inside.

2 Triaging the Everyday, Every Day

> I trust these [medical] people [in jail] because, well, it's a
> lot different [than prison]. A lot different. . . . I'm more
> familiar with these people.
>
> *Ladonna, a woman frequently incarcerated at the*
> *San Francisco jail*

THE TRIAGE DOOR

The door to the intake jail, CJ1, opened. Two police officers escorted a thin, bearded, handcuffed man through the entry. He wore a dirty shirt, ripped pants, and worn-down sneakers; he reeked of alcohol and urine. This particular door, which opened to a wide alleyway, was the only direct interface between the outside world and the space populated by inmates and staff.

When the CJ1 door slid open, nurse Charlie welcomed the police officers and the handcuffed man from behind a desk that faced the entrance. The officers motioned their charge to sit down, and handed Charlie a beige card with the man's name on it. Charlie then asked the man a series of standardized health questions. This was medical triage, the first thing to happen upon entering the San Francisco jail. Before criminal processing, before custody was transferred from the police to the Sheriff's Department, a nurse evaluated each person's physical and mental stability.[1] If the nurse detected urgent conditions, then medical (and often psychiatric) intervention diverted the person from criminal processing. Nurses might detect a wound acquired during the event that led to arrest, or one that had been festering for weeks. They might identify a person with diabetes who had not taken insulin for days and was at risk of going into a coma, or a pregnant woman withdrawing from heroin. Triage nurses sorted these new arrestees into various categories of health and disrepair.

Triage in CJ1 had the hallmarks of decision-making and prioritizing that characterize the medical triage seen in emergency rooms and disaster zones.[2] These processes contain not just a practical but a moral dimension, one that involves reckoning someone's health-related deservingness in the face of finite resources.[3] In jail triage, the criteria for this calculus of health-related deservingness were guided in part by official JMC protocols. Determinations about deservingness were also affected by the reality of tending people who might not otherwise get treated outside of jail, and whose treatment occurred in a space of punishment; in other words, it was an active, contingent process of care. CJ1 triage thus represented this complicated nexus between the precarity of the streets and the condition of confinement for receiving medical care. Because of Supreme Court decisions and professional regulatory apparatuses, jail medical triage is an expectation. But in the everyday interactions of triage, it is the moral register of reckoning the value of another life that is at play.

Attention to the everyday interactions of jail triage reveals the chronic nature of moral considerations, fostered by recidivism and patients who constantly cycled through jail. Its recurrent nature facilitated jail triage as a social process, and recidivism as an intimate relationship. Along with dynamic assessments of health-related deservingness, the relational nature of triage grounded its care in ambiguity. Triage staff saw their work involving urgent health care matters reflecting the deficiencies of their patients' lives outside of jail. In jail, then, triage involved not only individuals, but the inequalities outside of jail that constitute mass incarceration.

THE ANGRY CHAIR

"I call this 'the angry chair,'" Charlie told me one night in CJ1. He pointed to the empty blue plastic chair in front of him, in which new arrestees sat as a nurse performed the triage assessment. The chair, the stackable kind you might see at a church luncheon, was light and easy to clean; chairs just like it were located throughout the jail to support a wide range of jail

activities, from lawyer-client meetings to music classes, and their attend-
ant emotions. In CJ1, the blue chair structured the triage evaluation.
Charlie called it "the angry chair" because people who had just been
arrested were typically not in the most receptive of moods. "Everyone's
angry when they first arrive," he explained.

Constant movement and a charged energy surrounded CJ1. The background noise of deputies tapping on computers and socializing with co-
workers was punctuated by sounds from new arrestees in holding cells:
anguished sobs, calls for help, angry insults directed at no one in particular. This evening, likely in the throes of psychosis, a woman in a group
holding cell fifteen feet from where Charlie and I sat shouted nonsensical
phrases and banged her head against the door. She screamed in protest
when two jail deputies dressed in black uniforms grabbed her by the arms,
dragged her to a "safety cell" with padded walls, pushed her inside, and
closed the heavy iron door.

Meanwhile, next to the triage desk, a deputy's iPod blared the 1980's
song "Close to Me" by The Cure, accompanied by his keyboard typing.
Another deputy arrived to start his shift and cheerfully greeted Charlie
and me. "I brought some cookies from my favorite Polish bakery! You
should have some," he offered. From the staff's perspective, though CJI
was taking in people in various states of intoxication, aggressiveness, and
fatigue, the atmosphere was light and social.

CJ1 was a busy place for a nurse to be stationed. One year alone, according to JMC records provided to me, saw 24,233 triage encounters, an
average of 66 per day, mostly concentrated in late afternoon and nighttime shifts. Since CJ1 was the point of contact with the outside world,
people were constantly entering (police officers bringing in arrests,
inmates returning to jail from the hospital) and exiting (people being
released from jail or sent to prison for longer sentences). The triage nurse
assessed everyone who entered. Some arrestees stayed in CJ1 for a few
hours and were released; this often included women who were picked up
on prostitution charges. Others stayed in CJ1 up to twenty-four hours,
until they were sent to a housing unit in CJ2.

Deputies moved people in street clothes from holding tanks to curtained
dressing rooms, where they "dressed in" to standard-issue orange pants,
shirts, socks, shoes, and undergarments, before being shuffled in and out of

holding cells to have mug shots and fingerprints taken. Nurses, psychiatric workers, and deputies checked on those with severe mental illness or in withdrawal from alcohol and drugs.[4] Some arrestees lay on the floor or the wooden bench in their cells, while cellmates paced around them.

The centerpiece of the triage routine was a seventeen-item health screening questionnaire and a visual assessment of each patient in the angry chair. The interaction was guided by the jail's electronic medical record system, called CHART (discussed later in this chapter). During the triage interview, nurses would adeptly switch back and forth between a computer screen and the newly arrested person in front of them. Charlie, who had worked in the jail for over twenty years, paraphrased the standardized questions and switched their order, trying to sound like he had not asked the same series of questions thousands of times. Sometimes nurses averted their eyes from the patient to accomplish triage as quickly and impersonally as possible. Nancy, another longtime CJ1 nurse, read questions from the computer prompts in a detached monotone, firmly redirecting patients who offered information out of sequence.

The triage questionnaire programmed into CHART required the nurse to enter a response for each of the following prompts, a mix of yes/no, fill-in-the-blank, and open-ended questions:

Refuse to answer triage questions

General appearance

Urgent medical condition

Fever, cough, sore throat

Prescription medication brought in with patient

Primary care provider

Recent injury or trauma

Current abscesses or infestations

PPD status

Night sweats

Recent weight loss

ETOH [alcohol] use

History of diabetes

Are you suicidal

Drug use
Women-specific questionnaire
Last menstrual period
Are you pregnant

Later, during the "intake assessment," nurses asked a much more detailed set of questions for those remaining in jail. This occurred in a semi-private, glass-walled room in a different part of CJ1. Both of these initial evaluations in the intake jail sorted people into groups meriting different degrees (including none) of medical attention before incarceration could proceed.[5]

On the surface, jail medical triage appeared to process people as bundles of biological needs—many of which had been neglected on the streets—that needed to be addressed. Triage nurses screened patients for acute and serious medical ailments as a condition of entry, employing the triage questionnaire to discover lacerations, HIV, asthma, diabetes, or other acute and chronic conditions. Often, patients would reveal, either by direct admission or through signs like high blood sugar or difficulty breathing, that they had not been taking their medication; on many occasions, the last time patients had taken their medication was during their last incarceration. Triage nurses would intervene with the appropriate therapeutic, which would continue throughout the jail stay. Insulin lowered blood sugars; inhalers loosened wheezy lungs; anti-retroviral medications raised CD4 counts; and prenatal vitamins provided nutrients to pregnant women and their fetuses. These activities that comprise jail medical triage seem an extension of classic reductionist activities of carceral institutions: processing individuals into a collection of bodies, enveloping them in a therapeutic logic of control. But Charlie's moniker "the angry chair" reveals that triage interactions exceeded this institutional-level reading of triage as a controlling strategy; in fact, the patient's affective state and the nurse's interpretation of it were part of triage too.

DESERVINGNESS: SENTIMENT IN TRIAGE

During a mid-afternoon lull in CJ1, another longtime nurse, Lenny, reflected to me about his triage work, relaying stories of a diabetic patient who slashed the tires of a parked car in plain view of a police officer so he could come to jail to get insulin; and of patients so accustomed to the jail's routines of care that they asked for "my Percocets" as soon as they sat in the angry chair.

As he reminisced, Lenny conveyed both humor about the situation and annoyance with people's demands. "I don't know if we should be pampering them like this. You know, in [adjacent county] they have to pay a fee every time they request medical care." Lenny presented this fact to me as a good idea, to discourage people from asking for too much.[6] Lenny then looked around at the processing scene in CJ1 and adopted a different moral stance. "I like working here. After years of ICU [Intensive Care Unit] nursing, of med-surg at [a private hospital], here I feel like I'm serving the community." He gestured with his chin at the arrested people around us. "These people are social outcasts," he said compassionately. "At the end of the day, I know I've done something for the people in my community. I'm a Christian, and caring for these people is in line with my Christian values." This mix of cynicism and moral obligation exemplified Lenny's nursing duties in triage.

People like Lenny were constantly confronted with broader questions about society's responsibility toward "social outcasts" and, consequently, with questions about the distribution of medical care. Should jail triage nurses dose insulin to a returning patient with a dangerously high blood sugar, knowing he did not use insulin on the streets? The answer to this was always yes, since untreated hyperglycemia can lead to coma and death. But should Lenny order "Percocets," implicated in opiate addiction and an underground jail economy? That answer was less clear. CJ1 nurses performed their triage work amid the tensions of the state's responsibility to care for its citizens and questions about an individual's specific deservingness to be cared for. This made care a process filled with ambiguity, adapted to each triage encounter. Lenny's own conflicted stance against pampering and in favor of helping "social outcasts" illustrates the ambiguity at the heart of moral assessments of deservingness in jail triage. As Willen contends, the moral domain in which deservingness claims are articulated are deeply relational. That is, they are based on "one's sense of actual or presumed social connection to those whose deservingness is in question."[7]

In the age of mass incarceration, imprisoned people are understood in mainstream representations as criminals who have violated social and legal norms, are incarcerated to exclude them from society, and are thus undeserving. And yet, the emotionally laden processes of triage conceptualize these individuals' worth as humans, as triaging nurses consider how much and what kind of care people arrested for allegedly committing a crime deserve. Nurses in CJ1 triage could not help but bring to their work their own affective and moral stance on the state's responsibility toward the allegedly criminal body before them and the worthiness of that body.

What I observed in CJ1 triage was that nurses' assessments of deservingness had more to do with marginality on the streets and perception of patients' self-care than with their status as alleged criminals. The triage nurses' savvy in deciphering numerical codes for the arrest charges on a person's jail card was usually more a point of interest than a reckoning point of their patients' health-related deservingness. This was apparent to me as nurse Nancy looked at the back of a patient's jail card before triaging a patient. "5143–2, that's for theft. But see this—" Nancy pointed to a few other numbers on the card. "That means she has some outstanding warrants. She's going to be here a while," she said nonchalantly, and proceeded to ask the patient the standard triage questions. The patient's criminal history did not concern her. Part of the active work of triage involved sidelining knowledge of criminal charges in order to focus through a medical lens. This lens viewed patients' marginal social position as part of their medical profile. Another CJ1 nurse acknowledged this, in saying, "You know, people say these jail people are 'throw-aways,'" furrowing his brow. "They're not throw-aways, they're people." This nurse both acknowledged and rejected a dominant stance that devalued his patients in jail.

At each stage of the triage decision-making, nurses implicitly confronted the failures of society at large to equitably care for people. This was a stressful burden, particularly at the interface of healing and punishing apparatuses. Triage was an emotionally laden task that, though not reducible to politics, was affectively shaped by political dimensions of inequality and marginality. Lauren Berlant's conception of compassion is useful here, in recognizing that affect can be both political in its operational effects and intersubjective as a process. Both nodes are connected by the moral weight behind decisions about whether to act or to withhold action. Berlant writes: "In context [compassion's] power involves myriad anxieties about who among the sufferers deserves to be positively or negatively judged, and why, and whether there is any adequate solution to the problem at hand."[8]

Triage nurses' work in the responsibility-deservingness tension entailed such ongoing anxiety. As the sole clinical decision-makers in CJ1, nurses found their independence both rewarding and stressful. They feared "missing something" that would cause the patient further suffering and might invite reprimand from supervisors. Furthermore, their professional conduct was on public display. How nurses conducted themselves with patients, the degree of sympathy they showed (too much or too little), how much time evaluations took, how they extracted personal details from the patient—these dimensions of triage put nurses and their competency under personal scrutiny from police officers and deputies. A third source of triage anxiety stemmed from the fact that nurses were gatekeepers between the police officers and deputies responsible for the arrestee.[9] Police did not like to be sent to the hospital with an arrestee, and sometimes retaliated with public insults, ridicule, and other forms of harassment during current or future interactions in CJ1.

MEDICAL CLEARANCE AND THE ASSUMPTIONS OF TRIAGE

The express purpose of the initial triage was twofold: to identify people with urgent medical or psychiatric needs that required attention before they could be processed further; and to identify people with nonurgent medical or mental health issues who would, once admitted to jail, warrant medications, testing, or detailed clinical care. It is generally standard practice at jails and prisons to perform some version of medical screening at intake. The comprehensiveness varies; some facilities may not even require that medical professionals conduct the assessments.[10] Despite this variability, the near-universal existence of some medical screening upon entry presupposes ongoing danger from multiple sources. It presumes that the outside world can be dangerous for bodies that therefore need medical assessment; it presumes jail may be dangerous for bodies inside, if they have untreated medical conditions; it presumes inmates may expose other inmates to danger, such as communicable diseases;[11] and it presumes that inmates may be dangerous for the institution, if medical lawsuits charging "deliberate indifference to the serious needs of prisoners" ensue. The *Estelle* case created liability concerns for jails around inmates' health. Jail medical triage is thus, in addition to being a moral, relational filter to assess health-related deservingness, a risk management strategy that addresses potential dangers.

Two key health-based assumptions underlie the existence of this medical classificatory ritual in jail and the various presumptions of danger. The first assumption is that the daily outside lives of most people cycling through jail are "unhealthy." San Francisco jail health care providers witnessed this embodied ill health as people walked into the triage door: emaciation, obesity, lacerations, abscesses, track marks from injecting drugs, high blood pressure, bloodshot eyes, dirty clothes. Nurses were routinely confronted with the stigma of social suffering and structural violence. Nonetheless, they often attributed these visible signs of ill health to individual irresponsibility.[12] "They just don't take care of themselves," a nurse told me derisively after triaging a woman with scabbed-over bug bites on her face and the darting eyes of someone high on crack cocaine.

Amid this derision, nurses simultaneously understood that "their lives are hard." Not infrequently, nurses would list homelessness and poverty among other reasons for the "unhealthiness" of the patients they treated. Certainly, nurses screened for such downstream, medically legible consequences of structural vulnerabilities and the deficiencies of the safety net as housing deprivation, poverty, racism, and gender-based violence. Understanding these connections raised the possibility that jail could remedy outside suffering or limited access to health care. Nurse Stephanie, who had worked as a CJ1 triage nurse for over fifteen years, meticulously combed electronic medical records from the jail system and the community health system (to which all jail health workers had access). On a number of occasions, she discovered reports of sexually transmitted infections (STIs) that had been diagnosed in the community or a prior jail stay, but had yet to be treated, for a variety of reasons—patients had no address or phone through which to be notified; patients lacked the resources to get treatment; or patients did not trust the clinic at which they were tested.

Untreated STIs identified in jail triage thus hinted at a range of the medical safety net's possible shortcomings.[13]

Nurses and other jail clinicians were always negotiating what to do with the health conditions detected in the bodies before them, within the constraints and possibilities of CJ1. For example, since a chlamydia STI, which is often asymptomatic, is not a life-threatening situation, treating it in jail triage might seem like an unnecessary excess. If untreated, though, chlamydia could spread to others and lead to adverse health consequences such as pelvic inflammatory disease, infertility, ectopic pregnancy, and chronic pelvic pain. It is also simple to treat, with a single dose of inexpensive antibiotic. For triage nurses like Stephanie, treating this infection—acquired on the streets, tested for at a nontriage moment, but noted upon entry to jail—was a reasonable triage intervention.

The second health-based assumption behind the existence of medical triage upon entering jail and prison is that incarceration itself acts upon bodies and psyches. Therefore, people must be screened to, in theory, make incarceration proceed "safely"; indeed, many incarcerated people suffer physically and mentally from conditions of confinement and inadequate medical care. Jail medical triage is thus not unlike health screening to enter another total institution, the military, which assesses fitness for the violence of combat. A major difference, of course, is that a health condition may preclude someone from entering the military, but an illness can only delay (if a person is sent to the hospital) or qualify the conditions of incarceration.

This perspective on jail medical triage as readying someone for incarceration was not actively acknowledged by the medical staff at San Francisco. Doing so would suggest a subordination of the healing goals of medical care to the punitive goals of confinement. At the same time, the language used to define the final step of the triage process is revealing: "medical clearance." If the triage process detected an acute condition in a patient, the nurse would send the patient to the county hospital to be "medically cleared." Conversely, if no acute condition was detected, the nurse would sign his or her name on the new arrestee's custody card (the piece of cardstock with select information that followed a person through the jail), and jail processing could proceed with implicit medical consent.[14] Both stances of jail triage—screening the deficiencies of the streets and screening to further the carceral process—played out practically in the first decision that triage nurses made: to send someone to the hospital or not. In this capacity, triage nurses had notable, albeit short-lived, authority, as they could arbitrate, if not override, criminal processing by ordering hospital-level care.

Certain conditions, by JMC policy, required transport from the jail to the nearby county hospital.[15] This protocol helped medical decisions seem objective and uniform and, at least in theory, protected triage nurses from the inconvenienced gazes of police officers who would have to escort arrestees to the hospital. Diverting someone to the hospital also represented the risk-management orientation of triage; this was especially true for pregnant women and their fetuses. For example, if a woman reported using opiates (heroin or prescription painkillers), protocol required the triage nurse to perform a urine pregnancy test. If the woman was pregnant, she was immediately sent to the hospital for medical clearance, since withdrawal from opiates in pregnancy can be associated with miscarriage or other adverse pregnancy outcomes.[16] At the county hospital, obstetricians would assess a woman's risk for withdrawal and start treatment accordingly with methadone or buprenorphine. The pregnant woman would then receive medication at the jail, and be put into contact with a community program. This protocol mitigated risk for the fetus; it also mitigated the jail's risk of lawsuits.

While decisions about sending people to the hospital were protocol-driven, the decisions also relied on nurses' independent clinical judgment. One Sunday morning, nurse Stephanie was confronted with the dilemma of whether to divert a patient from jail processing to the hospital. Her patient, a quiet, unassuming man, answered "yes" to the question about whether he had a "current abscess or infestation." Many people came in with skin abscesses, often a consequence of certain injection-drug-use techniques.[17] Stephanie noticed a few small abscesses on the man's neck as they walked to a nearby exam room. When he removed his shirt, Stephanie observed a hot red abscess the size of a grapefruit on his left armpit. It was not an emergency, but, she thought, it looked painful. The cause of his abscess was irrelevant to her triaging, and she focused on the logistics of treatment.

Stephanie decided to send the man to the hospital because the abscess was too big to manage the next day in CJ2. She worried that if the man were released from CJ1, he would not get the abscess drained. She also worried that if he went to a jail housing unit, hospital transport would be delayed by having to see a clinician and then arranging a Sheriff's Department escort. It was easier here in CJ1 to send someone to the hospital, in part because of the single door to the outside world, and in part because the police officers were still in charge of the arrested patient. The grapefruit-sized abscess was not a life-threatening emergency. But Stephanie's triage algorithm was laced with empathy for the pain the mass was causing, and her awareness that structural forces on the streets and in jail would prevent the abscess from getting drained.

THE INTIMACY OF RECIDIVISM

Every jail medical staff person I spoke with at the San Francisco jail was keenly aware of the medically restorative role of jail, and that many patients did not tend their bodies on the streets. One prominent infectious disease doctor in the community, who was also the former director of the city's health department, declared publicly a number of times that some of his patients with HIV would not be alive if they were not cycling through jail.[18] In jail, a nurse handed them anti-retroviral medications, along with a comprehensive HIV treatment program that was part of JMC.[19]

In these and other cases, jail was life-saving. However, the jail's medical interventions were temporally limited. They offered brief interruptions in lives that were largely medically bereft. Most people returned to the streets and the conditions of chronic marginality that compromised their health and limited their access to health care services. Despite efforts to connect jail patients to community care, there was little the jail medical apparatus could do to alter the broader context of inequalities undergirding patients' poor health and the realities of mass incarceration. Ultimately, even with valiant efforts, jail could literally and figuratively offer Band-Aids.

And yet, jail's scope in ameliorating the difficulties of people's health was broadened by its regularity. Recidivism rates at the San Francisco jail hovered around 70 percent. Most of the people who left jail came back. Kima, for instance, would usually return within a few months—sometimes a few days—of being released. Recidivism statistics often depict repeated crime and repeated incarceration interchangeably. In this usage, though, recidivism is a statistical signifier of failure—failure of the individual and failure of the criminal justice system to reform prisoners into law-abiding citizens.[20]

The medical triage of jail as intervention in people's lives urges us to rethink recidivism beyond its numerical representation. For it is through recidivism that people cycling through jail have their bodily and mental states tended by professional caregivers on a somewhat regular basis. The story of triaging Kima demonstrates that recidivism is an intimate relationship. On one of her many arrivals to jail, nurse Charlie was at the triage station to welcome her. They had known each other for many years and had been in this configuration before. As Kima later told me, this moment in the triage station forced her to admit that she suspected she was pregnant. Kima said that when she saw Charlie in CJ1, she began to cry. "I was crying, but I was like, 'Charlie, I think I'm pregnant.'" She was scared, she explained, because she had been using drugs she knew were harmful to pregnancy. At Charlie's prompting, Kima gave a urine sample, and when Charlie confirmed her suspicions that she was pregnant, she "burst into tears." Kima felt familiar enough with Charlie that she could be emotional. She also welcomed his comfort. In this moment, we see the limits of a narrow understanding of recidivism as a statistic.

Care is sutured to recidivism. People enter jail, they leave jail, and they return. Within that cycle, jail has a legal mandate to provide care. This kind of chronicity compels an active imagining of patients' lives outside jail, in order to understand what has happened to their bodies between one incarceration and another. When Charlie triaged Kima and decided he should run a pregnancy test on her urine, he was partly guided by protocol that directed him to offer the test to a woman whose last menstrual period was over one month ago. But Charlie's decision was also informed by his knowledge of Kima individually. Kima's anxieties and tears provided information, as did past triage encounters that had revealed that Kima had unprotected sex with multiple partners on a regular basis.

Kima and Charlie had a relationship built through recidivism's repetitive temporality. Charlie noted that he sometimes saw his recurrent jail patients on the street, since the five-block walk from the jail to the subway station traversed drug corners where many people released from jail spent their time. Some people greeted Charlie with a smile, he told me, and even escorted him to the subway station. I too experienced this gesture and warm recognition from some jail patients on the street. "Hey!" one shouted excitedly when she saw me. "You put that IUD thing in me when I was in jail!"

The familiarity that enabled some triage moments to be intimate, like the one between Kima and Charlie, was also evident in the relationships arrestees had with the institution itself. People who had spent time in jail came to expect certain things. One man who sat down in Charlie's angry chair one day gruffly answered his questions with mostly monosyllabic responses. When Charlie asked if he had any medical conditions, the man grunted "back pain." "Any medications?" "Hydrocodones," the patient responded. "And I need a bottom bunk." He knew jail's amenities existed. Arrestees' memory of the institution was reciprocated in the institutions' memory of them; this came in the form of computerized records and interpersonal familiarity. So when this man requested his pain medication and a bottom bunk, Charlie checked the jail medical record system to confirm that he had indeed been prescribed a bottom bunk and pain medication in past incarcerations. Nurses also diligently checked the public health department's electronic medical record system and called pharmacies to verify the medications people were prescribed in the community.[21]

Another way in which recidivism becomes animated as more than a statistic in medical triage can be seen in the patients' cumulative electronic narrative, which complements the interpersonal familiarity. As I discuss further in chapter 4, computer technologies in jail cannot be simply understood as impersonal strategies of knowing subjects. In the criminal justice system, electronic records can be distinctly personal, compressing information about individuals into selective stories that then authorize approaches to punishment and justice.[22] The familiarizing role that CHART played in triage interactions prompted nurses to recall and learn details of prior incarcerations. The meaning of the acronym CHART is telling: "Correctional Health Assessment Record and Tracking." Tracking implies following someone through time; for CHART, that included both the current incarceration and the recurring ones. CHART thus partially encoded the intimacy of recidivism initiated by the entire triage evaluation.

The conditions of recidivism, physical embeddedness of jail within the community, and electronic records thus all fostered personal and institutional memory for the people who cycled through the jail. Intimacy,

Berlant writes, "involves relations that largely proceed by way of what goes without saying."[23] It is an unequal intimacy, to be sure, for jail patients did not have the same detailed knowledge of nurses that nurses had of patients. But the rhythm of recidivism and the predictable practices of medical screening anchored jail staff and newly arrested people in familiar ways of relating. These elements generated enough comfort that Kima could let her guard down and cry with nurse Charlie about her pregnancy fears. What Berlant calls "the normative promise of intimacy," is having compassion granted as part of everyday living.[24] We might assume that Kima's closeness to Charlie has its cathartic power by way of its contrast to uniformly antagonistic, distrustful, and abusive relationships with deputies; however, as we enter further into jail and its relationships in subsequent chapters, we shall see that these avenues of intimacy are part of the fabric of the institution itself, and are inextricably woven into elements of institutional violence.

The meaning people make out of their relationship with the jail is not reducible to the punitive aspects of the institution, but arises precisely because it is a place from which they expect a peculiar ambivalence of harshness and nurturance that is animated in the social engagements of care.[25] Understanding the recurrent, interactional nature of triage in jail allows us to see how emotion and politics are wrapped up in intimate sociality. Triage interactions in jail were repetitive, not only in the states of disrepair in which people appeared, but also in the actual people involved. That is, recidivism created a chronic triage scenario where the same questions, the same nurses, and the same patients appeared over a long and potentially unending period of time. The familiarity generated by this chronicity resists any simple politicization of the affect involved in jail triage interactions. Recidivism means that these Band-Aid moments of healing are recurrent and, in fact, as the public health director acknowledged, it is by the logic of recidivism that jail can be a life-sustaining safety net. In other words, recidivism becomes a key ingredient in the survival strategies of the urban poor.

TRIAGE'S PUBLIC PRIVACY

It is notable that Kima displayed emotional vulnerability during triage, especially given the public nature of the interaction. Charlie and Kima were stationed right amid the chaotic flux of CJ1; there was no screen and no door around them (except during the urine test). Deputies walked by or leaned against the adjacent counter filling out paperwork as the patient in the angry chair answered personal health questions. Two plainclothes police officers who arrested Kima hovered a few feet away, as was standard practice, since they were still "in charge" of this person. The police officers' proximity to the triage interview made it impossible for them not to hear the conversation.

This lack of privacy encroached on the usual expectations in Western biomedical practice of confidentiality between caregiver and patient, codified in regulatory codes of the Privacy Rule of the Health Information Portability and Accountability Act (HIPAA), which establishes medical privacy as a patient right.[26] In nonjail settings, health care providers are constantly reminded that people not involved in the patient's medical care are not privy to the patient's private medical information (without permission from the patient). In jail triage, being arrested hardly served as implied "permission" for an officer to listen, but that was functionally what happened. In some jails and prisons around the country, especially small jails with limited nursing staff, the triage is even done by a correctional officer. One justification given for the visibility of the nurses' triage work was that police officers and deputies could protect nurses from a potential assault by an arrestee. This was a legitimate concern. An administrator told me that there was one serious assault on a triage nurse, and several other attempts.

When I began working at the San Francisco jail's clinic, I assumed that there were official guidelines on how to navigate HIPAA. Instead, I learned that patient confidentiality was something to be negotiated in the face of constant surveillance. If a patient needed transportation to the hospital, jail health workers relied on deputies to make that happen, but were deliberate in omitting the medical reason for the transport. Sometimes, deputies would pressure providers into telling them.

Deputies were allowed access to pieces of medical information that jail medical staff disclosed, according to protocol. For instance, an inmate's "housing card," a five-by-eight piece of beige cardstock, denoted if the person had certain "high risk" medical conditions: pregnancy, tuberculosis, diabetes, detoxification from alcohol or opiates. Certain information about mental illness was also disclosed. This was done formally, by having deputies check in every fifteen minutes on inmates put on "suicide watch" in a safety cell, or informally, as deputies observed inmates visited by jail psychiatric staff.

The negotiation of patient privacy in the midst of an all-seeing carceral institution was magnified in CJ1 where medical triage and jail processing were spatially and procedurally intermingled. To adapt to the exposure of this clinical ritual, triage nurses adopted a variety of approaches. Sometimes they passively acquiesced, proceeding as usual with the question-answer triage routine. This caused some patients discomfort. Nurse Nancy, for instance, learned from the electronic CHART that a man she was triaging had a history of syphilis. She asked him, "Other than the STD, any medical problems?" The man gestured toward the police officers with embarrassment. "Jeez lady," the arrestee said angrily. He was, after all, sitting in the angry chair. Nancy's disregard for his privacy on a sensitive matter might be seen as a form of violence, removing his agency in determining who had personal knowledge about his bodily state.

Other times, nurses and patients spoke in code. On another patient's electronic medical record, Nancy could see that the patient was HIV positive. Instead of explicitly mentioning the diagnosis in her triage questions, she asked the woman, "Do you take anti-virals?" This coding was a gesture of care, protecting the patient from exposing a condition that carries tremendous stigma to the police officer. Triage nurses could also escort a patient from the angry chair to a small room a few feet away. This room resembled a storage closet more than an exam room, but it offered a bit of privacy from the rest of CJ1. Nurses could also defer questions to the more detailed "intake evaluation" that occurred later in CJ1, in a glass-walled room. Caregiving involved a moment-to-moment adaptation to this carceral presence, in which caregivers chose how they spoke with a patient under law enforcement's gaze.

This work of negotiating privacy with the patient was exemplary of the ambiguity of jail, in which gestures were simultaneously caring and violent. On the one hand, granting a private room for a medical exam contradicted the usual erasure of privacy characteristic of incarceration's panopticon. The private room reminded patients that despite surveillance, their sense of dignity still mattered. At the same time, these gestures of care harbored potential harshness, as there was no guarantee of benevolence from the nurse's gaze, even behind private doors or glass walls.

Nurses' willingness to craft a shared, private connection amid a public triage encounter within an institution of incarceration enabled intimacy. Intimacy, Berlant notes, encompasses the "range of attachments" people make in mediating the forces of collective experience in public and private domains.[27] The everyday work of triage in the jail created such opportunities for intimacy, such as a connection where Kima could cry to Charlie about her pregnancy suspicions while sitting in the publicly exposed angry chair.

Kima was used to the relative lack of privacy in CJ1. She was also used to Charlie. Her emotional display during triage was unexceptional for her. Charlie's warmth with Kima during this triage process of finding out about a pregnancy is hard to reduce to a technique of governance. This is not to say that Charlie's actions did not have strategic dimensions, for testing Kima for pregnancy was part of a larger triage project of patching deficiencies from the outside and making incarceration safer for poor, unhealthy (sometimes pregnant) bodies. But the exchange between Charlie and Kima reminds us that triage moments can cultivate emotional connections inside jail.

TAKING CARE OF TRIAGE

Despite the occupational stresses of the job, nurses liked working there. Most of them had worked at this job for over fifteen years. They liked the independence of their clinical decision-making; they liked the collegiality of working with the deputies in CJ1; and some felt gratification for helping those whom society treats as disposable. A few nurses even identified the constant action and interaction of CJ1 as "entertaining." Indeed, there were times in triage when I had to suppress laughter when patients who were psychotic or high on a cocktail of drugs would answer triage questions with elaborate non sequiturs. The chaos of the intake jail, a people-processing place that ushered people into a punitive space, could, disturbingly, be fun.

Triage was central to the jail's everyday rhythms of processing new arrestees and of tending to inmates living in jail. Triage was a task-oriented practice—nurses assigned to be in CJ1 did triage as part of their job; their tasks were part of a broader risk management role that health services played in protecting the jail from liability, while also responding to the deficiencies of the streets. Triage was also a process of negotiating what kind of care was deserved by a person enmeshed in the poverty of the streets or the rigidity of a jail system. These elements of affect and power in triage were not accessory to the technical decisions health care providers made in jail. Nor were they reducible to a broader political strategy of differentially valuing inmates' bodies. Triage diagnoses the deficiencies of the streets and offers a temporary, yet, because of the chronicity of recidivism, sustaining salve. These triaging endeavors themselves require care, in the ongoing and implicit commitment to work through and within the realities of caregiving in a space of confinement. The task is full of uncertainties and contradictions in who deserves what kind of care. In triage, ambiguity shows itself to be the cornerstone of care. This ambiguity pervaded the other clinical spaces of the jail and was routinized in the daily workings of the clinic.

3 Cultivating Ambiguity

NORMALIZING CARE IN THE JAIL CLINIC

A lot of them just be coming [to clinic] just to be
coming, just to see what they can get. So, they know.
They know which nurses they can manipulate and
which ones they can't. A lot of them women could be
me. . . . A lot of them I can sympathize with. I look at
them and I say, "For the grace of god, that could be me,"
but I just turned.

Adrienne, nurse in the San Francisco jail clinic

FROM COHERENCE TO AMBIGUITY

In the morning, one of the other clinicians, Vivian, stepped into the exam
room where I would soon start seeing patients. It had become a ritual, an
opportunity to talk about patients, vent frustrations, and tell stories about
things that happen only in jail. "This one's for your book," she would say.
Vivian had been working at the jail for thirteen years, providing the bulk
of routine gynecological and prenatal care to the women of the San
Francisco jail. Vivian came to her profession with a deep desire to help
those at the bottom rungs of society. Having grown up in the same San
Francisco neighborhood as many of the women cycling through jail,
Vivian now lived in the suburbs, with a very different life from the women
in her old neighborhood. She attributed her success to her parents, especially her mother, who fiercely promoted her education. In contrast, she
noted, other mothers from the neighborhood had abandoned their children for drugs, prostitution, and prison. Like most of the women in jail,
Vivian identified as black, and took pride in being a positive example.

81

Vivian saw her work in jail "as a kind of ministry," she said, to serve the women who came from her own community.

One particular morning, Vivian was exasperated. She gesticulated and shook her head and stopped and started over again, in narrating her frustration with Kima. Kima was now 32 weeks pregnant. She had been back in jail for two weeks for the third time this pregnancy. By this point in their pregnancies, women typically have prenatal visits every 1–2 weeks to measure their blood pressure, to check the fetus's growth, and to make sure there were no signs of preterm labor. But except for one initial visit, Kima had repeatedly "refused" to come down to clinic to see Vivian, despite the fact that Vivian kept her on the "sick call" list every day.[1]

Vivian was so exasperated with Kima's refusal to care for her pregnancy that she half-joked: "I'd like to get a court order for her to come down here for prenatal care!" Vivian's statement might, if taken out of context, seem coercive, paternalistic, or even punitive; on the surface, it is consistent with a carceral mindset that exacts reproductive control through forced obstetrical interventions.[2] But Vivian's comment was a joke. It arose from Vivian's understanding of the regulatory role that the courts played in both Kima's life and jail conditions more generally; the joke also emerged from the tension between Vivian's desire to help provide Kima with a healthy pregnancy and her respect for Kima's patient autonomy. The fact that it was partly in jest speaks to the contradictory nature of the work of providing care in a jail.

Moreover, Vivian's joke was grounded in empathy, in Vivian's understanding of why Kima was "refusing": Kima was angry to be in jail for the minor offense of shoplifting soap from Walgreen's, and this anger fueled her refusal; and because of a long-standing connection Vivian had to Kima's aunt in the community, Kima expected special treatment. Vivian confided, "She expects personal treatment but I can't do that. I have to be professional and treat her like a patient." To Vivian, it was only ethical to treat Kima as she would other patients. But Kima was hurt by Vivian's professionalism; she experienced it as a withdrawal of care.

Jailcare is infused with what Paul Brodwin calls "everyday ethics," in which frontline caregivers' ideals are constantly questioned and articulated through reflections of their everyday encounters with patients.[3] This is not the abstract terrain in which bioethics is typically debated. According to

Brodwin, "Everyday ethics is a matter of second thoughts and fleeting moments of self-doubt," and, I would add, reflective jokes like Vivian's.[4] "People reflect in passing on what they just did or witnessed someone else doing, and why it disturbed them. Afterward, they plunge back into the usual routines."[5] This active ethical engagement was part of the work of jail health care providers. It reflected the strangeness of folding medical routines into custody routines, of providing care to bodies labeled criminal.

The challenges that brought ethical questions into focus for jail health providers relate to two realities I introduced in chapter 2: the structural inequalities characterizing inmates' lives—and health—on the streets, and the constraints of the carceral environment. Jail's constitutive outside and its carceral structures informed the way in which health care workers carried out and reflected on their day-to-day work, reflections that included judgments of deservingness. These dimensions to everyday ethics in the jail clinic index a form of care that necessarily had to incorporate unique tensions and congruities in the realities of jail custody, clinical caregiving, and street life. Moreover, this form of care required clinic workers to cultivate ambiguity amid the apparent certainties of the carceral environment.

It would be easy to imagine a biomedical clinic in a jail reproducing the normalizing, controlling processes that Foucault saw as interdependent regimes of discipline in the prison and in the clinic.[6] Indeed, some of these carceral elements seeped into jail clinical practice. Simultaneously, jail health providers also worked to distinguish their care in the clinic from the punitive practices of the deputies. As one nurse told me: "There is that dichotomy that still exists.... They [the deputies] think of them [the inmates] as being less of a deserving person in terms of that we [clinic staff] are really spoiling them [with medical care]." This dichotomy resonates with what some scholars have emphasized as the seemingly incompatible goals of medical care to care and incarceration to punish.[7]

Jail health workers were constantly confronted with the incoherence of the ostensibly coherent domains of carcerality and biomedical care, and subsequently tended to these oppositions, fusing discipline and care in ways that were far more ambiguous than those described by Foucault. They did this through daily clinical duties, the work of defining inmates as patients and not prisoners, the medicalization of life in jail, and the aspiration to make care in jail equivalent to care outside of jail. Care arose as clinic providers sorted through the inconsistencies they encountered between punitive discipline and compassionate caregiving.

Everyday contradictions negotiated by jail clinic staff traced back to questions of whether patients were morally deserving of care or receiving excessive entitlements. Such attention to ambiguity in clinic workers' actions and relationships was the essence of jailcare—a kind of care that grapples with inequality writ large. Ambiguity, which resides in tension, involves polyvalence, uncertainty, and the coexistence of contrasting interpretations.[8] The ambiguity of jailcare asks fundamental questions about the moral worthiness of prisoners receiving care—people who, on the one hand, have ostensibly violated legal-social norms and may be seen as less deserving of services;[9] and who, on the other hand, are marginalized by poverty, addiction, and racism, and deserve care because of their structural vulnerability.[10]

PATIENT-PRISONERS

The space of the clinic in jail offered the possibility of transforming, albeit temporarily, a prisoner into a patient. When patients entered the jail clinic, which is spatially distinct from their housing units, nurses and doctors were ready to take temperatures, auscultate lungs, palpate masses, and ameliorate aches and pains. Behind the closed door of an exam room, patients shed their orange pants and sweatshirt for standard white paper gowns, momentarily making the space of incarceration look and feel like a clinic in the outside world. No guards stood in the exam room; nobody barked orders. The only routine was the biomedically familiar eliciting of a "history of present illness" and the physical examination.

This clinical routine corresponded to the staff's frequent affirmations that they were there to treat patients, not inmates. This sentiment was repeated in casual conversations, interviews, and when conflicts with deputies arose. Vivian had, several times, relayed with pride the story of her job interview:

> The last question I was asked was "So, how do you feel about taking care of inmates?" And, I told him, "Well, they're not inmates to me. They're patients

to me." I'm here to provide medical care. I'm not here to police them, judge them, that's something that's left to the legal system. I'm going to provide care to them whether they've committed a petty theft or they committed murder. If they're a serial killer, my job is to provide medical care to them, and do it efficiently, and provide good care to them. So, what[ever] their offense [was] that caused them to be incarcerated, that's not my concern. I'm not going to be naïve and think [otherwise], because I know I'm in jail because they're inmates and I'm *in jail*. But, they're patients to me. So, their *medical issues* are my concern. . . . And I tell the patients, "You're a patient to me, you're not an inmate."

That jail-based health care professionals reaffirm that the subjects before them are patients suggests the ever-present possibility of the reverse— that these professionals could slip and treat their patients as inmates. For this reason, inmates in clinical configurations are better understood as patient-prisoners.[11]

This potential to treat a patient as a prisoner arose from the reality of working in a place that houses people accused or convicted of committing crimes. Clinic staff navigated the jail's punitive and custodial missions, which were seen as contrary to nursing and medical care: "Their [referring to the deputies] [goal] is law enforcement and they don't see that we have different principles we care about. We don't care what [the patients] are here for, and [the deputies] are just convinced that they are making our streets safer," a nurse commented to me while waiting for deputies to bring patients to clinic. Although medical and carceral institutions derive their authority from similar places of normalization and control, jail medical staff actively worked to distinguish the two. The distinction between patient and prisoner, healing and custody, us (clinicians) and them (deputies) was formalized in orientation for new staff in the jail clinic. Practitioners were conditioned not to ask why patients were in jail. This instruction served dual purposes: managing patient perceptions—so that patients did not think providers were judging them for their alleged crimes or offering to assist their legal proceedings—and managing clinical perceptions of patients—so that clinicians did not view patients as, say, murderers, and then invoke moral judgment as to deservingness of care.

At the same time, as clinic staff carried out their daily work, they were constantly sorting the people before them along a continuum of patient and prisoner subject positions. While nurses did not directly ask why patients were in jail, they made small talk acknowledging patients' criminal status: "You back so soon? You just got out of here!" More pointedly, clinic workers heard details of patients' arrest charges from multiple sources—from deputies, from the local paper's police blotter, or from inmates themselves. Often, reviewing criminal stories was a voyeuristic fascination, something with which clinic staff could fill idle time.

One day, I watched staff gather around a computer screen to read about the patient who had just been seen in clinic. Someone heard that she had been arrested for allegedly robbing *Jeopardy!* host Alex Trebek in a San Francisco hotel room, and the staff's Google search confirmed this. After another patient unabashedly disclosed that she had stolen a $20,000 purse from a Barney's Department Store, clinic staff searched the department store's website for an online photo of the bag. Michael Jackson's "Man in the Mirror" gently played from the small radio at the nurses' workstation, keeping the atmosphere light. In these moments, alleged criminal acts were sources of gossip and humor for the staff, a way to minimize—but not dismiss—prisoner-based identity; this playful treatment of criminality allowed the clinic staff, at least in theory, to perceive morally culpable criminals as patients who deserved the health care they were providing.

Although she never asked, Vivian often heard arrest stories from patients. Most of the criminal stories disclosed to Vivian contained complicated but predictable elements of drug addiction, sexual violence, low self-esteem, unemployment, and lack of social support. Vivian took a therapeutic stance in order to treat these self-declared criminals as patients, offering life lessons about making better choices that sometimes sounded like a mother disciplining her child. Still, other clinical exchanges could disrupt efforts to see someone as a patient and not a prisoner or criminal. For instance, I have known clinicians who, upon placing a speculum in a woman's vagina to test for STIs, have discovered plastic baggies of drugs. At such exceptional moments of intersecting criminality and health, clinicians would quietly dispose of the stash, and treat the woman's vaginal infection with an antibiotic. In these and other scenarios, clinicians remained actively faithful to their mission to care for a patient, and actively rejected the at-times-tempting opportunity to punish a prisoner.

There were times when inmates themselves played with this patient-prisoner continuum, reinforcing stereotypical prisoner identities in clinic by manipulating staff, stealing items, or referring to themselves as criminals. One patient, Connie, smeared strawberry jam on a menstrual pad to fake a miscarriage, in the hopes she might be transferred to the hospital where, she later told me, she could stage an escape. Clinic staff filtered her report of vaginal bleeding through their description of the patient-prisoners as manipulative. The nurses even saved the jam-filled pad in a biohazard bag as evidence for me, making the clinical task of diagnosing a possible miscarriage feel like a crime scene investigation.

I once caught another patient, Nina, stealing a dispenser of liquid anti-bacterial soap. When I noticed the soap was missing from the exam room after I had seen her, I chased her down in the hallway and asked her to return the soap. She weakly denied the theft. Then I motioned toward the deputies with my eyes—a suggestion that I had the power to get Nina in trouble. She sheepishly pulled the elastic waistband on her orange pants, reached in, pulled out the soap, and handed it to me. I chuckled at her concealment tactic, not knowing what to do with this item stored in a less-than-sterile place. The deputies were barely watching our interaction, but asked, "Everything okay, doc?" I looked Nina in the eye as I covered for her. "Yep, all set, thanks."

Rhodes describes how prison workers are trained to presume that inmates in a maximum-security prison are manipulative.[12] I should note here that this haunting of distrust also exists for many patients in jail who may not trust the skills or compassion of the caregiver associated with the institution. Caregivers' trained baseline of suspicion of patient-prisoners means that empathy is an occupational hazard.[13] Yet nurses and doctors are generally expected to develop empathy for their patients. San Francisco jail clinic workers' responses to patient-prisoners' manipulations, then, were central to how they cared. When Nina stole the soap, I scolded her, trying to discipline her into a properly behaved patient and prisoner. I veered toward a carceral mindset of diminution and control, assuming a tone of voice I have never used with a patient outside of jail. Yet in the same breath, I assured deputies that "everything was fine"—a protective gesture toward my patient, and a subversion of the deputies' power to punish. This gesture also reinscribed my authority, which Nina had temporarily challenged with her theft from the exam room. Care is not simply that protective gesture, an apparent contrast to the punishment of a manipulative patient-prisoner. Care is that my gesture was simultaneously scolding and kind. Care emerges precisely in these moments of ambiguity, when disciplinarity involves human connection, intimate concern, and suspicion.

Clinicians working in jails must navigate these territories of culpability, criminality, moral judgment, and custody on a daily, moment-to-moment basis. I did not want to get involved in any formal disciplinary process or punishment of Nina—although I could have; and yet I felt compelled to warn her, sotto voce, "Don't do this again." Moments like these challenged clinic staff to assess their own roles in the system, to navigate their positions as patient advocates as well as disciplinarians. Clinicians had to equally cultivate skepticism and compassion, which became particularly visible in exceptional moments like theft. Clinic workers attended to the messiness of these two subject positions—patient and prisoner, or patient-prisoner—as a fundamental part of care. Patient and prisoner were neither fixed identities nor identities dependent upon the space of the jail, the clinic, or the housing units. Rather, both identities sat uneasily on a continuum that jail medical staff constantly recalibrated as part of their job.

EQUIVALENCE OF CARE

The tensions of the patient-prisoner continuum parallel the relationship between the world inside a carceral institution—where prisoners live— and the world outside—where patients are not presumed to have committed a criminal offense. This dynamic gets played out in the field of correctional health care in discussions of "equivalence," as the NCCHC affirms: "Medical care for prisoners must be equivalent in quality to the care which is available in the community."[14] Contestations over equivalence are moral in nature, as they consider individuals' health-related deservingness inside with respect to health systems outside.[15]

San Francisco jail health care providers continually contemplated the comparison of services inside and outside jail as part of their "everyday ethics." Equivalence was reckoned in terms of individuals' degree of self-care and in terms of access to health care systems. Vivian expressed frustration with the apparent high-quality care women access inside jail, and their lack of attentiveness to their health outside jail:

> We get them healthy, we get them a nice little plan, and now we get you an IUD [intrauterine contraceptive device]. You can come to any of the [community] clinics and continue their care [outside]. And then they leave and they forget about it all. "I have CIN3 on my pap [precancerous changes of the cervix] and I need to get a biopsy." And they forget it all [when they get out]. And then we make an appointment all over again and the appointment is April 28 and they get out April 27. Then they come back [to jail] and we start it all over.

Clinic workers critiqued patient-prisoners for not maintaining jail-initiated improvements to their health. Structural barriers and assumptions about patient-prisoners' street lives thus got collapsed into moral judgments about patient-prisoners' inability to take care of themselves. The lingering, usually unspoken follow-up questions to such narratives among jail health providers were, "If they don't take care of themselves outside, should we . . . ?" "Do they deserve . . . ?" And yet clinic workers did take care of them. Sometimes staff performed health care tasks as matters of routine, and sometimes these tasks were infused with compassion. Providers aimed to improve their patient-prisoners' health in ways they were unable to in the community. Here again is the ambiguity that constitutes the texture of jailcare.

MCRS AS SOCIAL SCAFFOLDING OF CARE

Not surprisingly, clinical care at the San Francisco jail relied heavily on bureaucratic practices. Constant documentation in CHART, following guidelines and protocols, and circulating various half-sheet, carbon-copy pieces of paper to request and deny medical care were all routine and integral parts of medical care.

Documentation has become important to the biomedical project of knowing the patient in certain formulaic ways,[16] and is also integral to the workings of any jail or prison; it is a classic technique of disciplinary power, organizing life into discrete, scheduled parts that regulate prisoners' behaviors.[17] At first glance, papers and computer screens seem impersonal and benign. Yet, as a rich anthropological literature has demonstrated, the practices and objects of bureaucracy can act as sources of violence and oppression, as their veil of neutrality erases individuals' humanity, creates distance in social relationships, and enables cruelty through anonymity.[18] In contrast, in the San Francisco jail clinic, bureaucratic elements are better understood through the rich social networks and affects they cultivate, and the meaning people invest in documents.[19]

Three forms were in constant circulation in the jail clinic milieu: medical care request forms (MCRs), refusal forms, and "chronos" (special privilege forms); these forms also circulated through CHART, for each piece of paper had to be documented. Functionally, these forms were essential to the work of care—they enabled patient-prisoners to request and decline medical care, nurses to triage their complaints, and clinicians to prescribe special privileges. These scraps of paper were also key objects through which patient-prisoners sought recognition and clinic staff worked through everyday ethics of care.

MCRs were 5" × 8-1/2" pieces of paper upon which inmates would request services from clinic staff. MCRs were such an integral part of daily jail and clinic life that, when I first asked what MCR stood for, many people could not tell me; the acronym itself had become the signifier for both the paper and its purpose. A stack of them lived at the guard tower in the housing units. Each day, a nurse was assigned the duty of sorting MCRs— sometimes over fifty a day—and deciding what to do with requests. In theory, the MCR nurse was supposed to see every person who submitted an MCR, and these face-to-face encounters, when they happened, imbued MCRs with sociality. In practice, the nurse decided when to see someone about an MCR.

It would be easy to read MCRs as a standard technology of modern medical and carceral apparatuses. But the ways that patient-prisoners and nurses engaged with MCRs made the forms a nexus of the desire to be cared for and the state's carceral burden to care.[20]

The content of MCRs from the San Francisco jail reveals a rich and diverse array of concerns that women wanted to communicate to medical staff, which was clear after I reviewed MCRs from a one-month time period. Some MCRs indicated specific symptoms such as heavy periods, pain, vaginal discharge, or stuffy noses; others requested specific medications or appointments with certain medical or mental health providers, while many requested things that might happen to fall (or not) under the clinic's purview, such as special diets, or creams for dry skin.

The minutiae and breadth of requests to the clinical apparatus revealed the intense medicalization of daily life in jail. Inmates knew the extent to which clinic staff controlled access to certain resources, and they tapped into this through MCRs. MCRs were vital means of seeking recognition of bodily and psychic experiences in jail. Whereas the intake triage in CJ1 responded to the effects of life on the streets, the everyday triage of MCRs responded more directly to the carceral environment and the discomforts of daily living that medically prescribed salves might soothe.

A closer look at the words used in some requests further reveals the role MCRs played in the moral economy of triaging people's deservingness of care. Many MCRs were crafted as letters to health care providers, with pleas and detailed explanations that served, the inmates hoped, to buttress their request for medical attention. Here are some examples, with original capitalization, spelling, and punctuation included:

Att: Adrian [mental health provider]. Can you plese [sic] come see me ASAP. I really need to talk to you. I feel like I am going crazy!

ATTENTION MEDICAL EMERGENCY 911. Need to see Vivian because my monthly is irregular and she told to put the slip and I'm bleeding realy heavey [sic].

Urgent Please. I would like to know if you can up my meds to a higher does [sic] and also could you please house me by self because I am tired of smelling ASS ALL DAY and all night and it is getting to the point where I am getting sick to my stomach

URGENT!! Attn: NP Please evaluate me for stronger pain meds for my lower back pain. I am in a lot of pain most of the time and Motrin *is not* strong enough. Thank you for your consideration.

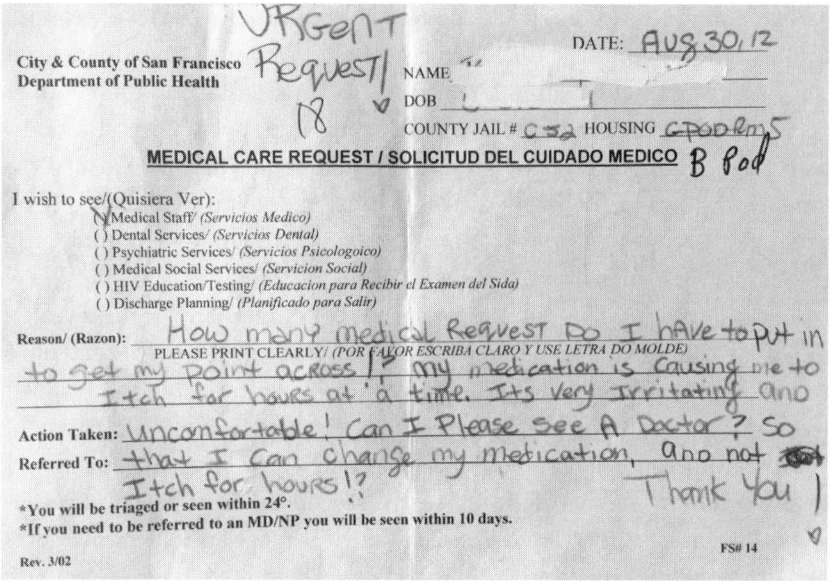
URGENT Request!!

DATE: Aug 30, 12

City & County of San Francisco
Department of Public Health

18

NAME

DOB

COUNTY JAIL # HOUSING GPOD Rm5 B Pod

MEDICAL CARE REQUEST / SOLICITUD DEL CUIDADO MEDICO

I wish to see/(Quisiera Ver):
(√) Medical Staff/ *(Servicios Medico)*
( ) Dental Services/ *(Servicios Dental)*
( ) Psychiatric Services/ *(Servicios Psicologoico)*
( ) Medical Social Services/ *(Servicion Social)*
( ) HIV Education/Testing/ *(Educacion para Recibir el Examen del Sida)*
( ) Discharge Planning/ *(Planificado para Salir)*

Reason/ (Razon): How many medical Request Do I have to put in to get my point across!? my medication is causing me to Itch for hours at a time. It's very Irritating and
PLEASE PRINT CLEARLY/ *(POR FAVOR ESCRIBA CLARO Y USE LETRA DO MOLDE)*

Action Taken: Uncomfortable! Can I Please see A Doctor? So

Referred To: that I can change my medication, and not Itch for hours!? Thank You!

*You will be triaged or seen within 24°.
*If you need to be referred to an MD/NP you will be seen within 10 days.

Rev. 3/02 FS# 14

Figure 2. A medical care request (MCR) form.

This sampling of MCR text provides insight into the ways that people scripted themselves as deserving of care. Calls of urgency attempted to persuade nurses to respond right away. While some people's requests were addressed immediately, some took two weeks, and others, it seemed to the women, were not addressed at all. Many women expressed frustration to me that they did not get adequate, timely attention; these same women also acknowledged that the health care provided at the San Francisco jail was more robust than at other jails they had been to.

Vivid explanations in MCRs like the putrid smell in someone's jail cell were attempts to garner sympathy. "Please," "thank you," and other pleasantries of polite address depict the requesting inmate as reasonable and courteous. Asterisks, underlines, and other crafted pen marks animated the MCRs as personalized pleas for recognition, attempts to persuade the MCR nurse of the worthiness of requests (see figure 2).[21]

One woman, Nina, submitted numerous MCRs to get Boost nutritional shakes to supplement the jail meals. Text from one of her many MCRs conveys her deep desire for recognition:

From Nina's MCR

Att: to Dr. David. Please→ I need to be put back on my Boost treatment because of my weight NOT being where it should be. Also I am NOT eating as much due to me having SWOLLEN INFLAMED GLANDS in MY THROAT. It hurts to swollow [*sic*] and it is causing for my left ear to hurt when I try to swollow [*sic*] my food. So it has caused me not to consume the amount of food I should be intaking [*sic*] to gain my weight. So I need to be put back on my Boost treatment. Please acknowledge my pleas in concern of my condition. Thank you! Thank you so very much! [*Signed with Nina's signature*]

Clinic staff had to triage her pleas through the tensions of her deservingness and the jail's clinical obligation to care. The nurses knew Nina well from her chronic incarcerations. Nina was thin, her face gaunt from her inconsistent food supply outside of jail. But at 5 foot 7 inches tall and 120 pounds, her body mass index (BMI) of 18.8 did not classify her as underweight, nor was she losing weight; she also did not have a diagnosed chronic medical disease that would merit nutritional supplements. The clinic distributed the limited supply of Boost shakes to those who needed them most. The clinician, therefore, denied Nina's request. Applying this clinical logic was one way in which providers clarified the moral uncertainties about what kind of care a person, and a person who came from harsh streets, merited.

The chronic conditions that kept Nina thin (but not thin enough to get the Boost shakes she wanted) were poverty and the structural violence of her street life as a drug addict. A few weeks after Nina's multiple MCRs for Boost, I passed her on the street. Her eyes had the alertness of someone high on crack cocaine. Bundled in a black hoodie, her sallow cheeks were just visible to me. Was she thinner than in jail, where she had three meals a day delivered to her? Possibly. Did she buy Boost from the Walgreens around the corner? Unlikely. In Nina's case, broader questions of care loomed in the background as clinic staff decided how to manage her MCRs for high-calorie shakes. What was the jail's responsibility in terms of tending Nina's thin bodily state? In this case, nurses smoothed the rough edges of her outside life into a neat story of normal BMI and weight stability that documented how she did not deserve nutritional supplementation.

Nurses never referenced the constitutional mandate from *Estelle v. Gamble*, and, in fact, when I asked them about it, most had never heard of the case. Nonetheless, in sorting through MCRs, nurses effectively made determinations about what counted as "serious medical need." These determinations were not straightforward yeses or nos; rather, the vernacular of "serious medical needs" was expressed through ongoing human interactions in which professional judgment was laden with questions about the institution's should's and should not's. The writing and triaging of MCRs were at the heart of such everyday, socially situated ethics. In this seemingly mundane bureaucratic artifact, frontline jail health workers and inmates worked through the ethical entanglements of courtroom mandates.

MEDICALIZING LIFE: THE PRIVILEGE SYSTEM

A second form that circulated through the intimate medical economy of the San Francisco jail was the "chrono" (see figure 3).[22]

The chrono consisted of a quarter sheet of carbon-copy paper upon which a jail clinician would handwrite medically authorized "privileges." Chrono privileges were not exactly luxuries. Minor things like bed rest, a bottom bunk, and a water pitcher, chrono privileges would be taken for granted on the streets but became privileges in jail because of the background of deprivation.

Chronos, like MCRs, were invested with inmates' desires for care and recognition from the institution. Moreover, the protocols and interactions surrounding the granting of chronos provide a window into the intense medicalization of daily life in the jail. Jail clinic staff controlled access to a number of privileged items that, outside of jail, were unremarkable and could be obtained without a third party: over-the-counter medications like Tylenol, peanut butter–free diets, a plastic pitcher to hold water, Vaseline, a bottom bunk bed, a warm compress. Chrono-granted privileges like medically authorized bed rest also offered reprieve from the jail's standard routine. Only a doctor's note could excuse someone without repercussion from classes, programming, and other required activities— ironically, activities meant to fill idle time in jail. Unlike the economy of

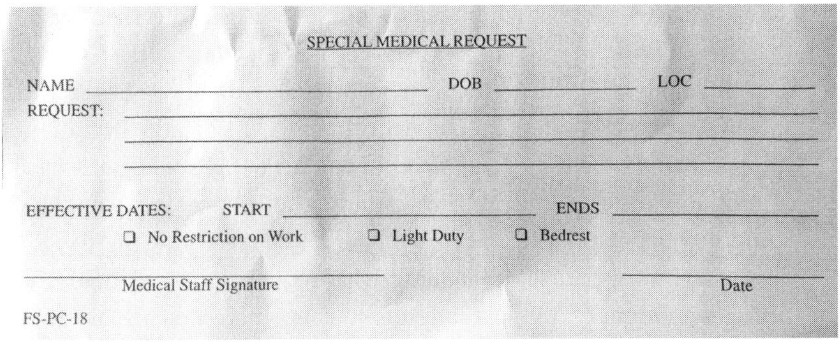

SPECIAL MEDICAL REQUEST

NAME ______ DOB ______ LOC ______
REQUEST: ______

EFFECTIVE DATES: START ______ ENDS ______
❑ No Restriction on Work ❑ Light Duty ❑ Bedrest

______ Medical Staff Signature ______ Date

FS-PC-18

Figure 3. A blank chrono form.

total institutions that Erving Goffman described, privileges from the clinic were not rewards for good behavior;[23] they were added accoutrements, granted if a medical professional deemed the person deserving.

Patients knew to ask clinicians for chronos. When I first began providing care at the jail, I willingly granted chronos for whatever women requested, not even knowing whether such things were possible: a pillow, an extra mattress, a second blanket. Years later, I learned that these orders were not fulfilled. I knew that some women exaggerated their symptoms and, as other staff would label it, "manipulated" me, but I did not take it personally. I wrote chronos in part as a gesture of compassion and in part as a conscious effort to try to soften the rough edges of institutional living for my patients. And I also saw my strategic use of white coat capital as a subtle act of subversion against the larger system of mass incarceration. But over time, I began to realize the complexities of indiscriminate chrono-granting.

In the carceral milieu of scarcity and deprivation, ice was a particularly contentious privilege. Clinicians would prescribe ice for a range of situations: menopausal hot flashes; the temperature dysregulation of heroin withdrawal; nausea; and to hydrate patients like pregnant women who would not drink the jail's metallic-tasting water at room temperature.[24] Partially because ice was a controlled substance in jail, many women wanted it. Over time, deputies felt that the number of women receiving ice had "gotten out of hand," resulting in longer pill call lines, complaints to deputies, and the bartering of ice for commissary items like Doritos.

Deputies would report ice charades to nurses and needle them about whether these women actually needed ice prescriptions. Once, when a nurse at pill call scolded a pregnant patient who had shared her ice, the patient's response was simple: "Oh yeah, I didn't use it all." To patient-prisoners, sharing ice was not a big deal—just part of the social network of life with other women in jail. To nurses and deputies, ice was a source of unregimented behavior.

There was no algorithm for dealing with requests for chronos, since they were dependent on clinical judgment. There were no rules to transgress or uphold, only individual decisions to arbitrate. In the course of these arbitrations, the medicalized privilege system challenged what it meant to care. Sometimes providers caved in to requests out of sympathy or fatigue from the persistence of the requests. Frequently, decisions about chronos weighed medical necessity against an understanding of what would happen in the outside world. By fulfilling or denying privileges, providers could inflict their own medicalized version of reward or punishment, providing or withholding amenities they thought the patient-prisoners did or did not deserve.

At the same time, constructing absolute equivalence between inside-jail and outside-jail in deciding when to grant special privileges risked ignoring the inequalities that characterized the outside world in which most of these women lived. Many clinic staff knew that for many of these women, the care they received in jail, including bed rest and nutritional supplements, could help smooth over—at least temporarily—inequalities from the streets. Medicalized privileges, solidified on the chrono form, were thus a moral endeavor and a convergence of the deprivation of punishment, of medical power, of revealing societal-level inequalities, and an individual's desire to be recognized.

"I REFUSE"

At the beginning of this chapter, I described an episode in which Kima "refused" prenatal care in jail. While prisoners have a constitutional right to receive health care, they also have a procedural right to refuse evaluation or treatment from the jail, a fact codified in NCCHC standards.[25]

Patients in nonincarcerated settings also can refuse medical care; what is different about a jail setting is that the categorical absence of autonomy turns a refusal of even the most mundane medical acts into an event worth documenting. On the surface, an event in a jail called "a refusal" seems confrontational, conjuring stereotypical images of a powerful jail worker and resistant inmate. Or refusals might be seen as providing patient-prisoners a brief moment of agency and freedom in an environment lacking those opportunities. But to read refusals in such formulaic ways would miss the nuanced ways in which care and discipline are entwined in the jail clinic.

Refusals were daily occurrences. While on rare occasions refusals involved confrontation, for the most part, deputies, clinic staff, and even patients treated refusals as a matter of procedure.[26] It was unremarkable, then, when one woman sitting on the clinic bench casually asked the clinic nurse, "Can I sign a refusal form?" Another woman followed her cue. "Yeah, me too." And another. "OK," the nurse responded with a shrug of the shoulders, "It's up to you." The refusing patient and witness made it official by signing a form—though sometimes the patient refused even to sign (see figure 4).

The form was a risk management strategy, explicitly shifting medical responsibility from the jail clinic to the patient, should any adverse health outcome or litigation ensue. Rarely did I observe attempts to explain or persuade, or even to inform the patient of "the risks involved with my refusal."

While nurses and clinicians may have responded to patients' refusals with casual acceptance or (more rarely) persuasion, they also, when patients were not around, interpreted what refusals signified. Refusal moments provided staff with an opening to make broader social commentary about the rights of and entitlements to health care. A few deputies told me why they thought patients refused: "Sometimes they don't want to get out of bed"; and "Some of 'em just don't like the medical staff." These reasons led many deputies and clinic workers to express the sentiment that "these inmates don't know how good they have it," critical of inmates who took their free, readily accessible medical care for granted to the extent that they could casually reject it. One female deputy, Deputy Harrison, became especially agitated when she vented her frustrations with medical refusals:

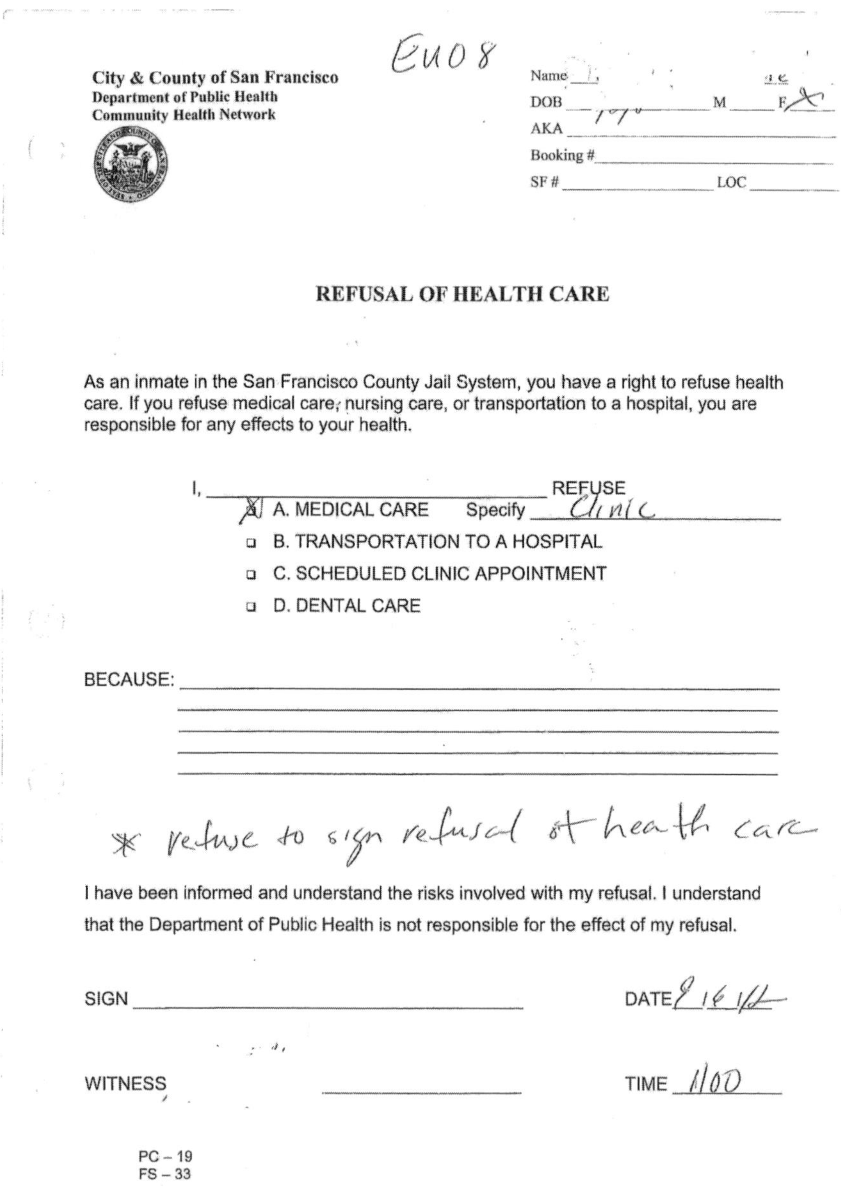

Eu08

City & County of San Francisco
Department of Public Health
Community Health Network

Name _____ ᴹ.ᴱ.
DOB _____ / 7 / _____ M _____ F ✗
AKA _____
Booking # _____
SF # _____ LOC _____

REFUSAL OF HEALTH CARE

As an inmate in the San Francisco County Jail System, you have a right to refuse health care. If you refuse medical care, nursing care, or transportation to a hospital, you are responsible for any effects to your health.

I, _____ REFUSE

☒ A. MEDICAL CARE   Specify ___*Clinic*___

☐ B. TRANSPORTATION TO A HOSPITAL

☐ C. SCHEDULED CLINIC APPOINTMENT

☐ D. DENTAL CARE

BECAUSE: _____
_____
_____
_____

✳ *refuse to sign refusal of health care*

I have been informed and understand the risks involved with my refusal. I understand that the Department of Public Health is not responsible for the effect of my refusal.

SIGN _____   DATE *8 16 14*

WITNESS _____   _____   TIME *1100*

PC – 19
FS – 33

Figure 4. A refusal form.

Excuse me, but that pisses me off, because . . . now you don't want to go to medical? You're on the medical list, you need to get up and go. "No, I don't want to go." I hear what you're saying. No. You need to go. Or they finally put them on the thing to go out to the county hospital. "I don't want to go because it's too early in the morning." So, it's always something for them. . . . It's like you put in all of these requests and now you don't even want them to take a look at it? You want it to be convenient when it's convenient for you.

This deputy saw refusals as an expression of inmates' sense of entitlement. Staff's interpretations of refusals reflected a familiar tension between the responsibilities of a welfare state to care for the most marginalized and the presumption that those recipients are lazy and entitled.

DOCUMENTS AS RELATIONAL

As part of the jail's audit culture, MCRs, chronos, and refusal forms were loci for social interactions in executing the work of care in an environment of punishment. Responses to the various forms of paper recognized inmates as patient-prisoners, simultaneously caring for them while also inscribing them in a system where deprivation, regimentation, mutual distrust, control, and opposition were standard. From inmates' narrative constructions of bodily and psychic needs on MCRs, to clinic providers' handwritten chronos, to mundane refusal scripts, bureaucratic objects provided a locus around which caregivers and patient-prisoners created the ambiguous intimacy we have now come to recognize in this medical-carceral milieu. This intimacy derived from the interface of clinic workers and patient-prisoners, through the chronicity of recidivism and through the intensity of medical management of daily life in jail.

Patient-prisoners and jail workers invested considerable affect in the documents, for it was through them that they worked through the moral stakes of what mattered to them on a daily basis—recognition, ameliorating the discomforts of incarceration, adherence to professional standards, sympathetic caregiving. The forms also furnished regular opportunities for providers to reflect on the boundaries of health-related deservingness for marginalized people confined in an institution. Bureaucratic practices were not simply instrumental tasks, but were vital to the mutual coexistence of punitive deprivation and concerned caregiving. Care in the jail was normalized as a perpetually ambiguous endeavor, which was imbricated into the regimented organization of time and tasks in the jail clinic, as the next chapter further explores.

4 The Clinic Routine

CONTRADICTIONS AS CARE

It's time to pass pills again.

Frequently heard from nurses in the San Francisco jail clinic

ROUTINES OF CARE

Just as reliance on documents in the jail clinic allowed certain kinds of care to flourish, so too did the predictable structure of the clinic's daily flow. The clinic's rhythms were organized by the regimented routines of its carceral host. Despite the potential for such intense bureaucratic structuring to displace the compassion and empathy we expect of caregiving relationships, to take too seriously the "administrative schemes for the prison [would miss] the extent and implications of slippage away from them."[1] Instead, the bureaucratic organization of the jail's clinical routine created gaps and possibilities for creative enactments of care that braided together violence and concern.

A closer look at the routine in the San Francisco jail clinic reveals that the rhythms and tasks were punctuated by a moral intimacy.[2] That is, caregiving interactions among nurses, clinicians, deputies, and patient-prisoners worked through the personal and moral stakes of desiring recognition, exercising professionalism, and articulating how medical resources should be distributed and who deserved them. These various moral domains were situated amid the state's carceral burden to care and the broader failures of the safety net. The chronicity of recidivism and the shared task of confronting the punitive regimes of the jail cultivated possibilities for intimacy. Thus the seemingly impersonal, disciplinary dimensions of care and the compassionate intimacy of care became mutually constitutive. To further understand this moral intimacy, I will describe an aggregate of a twenty-four-hour time period from the perspective of the clinical world of the jail.

CLINIC AREA RULES

First, it is necessary to be oriented to the material aspects of the jail clinic. The clinic area, called "2 South" by clinic and jail staff, was located in a separate wing of CJ2, on the second floor in the south end of the building. To get from the housing unit pods to the clinic required exiting through the pod's sliding metal door, walking to an elevator at the end of a long hall, getting out on the second floor, and walking through another hallway. Inmates were required to pass through a metal detector into the holding area. In the holding area, three dank cells contained inmates as they waited to be escorted to clinic, court, or CJ1 for release. The holding cells were uncomfortable, containing a hard wooden bench and a single toilet partially shielded by a three-foot cement wall. Depending on the security level of the inmates and on deputies' moods, they either left the glass doors of the holding cells ajar or locked them.

Deputies controlled when patients were escorted to clinic, which clinic staff often identified as "an obstacle" to caregiving, for it could sometimes mean that clinicians sat idle for hours, waiting to see patients while deputies were pulled for other duties or lunch breaks.[3] It provided a constant reminder that this clinic was in a jail. Jail clinicians became accustomed to this limitation and chose carefully when to accept deputies' constraints, and when to insist on immediacy due to a patient's serious medical condition. Caregiving was thus complicated with layers of negotiations, lists, moments of deputized authority, and categorical differences among prisoners, suturing the practical tasks of caregiving to custody routines.

The holding area led to a wide hallway, at the end of which was the main clinic area. A wooden bench and a few blue plastic chairs lined the walls at the entry, and health-education brochures on a variety of topics were available for patient-prisoners. The focal point of the clinic was a long, elevated, counter-like desk behind which nurses sat. The area brimmed with binders filled with protocols and shift schedules, medical reference books, stray papers from patients' medical records, a fax machine, and stacks of blank forms.

The white walls had dulled with time. Flyers were stuck to the walls with peeling tape, informing patients of things like their right to medical care and reminding them they were in jail: "Remain seated until called. Getting up, being loud, or being verbally abusive will result in disciplinary action." Another sign of the "Clinic Area Rules" provided more specifics of proper behavior (see figure 5).

This sign illustrates that the ambiguous nature of jailcare as both violent and nurturing could be displaced by predictable, clear elements of disciplinary control. While these rules would make no sense in a clinic outside of jail, they were logical in an environment where inmates were constantly told what and what not to do. The content here aimed to minimize annoyances for clinic staff, restrict access to amenities inmates did not have in housing units (ice and a scale), and maintain order. Despite this sign, I observed countless patients in the waiting area ask to step on the scale or for a cup of ice water. One nurse responded by placing a pitcher of cooled water and cups on a ledge in the waiting area, both to provide relief to women while waiting and to reinforce the rule that they should not ask.

Along the periphery of this central, open area of the clinic were seven doors leading to: a medication room; a "treatment room," with a stretcher, ceiling-mounted exam light, EKG machine, equipment to take X-rays, and cabinets full of various medical supplies; a lab room, where nurses drew blood for various tests and did urine pregnancy tests; a bathroom; and three examination rooms where clinicians evaluated patients in private.

I describe the layout of the clinic in part to set the scene, and in part to establish that, aside from a few regulatory flyers, the clinic looked and felt like any other. It was spatially, administratively, and financially separate from the rest of the jail apparatus. This separateness should not be taken too literally as the symbolic distinction between the goals of incarceration and the goals of medical care, as some scholars have done.[4] Rather, the distinction between the clinic and the rest of the jail, as well as the moments

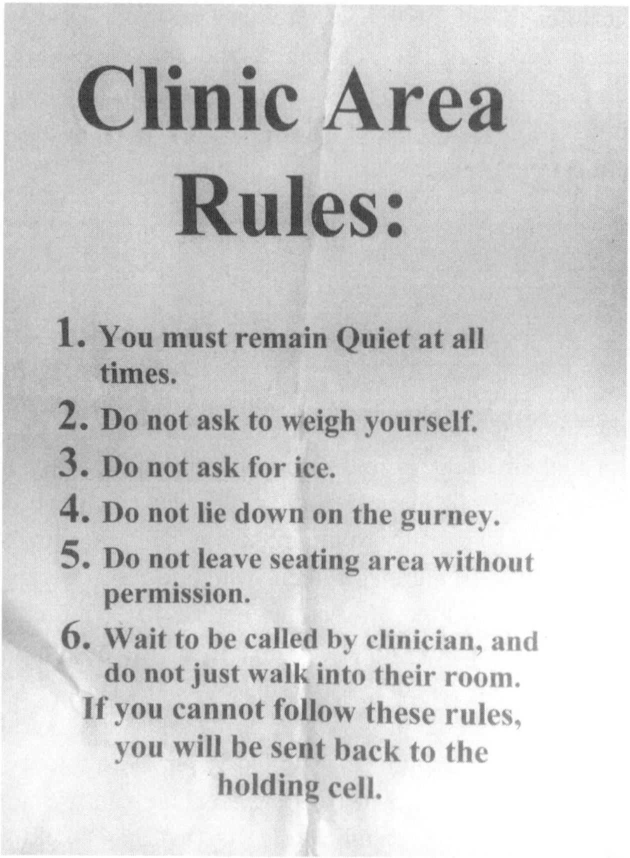

Clinic Area Rules:

1. You must remain Quiet at all times.
2. Do not ask to weigh yourself.
3. Do not ask for ice.
4. Do not lie down on the gurney.
5. Do not leave seating area without permission.
6. Wait to be called by clinician, and do not just walk into their room.

If you cannot follow these rules, you will be sent back to the holding cell.

Figure 5. Sign posted in clinic waiting area.

when that distinction fell away, fostered ambiguity in which providers worked through their "everyday ethics" to craft a form of care that works in this particular setting and with these particular patients.[5] I now turn to the routine of the clinic to explore the rhythm of this ambiguity.

6:30 A.M.: WAITING AND ACTION

The day shift arrived to relieve the night nurses at 6 a.m. The nurses enjoyed the calm before patients and deputies arrived in clinic. Nurse

Julie alternated between checking Facebook and typing her responses to MCRs on the ubiquitous turquoise glow of CHART. Becky, the nurse who would coordinate clinic that day, briefly reviewed the "Sick Call" list and started getting ready for "noon" pill call, still four hours away.[6]

By 8:30, the quiet was gone. The waiting area and clinic desk bustled with eight patients waiting on the bench. Becky wrapped a blood pressure cuff around a woman's arm and stuck a thermometer under her tongue, then scribbled vital signs on a scrap of white paper, and taped it, face-down, to the plastic bin next to Vivian's exam room door. Vivian stood at the threshold of the door and called the name scrawled on the paper, extracting the woman from the undifferentiated noise of the waiting area. Vivian and this patient knew each other from prior incarcerations, and there was familiarity as Vivian smiled, greeted the patient, and said "come on in."

The clinic was an intensely social space. Patients talked with each other about jail food, pop culture, people they knew in common, their cases, and when they might get out. A small radio next to one of the computers played R&B. As one patient exited the exam room, she danced to the slow beat. "This is one of my favorite songs!" she exclaimed. Nurse Julie barely looked up, but met her smile. The woman swayed down the clinic hallway, saying, "This is the closest we get to the outside, here in the clinic. Yeah. You ladies have a blessed day. Don't work too hard," to all of us sitting behind the clinic desk. This casual reflection summarized clinic workers' sometimes unintentional efforts to create a space that was separate from the punitive, disciplinary structure of the jail world, a space that was "closest to the outside"—filled with music and familiarity instead of deliberate deprivation. The clinic's routines—even the clinic's existence as part of the jail routine—allowed for this.

Another patient-prisoner, Quiana, was on her way to give a urine sample for a pregnancy test, a routine procedure for all patients in clinic for an Ob/Gyn related visit, before seeing Vivian. Quiana sauntered up to the counter to talk to nurse Julie, saying, "Guess what, Julie, they're going to drop my charges! I mean, I still have probation, but they're going to drop these charges." Julie smiled, showing friendly, casual interest. "Oh really? That's good." Julie knew Quiana well—she had been cycling through this jail every few months for over a decade.

In clinics outside jail, longitudinal relationships between patients and the clinic staff can also cultivate a sense of familiarity. But the kind of familiarity in which patients dance their way down the clinic hall or participate in chatty nonclinical exchanges about a legal situation would be unusual in a community clinic. One reason for this difference is that, in jail, the chronicity of recidivism creates a space for intimacy in caregiving routines that surpasses that of nonjail clinics. Quiana, like so many of the other patients, spent more time in the jail clinic than she did at any single clinic in the community. Another foundation for the intimacy was the connections that staff had to patients' families and geographies. Intergenerational cycles of incarceration meant that clinic staff knew cousins, mothers, aunts, and daughters. Vivian, Julie, and a few other nurses acknowledged that they had grown up in the same neighborhood as some inmates. These kinds of community overlaps would be less common in a prison setting, where inmates come from all over the state (or country if it is a federal prison).

Common history between inmates and workers was rarely discussed, but when it was, it took on several valences of sentiment. For some staff, common history signaled that although they had come from similar backgrounds as incarcerated patients, they had not ended up destitute and criminal. For others, like Vivian, common history prompted pity for the circumstances, which she incorporated into her caregiving:

> So they never had an adult figure or a parent. And they say "I've never had anybody who listened to me. I never had anyone who cared. So for you just to listen to me." And you can see their faces, I approach them and respect them because I'm treated that way when I go to see any of my doctors. And they'll say "Hi Vivian," or Miss Carter, or they'll hug me because I'm a hugger. . . . Shake my hand when they meet me. You have to earn respect. The way you earn respect on the streets is you curse someone out or you fight 'em. So I'm not using profanity. So they learn some socialization, just in the little time that they see us.

Despite her empathy for her patients' experiences, Vivian also criticized them, to me and to the patients themselves, for making bad choices about who, what, and where they spent their time. "It's always people, places, and things, I tell them. . . . There are people here [in jail] now I grew up with who made different decisions [than me]." This combination of relief, empathy, and valuing individual responsibility were representative of the ambiguity clinic staff cultivated in how they approached care.

Intimacy was also intensified because the staff had more frequent opportunities to interface with patients in the jail clinic than in the community. The management of health in jail necessitated constant human interaction, such as for regular, routine testing: tuberculosis skin tests for all people arriving in jail; vital signs every few hours for new arrestees withdrawing from alcohol or heroin; blood sugar checks for inmates with diabetes. Moreover, the clinic and its representatives were always conveniently there. There were no busses to take, no need to rearrange other activities or childcare, no appointments to get in the way. And at the San Francisco jail, medical care was free. In jail, where they had shelter, food, and other necessities, patient-prisoners could prioritize health care on their lists of things to do. Convenience circumvented structural barriers often articulated as major reasons marginalized populations do not access health care in the community. Jail filled in the holes of the safety net, providing "opportunities" for care.[7]

Some nurses attributed the frequency of visits to boredom, since coming to clinic was a way to break up the monotony of jail. Women came to the clinic for minor issues such as headaches, rashes, scrapes, or other things they could ignore or self-remedy at a drug store outside jail. By virtue of the jail's deprivation of access to resources, the clinic stepped in to provide—or deny—things these women could obtain in the community without assistance: an ice pack or a warm compress to soothe a wound; foot powder for itchy feet; Tylenol for a headache. Patient-prisoners had to go through the medical apparatus to procure these over-the-counter remedies, which provided yet another opportunity to interface with clinic staff. Then again, jail clinicians noted, many women did not buy Tylenol or foot powder at the drugstore when out of jail. Some could not afford it; some spent their money on vials of crack cocaine. Others, clinicians said, just did not prioritize caring for their bodies.

According to jail clinic staff, the increased frequency of visits for minor issues did not arise only as a matter of geographic and financial access. Providers noted that patient-prisoners' perceptions of health, health care, and embodiment changed as they transitioned from community to jail. Jail clinic staff speculated that the forced sobriety of incarceration affected patient-prisoners' bodies differently in jail.[8] For example, Vivian explained that the most common reason women came to clinic was vaginal discharge. Sometimes she diagnosed them with STIs or nonsexually transmitted vaginal infections.[9] Frequently, though, the discharge was just normal, physiologic secretions that, Vivian ascertained, these women were too high to notice on the streets.[10] Jail and the accoutrements the clinic provided temporarily reconfigured the reality of these women's bodily experience.

10:30 A.M.: PEDDLING PILLS

Nurse Becky tried to stay focused on her tasks, but patients' requests diverted her attention. Sometimes staff responded to these moments by ignoring patients, sometimes by interrupting what they were doing to respond, and sometimes by exasperatedly telling patients "No." Today, the low-level irritant of requests and complaints was too much for Julie. With a roll of her eyes, she declared, "These people get on my nerves!" The kind nurse Julie who had casually chatted with Quiana had disappeared. "You people need to sit down and be quiet! This is not a playground!" she ordered, sounding like a deputy. Turning to me, she shook her head, and repeated something I have heard her say numerous times: "It is not my job to regulate these inmates!"

Ironically, when, at a later point, I asked nurse Julie about her role in the waiting area, she summarized it as "keeping order in the clinic." Julie indeed took on a regulatory role in the clinic, through threats of punishment and by enforcing behavioral norms. As she explained:

> They would just like jump up and run into the clinician's room. And I have to tell them . . . "Okay, I have power in this pen. If anybody gets up and goes in that room again, I'm going to write you up." . . . You have to be very firm. And it's kind of like you almost have to talk to them like they're children. You know what I mean? And they don't like that because they consider themselves as adults. My thing is you consider yourself as an adult. Act like an adult. Sit down, behave like an adult and no one would have to—I shouldn't even have to say anything to you.

She saw her admonitions, infantilizing though they were, as justified in the face of rudeness and unruly behavior. In moments like this, the ambiguous suturing of violence and care expressed itself more clearly as the control that typified the deputies' custodial and punitive duties. Certainly, in moments of exasperation, clinic staff were susceptible to treating patients like prisoners. Even within a clinical space where patient-prisoners are cast as worthy of compassion, threatening and chastising were acceptable tactics for making sure the clinic's work of care proceeded smoothly.

While Julie was "keeping order," Becky was putting the final touches on her pill call cart. Four times a day, every day, a nurse pushed a medication cart through each housing unit to deliver everything from over-the-counter pills like Tylenol, to controlled substances like methadone, to other accoutrements of healing like ice packs or warm compresses. It was a ritualized process, with each nurse crafting her own lists and electronically charting which medications were dispensed. Pill call was a routine and integral part of the day, providing a mobile extension of the clinic into the housing units.

Suddenly, I was startled by a loud noise from the medication room. When I looked in, I saw Becky was using a hammer to pulverize Vicodin and Percocet, still in plastic blister packs, into a powder; in the pods, she would dissolve this opioid powder into a cup of water, ensuring the prisoner-patient could not store the narcotic in her cheek (known as "cheeking") to use for other purposes. When Becky had organized the medications and a pitcher of water, she called B-pod and got permission from the deputy to come.

Becky expertly maneuvered the unwieldy cart through a series of doors, a long hallway, and an elevator. The heavy door to B-pod magically whirled open—someone at the central command panopticon could see, via video camera, that we stood in front of the door. The pod deputy had already called out the women on the pill call list, so by the time we entered B-pod with the cart, they were dutifully lined up along the upstairs railing, a deputy standing by.

Pill call was the essence of directly observed therapy (DOT), a classic biopolitical technique popularized in the treatment of tuberculosis in the 1940s.[11] In jail, pill call's DOT was a naturalized function of incorporating biomedicine into institutional life. Pill call solved a practical problem: it was more efficient to send one nurse with a cart to patients in their pods than to send many patients to one nurse in the clinic.

One of the most notable aspects of pill call was how many people received narcotic medication. People came to clinic complaining of all kinds of aches and pains. Some pain narratives evoked uncomfortable living conditions—a hard metal bed frame and thin foam mattress that caused back pain. Some patients claimed they received pain medicine last time they were in jail; some cried as they described physical symptoms. Clinicians were trained to take pain seriously, yet acknowledged that some of the patient-prisoners performed pain to access opiates to trade, take for pleasure, or take to pass jail time. The issue of pain medication could never be resolved, for as soon as a clinician decided to order, increase, or deny opiates, other MCRs were submitted to increase the dose.

After a woman swallowed medication at pill call, she knew to turn away from the nurse and toward the deputy. She would open her mouth wide, lift her tongue, and prove that she was not hiding anything—although people found ways to conceal even with an open mouth. Some women turned this demonstration into a childish performance, sticking their tongues out in contempt like they might on a playground. Here, women remained docile as prisoners while mocking the distrust surrounding them.

While pill call was rife with regimentation, it was also intensely interpersonal. Pleasantries of "Hi, how you doin'?" were frequently exchanged. There was joking, such as a nurse greeting a patient by calling her "klepto" because she had been caught stealing stray soy sauce packets from a nurse's lunch a few months earlier. The patient smiled at this inside joke. Some nurses "passed pills," as they called it, with a "feel better," or a smile, inserting an affective dimension to the ritual.

In a nonincarcerated clinical setting, the nurse's smile would be unremarkable. But in jail, it was noteworthy. The sympathetic smile that accompanied the nurse's rule-governed pill pushing unsettled the division between her compassion and penal discipline. This is precisely the nature of jailcare that emerges in this charged environment. Even when a nurse delivers a pill with a tender smile, care is premised on an authority relation in which that nurse must directly supervise her patients taking their pills. The hierarchical foundation of care in turn creates possibilities in which affective connection becomes a transgressive element of care.

Other nurses did not even look patients in the eye on pill call. They buried their heads in their pill-taped lists. In this case, bureaucratic rituals provided a crutch for avoiding the intersubjective nature of nursing care, instead veering toward the impersonal affect of disciplinary power. This strategy helped stave off complaints from patient-prisoners, who viewed pill call as an opportunity to voice medical concerns to an agent of the jail health apparatus. "I was supposed to get my pain medication increased, why am I only getting one?" "I have this discharge and it itches real bad." "I put in a slip for medical three days ago, when am I going to be seen?" Nurses were unable to answer most of these questions on the spot, for they often stemmed from actions taken (or not) by clinicians. But patient-prisoners considered pill call the front line of the jail's medical establishment. Inmates held pill call nurses accountable for all clinic staff and systems. Nurses responded in various ways—sometimes with an "I'll look into it," or sometimes by looping prisoner-patients back into the bureaucratic circle by advising that they "put in another slip for medical."

Depending on the nurse involved, the response could be delivered apologetically, distractedly, or with annoyance. Or there could be no answer at all—just a glance at the list and a scribbled reminder note. Silence was a tactic some nurses developed to keep their cool amid the barrage of requests—a tactic sometimes perceived as rude by patient-prisoners, who might, themselves, hurl insults at nurses about incompetence. Becky explained how she coped: "Under my breath I'm like, you know, like I'll say something back, just to keep myself sane."

As pill call's DOT suggests, disciplinarity in the jail clinic milieu took several forms. It drifted between infantilizingly punitive regimes like Julie's waiting area admonitions and the medicalized microtechniques of care, such as directly observing the swallowing of medication. These moments all contributed to disciplining the patient-prisoners. But these moments were also the same ones that invited sociality, intimacy, and compassion. From a gentle smile to an annoyed shrug of the shoulders to detachment, nurses on pill call cultivated ambiguity precisely as a form of recognition.

12 P.M.: THE TEDIUM OF CHART

At noon, while deputies cycled through their lunch breaks, clinicians and nurses documented their morning work with patients. All their notes and medication orders were made in CHART. With its turquoise background, all-capital letter typing, and computer-mouse incompatibility, CHART appeared to be a relic from 1980s DOS-style programs. In fact, it was introduced to the San Francisco jail in 1996 as a response to a court order to have better continuity of care when inmates were transferred from one San Francisco jail to another. CHART was more than a repository of electronic medical information. It was an ongoing professional task, a medically narrated representation of time spent in jail. Because every patient's intake medical evaluation in the booking jail was documented, one could view how many times a person had been admitted to jail. Every pill given at pill call, every MCR submitted by a patient, every visit with a clinician, every measured blood pressure, was logged in CHART.

The ubiquity of CHART as part of medical caregiving in the jail cannot be overemphasized. Clinicians and nurses spent many hours of their days tapping on the keyboard. While it may seem an obvious sign of how technology has depersonalized medicine, an act of neoliberal efficiency, CHART was also a dynamic interface through which scripts about patients were narrated. The difficult patient, the pain-medication seeking patient, the psychotic patient, the irresponsible patient who does not follow up outside of jail, the "needy" patient with a multitude of minor complaints, the first-time jail patient, the patient who leaves jail and comes back—all these figures became codified in official documentation.[12] Subsequent providers could then read others' CHART interpretations of patients to calibrate how they framed patient encounters.[13] CHART enabled this kind of "institutional memory," and also projected future action.[14]

For instance, before I saw Connie, the pregnant woman who tried to fake a miscarriage with strawberry jam, I read the night nurses' account of the events. Despite the caregiving imperative to listen to the patient, CHART predisposed me to distrust Connie, and even to distrust the ostensibly objective findings of pelvic tenderness—which can be a sign of the dangerous condition of a tubal pregnancy—I found on her physical examination.[15] I had to weigh the CHART script that claimed manipulation (and the patient's own corroboration of this script) against signs of danger in the physical examination; I risked either looking foolish for unnecessarily transporting a patient to the hospital—a burden for the deputies—or missing a dangerous diagnosis.

Ultimately, fear of missing a serious condition tipped the balance.[16] I had Connie transported to the hospital—an action which I initiated in CHART, choosing option "M" under the category "disposition": transfer to emergency room. But this action did not clearly resolve opposing narratives, for I remained begrudging in my actions, and felt foolish for deciding to send a scripted "manipulator" to the hospital. Even in the acts of medical decision-making, the boundary between diagnosing disease or diagnosing manipulation was unsettled. CHART was a critical mediator of these engagements with ambiguity.

3:20 P.M.: AFTERNOON CLINIC

The morning shift of nurses had been replaced by the afternoon shift. "PM clinic" was the daily afternoon session in which nurses conducted routine checks: blood sugar checks for diabetic patients, skin-test screening for tuberculosis among new arrivals, blood pressure monitoring, dressing changes for wounds, lab draws, vaccinations, weight checks, etc. These orchestrations began once the deputies changed shifts at 3 o'clock, and once the afternoon "count time" of inmates in CJ2 was complete.

The atmosphere in PM clinic was decidedly more relaxed than during the morning clinic. In the morning, nurses scurried about getting patients ready for clinicians, and served as intermediaries between clinicians and deputies, who controlled the flow of patients. Clinicians were generally not around in the afternoon—they had left for the day or were busy entering information and ordering medications in CHART from the morning group of sick call patients.

In PM clinic, patients, nurses, and deputies in the waiting area chatted even more casually than in the morning. Unlike morning clinic, when deputies stayed in front of holding cells, PM deputy escorts would hang around the clinic, as they were always supposed to, to make sure inmates behaved. The nurses made small talk with the patients, asking "You back again?"; or talking about food—"You gotta try the barbeque from T-Dubs when you get out! It is sooo good." Laughter, bored silence, and, on occasion, yelling cycled through the PM clinic soundtrack. Regardless of content, there was a routine familiarity in the air.

A nurse called a patient to the lab room to get blood drawn for an HIV test, and to give a urine sample for a pregnancy test she had requested. While she was waiting, the supervising deputy hovered by the bench, fidgeting with a set of handcuffs that made a rhythmic ratcheting sound. He tried to banter with her, saying "Are you pregnant?" "You just a dope fiend." The woman responded, "Hey, that's not nice. That's not good for someone's self-esteem." The deputy gave her a look that said "Can't you take a joke?" Clearly, his position of authority made him feel entitled to joke with her in the form of harassment and to pry into her medical history. In response, she revealed herself as neither a hardened prisoner resisting authority nor a silent subject but as a vulnerable human whose feelings could be hurt. Even in the midst of a disciplinary relationship with the deputy, there was intimacy in this admission.

Later, when the nurse beckoned the patient to the lab room, she begged to stay after her blood had been drawn, to avoid the deputy. The nurse tried to soothe her as she tightened a tourniquet around her arm. The patient told the nurse about her weeks on the streets since her previous incarceration, about her children, and about her hope that she would get her life together this time. More than four minutes had passed. She was not pregnant. Here in the clinic's lab room, under the burden of prescribed biomedical diagnostic practices, intimacy emerged as the patient sought refuge.

6 P.M.: NIGHT SHIFT

The scheduled tasks of the day were almost complete—one more round of pill call before bedtime, around 8:30 p.m. The overnight crew—two RNs and an LVN—arrived, overlapping for a few hours with the 2–11 p.m. shift nurses. The night team responded to all the pods' urgent overnight needs. A "man-down" emergency or a phone call from a pod deputy would break up the monotony and require nurses to decide what was an emergency and what was not.

As midnight marked the shift's halfway point, nurses readied lists for the next day's sick call and transports to the county hospital for specialist appointments. After their 4 a.m. wake-up call and breakfast, patient-prisoners with hospital appointments would be called out and escorted

from the pods to a Sheriff's Department vehicle. Nearly every day, someone refused to be transported. Sometimes, that person wanted to get back
into bed for a few hours, or did not understand where she was going;
sometimes, she felt embarrassment at the prospect of being seen publicly
in orange clothes and chains; or she had a court appearance that day
which she did not want to miss. It was also routine for staff to sigh in
moral reflection. "They take this for granted. Do they know how long it
would take *me* to get an appointment like this?" 4:30 am pill call was the
night shift's last task. At 6 am, the morning crew arrived, and it was time
for another day of care to begin.

CARE IN THE ROUTINE

Describing the jail clinic through a temporally demarcated structure offers
several insights. One is that the jail and, by association, its clinic, organizes
its duties to punish and to heal by marking time. It is a predictable illustra-
tion of Foucault's observation that disciplinary power manages bodies by
managing relations of time. But to limit the interpretation to an expected
example of regulatory, governing power inside a clinic inside jail would
miss how humans actually work through the tensions imposed by the
intersecting regimes of medicine, carcerality, and an ineffective safety net.

Instead, the routine of the jail clinic opens the possibility of intimate
caregiving arising from bureaucratic routine and the very structures of
carcerality, revealing that affective dimensions of caregiving are not inconsistent with punitive aspects of discipline. It is not that caring relations
ontologically precede discipline, or that their grounding in mutual human
vulnerability comes before superimposed power arrangements. Rather,
care emerges from and within disciplinary routines. It may not always
take the romanticized form of clinicians holding patients' hands amid
grave physical and emotional suffering. Instead, it appears as a willingness
to sift through the ambiguity of a mandate to tend the needs of women
who, by virtue of being in jail, are categorized as socially deviant, and who
may exhibit behaviors that reinforce that characterization.

At every level of the jail clinic's routine, health care providers were confronted with the morally ambiguous question of worthiness—did inmates

deserve this HIV screening test? Did they deserve to be in jail? Was it fair that inmates received more extensive health care services in jail than many people received in the community? As one nurse asked, "How you going to think you deserve this, but you done killed somebody?" The clinic had to confront both the fact that its patients were arrested for allegedly committing a crime and that tremendous health inequalities existed outside of jail, with ineffective safety net services. Ambiguity flourished within these conflicting realities.

Clinic staff sometimes suppressed recurring questions of deservingness by approaching their routines and patients as they would at any other clinic; or they sometimes enlivened the ambiguity with shoulder shrugs as they dispensed a pill, or with a casually critical conversation among themselves. These small gestures within the routines of medical care became important opportunities to negotiate ambiguities. An eye roll, a tender smile, a rude side comment, or a joke became ways through which clinic staff diffused the tensions they felt in deciphering patients' worthiness of care. These same ambivalences enabled clinic workers to care for patients in ways that exceeded the punitive dimensions of the carceral milieu.

Much of the negotiating over the moral status of the patient and the moral position of the caregiver was made possible by the reliance on biomedical diagnostic technologies that have been critiqued for displacing the intimate exchange of caregiving relationships.[17] The jail clinic set up a counterpoint to this displacement. On the surface, its bureaucracy and technical diagnostics seem to depart from a notion of romanticized human connection within caregiving.[18] Instead, what I hope the routine at the San Francisco jail clinic has shown is that rote technical practices and the human intimacy of caregiving are not necessarily divergent. They can be mutually enabling. They allow an ethos of compassionate care not to contradict an ethos of punitive discipline, but to form within it.

CULTIVATING AMBIGUITY

Understanding the jail clinic is not a matter of labeling certain moments as care when they provide kindness in a cruel place. Instead, it is about seeing relationships, affects, gestures, and routine procedures in often contradictory forms. These everyday human engagements in the jail clinic wrestle more broadly with what it means to care for another person. Seeing intimacy and human connection in rote bureaucratic acts enables possibilities of care even within larger systems that sustain hierarchy and inequality. Perhaps the ethos of the jail clinic that is embedded within and arises from an oppressive system of mass incarceration and from an ineffective safety net marks the care that is all around us, even beyond the physical walls of the jail.[19]

Part I of this book has explored the contradictory forces that comprised the caregiving endeavor within the San Francisco jail clinic apparatus. The terms of practicing care were persistently constrained and interpreted by ethical, bureaucratic, and disciplinary concerns. These tensions gave rise to forms of care that, rather than being concerned with resolving contradictions, grappled constantly with the intersecting realities of inequalities on the streets, restrictions of incarceration, and desires to care. In Part II, I extend these complexities of care and carcerality to the rest of the jail beyond the defined clinical space. I describe the ways these ambiguous intimacies of care took shape in the relations conjured by women's reproduction and motherhood in jail, and ultimately to women's conflicting desires to be cared for by the institution.

PART II

5 Gestating Care

INCARCERATED REPRODUCTION
AS PARTICIPATORY PRACTICE

I just don't think a pregnant person should be incarcerated
in jail, even though sometimes maybe they don't care. But
I've seen quite a few that keep coming back here pregnant
and, in some sense, I think some of them actually get better
treatment and take better care of themselves and their
babies in jail, as opposed to them being outside. . . . I think
being in jail is like a safe haven for them.

Deputy Lewis, female deputy at the San Francisco jail

"BETTER OFF IN JAIL" OR "NO PLACE FOR A PREGNANT WOMAN"?

Alisha was trying to make things work. At age 32, she was pregnant with her third child. She did not have custody over her other two children, though she dreamed of being reunited with them, and was determined to raise this child to whom she would soon give birth. Alisha had enrolled in a methadone maintenance program for pregnant women, and only rarely used street drugs.[1] She attended most of her prenatal appointments, which were frequent due to a pregnancy condition, shortened cervix, which increases the risk of preterm birth. Alisha had also recently assaulted her ex-girlfriend, who had stolen the money with which Alisha was paying for housing. A judge mandated that Alisha attend a fifty-two-week-long domestic violence class, which she did. But she missed a few classes, both because of frequent prenatal appointments, and because she was fatigued from her cocktail of psychiatric medications and methadone.

At a subsequent court appearance, she also admitted to occasional use of drugs. The judge and probation officer initially recommended Alisha to an outpatient drug treatment program.

But then, Alisha told me, they factored in that hers was a "high risk pregnancy," due to her shortened cervix and drug use. "They was worried about the baby," Alisha told me, rubbing her pregnant belly under an orange jail uniform. "So they remanded me to custody, because of the baby." The judge considered pregnant Alisha to be "better off in jail," believing that the carceral environment would be better for the pregnancy than her current life. In jail, she would be escorted to on-site prenatal appointments and would be kept away from drugs and other behaviors deemed harmful to the fetus. Had she not been pregnant, Alisha believed, the judge and probation officer would not have sent her to jail. There was no anger in her voice as she told me this. Alisha was resigned to this protectionist conviction, even as it was accompanied by a moral judgment about the inappropriateness of her maternity behavior. Perhaps she was accustomed to the state's intervention in her life, after her long-standing involvement in the criminal justice system, her enrollment in publicly funded Medicaid during pregnancy, and her hypermanaged daily attendance at a methadone maintenance clinic.[2] Perhaps the state's involvement in Alisha's current pregnancy, by way of incarceration, was merely an extension of what she already knew. Ultimately, Alisha stayed in jail for three months, and was released to a residential drug treatment program when she was 36 weeks pregnant.

In contrast, a different judge made a different assessment about the appropriateness of pregnancy in jail for a woman named Maria. Maria was 28 weeks pregnant when she was arrested for the first time, for a nondrug-related, nonviolent offense. A quiet woman who spoke only Spanish, Maria kept to herself in the pod. She had received regular prenatal care in the community, lived in a house with family members, and had no history of drug addiction. Her daily life outside of jail had little of the instability that characterized Alisha's. I saw Maria for a prenatal visit in the jail clinic on her second day at the San Francisco jail. She had just had a court appearance, and the judge had decided to release her from jail the next day. "Jail is no place for a pregnant woman," he had told her. He was referring to the material deprivation of incarceration that seemed unsuitable

for a pregnant woman's needs: uncomfortable beds, food only at scheduled mealtimes, close living quarters, and in general (though not at the
San Francisco jail), inconsistent and substandard prenatal care.[3] Maria
left jail the next morning and never came back.

One judge's ruling that Alisha should be in jail and another's that Maria
should not might seem to indicate the arbitrariness of the criminal justice
system. More broadly, these decisions reflect the state's deep and persistent
involvement in regulating women's reproduction, especially poor women
of color. The management of women's pregnancies in a carceral setting
represents a convergence of the racialized, gendered, and economic dimensions of mass incarceration with the politics of reproduction, the differential valuing of lives, and the ways that state institutions regulate women's
bodies. It is easy to see the management of pregnant inmates as an exemplary site for controlling and valuing (or devaluing) women's reproductive
behaviors along differentials stratified by race, poverty, and addiction—
what Morgan and Roberts have called "reproductive governance."[4]

However, an understanding of the entanglements of incarceration and
reproduction should not end with a story of producing governable subjects. For as we have already seen, relationships in jail are grounded in
unsettling contradictions between caregiving and carceral discipline.
Exploring the experiences of women like Alisha, as well as the management of their pregnancies, reveals how the relational tensions of carcerality shape both the moral claims of people charged with taking care of prisoners and their gestating fetuses and the maternal sentiment of poor,
marginalized, reproducing women. In turn, pregnancy in this setting
sheds light on the vulnerabilities of the institution itself. Furthermore, the
intimate and contradictory interactions between jail workers and pregnant inmates amplify and are amplified by the uncertain status of the
incarcerated woman's fetus, which remains a liability risk for the institution. Thus the pregnant inmate and her fetus challenge the institution to
think about how it cares for all those inside its walls. I explore these challenges in this chapter, first by giving an overview of incarcerated pregnancy on a national scale, and contextualizing these processes in the contradictions encapsulated by the pregnant inmate. What happens on the
ground at the San Francisco jail then reveals how, through the custody
and medical staff's management of pregnant inmates, the jail articulates

what kind of care these women—and their fetuses—deserve. Through risk management, moral judgments, and gestures of care and control, the jail both challenges and reinforces expected norms of punishment and maternity.

GOVERNING REPRODUCTION THROUGH INCARCERATION

The reproductive experiences of incarcerated women exemplify modern state projects to manage life at the population level and at the level of the individual pregnant prisoner whose behavior is regulated by the conditions of incarceration. It is worth acknowledging these real political dimensions, for they are critical backdrops for the day-to-day interactions surrounding pregnant women at the San Francisco jail; these predictable politics in which reproduction is controlled also serve as a foil to more surprising ways that care can be engendered in a carceral setting when the reproduction of future generations is involved.

Racialized mass incarceration and the criminalization of poverty are themselves techniques of differentially regulating reproduction.[5] Most incarcerated women, in their 20s and 30s, are removed from society during the prime of their reproductive years, precluding many (at least those with long prison sentences) from reproducing. For the two-thirds of incarcerated women who are already mothers, time behind bars can disrupt their ability to parent—although, as I show in the next chapter, jail can also create new visions of motherhood to which these women aspire. When they go to prison or jail, they risk having their parental rights terminated if their children are in foster care for more than fifteen months.[6] These systematic carceral infringements on reproduction disproportionately affect women (and communities) of color. Giving birth while in custody creates readier pathways for those newborns to go into state foster care systems, if there is no designated guardian for the baby. Given the disproportionate incarceration of young black women, this perpetuates the racialized disruption of parental relationships and institutional management of the next generation. An extreme example of prisons controlling reproductive capacity is the coercive sterilization of incarcerated women. A 2013 report revealed that nearly 150 women in California prisons were unlawfully sterilized from 2006 to 2010.[7] One prison doctor interviewed for the report justified the actions by saying the sterilization operation was cheaper than these women having more babies, which the state would then have to support. This practice suggests that state projects aimed at suppressing the reproduction of the poor and women of color are not merely historical lessons in eugenics. Rather, they are evidence that certain women's reproduction is devalued while others' is encouraged.[8]

Disturbingly, medical literature has documented that women who are incarcerated during pregnancy have lower rates of preterm birth, stillbirth, and low birth weight, when compared to women of similar demographics in the community.[9] The explanation given for these epidemiologic findings is that incarceration removes a pregnant woman from an unhealthy environment, like the reasoning of the judge who sentenced Alisha to jail-time in her pregnancy. This sentiment has also been widely translated in some states into criminal convictions of pregnant women who are perceived to be harming their fetuses in a variety of ways, like using drugs.[10] Such laws incarcerate women in order to multitask: at once punishing women for "bad behavior," while protecting the fetus from "dangerous" mothers.[11] Such policies elide the underlying structural forces that constrain these women's choices, and fail to adequately invest in noncarceral efforts that could assist them. Moreover, they correspond to conflicting constructions of risk. On the one hand, structural inequalities make pregnant women who are enmeshed in the criminal justice system at higher risk for poor health outcomes compared to the general population. On the other hand, pregnant women are expected to take personal responsibility for individual and social failures.[12]

Because there are no mandatory health care standards or oversight systems for prisons and jails, for the approximately 3–5 percent of incarcerated women who are pregnant at any given time, the nature of pregnancy services is wildly variable.[13] A comprehensive review of pregnancy care in state prisons documented that thirty-eight states had insufficient or no prenatal care, or inadequate arrangements for childbirth.[14] In a Department of Justice report, 54 percent of pregnant women in state prisons indicated that they received no prenatal care.[15] At some jails, "prenatal care" consists of a nurse checking a pregnant woman's blood pressure and weight, but no comprehensive care from a prenatal care provider.

I have heard from women in other states who say prison doctors have shamed them for being incarcerated and pregnant, and delayed aspects of their prenatal care as punishment. Custody staff, who have no medical training, are usually the first point of triage for subtle symptoms of pregnancy such as bleeding and cramping which, even when mild, can be signs of labor, miscarriage, preterm labor, or other conditions. Narrative accounts, lawsuits, and media reports also chronicle neglectful prenatal care for pregnant women at facilities across the country.[16] As an expert witness, I personally have reviewed cases from other county jails where pregnant women's bleeding was ignored, and they miscarried or gave birth to still- and live-born babies in their jail cells.[17] These harrowing instances are not exceptions on a national scale. They should not be forgotten as I further describe the conditions at the San Francisco County Jail, where pregnancy care was comparatively thorough and attentive.

Many incarcerated women end up giving birth in chains. They usually cannot have visitors in the hospital while giving birth, which reflects the isolation many incarcerated pregnant women feel throughout their pregnancies. Women who give birth while incarcerated, of whom there are approximately 1,200–1,500 per year, are typically separated from their children at birth.[18] Other pregnant women who want to terminate their pregnancies are frequently denied access to abortion, despite clear legal precedent that asserts that they retain this right while incarcerated. Notably, abortion was easily accessible for women at San Francisco jail.[19]

These examples show that, whether being prevented from reproducing, disabled from maintaining preexisting motherhood, forced to continue an unwanted pregnancy, receiving inadequate reproductive health care, or actively giving birth, reproduction in prison is a critical phenomenon upon which problems of poverty, racism, gender roles, oppression, and societal responsibility converge. These processes signify a broader devaluing of these women and their reproduction.

Much effort has been expended to explore the consequences for children of having incarcerated mothers.[20] Most of these reports demonstrate that children born to incarcerated women, especially if they are placed in foster care, carry a high risk of being incarcerated themselves as adults. But surprisingly few scholars have explored the experiences of motherhood and the politics of reproduction from the level of everyday experiences of incarcerated women and the people managing them. Existing narrative representations of women's pregnancy experiences convey institutional neglect and callousness, and emphasize the conditions I described above—sparse medical care, humiliating shackling during childbirth, and the pain of being separated from their children.[21] These various reports of incarcerated women and reproduction rightly point out how women's reproductive capacity is always already enmeshed in patriarchal regimes of control.[22] Many of these representations humanize the plight of women prisoners through their status as mothers, a depiction that romanticizes the symbolic, affective dimensions of motherhood; such strategic romanticizations of motherhood may appeal to policy makers who could then improve conditions.[23]

To be sure, the stories of Evelyn, Kima, Alisha, and other women in the San Francisco jail whom I describe are rife with evidence of the state's deep regulatory involvement in every aspect of women's reproduction and the criminalized politicization of motherhood.[24] But existing accounts of the intersection of reproduction and incarceration are so focused on power dynamics and the oppression of women that they leave little room for understanding what is at stake for reproducing women suspended in the criminal justice system and for the guards and medical personnel who are charged with managing—and caring for—them.

FAVORITISM

Tenisha approached the deputy watchtower and asked Deputy Brody if she could get some hot water. Tenisha held a shrink-wrapped bowl of Ramen noodles in her hand, the noodles thirsty for rehydration and Tenisha hungry for an evening snack she had purchased from the jail commissary. She was five weeks pregnant and her appetite had increased as soon as she learned she was pregnant, during her intake evaluation in CJ1, the booking jail, a few days ago. It was now 8 p.m. in B-pod, past the window of time when inmates were allowed to use the microwave in the pod's pantry. Deputy Brody reminded Tenisha that she could get warm water from the tap, but could not use the microwave. Tenisha sighed. Then Deputy Walker, the other pod deputy for the evening, chimed in to override her colleague's enforcement of the rules. "It's OK. I authorized it. She's pregnant."

Deputy Walker's declaration hung in the air. She meant it as an obvious justification for Tenisha to use the microwave off-hours, though Deputy Brody also knew that Tenisha was pregnant: her housing card had the word "pregnant" written on it in blue ballpoint pen. Yet this knowledge did not move Deputy Brody to bend the rules. Her authority momentarily displaced, Deputy Brody quietly swiveled her chair back to some paperwork. Tenisha steeped her Ramen in microwaved hot water and went to her cell to enjoy the noodles.

That same evening, Tenisha walked up the stairs, which involved passing by the watchtower. Deputy Walker stopped her, asking, "How far along are you?" Even if she had been five months pregnant, it would have been hard to tell under her baggy orange sweatshirt. "Five weeks," Tenisha responded. Deputy Walker used this as an entrée to start a conversation about raising children. Tenisha, realizing it was going to be a long chat, got herself comfortable on the steps. They soon learned that Deputy Walker had a daughter in her late teens, and Tenisha had a fourteen-year-old son.

For the next half hour, they shared their perspectives on spoiling children and teaching them discipline. Tenisha told the story about her arrest, which, in her mind, arose from a misunderstanding during a dispute with her son. Deputy and inmate reminisced about their childhoods, eventually realizing that they went to the same high school, twenty years apart. They laughed, agreed with each other's parental insights, and talked about old teachers. Had my eyes been closed, I could have imagined they were two friends getting to know each other over a cup of coffee. But then I would have opened my eyes to see one woman in an orange jail uniform and the other in a guard's black uniform, with handcuffs attached to her belt.

A few minutes after their conversation ended, Tenisha called from the upstairs balcony and asked Deputy Walker if she could read the newspaper lying on the watch tower desk. Deputy Walker looked furtively at a cell that housed a woman—not pregnant—whose multiple requests for the newspaper she had denied—"Because I'm not done reading it," Deputy Walker had told her. The other nonpregnant woman was not looking, so Deputy Walker quickly passed the paper to an inmate walking up the stairs, who then discreetly passed the item to Tenisha on the upper level.

Numerous examples like this show pregnant women getting tender care, sometimes furtively delivered, from the deputies. I observed kindness in the pods when deputies called pregnant woman to the watch tower, just to ask "How are you feeling?" It was not uncommon for deputies to transgress their own rules and give pregnant inmates an extra meal tray or bags of chips from their work-issued meals. And some deputies even stealthily brought in outside food like shrimp and steak burritos for pregnant women, delivering the food with a wink of the eye. "It's for the baby."

Deputy Walker's favoritism toward Tenisha, sparked by knowledge of her pregnant status, was not uniform. Not every pregnant woman in the San Francisco Jail was treated with this tenderness by every deputy or medical staff member. Some deputies strived to adhere to the conventional wisdom that all prisoners should be treated the same and ignored pregnancies as much as possible. For instance, a few days later, I watched Tenisha in the holding area near the clinic flaunt her bag of ice to a deputy, telling him, "You know why I got this? I'm pregnant!" He nodded his head without looking at her and without saying a word—until she left, when he said to me and the other deputies, "Now why should I care?" For this deputy, the inmate's pregnancy was as inconsequential as a stubbed toe. These stories of quotidian moments between deputies and a pregnant woman expose the ambivalence surrounding reproduction in jail: the mixture of exceptional concern and standard disregard for pregnancy. At the heart of this ambivalence are the numerous discordances of a pregnant woman and fetal subject being in jail.

PREGNANT INMATE AS CONTRADICTION

Pregnancy is a socially complex state to which anthropologists have long been drawn.[25] A classic interpretation views pregnancy as a liminal state between the social status of a woman and of a mother, between the uncertain living fetus and birthed, living child.[26] Furthermore, pregnant women are highly valued because of their biological capacity to enable social reproduction. Such reverence for Tenisha's pregnant status in jail inspired Deputy Walker to bend the microwave rules and to deny a nonpregnant inmate the daily news. For the same powerful reason they are revered, pregnant women are also feared: they generate cultural anxieties about the social order they have the power to reproduce. This coexistence of reverence and fear contributes to pregnant women having an ambivalent and, relatedly, ambiguous symbolic status.

The fetus, too, is replete with ambiguity. Indeed, the fetus cultivates a plethora of biomedical, religious, cultural, and moral values whose contradictions speak to existential questions about personhood.[27] In the United States, the fetus is imagined as the ideal citizen, at once a *tabula rasa* for all of life's potential and a figure already deeply entangled in social, economic, gendered, and political discourse.[28] Deputies and jail health care staff brought these cultural understandings of the fetus with them to the situation of pregnant inmates.

The ambivalence of pregnancy is tied to both the symbolic value ascribed to the fetus and the mother's role in nurturing it. We now take this interdependence of the maternal-fetal unit as a biological and social fact. However, Lorna Weir has carefully argued that the biomedicalized connection between pregnancy behaviors and fetal health is a relatively new understanding, emerging in the 1950s when the epidemiologic concept of "risk factor" developed.[29] This shifted the threshold of when we believed life began from the moment of birth to the time of in utero gestation. The fetus became an "at risk" entity. Prenatal care developed to optimize fetal life in the present, rather than deferring to the future, after birth. The perinatal threshold of life, rather than the birth threshold, made pregnancy an obvious site for risk governance, authorizing the management of how pregnant women should behave and what they should (and should not) consume.

Because the fetus is viewed as highly dependent on its maternal host, it is a vulnerable figure who, in turn, renders the pregnant woman vulnerable, more susceptible to harm. Additionally, the biomedicalization of our contemporary moment has meant that pregnancy is seen as a physiologic state of increased needs which, if fulfilled (ideally through biomedical interventions), can mitigate the vulnerability.[30] State and biomedical apparatuses, as Weir and others have elaborated, intervene with pregnant bodies because of their precarious and needy status.[31] The presumed vulnerability of pregnancy and of the fetus incites protectionist stances resulting in the incarceration of pregnant women who behave dangerously—like that of the judge who sent Alisha to jail at 26 weeks.

This status of the fetus as vulnerable and at risk comes to bear heavily on the entangled nature of risk management protocols in jail.[32] If anything happens to the pregnant inmate that endangers the fetus, the institution is open to lawsuits. Thus, prenatal care and living accommodations for pregnant women, like a bottom bunk, are intended to reduce the risk of harm to the fetus and, in turn, help protect the institution. The jail-specific protocols for managing pregnant women are thus rooted in such risk management approaches, and frame the relationships between pregnant inmates and jail staff.

Beyond its invitation to regulate, vulnerability also enmeshes individuals in social relationships, given "the fact that one's life is always in some sense in the hands of others."[33] Apprehending another's potential for injury reminds us of our own vulnerability, which can evoke empathy and be a basis for care.[34] Accordingly, pregnancy, particularly with the cultural ascription of vulnerability, can engender relationships of care. After all, Deputy Walker, a mother herself, was moved to provide special care for her pregnant charge, Tenisha.

Pregnancy is thus shrouded in ambiguity. Ambiguity, as I explored in chapters 3 and 4, entails the coexistence of multiple, often contradictory, interpretations or phenomena. Pregnancy is at once a valued force of social and economic reproduction, a potential threat to existing social orders, an act of gestating a being whose vital status is uncertain, and a state of vulnerability that opens the pregnant body to regulation and care. These registers all contribute to pregnancy's ambiguity. Jail amplifies that ambiguity. What to make of a fetus—that innocent, idealized citizen—in the womb of someone being punished for committing a crime? Does this mean the fetus is incarcerated? Is jail responsible for caring for the fetus? Will the mother's criminality be reproduced in her offspring? How could a female who allegedly broke the law and transgresses gendered norms of passive femininity also be maternally nurturing?[35] What forms of life are possible in such a setting?[36]

The pregnant inmate thus challenges its carceral host with numerous contradictions.[37] Not only does she contain the contradictory categories of certain living subject (woman) and uncertain living subject (fetus) carried by all pregnant women; she also embodies characteristics of life-giving and life-depriving, gestating as she does in a carceral dwelling designed ostensibly to deprive and dehumanize. Certainly, contradictory figures challenge others to sort through their cultural values, to affirm and question what they believe.[38] This ambiguous figure—the pregnant inmate—thus prompted jail workers and inmates in the San Francisco jail to negotiate the tension between what kinds of care can emerge in a punitive context, and against the backdrop of marginality these women experience outside of jail.

PREGNANT INMATE AS MORAL SLATE

Pregnant woman in their midst triggered deputies to broadly question who should and should not be reproducing. Even if the full belly was not visible through the baggy orange clothing, the "pregnant" label on the housing card marked a woman's status, and offered a constant, low-level reminder of the fetus and all its political baggage. This discordant situation prompted deputies to map values of motherhood and reproduction onto the figure of the pregnant inmate. Jail staff articulated reproductive ideologies as they contemplated the problems raised by pregnant inmates.

One day when I sat with the deputies in the holding area, Nicole, a woman who had recently had an abortion while incarcerated, walked from the holding cell to the clinic to see a clinician for a post-procedure follow-up. After she left the holding area, Deputy Carter began to talk about her. He had noticed that her housing card no longer said pregnant. Deputy Carter assumed, correctly, that Nicole had terminated the pregnancy—although the change in pregnancy status could have also signaled a miscarriage. "I don't want to sound like I don't respect life and all, but maybe it's a good thing she's not bringing a baby into this world. I mean, some of these people shouldn't be having babies they can't take care of." Another deputy nodded his head in agreement, similarly adjudicating who should and should not reproduce, based on their ability to display maternal norms, to raise their own children, to not use drugs, and to be upstanding citizens.

The conversation led Deputy Carter to reminisce about Raquel, a woman who had been in and out of jail several times a year for the last twelve years. She had delivered six babies while in custody—I myself took care of her during one of these pregnancies—and all of them were funneled immediately into foster care. Deputy Carter recalled watching over her in the hospital nursery after one of her deliveries. Deputy Carter folded his arms in front of him, as though he were rocking a baby while he described Raquel cooing and bonding in the nursery with her infant. A social worker from CPS then arrived in the nursery, to inform Raquel that she was looking into the case.

"As soon as this lady walked away," Deputy Carter recalled, "Raquel practically dropped the baby back into the basket and says 'I wanna go back now.' And all that tenderness, all that mother love went away in an instant. I mean, not meanly, but, she was done with that baby." The deputies agreed that this kind of woman should not be bringing babies into the world. Here, moral notions about reproduction—about the ideal, loving mother—were small talk, part of how deputies filled their downtime.

The tone among this group of deputies, all male, was one of resigned cynicism. Other deputies expressed anger. One male deputy, Deputy Randolph, summarized some female deputies' feelings about the pregnant women in jail:

> There are a number of female prisoners who come through here, repeatedly over the years, pregnant. It really causes a pretty deep negative emotional response with the female deputies. They just are angry about it. That's a very complex thing. They're angry about it, because in their perception the woman is irresponsible. She's not practicing any kind of birth control. She wants the county to pay for all this, to take care of this, somebody else to take care of the baby. They're angry because they feel bad for the babies.

Though he characterized the anger as being specific to the female deputies, it was clear through his sighs, his shaking head, and his gesticulating hands that Deputy Randolph, too, felt anger toward pregnant inmates.

As they freely expressed among themselves their judgments about the reproductive limits of women in their custody, some deputies, as I observed, maintained professionalism in front of the pregnant women. Other deputies did not. Evelyn had reproductive insults hurled at her by some deputies, as she told me: "One deputy told me I needed drug rehab, not a baby, that I shouldn't—Why am I bringing another child into the world? They said I should be—I should—She was being really rude. She basically was saying because I'm an addict, I shouldn't have kids. Like, I should go to a drug rehab and not—She told me I needed to get an abortion, basically. That's what she told me." Whether they kept their comments to themselves or shared them directly with the inmates, deputies encountered pregnant women as an opportunity through which to consider a broader cultural narrative about motherhood and the societal burden which these women's children, extracted from their custody by social services, created.

INSTITUTIONAL VULNERABILITY

Another element of a pregnant prisoner's status as an ambiguous figure was that while she could be vulnerable to the whims of the institution, she also could be a liability and reveal the institution's weaknesses. Although, in general, most pregnancies proceeded uneventfully, obstetrical complications could arise for any pregnant woman—bleeding, miscarriages, preterm labor, stillbirth, to name a few. If any of these things happened while a pregnant woman was incarcerated, the jail would be held accountable. To complicate matters, fights occasionally broke out in jail, a hazard particularly for a pregnant inmate. Jail could be risky for the pregnant woman, and the pregnant woman could be risky for the jail. The San Francisco jail administration indirectly revealed its stance that jail and pregnancy were a potentially dangerous combination when Deputy Lewis announced her pregnancy and was reassigned. Starting in her first trimester and lasting the remainder of her pregnancy, she was removed from the role of "pod deputy," where she interfaced and managed inmates constantly, and risked dealing with violent inmates. Instead, she was assigned to work in the central command tower, watching security camera screens and pushing buttons to remotely permit other people's movements through metal doors. By working security from a distance, without direct inmate interaction, the deputy could protect her fetus from the jail's inmates, and the jail could protect itself by avoiding an occupational injury in a pregnant woman.

At a pragmatic level, the contradictory figure of the pregnant prisoner, with her highly dependent fetus, was seen as a looming threat to the institution. Deputy Allston shared her fear with me: "It does feel like a liability, because one of them can trip and fall down these stairs and is maybe a lawsuit ready to happen." This is not merely theoretical: many jails and prisons across the country have had lawsuits brought against them for neglectful care of pregnant women and adverse fetal or neonatal outcomes.[39] The liability of having a fetus in jail meant that deputies had to be hypervigilant of pregnant women—from watching how they walked up and down stairs to retrieve their meal trays, to maintaining a low threshold for transporting a pregnant inmate to the hospital, where she and the fetus could get a more comprehensive evaluation than at the jail. For behind a pregnant woman's symptoms of pain, bleeding, or even, as Deputy Randolph joked, "a hiccup," lurked the potential for fetal harm, for perceived neglect, and for subsequent legal consequences. In jail, the fetus's and pregnant woman's interdependent vulnerability thus reciprocally made the institution vulnerable. It also inverted the usual power vector between an inmate and a jail worker. Because the pregnant woman, by virtue of her fetus, was a threat to the institution, she therefore possessed power over jail staff, who had to care for her accordingly.

This vulnerability and powerful threat of the pregnant inmate blurs the line between penal logic that tries to tame the threat of an inmate and caring concern for the mother-fetus unit. That is to say, it was sometimes difficult to discern whether the increased attentiveness to pregnant women represented jail staff's fear of liability, or their genuine concern for the well-being of the woman and the fetus. Alisha experienced the deputies' attentiveness to her pregnancy state both as nagging control and compassionate concern. "Sometimes they [the deputies] treat me okay. Some treat me special. And some of them just, is like, really cold and rude. . . . They'd be like: Well don't do this, and don't do that." One day, she ran up the stairs to get her meal tray, and a deputy scolded her to "slow down" and "hold onto the rail." Another day, she danced to the music playing on the pod's boom box during free time, and a deputy told her she should not be dancing, "because of the baby."

Alisha was annoyed at their micromanaging, policing comments: "Just because I'm pregnant, I mean, I can't dance? Sometimes it's bothersome." And yet she recognized that within the discipline was a hint of concern and care. "But sometimes it's good to know that people care." Alisha recalled one deputy's worried response when Alisha told her she had not felt the baby kick that day: "I guess she [the deputy] had been pregnant before, so Deputy K. was like: 'As a woman, I'm going to take you now to medical. If you have to go down to medical 100 times a day so you can feel safe to know that your baby's all right, then that's what you've got to do.'" Alisha sensed ambiguity around the object of care. "Is it that they care about me, or is it just the baby?" The answer to Alisha's astute question was never clear.

Deputy Allston explained that the more frequent hospital transports for pregnant women were a burden: "It taxes the staff because we have to go all the way to the hospital and come back. That takes away another deputy from our minimum. So, we rarely have enough staff to cover what we need to cover, and then on top of that, take on another added responsibility of a pregnant [woman]." One night, I was on call on the Labor and Delivery unit at the county hospital. At about 10 p.m., a woman in an orange jail uniform walked onto the unit with her wrists cuffed in front with blue plastic handcuffs and a male guard by her side. I recognized both of them. The patient was Evelyn, who was now 37 weeks pregnant, and the deputy was Deputy Faderman, whom I had gotten to know during his afternoon shifts at the jail.

I knew from the night nurse at the jail, who had called the hospital, that Evelyn was here because her water may have broken. But Deputy Faderman did not know these details. He presumed that the jail nurse ordered the transport because Evelyn might be in labor, because labor is the most common medical event for a woman in the final weeks of her pregnancy. Evelyn had no contractions in the van ride from the jail to the hospital (having your water break does not necessarily occur with contractions). So while Evelyn was behind the curtain changing into a hospital gown, Deputy Faderman turned to me with a roll of his eyes and said sarcastically, "Yeah, *she's* in labor." He assumed she was gaming the system—a common assumption about prisoners, as discussed in chapter 3. The end of his shift was nearing. He was annoyed that he had been dispatched to the hospital, that he was going to have to stay on duty past when he had expected, and that the liability threat of a pregnant inmate meant he had to do this for a woman who was not in labor. By treating pregnant inmates as nuisances with excess needs, jail staff attempted to place these uncertain, liminal figures with their at-risk fetuses back into the familiar, mundane category of inmate.

These risk management approaches to pregnant inmates derive from notions of fetal personhood and questions over the state's role in protecting the fetus. Whether through regulations on abortion, the nuances of performing fetal surgery, the prescriptive nature of prenatal care, or expectations of pregnant women's behavior, the politics of constructing the fetal subject conjure a protectionist stance.[40] This was on full display in the jail, where the fetus was the locus of liability. The fetus was thus integral to the means of disciplining and caring for the incarcerated maternal body.

NORMALIZING PREGNANCY, NORMALIZING JAIL

Incongruous as it might seem, pregnancy in jail also invited normalizing gestures. In the introduction, I described how Kima, 34 weeks pregnant, performed a dance at the talent show in D-pod. She also recited poetry and sang, quite beautifully, a rhythm and blues song, "No Matter How Hard It Gets." Kima performed comfortably, joyously, and was energized by her podmates' cheers. She was at ease, rubbing her pregnant belly to her fellow inmates' encouraging words. There were no gifts, but the celebratory, supportive tone of the talent show gave the event the feel of a baby shower. Having learned from Kima about some of the places where she spent her life—at the subway plaza teeming with commuters and drug dealers, in daily rent hotel rooms, and in the small apartment of her frail mother (herself a recovering addict who had spent time in jail)—I surmised this was more of a celebration than Kima would have gotten outside of jail.

Coincidentally, just a few hours earlier, I had attended a baby shower in the deputies' break room for Deputy Lewis, who was now 36 weeks pregnant, and who had survived five months of the safe, uneventful work assignment in the control tower. Pizza, a frosted cake, and "It's a boy!" banners made it easy to forget we were in a jail. Yet Deputy Lewis's black Sheriff's Department uniform clung awkwardly to her pregnant belly; clearly there was no maternity size. There was also no maternity jail uniform for Kima—just an extra, extra-large thin orange T-shirt that made it hard to discern whether Kima was pregnant or obese.

Another way in which aspects of pregnancy in jail were normalized was in deputies' responses to pregnant inmates who conformed to maternal conventions. When women displayed culturally appropriate maternal emotion, deputies conjured sympathetic responses. This was the case when Nellie had a miscarriage at the San Francisco Jail. Nellie, like so many others, first found out she was pregnant when she got to jail. At 39 years old, she had given birth to the first of her nine children when she was 13. It had been twelve years since her last pregnancy, so Nellie was quite shaken to learn, in CJ1, that she was pregnant again.

It had also been many years since she had been in jail. Nellie lived two hundred miles from San Francisco, and only got into trouble when she had traveled to the city a few weeks earlier to make some "fast money," by prostituting and selling drugs. It was Christmas time, and she needed money to buy presents for her nine children—none of whom she had raised but all of whom were still in her life—and three grandchildren. But her activities landed her to jail, where she found out she was seven weeks pregnant. Initially, she had wanted an abortion. Then as the days passed in jail, she had decided to continue the pregnancy, thinking that maybe the pregnancy and a new baby would help her get her life back on track. The day she excitedly affirmed her resolve to keep this baby, I performed an ultrasound to measure the progress of the pregnancy. But in a cruel twist of fate, the embryo had no heartbeat. Within minutes, Nellie's transformed pregnancy hopes were transformed again. She was visibly upset, her eyes swollen with tears, when she returned to D-pod.

An hour later, Deputy Anderson called me from D-pod. A tall, white woman with hair slicked back into a tight, long braid, Deputy Anderson was someone I had never seen smile. She had a quiet demeanor, but like anyone in charge of jail inmates, she could get loud and authoritative at any moment. In a business-like tone, Deputy Anderson asked, "Is Nellie pregnant?" I hesitated, concerned about protecting Nellie's privacy. Deputy Anderson jumped in, "She told me that she had a miscarriage, so I just want to know if I need to take 'pregnancy' off of her housing card."

Since Nellie had clearly shared the news with Deputy Anderson, I felt authorized to confirm the medical facts. "Well, there is no heartbeat, so the pregnancy isn't viable. But it's still inside her, and we're working on a plan to take care of that," I informed her. As it turned out, Nellie later told me, Deputy Anderson had noticed Nellie's sadness upon her return to D-pod after clinic. "Are you OK?" she had asked Nellie. Nellie, at ease with Deputy Anderson as with all of the women in D-pod, had had no qualms sharing her sad news. In fact, she wanted their support.

During the subsequent week, when deputies asked Nellie about her pregnancy, she tearfully told them the news. She felt, she said, warmed by their kindness when they told her, "'Oh, I'm so sorry to hear that. I'm really sorry to hear that you had a miscarriage.' They were very concerned and very supportive." The kindness continued when Nellie went to the hospital for a procedure to end the miscarriage. Hospital deputies let her watch TV, and fed her homemade barbequed chicken they had brought into work that day. "Oh my god, I tore it up, it was so great. They just treated me like I was a princess," Nellie recalled with amazement. Jail medical staff were also supportive, Nellie noted. But it was the deputies, with whom she interfaced more regularly, whose kindness surprised and even sustained her.

Nellie's response to her miscarriage, at least outwardly, was the appropriate and expected one: grief. Unlike the woman whom the deputies disparaged for not lovingly holding her newborn baby, Nellie elicited sympathy. Her conventional affective response to reproductive loss enabled jail staff to deem her a deserving subject, worthy of caring gestures like barbeque chicken and words of solace. Here, the figure of a pregnant inmate allowed jail staff to affirm their moral sense that women should feel attachment to their fetuses and newborn babies. What first appeared as an inconsistency of categories—Nellie's pregnancy and incarceration— emerged as a normative yet ambiguous experience in which a woman grieving over miscarriage could elicit compassionate concern from those with power to manage her daily life. Nellie's emotions normalized the miscarriage in a jail, while Kima's performance normalized the fact that jail was part of her pregnancy. The intersections between life in jail and reproduction were entwined in evaluating someone's deservingness of care, and refracted through jail staff's assessment of whether the pregnant inmate herself cared about the pregnancy. Such assessments included women's affective responses as well as jail staff's assumptions—often accurate—

that many of these women used drugs on the streets. Jail staff advanced a maternal ideal in their approach to deservingness, which normalized incarcerated reproduction. Part of this normalizing process was the notion that jail could be a space to cultivate "healthy" pregnancy behaviors (such as avoiding drugs) and appropriate maternal sentiment.

HYPERMEDICALIZING PREGNANCY

The jail clinic staff were as equally involved as deputies in managing the ambiguity around the status of pregnant inmates. Pregnancy magnified the medicalization of the comforts of daily living that already existed in the jail, for pregnancy activated a special cascade of medically prescribed privileges. As soon as medical staff knew that a woman was pregnant, they ordered a series of pregnancy-justified amenities: a chrono for a lower bunk to avoid the fall risk of climbing up to a top bunk; ice to encourage hydration; a daily prenatal vitamin; and a pregnancy diet. The pregnancy diet included an additional bologna sandwich at lunchtime, and an evening snack of a carton of milk and a piece of fruit.[41] These few additives to jail life were highly coveted.[42] For instance, a bottom bunk not only eliminated the inconvenience of climbing to the top, but allowed the bed's resident to entertain other inmates. And ice, as I described in chapter 4, was a treat inmates often traded. In the pods, these privileges also reminded the pregnant women, other inmates, and deputies of this woman's gestating state.

As previously discussed, pregnancy in Western societies has become a highly biomedicalized event. It requires prenatal visits, lab tests, screening for genetic abnormalities, ultrasounds, weight checks, urine testing, and blood pressure monitoring. The "technocratic model of pregnancy" has been well documented in the literature as a regime of care premised on a pathologized understanding of pregnancy.[43] The medicalized management of pregnancy and birth have made them hallmarks of a risk society, where a focus on dangers that can befall the fetus becomes justification for a scale of intervention, surveillance, and moral judgment that is widely critiqued for constricting women's freedoms. Khiara Bridges has explored how this model of pregnancy is woven into the social management of poor, black, pregnant women receiving state-sponsored prenatal care at an urban safety net clinic in the New York.[44] In exchange for free prenatal care and other social services, Medicaid infrastructure demands that these women disclose extensive, private details about their home lives. Certain aspects of their lives—such as strained relationships and substandard housing conditions—are translated by the Medicaid system into pregnancy risks. These risks then authorize the publicly funded health system to further intervene in women's pregnancies with more testing or clinic visits. The pregnancies of poor, black women are excessively medicalized, Bridges argues, by the public system upon which they rely.

Moreover, Bridges continues, this model categorizes their pregnancies as "high risk" due to inadequate nutrition, poverty, unstable housing, unemployment, and poor social support, connected to an epidemiologic discourse of negative pregnancy outcomes like preterm birth and low birth weight. Translating these women's poverty into risk, Bridges writes, homogenizes an individual woman's experience of marginality into that of a population, which therefore authorizes increased state intervention.

This perspective on excessive medicalization is relevant for understanding, and for nuancing, the medical management of pregnancy in the San Francisco jail—which, as I have discussed, disproportionately housed poor and black women. For example, in our clinically based discussions about patients, Vivian and I routinely described pregnancies as "high risk," because of coexisting drug addiction, mental illness, domestic violence, sexually transmitted infections, and various factors that could be traced to these women's poverty. This trope that defines incarcerated women's pregnancies as high risk because of their pre-incarceration lives can also be found in the scant medical literature about pregnancy among incarcerated women.[45] Simplifying a range of complex life experiences that all have deep political and economic contexts has its dangers, to be sure, as Bridges delineates. And yet the category of a "high risk pregnancy" can also signify providing care and services for women who have otherwise been neglected. I myself have found the categorization, politically laden as it is, strategically useful when trying to convince practitioners at other jails and prisons about the need to improve services for pregnant women.

The clinic at the San Francisco jail explicitly aimed to provide prenatal care that was equivalent to community standards; the clinic followed the prenatal care guidelines used at San Francisco's publicly funded health department clinics, which were much like the one Bridges described.[46] In jail, however, prenatal care surveillance occurred every one to two weeks, even in early pregnancy, as opposed to every four weeks at the community clinic. One might say that, along with the system of medical privileges that authorized ice and bottom bunks, the San Francisco jail *hypermedicalized* incarcerated women as a strategy of reproductive governance. Another perspective is that hypermedicalization protected the jail from liability. These interpretations are certainly valid readings of disciplinary practices; but they overlook the intimate, relational aspects of care that comprise these medical surveillance routines in jail.

The protocol for frequent prenatal visits at the jail was formalized by Vivian and myself. Our reasoning included a predictable risk discourse that asserted that these women's pregnancies, by virtue of coexisting malnutrition, mental illness, and addiction, were more likely to include complications that could harm the pregnant woman or the fetus. Moreover, we knew that many of these women were not accessing prenatal care in the community. Jail prenatal care was a way to offset the medical absences in their nonjail lives.

But Vivian and I also discussed the high frequency of visits as an intentional desire to provide these women with recognition. Many of our patients had disclosed their fears about being pregnant in jail—fear of being neglected or alone, fear that something might happen to their baby, fear about being separated from their newborns after birth. Vivian and I intended the interface between our patients and medical staff to allay some of these fears, provide patients with recognition of their pregnant state, and offer recognition of the women themselves. We wanted them to feel cared for. We wanted to offer the opposite of deliberate indifference.

Frequent prenatal visits enhanced the familiarity between clinicians and pregnant patients. The absence of insurance company mandates for a certain productivity level, and our ability to defer other patients, meant that we could often spend longer with a patient in the jail clinic than at a community clinic. Moreover, recidivism also contributed to our familiarity. Kima and Evelyn, for instance, were each incarcerated several times during their pregnancies. The convergence of these three jail-specific temporalities—more frequent prenatal visits, longer visits, and recidivism—enabled intimate relationships with pregnant patients. In the exam rooms, Vivian and I both rushed through standard questions about contractions, bleeding, and fetal movement, for we had come to expect that our pregnant patients wanted to talk: about their excitement and fear, their boyfriends, their other children, their childhood sexual abuse, their drug addiction as salve for the abuse, their intentions to attend or disinterest in attending drug treatment programs. As Vivian had said on a number of occasions, "Sometimes they just want someone to listen to them."

I started seeing Evelyn for prenatal care in the jail when she was about five months pregnant. The first visit was quick. She was still coming down from drugs and was not up for talking much. The second week was also quick: one of the deputies was waiting to take his lunch break. But in the third week, Evelyn was clean and the deputies did not bother me about time. So I decided to try to get Evelyn to talk about her addiction. Instead of asking a question about how much crack Evelyn smoked, I started with "Evelyn, what do you like about crack?"[47] Her usual single-word answers were insufficient for that kind of question. We sat in an extended silence, the way one minute of quiet can feel like an hour. She slowly nodded her head. "It feels good. It feels real good. . . . Mostly it just helps me forget." It helped her forget, she explained, about how her father and uncle had abused her as a child—something, she told me, she had barely talked about in the last fifteen years. She first started using drugs as a young teenager to help ease the pain from that trauma, a common pathway for so many women who are in the criminal justice system. Although abuse was the main reason that the child welfare system had removed her from her aunt's home, none of the group homes, foster homes, or juvenile detention centers she passed through provided the mental health care she needed. So she turned to drugs.

Evelyn narrated her current struggles, and continued to open up to me the following week, during her next prenatal visit: "I want to get off drugs, I want to stop using, but it's hard. I'm getting out soon, and I have no place to go. I'd go to Whitman House [a residential drug treatment program for mothers and children], but they told me I can't go back, since I left once before." Evelyn was figuring out her options, anticipating release soon. I felt inept at helping her—her knowledge of safety net services in the community far eclipsed mine, and she had already looked into every idea I offered.

During these long, intense clinic visits, I learned a lot about Evelyn—more than any of my patients in the community. She had a witty personality and a sly, charming smile. I was sad when I learned that she had been released— an unsettling feeling, to be sad that someone had been released from jail. But I knew what the streets meant for Evelyn, because she had told me. I knew that the dangers she encountered on the streets were absent in jail. Indeed, a month later, I ran into her, high on crack, at 16th and Mission Streets, in the scene I described at the start of the book. When Evelyn returned to jail six weeks later, our weekly prenatal visits continued.

The frequency of prenatal visits in the jail clinic enabled a kind of intimacy that is more difficult to achieve in the community, where overbooked schedules and the exigencies of insurance companies and Medicaid constrain time. This is not to say that jails do not care for a large number of patients, nor is it to say they work without time constraints. Rather, in jail, if some visits take longer, a waiting patient can easily be seen the next day, since waiting is part of the temporality of jail anyway. Moreover, recidivism was, tragically, built into many patients' lives. Frequent pregnancy visits in the San Francisco jail capitalized on that recidivism, an ambivalent position in which misfortune is exploited to cultivate an intimacy of care not as common on the streets. As we saw with triage upon entering jail, recidivism becomes the substrate for intimacy. On the other hand, enhanced prenatal surveillance in the jail clinic reinscribed women into disciplinary regimes characteristic of jail's insidious violence. This is the essence of "jailcare," the kind of care born out of ambiguity—that is, the recognition that jail can in some ways be more nurturing and healthy than life on the streets.

"INSTEAD, THE POLICE IS DOING IT!"

The jail clinic's hypermedicalization of pregnancy, at one level, appeared to be a technique to sort this contradictory figure of a pregnant inmate into a recognizable category of pregnant patient. In dealing with this anomaly, jail medical staff, as well as deputies, articulated what kind of care these women deserved in jail, like regular prenatal care equivalent to what they could find for free in the community, ultrasounds, blood pressure checks, and a procedure in which the fetal heart rate was auscultated with a hand-held Doppler machine.

Certain aspects of the jail clinic distinguished it from a community prenatal clinic. For instance, providers had conversations with women in their third trimester about signing official forms with jail case managers to designate where the newborns would go, should a woman give birth while in custody. Sometimes they would go to a responsible and willing family member or friend, or sometimes they would enter foster care (nursery programs to keep mother and child together did not exist at the San Francisco jail, and generally jails have too much flux to make such a program feasible). Other aspects of pregnancy care in the jail, even as the clinic worked to neutralize the carceral quality of the environment, enabled ambiguity to flourish. Shante's experience of a miscarriage, which differed from Nellie's, is a key example of this.

It was late afternoon in E-pod, after dinner, when Shante's bleeding and cramping started. Eleven weeks pregnant, Shante had been unsure about whether this was the right time in her life to have a baby: she worried about her financial ability to support a child, her unstable housing, and whether she would get support from her boyfriend, who was also in jail. But when the bleeding started, her ambivalence faded. Fear and devastation set in. The pod deputy called the clinic and a nurse came to E-pod. He took Shante's blood pressure and pulse, told her she was fine and that she could wait for her scheduled clinic appointment in two days. Shante said she felt neglected, but had little ability to do anything. The next day, when her bleeding increased, Deputy Sinclair called a nurse back to the pod. This time, nurse Patrick saw the amount of blood in the toilet, and had Deputy Sinclair escort Shante to C-pod, the medical unit, where he could keep a close eye on her. Patrick discreetly arranged for a hospital transport, and called the emergency room to prepare them for her arrival. From a purely clinical standpoint, he gave appropriate medical care.

For Shante, this medical experience was a nightmare. For over two hours, she sat bleeding through her clothes in a wheelchair in C-pod, scared and unaware that Patrick planned to send her to the hospital. Sheriff's Department rules prohibited medical staff from telling patients about transport for higher levels of medical care, since in theory, patients could phone friends to help stage escapes. This interdiction was another risk management strategy—designed to insure order and discipline. But such a strategy destroyed Shante's hopes that nurse Patrick was concerned about her. While she unknowingly waited for the transport vehicle, Patrick continued with his other nursing tasks in C-pod and barely said a word to Shante.

Despite what she perceived to be neglect from the nurse, Shante did not feel alone. Notably, Deputy Sinclair waited with her in C-pod. The gesture was procedurally unnecessary: there were plenty of deputies in C-pod to watch over Shante. But Deputy Sinclair had experienced a bleeding scare in pregnancy herself. She tried to reassure Shante by sharing her own story, conveying how she went on to deliver a healthy baby boy and telling her, "Everything's going to be OK." She massaged Shante's shoulders. She helped Shante go to the bathroom to change her blood-soaked pads. In staying with her, and in disclosing her own pregnancy experience to Shante, this deputy offered an empathetic response. What made Deputy Sinclair's care for Shante even more nurturing was the fact that they had an eighteen-year connection. In a disturbing intergenerational coincidence, Shante's mother had given birth to her while she herself was incarcerated, at a jail in a different part of the state. Deputy Sinclair had worked at that other jail at the time, and had met Shante as a newborn. This connection since birth meant that Shante felt especially at ease with Deputy Sinclair. Perhaps, too, it was this connection that made Deputy Sinclair particularly attentive to Shante's situation.

Reproduction in jail enabled shifts in the sentiments one might expect. Shante expected compassion from her nurse and disregard from her guards. Instead, nurse Patrick followed procedure and went about his business. She read this as indifference. As Shante declared a few days later: "Medical staff, and the whole medical system, is full of shit. Like they don't care about you here. Like they do anything, they give you anything. They tell you to do this, they tell you to do that, they don't tell you to do this when you really need to do that. So it's like they don't care." However, Shante felt compassionate concern from a uniformed agent of the jail's disciplinary apparatus. Deputy Sinclair did "everything that the medical staff should have been doing. But instead, the police is doing it," Shante noted.

Shante was transported to the hospital and then back to jail. She finished passing the pregnancy in the bathroom of the jail clinic the next day as

Vivian was preparing to see her. Shante's pregnancy loss brought into relief different relationships of care in punitive confinement. The contradictory characteristics of a pregnant incarcerated woman experiencing a loss draw our attention to the complex and encumbered ways that jail staff negotiated what kind of intersubjective care inmates deserved. Deputy Sinclair was guarding her charge—but also believed that bleeding in pregnancy made Shante deserving of the solace she could offer. Nurse Patrick's approach involved a clinical calculus; this pragmatic form of care was refracted through the jail's risk-oriented rules that necessitated that he conceal the hospital plan from Shante—a move that made Shante feel uncared for.

SPECTRAL AMBIGUITY: SHACKLING PREGNANT WOMEN

Pregnant women in jail can also be seen as anomalous because their bodily processes mark them as distinctly female in an environment designed for males. Feminist criminal justice scholars have enumerated the ways in which the U.S. prison system is distinctly gendered.[48] From linear, noncommunal architecture to toilets, from jumpsuit uniforms to male-centered programming, from an inability to deal with women's health issues to misrecognition of women's different pathways to crime, these scholars have consistently exposed the highly gendered nature of the U.S. carceral system.

The visible physiologic changes of pregnancy, a state that has classically essentialized women to their reproductive capacity, present a stark challenge to a system that homogenizes all subjects into a hierarchical and masculine environment. While pregnant women make up less than one percent of the incarcerated population, the impact of the imprisoned pregnant female body is significant, as noted by deputies who worried that pregnant women and their fetuses were a liability for the institution.

It is hard to think of a practice that more graphically illustrates this categorical clash between pregnancy and a male carceral system than the shackling of pregnant incarcerated women. All inmates, male and female, are restrained when transported outside of a correctional facility to a court appearance or to the hospital, to prevent them from absconding. Restraints may be applied in a variety of ways, usually in combination: iron chains around the ankles and the abdomen; handcuffs around the wrists, behind the back; chains connecting one prisoner to another, reminiscent of chain gangs from slavery days.

These techniques of control—ostensibly to ensure "public safety" when presumed dangerous criminals are in public spaces—make little sense and pose medical risks for pregnant women. A woman in labor would have a difficult time escaping in between painful contractions, not to mention the fact that most incarcerated women are not "dangerous criminals," but are arrested for nonviolent crimes. Moreover, the medical risks of shackling pregnant women are clear, with potential for maternal or fetal harm if a woman trips because shackles impair her already-compromised gait, or if an obstetrical emergency arises and iron chains obstruct medical interventions.[49] Numerous medical professional organizations have condemned this practice on medical and human rights grounds.

Nonetheless, pregnant women are still shackled in this country. As of 2016, only twenty-two states had laws prohibiting this practice during labor, and some, but not all, of those laws restrict it at other points in pregnancy.[50] Even in states with laws, shackling in labor still happens, revealing the vast gap between policy and practice.[51] Mothers and advocacy groups condemn this as a human rights violation—lack of dignity, humiliation, exacerbation of pain—when working publicly to end this practice. Images of women writhing in pain, laboring in childbirth, while locked in chains, offer a vivid rendition of state power circulating through women's reproductive bodies, an instance par excellence of the state's spectral force—fantastical performances of state power in everyday routines.[52] Meanwhile, this spectrality comes not from the mere technology of restraints, but from the graphic, bodily experience of iron chains constraining a woman at a moment culturally scripted to be one of the most intimate moments imaginable: childbirth.

As an obstetrician in Pennsylvania in 2004, six years before the state passed an anti-shackling law, I delivered the baby of a woman who was shackled, and felt powerless to ask an armed guard to remove the restraints. Colleagues who deal with this in other states have told me with great emotion about the challenges of caring for shackled patients and negotiating with guards to remove chains. One obstetrician told me that she had to delay an emergency C-section by over thirty minutes because the privately contracted guard did not have a handcuff key. On labor and delivery units, shackling is usually confronted as conflicting discourses on threat: from the guards, threats to public safety if she is not restrained; from medical staff, threats to maternal and fetal well-being. The friction positions the fetus in uncertain terrain. Who exactly is being shackled and who exactly is at risk? The fetal subject, interposed between the incarcerated subject and the oppressive carceral apparatus, problematizes the goals of discipline and punishment, and calls into question the kinds of life that can be subjected to such repression.

It is a visceral image, a woman giving birth in chains. But the vividness of this practice becomes normalized in its everyday unfolding. In states where no laws prohibit the practice, shackling pregnant prisoners is a matter of routine; it is done because it is what is done with all prisoners transported off site. The fact that pregnant inmates are shackled by default, and that laws must be passed to disrupt it, signals the implicit gendering of a carceral system designed for men. And yet this exists alongside practices and sentiments of jail staff who respond sympathetically to women who display culturally appropriate maternal behaviors and emotions around their miscarriages or impending births. The carceral approach to pregnant women reveals the system to be deeply involved in responding to and reinforcing traditional gender norms. Despite decades of activism and scholarship to disentangle female gender identity from reproduction, incarcerated pregnant women put a microscope on the ways that carcerality engages broader discourses of gender.

BANALITY OF SHACKLING

In San Francisco, shackling was rarely an issue when pregnant women were brought from the jail to the hospital for childbirth. This was due to a 2005 California law prohibiting the shackling of pregnant women during transport for labor, labor, and postpartum recovery and due to the Sheriff's Department's compliance. However, not all California counties complied with the law. Furthermore, the law implicitly permitted shackling at other points in pregnancy, though the same medical risks apply outside labor. The day Alisha was released from jail, 36 weeks pregnant, I watched deputies put handcuffs around her wrists to escort her from E-pod to the jail exit. Deputy Gibson saw my jaw drop, and anticipated my response. "Don't worry, doc. It's just procedure," he told me as he shrugged his shoulders.

Policy discussions of the practice sometimes focus on procedural banalities rather than exposing the graphic intimacies of chaining a pregnant woman.[53] I worked closely with advocacy organizations to help expand California's 2005 law to outlaw shackling at any point in pregnancy, and to ensure greater compliance with the original law. At a lobbying meeting in Sacramento with the state organization that oversees county jails, the discussion focused almost entirely on procedural details. We met with an administrator in the state's jail regulatory board; he was a middle-aged white man named Alex with an ill-positioned comb-over, pungent cologne, and the air of a bureaucrat. Alex insisted that the reason this law had been rejected for the past two years was that once shackling restrictions became law, the jail oversight board could not include the law in its official Policies and Procedures code and would have no authority to enforce the law, which would be under state jurisdiction. I did not fully understand the technical distinction, which seemed little more than a bureaucratic web of confusion.[54]

Alex spent nearly forty-five minutes explaining this conundrum. The lobbyists were all women, and he peppered his explanations with patronizing comments such as, "There's been incremental change; each year, you gals are making progress on this." His arguments revealed the irony that the incarcerated women themselves were being omitted from the discussion. Alex declared that this law was not about shackling pregnant women. "It's not like they [people who work at jails] think we should shackle pregnant women!" He smacked his hand on the table, to parody someone who would think women should be shackled. "No, that's not what this is about!" It was a sarcastic gesture, to emphasize Alex's point that this law, and the discussion in the conference room, were merely a matter of the technical difference between a statute and a procedure.[55]

Alex's redirection away from the affected subjects, pregnant incarcerated women, was perhaps a symptom of his unwillingness to confront the uncomfortable inconsistency between pregnancy—biologically female—and incarceration—systematically oriented to males. Instead, his focus on bureaucratic matters sustained the myth that "prison is the great equalizer," treating everyone with equal harshness.

As with any handcuffing, shackling a pregnant prisoner brings guard and charge into close contact. Shackling, part of the carceral routine of violence, requires guards to touch prisoners' hands and any other body parts being restrained. It is another instance through which the exceptional circumstance of pregnancy in jail cultivates ambiguity in the relationships of discipline and care. The pregnant inmate can alternately serve as a figure who deserves special care, to a liability who deserves hypervigilance, to a security threat who deserves iron chains. Nicole, the woman who was pregnant in jail until she later decided to have an abortion, went to the hospital one day because of a severe case of pancreatitis. In preparation for hospital transport, a deputy handcuffed her, cuffed her feet, and put a chain around her belly. Nicole told him that she was pregnant. But, disregarding her protests as well as the jail's written policy, he left her, she said, "all shackled up. He didn't really care about me saying what I had to say; he just did what he had to do and walked out." Then Deputy Lucas walked by and noticed that Nicole was fully shackled. He also knew that she was pregnant. He consequently removed everything except the handcuffs, and loosened them to make sure they were as comfortable as handcuffs could be. He also offered Nicole an apology, commenting, "You know, we shouldn't be cuffing a pregnant woman like that." That act of kindness and the apology were exceptional and meaningful to Nicole in this moment created by shackling.

Shante was transported to the emergency room shackled during her miscarriage, and she experienced ambiguous emotions, too. The second deputy guarding her (not the one who knew her since birth) both helped Shante as she changed her pads and, when it was time to go to the transport vehicle, shackled her as a matter of routine. Shante felt angry and disempowered as she recalled that moment: "She shackled my ankles and she shackled my stomach, my hands to my stomach, and I'm thinking in my head like I don't know too much about the legal system and these shackles, but I know I have rights as a pregnant woman. My stomach is not supposed to be shackled. But I ain't saying nothing. I'm like okay, whatever, 'cause obviously I'm not going to get nowhere. So she shackles me up and she makes me walk." Despite her indignation, Shante felt comforted by this deputy, too. In the hospital, the deputy stayed with Shante while doctors and nurses came in and out, and eventually confirmed the diagnosis of miscarriage. Shante recalled that the deputy "did some things that, to me, wasn't okay, like the shackling and stuff like that, but she was very soothing and she was very helpful."

The discretionary use of restraints on pregnant women is not only a matter of statutes and procedures—to which it was reduced by bureaucrat Alex—or threat—as highlighted by disputes over security logic of public safety and medical logic risk of harm to the pregnancy. Nor is it merely a degrading and emotionally scarring display of state power. Shackling of pregnant, incarcerated women certainly is all of these things; that it is experienced as cruel and unusual punishment by the women who are themselves shackled cannot be minimized. But, as examples of moments in which restraints were used in San Francisco suggest, shackling and pregnancy unsettlingly juxtapose the possibilities of compassionate concern and violent degradation in carceral practices.

INCARCERATED REPRODUCTION AS PARTICIPATORY PRACTICE

It would be easy to read the jail's approach to pregnant women as "reproductive governance" that coerces them further into state regulatory apparatuses: the hypermedicalized prenatal care they receive in jail; the special privileges they receive to mitigate the discomforts of living in jail; the way they are shackled in childbirth; and their newborns' immediate entry into state institutions either of foster care, CPS, or Sheriff's Department–coordinated visits with their babies. These could then connect to narratives about poor, black, reproducing women's entrenchment in regulatory mechanisms that perpetuate their marginality.[56] But such an interpretation overlooks the everyday experiences in jail through which their reproduction unfolds.

Pregnant incarcerated women, deputies, and medical staff came together in a variety of ways to nurture and discredit these women's reproduction. Jail staff interchangeably treated some pregnant women as exceptional and worthy of special treatment; others disparaged them as unworthy of reproducing. Sometimes pregnant inmates were understood as threats to the fetus and the jail, and were regulated and shackled; other times, pregnant inmates were loci of sympathy from jail staff.

Pregnancy, that thorny reminder of potential life, brings into stark relief the dynamics of incarceration: the desire to punish women judged to be bad mothers and the desire to care for them as they nourish the next generation. The fetus is not, of course, a *tabula rasa*, for the care of pregnant women in jail presupposes a range of assumptions about her future child. A fetus in an incarcerated womb is already enmeshed in forces of structural inequalities that shape its host. Certainly, the relationships and practices around reproduction in jail work through these inequalities in a variety of managerial and intimate registers. They reveal not only that individual vulnerability renders people susceptible to governance and care, but that the institutions entangled in those practices are themselves vulnerable. In our cultural narrative about pregnancy risk, pregnant women are expected to "take responsibility" for themselves and their gestating fetus; but on the surface, jail would seem to constrain a woman's ability to do so. The jail then steps in to facilitate such normative expectations of pregnant women's behaviors. Reproduction and incarceration come to shape each other, as reproducing women and the carceral apparatus give each other pause—in part because both endeavors have the politics of life at their core—to figure out what kind of care people marginalized by institutions and structural inequality deserve.

Reproduction is revealed as a participatory practice for inmates and jail workers, a phenomenon that will become even more apparent in chapter 6, when I explore more deeply pregnant women's gestational trajectories. These people engage in a complex and often-contradictory mix of intimate concern, struggles to promote and perform normative motherhood, and the imposition of controlling—even punitive—strategies. Throughout, they cultivate ambiguity in the way that carcerality constrains and cares. Through these apparent contradictions between pregnancy and incarceration, inmates and jail workers alike actively figure out what kind of care alleged criminals, marginalized by an ineffective public safety net, deserve. Ultimately, incarcerated reproduction articulates what is at stake in an environment that lays bare broader social inequalities.

6 Reproduction and Carceral Desire

Jail brings me back to what being a mother is.

Karen, frequent San Francisco jail inmate

It was a mild winter day in San Francisco when Kima was arrested on charges of drug possession. For Kima, the arrest was not a disruptive event. At her lawyer's urging, she had calculated that it was her seventy-first time in jail since her eighteenth birthday, fourteen years earlier. She knew not only the routine, but also the people who worked at the jail. So it was familiar when triage nurse Charlie, who had worked at the San Francisco jail for over twenty years, asked her the standard questions during the intake medical evaluation in CJ1. The routine intake questionnaire I described in chapter 2 included, for women, questions assessing the possibility of pregnancy: "Are you pregnant right now? Was your last period more than thirty days ago?" "I don't think I've missed any periods," Kima told Charlie. Still, Kima had sensed she was pregnant. As she later related to me, "I had morning sickness, change in moods, craving a lot of stuff. So those are three signs that I'm pregnant, and those are the signs, especially the mood part, 'cause I get really mean to certain people." Kima had been pregnant three other times. She knew her body.

Although Kima laughed as she recounted this moment with Charlie in CJ1, she told me she had cried as she confessed to Charlie that she might be pregnant (a scene I described in chapter 1), afraid her suspicions would be confirmed, she admitted. Kima composed herself as Charlie escorted her to a private exam room with a steel toilet shielded by a half wall of concrete. She urinated into a small paper cup and watched as Charlie squeezed four drops of her urine onto a pregnancy test cartridge. Two pink lines appeared. Kima was pregnant. "Congratulations!" Charlie bellowed. Kima burst into tears. As she later explained:

> I had came in for a drug possession and I was using. I was in my active addiction, so like I said, it's something about knowing but not knowing that makes me not accountable or makes me think I'm not accountable, but then if I go to the doctor, then I know that I have to be accountable. So when I was out, I didn't go to the doctor even though I kind of knew I was [pregnant]. I kind of knew I was, but I wouldn't go to the doctor. Now here I am knowing for sure that I am, so it's just—it was really—I was really scared.

On the streets, Kima's bodily changes convinced her that she was pregnant. Yet she required medical confirmation, in the context of jail, to stop feigning ignorance. Now, she confronted the cultural weight of moral responsibility expected from a pregnant woman for her fetus.

Kima, somewhat consciously, suppressed her own embodied sensations to deny that she was pregnant. At the same time, she internalized society's judgments that equated her behaviors with moral choices. She knew she should not smoke crack during pregnancy. She also knew, as Knight has vividly described, that drugs and pregnancy activated an array of medical and state interventions that aim to protect the fetus from harm, while inscribing women in coercive regimes.[1] So on the streets, Kima deliberately avoided the medical system. Without medical affirmation of her pregnancy, she did not feel like a bad pregnant woman who was harming her fetus. In jail, via the routine medicalization of her processing, Kima's denial was punctured by the objective confirmation of pregnancy by a medical professional.

Kima was ambivalent about the pregnancy. On the one hand, she said, "I was happy because I knew I was going to have my baby. I was going to have this baby. That was for sure." But she was also terrified. "The scary part was knowing that it didn't stop me before. I didn't stop myself before. I used with my other child. . . . So that was all I was worried about, was scared that—I didn't want to mess up this baby." The tears when Charlie congratulated her on the pregnancy were the materialization of her ambivalent sentiments about this pregnancy, about her addiction, and about motherhood in general.

Pregnancy ambivalence is certainly not unique to the carceral setting. Without jail, Kima might eventually have gone to a doctor's office. She might have had a similarly mixed response of joy and fear. She might have felt guilt over her drug use, having already internalized expectations of what comprises healthy pregnancy behavior. But jail magnified and reframed these tensions. Jail imposed incessant behavioral regulation, along with morally inflected punitive sentiments and discourse about prisoner rehabilitation. As Kima and other women's pregnancies progressed, these carceral features permeated their preparations for motherhood. So did the intimacy of care that we have already seen emergent in the routines of discipline. This care was linked to ethical demands on pregnant women (that they act in certain normative ways) cultivated in jail, such that jail became a cohesive part of women's experiences of managing their motherhood.[2]

Although Kima could have refused the urine pregnancy test, she did not. Her willingness to confront the reality of the pregnancy here in jail was enabled, in part, by her familiarity with and trust in Charlie, built over years of intimate recidivism. Kima felt comfortable being vulnerable in front of Charlie. And she knew what to expect from being pregnant in jail: eight years earlier, she had given birth to a daughter while she was incarcerated at the San Francisco jail. Kima had used drugs throughout that pregnancy and, as a result of this and her ongoing use, she did not have custody of this daughter. "I still feel a teeny bit of guilt behind the fact that my addiction was so strong that I couldn't stop using for the sake of my baby. . . . I didn't want to travel down that same road with this baby." While she felt "guilty" for using drugs in pregnancy, Kima did not equate jail with punishment for that behavior. Instead, both pregnancy and jail were full of possibilities.

Kima used that moment with Charlie in that small exam room in CJ1 as an opportunity for reckoning: "I had a chance to get this one right." This hope was commonly expressed by pregnant women who passed through the San Francisco jail. Jail played a unique role in constructing such aspirations of transformation, as well as ideas of what motherhood could look like for these women. Understanding how jail framed women's own narrative commitments to pregnancy and motherhood builds on the notion, developed in chapter 5, that incarcerated reproduction is a participatory practice; the institution itself, not only the people working and living within it, is a critical participant as well.

RESCUE

The notion that incarceration can be a transformative experience has been widely explored.[3] Historically, these principles have manifested in policies aimed at rehabilitating the prisoner, or "correcting" his character (hence the categorical term "correctional institution" for prisons and jails).[4] While mid-twentieth-century prisons emphasized rehabilitation, numerous accounts have documented a decline in such commitments in the age of mass incarceration, though these impulses have not been universally displaced.[5] As we have already seen with the busy daily programming schedule and with policy makers' commitments at the San Francisco jail, the hope that incarceration can transform an individual still existed despite the preponderance of "warehouse prisons."[6] Pregnancy, too, is marked by its transformative potential as it gestates new life. In combination, jail and pregnancy become fulcrums for each other's potential for transformation. Evelyn's desire to be in jail during her pregnancy reflected that interaction.

Evelyn was released from jail when she was 26 weeks pregnant. She had no place to sleep, and quickly spiraled into her familiar life of smoking crack cocaine, shooting heroin, not sleeping, and selling drugs. Her Aunt Vera, who had partially raised Evelyn until she was swept into the institutional life of foster care and juvenile detention, had tried to rescue her. Late one night, Aunt Vera drove forty-five minutes from her quiet suburban home, where she was raising Evelyn's four-year-old son Adam, into San Francisco. She combed the dangerous streets by herself, until she found Evelyn, pregnant and high. But Evelyn rejected Aunt Vera's offer to take her in. Later, Evelyn told me that she did not want Adam to see her in this state, coming down from drugs, disheveled, and sleeping for days at a time while her body recovered. Though Adam knew Evelyn as his aunt, and believed Vera to be his mother, Evelyn hoped that someday she could tell him the truth. It was important to her that she shield her son from her current desperation.

So Evelyn stayed on the streets. When I ran into her there at the 16th and Mission subway plaza, a few people around her, when they learned I was her doctor in jail, chided her "Evelyn, you shouldn't be doing this stuff, you've got the baby!" Their concern did not, however, stop them from selling Evelyn drugs. Evelyn felt that no one cared about her. Eventually, Evelyn did ask for help. She did not ask Aunt Vera, the county hospital, the Homeless Prenatal Program, or any number of drug treatment programs she had attended in the past. No, Evelyn did not seek out the safety net services ostensibly designed to help her. Instead, Evelyn went back to jail. Citing violated parole and outstanding warrants, she turned herself in to the police on her corner. "I just wanted to be in jail where I knew that I could eat, I could sleep, and that even if it's not the best of medical care, I was going to get some type of care."

Evelyn knew what to expect from jail: institutionalized living she had been accustomed to since age 9, a bed, water, food, familiar faces, prenatal clinic visits to which she was escorted, and the complex mix of tenderness and discipline I have documented in the San Francisco jail. Deputies and medical staff knew, and some even liked, Evelyn. Deputy Lucas endearingly called Evelyn "Toothy" because, he told me, of the sly, toothy grin that he often saw on her face in jail. I later learned that this was Evelyn's street name, and that its etymologic roots had nothing to do with Deputy Lucas. Nonetheless, Evelyn could feel comfort and familiarity in jail.

Where life on the streets had failed her, jail was a place of comfort. Or, as Evelyn tragically put it, "I didn't get arrested, I got rescued." This unsettling desire for the constrained reality of a carceral institution should lead us to question the role of state institutions in governing people's emotional states. Lynn Haney's study of a group home for imprisoned mothers struggling with addiction in California describes a therapeutic model geared toward regulating women's desires—for food, boyfriends, drugs.[7] In this community-based carceral setting, official mantras of empowerment and staff involvement in women's minute decisions attempt to transform what women want in life: a healthy lifestyle instead of drugs and "bad boy-friends." If mothers' desires could be directed toward "healthy" choices, the logic goes, then healthy behaviors will follow. The carceral regulation in this program targeted desire in order to produce normative maternal subjects.

Evelyn's desire for jail may be seen as a mutated consequence of these kinds of treatment discourses, a symbolic violence in which Evelyn cannot see that her longing for a space of punishment while pregnant is itself a form of violence. Evelyn desired an environment that was, in contrast to the street corner at 16th and Mission, not teeming with drugs—an environment that was more "healthy." But we cannot stop at an analytic where we merely see Evelyn's emotional state as regulated. For her desire was produced by the comparative material realities of her life inside and outside jail; her carceral desire is a reflection of broader social failures. Evelyn developed a "cruel optimism" in which she could feel comfort and intimacy from a punitive state institution, a cruelty that was imbricated into her maternal existence.[8] Accompanying Evelyn's recognition of jail's benefits was a memory that was instilled by the chronicity of recidivism and that consisted of feeling cared for by the institution. Rescue was part and parcel of this form of institutional jailcare that made recidivism into an intimate, intersubjective process and not simply a statistical failure.

This sentiment of appreciating jail was not infrequently expressed by the women at the San Francisco jail. But it was more pronounced among pregnant women or mothers who reflected on their prior pregnant incarcerations. In explaining the sense of relief jail gave them, these women focused on their developing fetuses, and noted their concern about doing harm. Kima expressed her gratitude for jail during two of her pregnancies:

> Well, part of me was really grateful. In 2004, when I had my daughter, I was really grateful. I was grateful that the police came up with some bogus charges and sent me to jail, because here I am. If I would've not gone to jail, I would've not stopped. She would've been born with drugs in her system. And I did give her—I mean, well, my higher power did send me to jail, gave her a break. So for the last two and a half months she was clean, and she clean now, so that's the most important thing.

Jail provided a built-in mechanism for sobriety, which Kima recognized to be beneficial for her daughters. More generally, Evelyn, too, believed that jail would be good for her pregnancies. The institution recognized pregnancies with medical care, special privileges, and parenting classes; in turn, pregnant inmates recognized their gestating fetuses in different ways than they did on the streets. The medical protocol built into jail processing, with its mix of risk management, medical clearance, and care, allowed Kima to displace her initial denial of pregnancy on the streets with overt awareness in nurse Charlie's CJ1 exam room. For Kima and Evelyn, it was jail, not pregnancy alone, that oriented them more toward their fetuses, a harm reduction strategy they both explicitly and gratefully identified. Because these women were already entrenched in institutional regulation, they also knew the value of having a baby born clean, for that increased their chances of child custody.

It is important to recognize that incarceration can shape maternal desire in directions other than the desire to give birth or be a mother. For some women, incarceration meant avoiding pregnancy. I took care of plenty of patients in jail who wanted to terminate their pregnancies, and who often gave similar reasons as nonincarcerated women for wanting abortions—not the right time, unable to afford a child. But sometimes their reasons were produced distinctly by the carceral environment. For instance, one patient told me she wanted an abortion because she would be serving her prison sentence soon. "When I go to prison, I fight. That's how I do my time." Pregnancy would cramp her prison fighting style, so she wanted an abortion. Other patients' considerations involved their previous children. "I don't want to burden my auntie with another one of my kids," one patient told me. She knew that as "an addict in jail," she would be less likely to be able to care for a baby. For such women, desire for abortions was entangled with incarceration. Incarceration itself thus became imbricated in how they managed their fertility.

REDEMPTION

The pregnant women I have been discussing were conditioned to see their actions on the street as the result of bad choices. Several scholars have explored this neoliberal phenomenon in which personal responsibility is affixed to pregnancy and drug addiction,[9] and women who use drugs in pregnancy are marked as social and individual failures.[10] These supposed personal failures then act to justify intense state and medical intervention to rescue the fetus and the pregnant woman.[11] In this narrative, pregnancy offers a chance for rehabilitation, as the newborn invites a reimagining of alternate circumstances. In analyzing women's narratives of their experiences of addiction while incubating life, Sheigla Murphy and Marsha Rosenbaum argue that, "impending birth represented choosing life, an opportunity for redemption for past failures, hopes for the future, and a chance to claim a socially acceptable and respectable identity."[12] Given the symbolic currency of the fetus, this interpretation makes sense. In popular culture and abortion debates in the United States, the fetus is widely imagined to be the idealized, innocent citizen.[13] It is venerated as a hopeful symbol of the future, of social reproduction. Similarly, in times of personal and economic insecurity, some women experience motherhood as an anchor; they map their desire for security onto the mother-child connection, onto their maternal practice.[14]

Both pregnancy and incarceration independently offer themselves as possibilities for transformation and redemption, even as those possibilities are geared toward a particular, idealized way of being. In jail, Evelyn and other mothers attended Sheriff's Department–sponsored parenting classes, which conveyed standard models of mothering—ones which promoted things like reading to your children at bedtime, not recognizing that many of these women could not afford books. Accordingly, being pregnant and incarcerated are synergistic domains of experience that entice women like Kima and Evelyn into normative maternal ways of being. At the same time, because the insecurity of their lives outside of jail ensures their reincarceration, pregnancy in jail also offers forms of motherhood they can experience only in jail. All of these factors conspired to enable deep reflection by Evelyn to change and to be a mother for this child, a contemplative process I witnessed during this incarceration.

I spent a lot of time with Evelyn during the final weeks of her pregnancy, in the pods in jail and when she was hospitalized for a few days at the county hospital for having more frequent seizures, something she had suffered from since childhood. We talked many times about the future she imagined. Here is an excerpt from one of our conversations in which she discusses her last pregnancy. At that point, five years ago, she had been released in her second trimester from jail to "Revelation House," a residential drug treatment program for mothers and children:

> I stayed about maybe a month and a half, which is one of the longest times I've ever stayed at a program up 'til then. Like, I have been to programs before, and I just go, stay a day, eat, gain some weight and then leave. . . . But like the house is right across the street from Westside projects. So people would buy their dope, and then there was an abandoned—like a house where nobody lived next door. And I think what triggered me is I was outside sweeping the porch, and a guy was smoking crack. And he blew it, and the wind blew his smoke, like, right in my face. So then I was like: Oh, I want to go use. So I left that day. . . . I really wanted to change. Like, but then I think I got scared. I have a tendency to be self-sabotaging. Like, I let myself only get to a certain point, where I do good for a certain amount of time. Then for some reason, I start thinking like I'm not good enough or I'm not worthy enough to be clean or have a normal life. So I start—I purposely mess up.

Her self-critique is rich with therapeutic language that attributes misfortune and the power to overcome it to individual will. This kind of therapeutic script is deeply entrenched in community drug treatment programs for women.[15] In directing women to focus on their emotional and psychological flaws, rather than the concrete social and economic factors structuring their lives, many contemporary treatment programs' "therapeutic agenda turn[s] injustice into an emotional issue."[16] Both Evelyn and Kima had been in and out of programs, often mandated by court to attend such places as a condition of their release. Evelyn's ruminations about self-sabotage reflect this therapeutic approach to transform structural vulnerability into personal failure in order to recalibrate one's desires.

Yet even while Evelyn ascribed her failures to her own choices, she also blamed the safety net that had abandoned her. Referring to her most recent release from jail, three months prior to this interview, she said:

> But it's not that I started using again 'cause I wanted to. I started using because it was so hard to get anywhere. I got released with nowhere to go. I had been being told I was going to a drug treatment program my whole time in jail so that I didn't have a backup plan. So then when I went to parole to

try to get into a program, my parole agent was like, there was no beds. Everywhere he called there was no beds. There's no beds. There's no beds. There's no beds. So I started selling dope, and then of course, to stay up longer, I started using. And it kind of—it really hurt because I didn't want to use. But it's like, I felt like that's the only option I had, like use to make money, use to eat, use to use.

Having transitioned from the desperation of the streets to a space of contemplation in jail, Evelyn saw this pregnancy as an opportunity for change.

But, like, I'm nine months pregnant now, about to go back to Revelation House, and it's very important for me to change my life. . . . Not just for my child, but it just gets to a point where enough is enough. And plus, I'm just tired of being a dope fiend. Like, I know I'm worth more. . . . Yeah, in jail, I'm thinking about my baby and then just looking at my life. Like, at least in jail, you're able to get a little bit of get-back. Get-back is where you're back to your normal self. A lot of people are happy when they go to jail because they gain some weight. They get to rest, and then their run starts all over again.

Woven into this desire to change was her internalization of a broader cultural narrative that devalues the reproduction of poor, black women who struggle with addiction; she knew she was worth more than conveyed by the ubiquitous messages which diminished her sense of value to society. Evelyn identified the version of herself that appears in jail as her normal self. In this "get back" phase, she actively prepared for change, planning to stay sober, go to a treatment program, learn to parent, and get a job as an office assistant or a chef's assistant. Any day now, she would be leaving jail for the same Revelation House she had left during her last pregnancy. I asked Evelyn what made this commitment to change in pregnancy different from other get-backs:

Somebody once told me that I might have a lot of runs left in me but how many get-backs do I have? Not only do I have a chance to raise one of my kids for the first time by myself, like I said, you can only go so far. I don't want to get high no more. I don't ever want to have to sleep in the subway station with the mice running over my feet or wonder where my next meal's going to come from or—and I couldn't imagine bringing a kid into an environment like that. And not only that, my auntie—she's not taking this kid. But she has no intention of raising another one of my kids. She—and she's right. It's a time where I have to stand up and be a woman and raise my own kid. I'm the one who keeps having them. So I can't keep having kids and put it on this person, this person, this person. It's a time where I have to be responsible for me. So it's a choice that I made to have another kid, so I have to raise this kid myself.

Evelyn imagined a finite number of "get backs," which each release from jail provided. Pregnancy and her guilt for relying on her "kin of last resort" challenged her to make the most of her next "get back."[17] Evelyn's first son had been born ten years prior, while she was actively using drugs. Although family members tried to assume legal custody of him, the state swept in while Aunt Vera was sick in the hospital, and fast-tracked him to adoption. Evelyn gave birth to her second son sober, while she was incarcerated, and Aunt Vera was able to immediately take baby Adam home with her to raise him as though he were her son.

Evelyn felt personally responsible for avoiding such reliance on family in order to solidify her maternal identity. I have heard similar affirmations from other pregnant women in jail, conditioned to believe that making the "right choices" would lead them to become responsible mothers. Evelyn clearly identified this "get back"—a contrast to her rock bottom on the streets—as a reason this time in jail would be different. Whereas her other stints in jail were just part of what she (and many others, including policy makers) had called "a revolving door," her incarceration while pregnant had become a deeply moral experience for her. In this monologue, Evelyn articulated all that was at stake for her in this moment: a sense of self-worth, the ability to overcome her addiction, the experience of caring for another, the desire for maternal transformation, and connections to other humans and institutions alike.

Evelyn's commitments to change were not about rehabilitation. Rehabilitation, as James Waldram has deconstructed, implies restoration to a previous state. In his ethnography of treatment of incarcerated sex offenders, Waldram argues that the purported aspiration for prisoner treatment is more akin to "habilitation," a transformative rather than restorative process: "the idea is to create moral individuals who emerge from prison as 'fit' for society."[18] Likewise, the combined experiences of incarceration and pregnancy invited Evelyn to transform herself into a morally fit mother. Although she had given birth twice in the past, this was an identity she had yet to develop. Evelyn's current pregnancy did not so much offer a return to some prior maternal state, to rehabilitate, as help her identify that she had had similar desires for change during her last pregnancy. Now, pregnant in jail again, Evelyn wanted a new life. She wanted to habilitate to motherhood. Evelyn's desire for this maternal future also reflects her deeply contingent present. The kind of motherhood to which she aspired—to be drug free and raising her baby herself—depends on an astonishing array of racialized discourses and coercive state apparatuses that make her maternal aspirations nearly impossible to achieve.[19]

Both pregnancy and jail bring the future into the present. Pregnancy, with its circumscribed nine-month duration, signals the inevitability of childbirth and a future with a baby. Because most of these women had had prior children removed from their custody by state agents, though, they knew that a future with their baby was tentative. Being separated from their existing children, either by CPS or jail, made it hard for these women to fulfill normative expectations of mothering.[20] In contrast, the physiologic connection between mother and fetus made pregnancy a unique time of togetherness in the present, which even jail could not disrupt. Having such time "together" with her fetus in jail enabled feelings of motherhood to be cultivated in ways that separation from actual children in jail made difficult.

Just as pregnancy implicitly foreshadows a future after birth, jail, too, signals a future in its own way, as release, for most, is inevitable.[21] Indeed, even as they lived out the interchangeable monotony of the daily routine in jail, inmates in San Francisco talked constantly about their plans for release. Programming in the pods factored into both the present and the future, as it helped inmates occupy their time, and, at least in theory, prepared them with life skills (including parenting) for release.

Evelyn contemplated the synergistic futures of childbirth and release from jail. She conjured both memories of her life before this incarceration—where addiction, trauma from childhood sexual abuse, poverty, and CPS denied her a life with her children—and the hopes for her maternal life after jail. Her narrative is complex, juxtaposing her sense of individual responsibility and her disappointment at the failure of the safety net ("there's no beds") as it exposes the contingence of her present and the irony of her hopefulness.

The redemptive potential of an incarcerated pregnancy is also culti-vated at the institutional and policy level. At the San Francisco jail, mater-nal bonding was actively promoted. The Sheriff's Department contracted with a program called "One Family" that coordinated parent-child visits, taught parenting classes, and helped parents implement their CPS plans from jail. At one point during my fieldwork, Sheriff's Department admin-istrators approached me and a few others from the jail's clinical services to help them brainstorm ways to improve conditions for pregnant women. During our initial meeting and later at a public press conference held on Mother's Day, the Sheriff's Department voiced an interest in promoting mother-infant bonding when the babies were born to reduce recidivism. In such a framing, motherhood becomes a source of salvation. The Sherriff's Department hoped the sense of responsibility cultivated in the mother-infant bond would keep women out of jail. One result of these meetings was to increase contact visit frequency for mothers and new-borns.[22] A senior administrator in the Sheriff's Department talked to me about starting a "nursery program" in the jail, although the plan never progressed beyond the conversational phase.[23]

The oldest prison nursery program was opened in 1901 in Bedford Hills, New York. It is still in operation, along with similar programs in thirteen states and at Rikers Island jail in New York City.[24] In these programs, preg-nant women and new mothers live in a special wing of the prison with their babies, attend parenting classes, and are officially given the time and space to bond with and care for their babies. Documentaries about these pro-grams are infused with hope and the romanticized ideal of the mother-infant bond.[25] Perhaps this romanticization offsets the disquieting possi-bility of an infant starting its life in prison, a possibility that raises stark questions about what forms of life are possible behind bars. Is it possible for a newborn infant to flourish in a space of punishment? Proponents of prison nurseries rely heavily on the generally accepted notion that the maternal-infant bond is important not only for the baby, but also the crimi-nal mother, and the criminal justice system, with research documenting recidivism reductions.[26] Proponents of these programs also cite statistics showing that children of incarcerated parents are more likely to become incarcerated as adults; they hope early maternal bonding will mitigate this risk. Incarcerated reproduction thus generates the imagining of future intergenerational change. This focus on reducing recidivism and disrupting generational cycles of incarceration again shows how risk management strategies are central to incarcerated reproduction.

Normative motherhood promoted by nursery programs emphasizes sacrifice, self-restraint, and dedicated attention to the baby; the concern for reducing recidivism statistics is the state's affirmation that normal motherhood does not involve incarceration. But this future-oriented perspective does not adequately address the material and emotional realities of women's lives outside prison or jail, the realities that could make a different future possible.[27] Moreover, while nursery programs and the San Francisco jail invest pregnancy with the power to establish anew or reestablish motherhood, policy efforts rarely involve a realistic vision of what that maternal life outside jail would look like. And so desire for jail remains.

Despite the hopefulness of the Sheriff's Department's leadership, many of the deputies and medical staff who interfaced constantly with these women took a cynical approach to pregnant women's proclamations about transformation. I noticed some jail staff nodding their heads as they listened to these proclamations, then furtively rolling their eyes, or later, telling disbelieving stories to each other about previous children the women were not raising. Recidivism manufactured this cynicism, for jail staff saw these women over and over again, pregnant, not pregnant, and pregnant again.

"JAIL TALK"

One mother of an incarcerated pregnant woman was similarly pessimistic. Her daughter, Daisy, was six weeks pregnant in jail. Daisy was addicted to heroin and, despite periods of sobriety, had ceded custody of her four other children to her mother and sister. Daisy, too, talked about this pregnancy as a chance to turn things around. She had relapsed four months ago, but framed it as a way of coping with her grandmother's death. She could get clean for this pregnancy, she declared. As I helped Daisy prepare for her release, connecting her with community resources and making plans, she broke down. "I want Saturday mornings," she pleaded, sobbing. "I want Saturday mornings with my kids. Cuddling in bed, watching cartoons." Her incarceration allowed her space to fantasize about normal motherhood. Daisy wanted to "get things right" not only for this pregnancy, but for all her children.

Two weeks after her release from jail, after she had missed doctors' appointments and an intake at a methadone clinic, I called Daisy's home. Her elderly mother picked up the phone. She knew Daisy had relapsed. When I told her about Daisy's impassioned declarations to change, she told me she had heard such things before: "All that cryin', that wasn't nothin' but jail talk."

Jail talk. Daisy's mother's phrase suggests that being in jail supplied her daughter with the language for a trajectory of transformation, one that Daisy had yet to follow through once she left jail behind. Likewise, all the pregnant women I encountered at the San Francisco jail narrated some version of jail talk in interviews, in informal conversations in the pods, or in the clinic exam room. Whether or not their narratives were realistic, they focused on pregnancy as incitement for change on behalf of the lives they were gestating.

This notion of "jail talk" recalls E. Summerson Carr's analysis of therapeutic talk in a drug treatment program for homeless women.[28] These patients were well aware of the importance of scripted linguistic performances in which they took responsibility for their actions and committed to change. The recovery language they were supposed to adopt reflected their inner emotional states, including those of denial, desire, and shame. Women in this treatment program learned to speak "the language of inner reference without abiding by its principles."[29] Carr calls this "script flipping," the conscious performance of recovery linguistics with the intention not to act according to that script.

Like the women in the program Carr describes, pregnant women at the San Francisco jail used language about their inner states to articulate changes they saw as necessary for successful motherhood. This is not surprising, since most of these women had spent time in drug treatment programs like the one in D-pod at the San Francisco jail. Here, they were steeped in therapeutic discourses of recovery and self-motivated change.[30] Other nonpregnant women in the jail had told me, smirking, how they frequently convinced judges of their commitments to recovery in order to be released from jail to drug treatment programs—only to abscond after one day. Pregnant, incarcerated women in San Francisco discussed their desire for transformation so frequently that their language might similarly be read as performative. Most of them, like Evelyn, Kima, Daisy, and Alisha, already had given birth to children whom they were not raising, so these children were historical referents to scripts in which their mothers were "getting it right *this time.*" They knew these to be appropriate scripts for CPS workers, who would make custody determinations after birth. So pregnant inmates had strategic reasons to rehearse and perform these scripts about maternal transformation in jail.

In the case of jail talk, the intentionality of the performance was less relevant than for Carr's script flippers. What mattered was that jail gave them an opportunity to craft a narrative of change and to assert their desire for motherhood. As well versed as these women were in therapeutic discourse about individual responsibility, they knew, too, that cycling through jail was related to the failure of the public safety net. As Evelyn said, "It's not that I started using again 'cause I wanted to. I started using because it was so hard to get anywhere. I got released with nowhere to go." Evelyn's "jail talk" accompanied an experiential understanding of the care and comfort she found in jail, a remedy for "nowhere to go."

I became quite captivated with Evelyn's jail talk. It seemed consistent, insightful, and impassioned. And she was making concrete plans, a sign of the normative, futurist-focused action that our capitalist reality so venerates.[31] Over the course of the time we spent together, Evelyn told me that she planned to name this baby, her first girl, Carolyn. This was her deceased mother's name, but Evelyn insisted she had also chosen it because of me. When I left the jail at night, she would tell me not to get out of the subway at her corner because it was unsafe. She was looking out for me. It was hard not to have faith in Evelyn's jail talk.

As she approached her due date in jail, Evelyn told me furtively about occasional contractions she was having. She did not want to tell the nurses, who would transport her to the hospital. Evelyn was awaiting release to Revelation House any day now and did not want anything—hospital transport or spontaneous labor—to interfere. She wanted to give birth out of jail and leave the hospital with her newborn in her arms. I wanted this for her too, and drew on my clinical judgment to reassure her that with only a few contractions an hour, she was probably not in labor.

Evelyn was released from jail while still pregnant. A few days later, a case manager from Revelation House escorted her to the county hospital, where I met them for Evelyn's first prenatal visit outside of jail. Evelyn wore a gray and pink–striped track suit that a woman from the program had loaned her. Her hair was still in the braids that her cellmate in jail had tightly woven. She smiled her charming grin and chatted up everyone in the clinic, from other patients to ancillary staff. At Revelation House, Evelyn was attending group therapy and getting her dorm-style room ready for her baby. She was habilitating. A few days later, nonincarcerated and sober, Evelyn gave birth to baby Carolyn. The change she had imagined in jail seemed to have arrived.

A BABY GIRL IS BORN

Kima was also working on plans to enter a residential drug treatment program for mothers and children upon release from jail. She was still incarcerated when she went into labor early one morning in C-pod and was transported by deputies to the county hospital. Once admitted to the labor and delivery unit, Kima was almost like any other nonincarcerated patient. She wore a patient gown; she was hooked up to an electronic monitor to track her baby's heart rate; she had an IV infusing fluids; an epidural numbed her pain. Unlike other patients in labor, however, Kima had a uniformed guard outside her room, ensuring that she, even with numbed legs and regular contractions, would not escape. At 1:30 p.m., Sheriff's Department rules allowed Kima to have visitors for twenty minutes. Deputy Oberton was not supposed to allow more than one visitor at a time, but he allowed both Kima's elderly, hunched-over mother and stepfather to share in the excitement of the imminent birth, saying, "Especially when, you know, there's a kid. It's up to our discretion. There's a gray zone." To offset his rule-bending, Deputy Oberton stood in the corner of the room instead of outside, until time was up. Then he gently interrupted the conversation, exchanging well wishes and smiles with Kima's mother. They had known each other for a long time—Kima's mother herself had spent years cycling in and out of jail when Kima was growing up.

An hour later, Kima was fully dilated and ready to push her third baby into this world. She took a deep breath in and cried with anxiety and anticipation, "I'm scared! I'm scared!" Then she announced she was praying to God to help her push the baby out. Within seconds, she returned to the outgoing, unhesitating Kima I had seen dance to Beyoncé a few weeks earlier. With only a few pushes, Kima birthed baby Koia. I placed the baby on her mom's belly. After a few moments of staring into her newborn's eyes, Kima picked up the hospital phone she was privileged to use while outside of jail. She called her eight-year-old daughter, cousins, aunts—thrilled to share the news with everyone, and make sure they were ready to help. Deputy Jenks unobtrusively entered the room and wished Kima congratulations; Kima welcomed his warm wishes, smiling a "thank you" at him.

Kima would be going back to jail after the routine postpartum hospitalization, and her older sister had agreed to take care of baby Koia until her release. She was making the most of her two postpartum recovery days in the hospital—keeping her baby in her hospital room instead of the nursery, singing made-up lullabies, and breastfeeding. Kima was not surprised when, the day after giving birth, a CPS worker came to interview her. She had had previous involvement with CPS, and expected they would visit her as a matter of routine. But Kima's joy changed to disappointment and anger when the CPS worker told her that her sister had an active CPS case and could not take baby Koia into her custody. When the CPS worker left, Kima frantically called everyone she knew, desperate to find her baby a temporary home. She cradled Koia and held the phone against her ear with her shoulder. Forty-five minutes later, a nurse entered the room and announced "Kima, I'm going to have to take your baby to the nursery right now."

We were both confused by the edict's urgency and the nurse's coldness. As it turned out, the CPS worker had decided to put a "police hold" on Kima's baby. This meant the baby could not leave the nursery, and Kima needed a guard to escort her to visits. Kima was devastated. She wailed and pulled her baby closer to her chest. "Why is God doing this to me? Why? All these other women get to go home with their babies. I want to spend every minute I can with my baby, because soon, I'm going back to jail." She bargained with the nurse for forty-five more minutes with Koia, then breastfed intently while she alternately explained to Koia what was happening in a high-pitched baby voice, and railed against the CPS worker. Kima got no sleep that night—not because of a crying newborn, but because of her anguish.

The next day, Kima's anger had softened. I found her sitting in a wheelchair in the nursery, a deputy ten feet away. One arm was handcuffed to the wheelchair, and the other arm held her baby against her breast. Kima told me she was embarrassed about the handcuffs, that the other parents in the nursery were staring at her. She was also excited: her cousin had agreed to take her baby and Kima had found out she was going to a drug treatment program in two weeks. Two weeks, she counted, and then a one-month trial period at the program, and then she could be fully reunited with Koia. As Koia settled into her latch on Kima's breast, Kima drifted off into a light, contented sleep.

Kima's childbirth and postpartum recovery represent a confluence of institutional forces: the biomedical birth, the jail, and the state-sponsored child welfare system. Moreover, Kima's birth experience diagnosed institutional inconsistencies in their most intimate manifestations.[32] Women in childbirth are often surrounded by family, but Kima's incarcerated status meant that because the final stage of labor did not occur between 1:30 p.m. and 2:30 p.m., she was denied family support. "It's a hard time," Kima reflected. "It's not the most comfortable position to be put in, to actually be in custody and giving birth, 'cause your family can't come to see, to push you forward to have the baby." The justification for this restriction was thin: following procedure. Likewise, the unpredictability of childbirth highlights the arbitrariness of the hospital visitation hours rule. At the same time, even while maintaining some rigidity in rules about visiting hours, Deputy Jenks was inspired to bend the rules and let visitors in. "Especially when, you know, there's a kid. It's up to our discretion. There's a gray zone," he had said. In this decision, he cultivated ambiguity between institutional requirements and cultural reverence for childbirth.

Kima tried to maximize opportunities for bonding with her newborn infant and to create a semblance of normality in her mothering activities in the hospital room. Yet the CPS police hold that redirected her efforts to the nursery alone exposed the absurdity of the system. On the one hand, Kima was not discouraged from breastfeeding—even though she would soon be going back to jail without her baby. In fact, the San Francisco jail was notably supportive of breastfeeding: official policy allowed a woman to pump breast milk in the pods, store the milk in clinic, and have it picked up by the infant's caregiver.[33] On the other hand, Kima's intimate encounter with her baby in the hospital nursery was inhibited by having one arm chained to a wheelchair and a guard towering over her. Care (as the enabling of breastfeeding) and violence (as constraining its possibility with chains) graphically coexisted in this moment.

Indeed, the police hold placed on baby Koia reflected back on the various institutions that professed to protect (Child Protective Services), punish (jail), and heal (hospital). When Kima telephoned a CPS supervisor, she was told the police hold was unnecessary, and that a standard CPS hold, in which the baby is kept with the mother in the hospital until CPS confirmed the safety of her designated guardians, would have sufficed, especially since an incarcerated mother has a de facto "police hold": an armed law enforcement agent posted outside her room.

The CPS worker's decision was thus procedurally unnecessary in order to protect the child; it might even be viewed as punitive, depriving Kima of maternal comfort simply because she was incarcerated. This experience became a traumatic memory for Kima, one she alluded to with anger and pain months after Koia's birth.[34] In this scenario, the jail system was a bystander to CPS's extreme actions. The deputy outside Kima's room when the police hold went into effect told her he would take her to the nursery as often as she wanted. "The last thing I want to do is come between a mother and her newborn baby," he told her. But the jail also set the conditions of possibility, for Kima had to make arrangements for the baby whom she could not take back to jail. Moreover, the county hospital and the nurse who abruptly moved Koia from her mother's arms to the nursery were also complicit in Kima's experience of institutional care and violence. The convergence of these carcerally inflected institutions ultimately revealed limits to the imagined redemptive possibilities of Kima's incarcerated pregnancy. CPS's disruption of her finite opportunity for newborn bonding, and her inevitable return to jail, precluded the very normative motherhood for which Kima yearned.

Kima's experience shares many qualities with other incarcerated women whose births I have attended. There was also variability. Mimi, for instance, gave birth at the hospital between 1:30 p.m. and 2:30 p.m., so her mother was by her side. Since her mother did not have a criminal record like Kima's mother and sister, she was able to care for the baby. Another inmate, Kaylee, was relieved that her newborn was placed into temporary foster care instead of going to her inebriated boyfriend, the baby's father. Yet another variable quality to the experience of giving birth while incarcerated is that, as discussed earlier, hundreds of women in other counties and states give birth in chains. The variability of childbirth experiences sheds light on the institutional webs in which these experiences were enmeshed. The outcomes of their reproduction cannot be understood solely through a lens of individual choice, like becoming pregnant, using drugs, or committing a crime, or through a lens of "reproductive governance" where subjects are produced by technologies of control. Rather, "choices" and "control" were animated by individuals in a complex system of carceral and caring relationships where motherhood was made.

"JAIL BRINGS ME BACK TO WHAT BEING A MOTHER IS"

Kima had two more weeks in jail before she was to be released to Whitman House. She continued to pump breast milk for her baby, which the clinic stored in its freezer.[35] A staff member from One Family, Claire, coordinated the transfer of milk to the baby's guardians. When a piece of the breast pump broke, Kima repaired it with string from the end of an unused tampon. She was committed to providing breast milk for Koia.

During that two-week period, Kima had several contact visits with her baby. I waited with her before one of the visits. She fantasized about all the things she would do with Koia in the years to come:

> But being that I do believe that I can do it, I know that this has got to—this is my last time. It's so much that I've got to look forward to. Crawling on the floor with my baby. I mean, who wants to not crawl on the floor with their baby? Like it's just going to be so fun 'cause I've been chasing her around. I could just see it now, just certain things, singing with my baby. It's like I want to be able to teach my daughter how to say excuse me when you're talking behind somebody or bumping into somebody or asking for something to say please and thank you. That's exactly what my plan is, to teach my daughter how to be a young lady, a little princess and act accordingly, and know that she's tough, she's a fighter.

The imagined future of a normative motherhood was very much a part of what sustained Kima in the present reality of jail. It was part of how motherhood was cultivated despite physical separation from one's child.

At 4:30 p.m., it was time for her visit. Time to cuddle with her baby in a windowless jail classroom with stained institutional carpet. Koia's guardian had driven the baby to jail, where Claire, the family program worker, then brought her in her car seat carrier, up to the fifth-floor visiting room. The location of these newborn visits—a room in the administrative wing of the jail—suggested that the housing units of the jail were no place for a mother and infant. After performing a standard pre-visit strip search, a deputy escorted Kima to the room, where she rushed to picked her baby up from the carrier. Koia wore a onesie embroidered with "Sugar and Spice." Kima wore her standard-issue orange uniform. The two had about two hours together in this room that looked like a preschool classroom, including bright posters on the walls. One Family worker Claire watched closely.

Kima condensed as much maternal practice into those two hours as possible. She sang made-up songs to her baby about love and, when the time came, about poopy diapers. Kima spread a changing pad Claire provided on the floor and changed baby Koia's diaper. When the baby cried, Kima held her close and rocked her back and forth. Then she guessed her baby was hungry, arranged herself in a blue plastic chair, lifted her shirt, and pushed her right nipple into Koia's screaming mouth, using her rolled-up orange sweatshirt as a lap pillow. Claire and I watched closely as the baby tried to latch, suckling for only fifteen seconds before starting again to cry. Kima was patient, knowing her daughter had only seen her nipple a few times during her ten-day life. After a few position changes, Kima calmly covered up her breasts and asked Claire to mix a bottle of formula (with supplies paid for by the Sheriff's Department budget), which her baby happily imbibed. When the visit ended, Kima was sad to say goodbye, but also energized about getting out in a few days, when she could see her baby more regularly.

Jail enabled these nested moments of motherhood. It did so with help from organizations like One Family, with which the Sheriff's Department contracted to coordinate parent-child visits, conduct parenting classes, and serve as a liaison with CPS. This last arrangement was, according to

Laura, who also worked for One Family, unique for a jail. One Family staff communicated directly with an incarcerated mother's CPS worker to make sure the CPS plans for supervised visits or drug treatment programs, for instance, were continued in jail. As Laura explained, "Just because she's here doesn't mean she can't do it. And then we do all of that work with her inside. And so—and we're going to the judge and saying, 'No, mom is doing all the things that you stipulated. The visits are going well.'" This is a step beyond the ways that jail can facilitate child custody potential, such as enabling a "clean birth," as Kima was grateful for. Here, jail workers actively worked to fulfill the requirements to achieve child custody after jail.[36] This collaboration between CPS and the jail might seem an obvious continuation of institutional forces that control a woman's ability to be a mother to her child.[37] But it also shows the jail's active promotion of possibilities for child custody.

For women with newborn babies, One Family coordinated up to three visits a week. Claire had worked in this program for the Sheriff's Department for several years, and knew many of the women, including Kima, well. She also knew that these visits allowed mother and child to spend time together, supervised by a nonuniformed civilian employee, but never allowed inmates to forget they were in jail. Laura informed me that women were strip-searched before and after their visits to prevent the acquisition of contraband. I was naively unaware of this protocol, since I would met Kima and other women in the visit room. Kima never mentioned it—perhaps because she was so accustomed to such surveillance. Strip searches are traumatic, particularly for women who have experienced sexual assault in the past, who may then be re-traumatized by the search. Laura worried that these pre- and post- visit strip searches were especially traumatic for mothers after intimate visits with their babies, which often made them emotionally vulnerable.

Claire, Laura, and their colleagues also taught parenting classes, which Kima had taken several times, even before she was pregnant with Koia. The content of these classes was based on a standardized curriculum for incarcerated parents used at prisons and jails across the country, and focused on specific skills that involve caring for a child, as well as more general social interactions, behavior management, and problem solving.[38] The existence of such classes presupposed a future outside jail where women, equipped with skills to care for a child, and ingrained with principles like self-restraint and sacrifice, could be mothers. At times, we all wondered whether these classes were futile for someone like Kima, who had taken them many times yet never had the chance to apply the knowledge she acquired to raising her children outside of jail. Indeed, Laura criticized the curriculum for presenting a "middle-class motherhood" and for focusing unrealistically on the long-term future without considering their immediate needs for things like housing and other resources to raise their children. Yet she identified the value of these classes as "a mom's club," a chance for women to talk to each other about motherhood. Sometimes the classes were hard for the mothers, she said, because it brought up feelings of loss or jealousy of things they did not have as a child, like a parent reading to them. Regardless of the long-term impact on incarcerated women who imagined raising their children, these moments that focused on maternal practice constituted Kima's sense of being a mother. Taking the parenting classes was itself a practice reflecting a sense of maternal responsibility. Kima's recidivism enabled her to continue to participate in motherly activities, even in the physical absence of her children.

Indeed, women continued to tell me how much they appreciated the parenting classes. One woman, Karen, in her early 40s, attended classes even though her three children, whom she did not raise, were grown. Karen spent most of her addicted adulthood cycling between the streets and jail. She had left the childrearing to the children's father and her own mother, but visited her children when she could.

Karen hoped the parenting classes would help her now to be a good grandmother. The camaraderie she felt with other women in the pods who were mothers also energized her maternal sentiments. Volunteers from a local church would periodically record women's audio messages to their children and send the cassette tapes out in the mail. Some women could provide no addresses—and I could not help but think that very few people still had the ability to play cassette tapes. Nonetheless, this activity demonstrates the range of opportunities available for women to behave as mothers in jail. It also contextualizes the feelings of many women, that jail possessed resources for motherhood that life on the streets lacked. As Karen wistfully summarized, "Jail brings me back to what being a mother is." Ironically, this vision of motherhood in jail did not require physical presence of one's child.[39]

Sandra Enos interviewed mothers in prison to explore how they construct and manage motherhood while incarcerated.[40] She found that women employed a variety of strategies, from micromanaging their children's caretakers, to denigrating inmate mothers who used drugs in front of their children, to demonstrating their maternal fitness to official agencies. Regardless of strategy, women's identities as mothers were tended and preserved in prison. Barbara Owen's study of women in prison identified a similar attentiveness to motherhood in prison, with many women expressing a desire to eliminate criminal behaviors for the sake of caring for their children.[41]

What Enos's and Owen's analyses did not fully capture was how, for some women, the intensity with which they focused on motherhood while incarcerated contrasted starkly with their lack of involvement on the outside.[42] Claire, the One Family worker, recognized this to be true for many of the women she tried to help. Claire worked hard to coordinate parent-child visits for inmates, though she knew some of these women only saw their children when they were in jail. "I'll call up some families to arrange dropping off the kid and they'll say 'well, she never sees them when she's outside of jail, but I guess we'll bring the baby in.'"

Jail provided these women direct access to these coordinating services, with fewer logistical barriers than those imposed by city agencies on women who lacked custody of their children. Moreover, jail provided a sober pause where some women, surrounded by other inmates who hung pictures of their children in their cells, idealized their roles as mothers.

On Mother's Day, the jail always arranged a celebration, though it struck me as a painful reminder to women of their separation from their children. In 2015, the jail gave permission for a local musician to hold a concert and record an album in CJ2 on Mother's Day.[43] On the song tracks, one can hear women in the background singing and clapping, and a few even reciting their own poetry. The CD liner notes reflect the musician's sense of empowerment and the empowerment expressed by the women, too. Clearly, the San Francisco jail went to great lengths to cultivate motherhood despite the carcerally imposed separation. It was hard to ignore that, despite these thoughtful institutional efforts, the versions of motherhood available to women in the San Francisco jail were limited. While two-hour contact visits several times a week is more than many jails and prisons facilitate for new mothers, cramming mother-infant time into these discrete segments cannot fully prepare a person for the full extent of parental caregiving, such as dealing with a crying baby in the middle of the night. What pregnant women and mothers in jail had access to was a simultaneously idealized and restricted version of motherhood.[44]

RECIDIVISM AND TRYING AGAIN

As with the women in prison whom Owen and Enos interviewed, incarceration could foster contemplation about reproduction.[45] Patients I took care of in the jail clinic asked me to start them on a method of birth control, because they wanted to get their lives together and focus on housing, employment, and already-existing children, without an unintended pregnancy. Other women came to me to remove their intrauterine contraceptive devices (IUD), so they could plan to have another baby. Alexis, a woman whose twins I had delivered two years prior and whose mother was raising her five children, told me as I removed her IUD, "I think having another baby is going to slow me down and I think I'm ready. . . . It's time for me to grow up."

So when Kima was released from jail on Labor Day, she was full of enthusiasm to be a mother to baby Koia. But when she got to the jail lobby, she later explained, "Nobody was downstairs far as like my case manager to drive me to the program, even though that's a very lame excuse for me not making it that day. I didn't go." Instead, she hit the streets. The drug-filled Tenderloin District she spent much of her time in was only five blocks away. "I smoked some weed, and then I went and smoked some crack, and then I went to the program the next day. Everybody was really happy that I called and showed up. So I ended up having some having some clean pee, so I gave them some clean pee." Kima giggled at this detail, which she told me from jail, two and a half months after her Labor Day release. She was at Whitman House for only two weeks. While there, she attended group therapy, parenting classes, supervised visits with her baby, and rested comfortably on their beds. She also, on a pass to leave for a few hours one Saturday, went to a friend's house and got high before returning to the comforts of Whitman House. A few days later, she quietly walked out the front door.

And here she was again, in jail. Now I knew why the staff at Whitman House had not allowed me to visit Kima when I called them—Kima had no longer been there, but they could not tell me that. Now I knew why Kima had not come to her postpartum clinic visit at the county hospital, where we were supposed to discuss birth spacing and contraception: she was high on the streets. With multiple stints in therapy, Kima was well versed in taking individual responsibility for her failed attempt at reunifying with her baby. In jail, several weeks after leaving Whitman House, she confessed to me, "I kind of like set myself up by doing that in the first place. I got to give myself a chance. It's not the fact that I got away with using [before going to Whitman House]. It was the fact that I didn't give myself a chance by staying clean. I let them not showing up be a reason that I went and got high. And so I kind of set myself up again." Koia was still only three months old. Legally, Kima still had time to gain custody of her daughter, for whom her cousin was caring, and whom Kima hadn't seen in two months, as the courts were still adjudicating custody.

Armed with this proclamation about taking responsibility, Kima proceeded to tell me that she wanted to try again to be a mother. But trying again did not mean reuniting with Koia. "If they say in court 'no,' then it's no. It's nothing I can do about it. And they may well just say no, Dr. Sufrin, 'cause I didn't—I never unified—I failed the unification services with my daughter, my older daughter." Her past CPS experiences convinced her that legal custody of Koia was a lost cause, something over which she had no control. But Kima had already hatched another plan for motherhood. On the streets, after leaving the drug treatment program she hoped would reunify her with her newborn daughter, Kima had tried to get pregnant again:

KIMA: I tried to get pregnant by this Mexican and white boy. Oh, yes, I did. I tried that. I tried to get pregnant because I—'cause I'm going to have a baby and they're not going to take it. I will end up having a baby that they can't take, so—I know that sounds kind of fucked up, 'cause it's like, well, damn, you don't have none of your kids, but still.

CS: And what do you think would be different this time?

KIMA: I don't know, but I'm going to end up having a baby that they can't
       take, 'cause the social worker told me that if I don't—if I'm not in jail
       and I'm not using, they can't take a baby from me. If I have everything—
       If I get pregnant and I don't test dirty, and I give birth and I'm not in
       jail, how can they take it if I'm there, if I'm doing right? So that's
       my—If I was pregnant right now, I would be happy because—
       not saying that I can forget about my other children. I mean, that's
       not what it is, but just to try to have one that I can keep, so that
       I can keep it.

She alternated between childish laughter and a serious tone as she told
me about her attempts at pregnancy. I struggled as I listened to Kima
outline this logic. It tapped into age-old debates about structure versus
individual agency in shaping the conditions of people's lives. In this
moment, Kima unsettled my usual reliance on understandings of structural violence as my source of empathy, for I was frustrated with her willingness to give up on baby Koia.

Nevertheless, to Kima, this was an organized, sequential plan. Perhaps
for someone whose reproduction had been continuously managed by various institutions, and whose drug addiction also shaped her reproduction,
Kima's plan was logical. She had come to expect that her reproduction
required the involvement of state institutions—namely jail, the courts,
and CPS. Each child involved a trial period of varying lengths, in which
Kima had to prove herself a fit mother. She had yet to succeed. It is not
hard to imagine how the trial mentality could produce her apparent non-
chalance—she could just try again. Kima believed a clean pregnancy—not
an easy task for someone with long-standing addiction—would overcome
the regulatory obstacles that had impeded her success. Kima's past experiences produced an experimental approach to pregnancy. It was a pragmatic calibration of her maternal sentiment.[46]

Moreover, Kima had spent many of her reproductive years in and out of
jail, with only an occasional stint in prison. Each jail release equipped her,
at least in theory, with a reentry script to reorient herself to a different way
of being. The repetitive nature of these reentries differed from the context
of mothers in state prisons whom Owen and Enos interviewed;[47] while
these women may have been in prison before, their prison-induced aspirations to be better mothers had a singular chronicity to them. Instead, the

intimate recidivism of the jail reality provided Kima with hope. She could try her hand at motherhood and custody of her child, *again.*

This is not to say, as Kima declared, that "I can forget about my other children." Kima was capable of imagining the next pregnancy would be better, while still loving baby Koia. Jail facilitated this mixed aspiration; it nurtured Kima's maternal emotions. When Koia was five and a half months old, Kima returned to jail. She asked me for copies of the pictures I had taken at Koia's birth, which she taped to her cell walls—walls she did not have in her precarious life on the streets.[48] Having barely visited Koia in her six weeks out of jail, and facing the termination of her parental rights, Kima still wanted supervised visits with her baby. So Claire, the One Family worker, arranged for them again. The visits, Kima said, made her both "happy and sad." She was happy to see her baby. She was sad that, because the baby identified Kima, her own mother, as a stranger, Koia cried so much.

On one particular visit day, Kima was irritable and upset over an argument with some women in E-pod. When it came time for her visit with Koia, Kima was distracted. She played with Koia but complained to me and Claire about the drama in the pod. I was sad to see Kima wasting her limited time on such trivial he-said-she-said matters. Then Deputy Murphy stopped by to admire Kima's adorable baby. Kima put her baby down in the carrier, and took the opportunity to tell Deputy Murphy about the argument. She asked Deputy Murphy to transfer her from E-pod to B-pod. Deputy Murphy, familiar with Kima's impulsivity, took a deep breath, put a hand on Kima's shoulder, and said, sympathetically but with a hint of reprimand, "Kima, you can work this out. You need to think about the big picture. You need the programming in E-pod." Attending programming, after all, might help her gain custody over Koia, although we all knew the cousin's adoption of baby Koia was likely to be approved in a few days. Deputy Murphy had succeeded in mollifying Kima for now. They hugged. Kima went back to holding her baby and singing, as Deputy Murphy, Claire, and I watched. We also watched as Kima slipped Koia's partially soiled diaper into her bra, a multisensory reminder of her baby that she would discreetly keep in her cell until a deputy would find and confiscate it.

This visit exemplified the intimate ways that jail and reproduction are deeply entangled with each other. It was the ostensibly punitive but tragically normative space of the jail that enabled Kima to connect with her baby in ways she did not outside of jail. She could behave as a mother inside in a way she could not outside. What's more, solace and instruction from a deputy directed her back into the maternal moment. These moments were glimpses of maternal possibility for Kima, enough to sustain her institutionally produced desire to try again with another pregnancy.

CARCERAL DESIRE

The jail pregnancy experiences of women like Evelyn, Kima, and others illustrate how carcerality and motherhood are co-produced. Despite the hypermedicalized, morally judging management of pregnancy in jail discussed in chapter 5, women could still yearn for jail and the various kinds of maternal sentiments it enabled. Even as safety net services like free prenatal care or residential drug treatment programs existed in the community, these women were deeply inscribed in a reality where jail enabled certain elements of reproduction that other regulated services like CPS and drug treatment programs could not fulfill. We have seen how some women came to desire the reproductive comforts of jail, such as prenatal care, parenting classes, coordinated visits with their children, or even a wall on which to hang photographs. The intimacy of a mother's bond with her newborn, down to the very corporeal act of breastfeeding, was simultaneously enabled and deeply regulated in jail. Desire for jail and desire for normative motherhood are complex affects to house in the same person, and in the same carceral institution. Of course, other pregnant women, especially at other jails and prisons with systematic mistreatment and lack of services for pregnant women, have little to desire from jail.

Nonetheless, such desires, and the jail's efforts to manage reproduction, implicitly diagnose the failings of a broader system that has perpetuated these women's marginality and devalued their reproduction, a system in which they expected their reproduction to be adjudicated by institutions. Women's ideas of normative motherhood, and their opportunities to practice those ideals, were uniquely available in jail, in ways they were not on the streets. The desire for jailcare and its maternal possibilities have the potential to elicit dangerous parallels to problematic narratives of the welfare queen who leeches off institutional resources; but such a comparison overlooks the ways that jailcare is made possible by the institutional failures of the safety net and by the legal mandate that requires carceral institutions to provide medical care. Incarcerated reproduction reveals the fundamental equivalence of the carceral and medical-social safety net in our unequally structured society, particularly for poor, young women of color.[49] Motherhood in jail and jailcare's constitutive frayed safety net are chilling demonstrations of how mass incarceration is a matter of reproductive justice, for they complicate women's abilities to parent their own children in the ways they would like.[50] The carceral desire that was disturbingly woven into their reproduction sets the stage for thinking about how some of these women came to feel cared for by controlling deputies and came to see jail as home, processes I now turn to in the final chapters.

7 Custody as Forced and Enforced Intimacy

You know, the bread and butter of any sheriff's department is custody.

Deputy Faderman, male deputy at the San Francisco jail

CUSTODY: THE EVERYDAY WORK OF JAIL

As Kima and Evelyn gestated their pregnancies in jail, they did so surrounded by uniformed officers whose explicit job duty was called "custody." This core function of jails, which goes hand in hand with its punitive role, is the substrate for the intimacy—regulated as it might be—which pregnant incarcerated women could experience with the institution. Historical trends of ideologies of punishment in the United States and their translation into the daily operations of prisons have been extensively explored, from repentance to rehabilitation to warehouse prisons.[1] What has remained constant over these eras—though infrequently acknowledged throughout these shifts in penal management—is the function of carceral institutions to keep and guard people in one place. As such, jail—perhaps even more so than prison because jail houses those awaiting trial—involves not only punishment, but what is called "custody."

Custody is common parlance among jail and prison workers to describe the basic activity of keeping those within the walls of a carceral institution safe. Those less involved with the daily workings of jails tend to describe inmates as "incarcerated"; those with greater daily involvement describe inmates as "in custody." In fact, the division within the San Francisco Sheriff's Department that managed the county's jails was (and is) called the "Custody Division." The department's mission statement provides a practical explanation of what its Custody Division does:

> The Custody Division is the [Sheriff's] Department's largest division. This division is charged with the operations of all six of our County Jails, the Hospital Ward, the Classification Unit, and the various Jail Programs. The division strives to maintain a safe and secure jail system and to facilitate an environment in which the various educational and rehabilitation programs can accomplish their missions. These in-custody programs offer a variety of educational, vocational, substance abuse treatment and violence intervention classes.[2]

This description reveals custody's complexity. Custody entails maintaining safety, and also, at least according to this official statement, entails encouraging individuals to transform and rehabilitate themselves to escape the cycle of incarceration. Nonetheless, the sentiment of this description of custody is of concern and investment. Custody, then, is also a form of care. In jail, custody most obviously takes shape through reinforcing safety and security, but has practical and rhetorical roots in more affective forms of care. These two dimensions of custody—control and care—coexist at each moment.

Foucault's description of pastoral power is useful in considering the link between custody and care. Foucault points to a shepherd, who provides food and security for each individual sheep, treats the wounded, ensures his flock's welfare, and thus has power over them by controlling their well-being; "pastoral power," Foucault writes, "is a power of care."[3] Foucault does not linger on these aspects of pastoral care.[4] Instead, he demonstrates how pastoral nurturance leads to the eventual exploitation of the herd. Pastoral power, in Foucault's account, serves as the genealogic precursor to modern forms of power and governmentality that center on regulating the conduct of the population, the normalizing effects of disciplinary power. This mix of power and daily tending in pastoral power is precisely where jailcare, the simultaneous intimacy of custody and care, brews.[5]

Pastoral care thus enacts both benevolence and power, and renders inseparable the kindness of care and the control of subjects. So too are these nodes inextricable from each other within the everyday routines of custody in jail. The daily work of pod deputies consisted of practices that could always be justified as ensuring safety, but also gave rise to nurturing gestures. For instance, I saw deputies break up a fight by spraying pepper spray in an inmate's face, then anxiously bring her to clinic in order to flush the caustic chemical out of her eyes. Safety was achieved through a knotty entanglement of control and benevolence—what I call pastoral custody—that acknowledges the many contradictory tasks and affects of facilitating the minutiae of inmates' daily existence. The collective space of the jail and the deputies' job description resulted in close and constant spatial proximity, as well as intimacy around personal bodily processes and social interactions. The job of custody, then, required both forced and enforced intimacy generated by the jail's conditions.

UBIQUITY OF PUNISHMENT

The punitive discipline that has come to characterize modern carceral institutions manifested itself in the rhythms of regimentation, constant surveillance, and power configurations of the San Francisco jail. This was visible in, among other things, a long list of deputy-enforced rules and schedules posted in every pod. In the midst of my discussions about care, it is crucial to describe some of these routinized moments. For affect and intimacy in the jail should not be understood as merely disruptive to the expected punitive interactions; rather, the intersubjective tendencies of care are woven into degrading forms of punishment. Thus, even when caregiving within the jail clinic or housing units appears a "successful" salve for experiences of abandonment on the streets, the intimacies sustain problematic regimes of incarceration.

For women in the San Francisco jail, the punishment of being separated from the world outside jail included the psychological pain of separation from children and other extended family members. In addition, punishment included constant surveillance from deputies, who sat on their elevated, tower-like platform in the center of the pod, along with routinized and degrading diminishment of autonomy, such as the inability to freely choose when they could shower or read a book, or when and what they could eat for meals. Women at the San Francisco jail were dependent on deputies for access to all of their basic needs like food, water, hygiene, and sleep. Punishment was also experienced as the deprivation of small comforts such as a pillow.

Women also felt punished by what they perceived as unhygienic conditions. When I open-endedly asked women what they thought about medical care in jail, many of them complained about unsanitary conditions, and being forced to live in close quarters with disheveled people coming straight off the streets. One woman detailed her disgust with the environment:

> This jail is like by far the worst I've been in. I'm not going to lie to you, as far as disease control and just Ugh! It just really scares me. This lady came in here. She had lice and scabies. They didn't get rid of the mattress. They just threw me in that room. . . . Some lady literally defecated on the carpet, left it there, someone stepped in it, tracked it on the carpet. Why is the carpet here in a jail anyway? Women leave their [menstrual] pads around. San Francisco needs to get it together. I swear to God, I've never in my life seen anything this nasty. I am terrified about what I'm exposed to.

This woman lived in fear. She and others protested that being in jail did not mean they deserved these conditions. The filth they perceived was thus part of the punitive reality these women faced.

Humiliation, lack of privacy, and mockery were also parts of the punishment. Deputies knew every time a woman had to relieve herself, for inmates had to ask for permission in order to use the bathroom. They knew when a woman was menstruating, because they controlled access to pads and tampons. I watched an inmate hand a grievance form, in which she requested a transfer to another pod because a deputy was being mean to her, to her pod deputy, whose job it was to send the form to the supervisor. I then watched the deputy read the complaint and burst out laughing. "You can't choose your deputy! This isn't something you can grieve," the deputy said to her, still laughing. Deputies constantly laced insults into the orders they yelled at inmates. At dinnertime one afternoon, for instance, Deputy Walker chastised inmates for not following her instructions to line up on the right side of the stairwell to await their meal tray. Deputy Walker wore flaming red lipstick to match her anger: "Can you not follow simple instructions? Are you all that stupid?" She then turned to me and cackled, explaining that, having worked at the jail for decades, she had a system for making sure the women behaved. I thought about how each deputy had her own set of instructions, and how hard it must have been for inmates to remember how "to behave" properly for each deputy.

The arbitrariness to deputies' rules created ample opportunities for punishment and verbal abuse. If inmates talked back, as Evelyn and Kima sometimes did, they might be placed on "ad seg," higher security housing, in which inmates were confined to locked cells twenty-three hours a day and denied participation in programming or social activities in the pod. The effect of this exclusion was magnified by the fact that people in ad seg could see activities happening. Evelyn's self-proclaimed anger issues from her first ten years in and out of jail were a permanent part of her jail record, such that, even though she was calmer now, she was automatically housed in ad seg every time she arrived in jail—punished preemptively with jail housing isolation.

In addition to these controlling forms of punishment and verbal abuse, there was also physical force. I watched as a psychotic inmate, presumed to have violent potential, was pinned down by four deputies, placed in handcuffs, and dragged with an entourage of guards to a concrete block "safety cell" in the medical housing unit. Although I did not personally witness fistfights (perhaps my presence in the pods influenced people's behaviors), I heard firsthand from deputies and inmates who had engaged in fights with each other.[6] Evelyn recounted the days when she assaulted and was assaulted by deputies:

> Like, okay, you might get in a couple good licks when it's just you and you're fighting a deputy one-on-one, but once all the other deputies rush in—and it's never female deputies. It's like you fight a deputy and all these men come in. And then the elevator ride from say B-pod to Lower C-pod or Upper C-pod safety cell is really, really hard because, like, there's no cameras, so we're prone to getting our ass whipped in the elevators. Like I got my finger broke one time. I had a 300-pound deputy step on my back, like twist— They're not—the male deputies don't take in consideration that we're females. So okay, I understand I assaulted one of your co-workers, but I'm a girl. I'm not a guy. And they slam us; they twist our arms.

Cameras were predictably located throughout the jail for panoptic surveillance of inmates and staff; but the elevators were, for unclear reasons, surveillance-free. In her recounting, Evelyn admitted to some degree of complicity in the violence. She also described excessive force in the unmonitored elevators, where inmates were usually handcuffed. There were other instances, described by Evelyn and other women, of inexplicable, unprovoked physical assaults, in full view of cameras and other people.[7]

The San Francisco jail was thus saturated with well-documented, classic, degrading elements of carcerality, as well as with violence and arbitrary, punitive deprivation seen in today's "warehouse prisons."[8] As John Irwin summarizes in describing the San Francisco jail in 1985: "[Inmates] are impersonally and systematically degraded at every step in the criminal justice process."[9] He continues, writing, "most deputies embrace and help sustain the theory that prisoners are worthless and deserve their deprivation.... [They] must consciously reject more humane and tolerant conceptions of prisoners."[10] While this may be a baseline logic for many jail workers, the fact that it takes a "conscious rejection" leaves open the possibility for alternatives to this model, such as nurturance.

CUSTODY AS SAFETY

To explore the pastoral care of custody as it played out in the San Francisco jail, let us begin with the start of a deputy's work shift, called "muster." The name of this ritual is an unironic reference to the military practice of assembling and inspecting troops. Fifteen minutes before the changing of the guard (6:45 a.m., 2:45 p.m., and 10:45 p.m. each day), the oncoming group of deputies routinely met in a cramped, windowless conference room on the fifth floor. Deputies entered the room ready to work, dressed in black Sheriff's Department uniforms and adorned with enforcement-gear belts: handcuffs, stick, pepper spray, flashlight, walkie-talkie.[11] Their uniform and accessories represented the so-called safety and security mission of custody, and signified guards' readiness to injure an inmate who crossed the line that constituted safe behavior.

The structure of muster was the same every day: deputies trickled into the conference room, collected their food vouchers, greeted each other and made jokes, and awaited the arrival of senior officers. The charge nurse for the shift was supposed to attend muster, but he usually just dropped off the lists of inmates coming to clinic and lining up for pill call. Shift supervisors—more highly ranked senior deputies, lieutenants, or captains—would then file into the room and sit at the front. The "watch commander" of the day would take attendance by announcing each deputy's assignment for the shift (which usually remained the same for one month's time).

New announcements were read from the "muster board," a clipboard with a cumulative stack of official departmental memos from the year. The range of muster board announcements was varied: beware of the recent resurgence of "tomahawks" (creative repurposing of the safety razors inmates used to shave); an inmate was court-ordered to have a free phone call; a nurse was fired and her jail clearance revoked after having romantic relations with an inmate; in-service training dates were set for a suicide prevention module; overtime shifts were available.[12] The messages were efficiently and unidirectionally announced, from supervisor to lowest-ranking deputy. As they listened to the routine, deputies joked with each other and distractedly completed crossword puzzles. After information was communicated, deputies dispersed to their posts to carry out their duties.

I spend this time describing muster to frame custody as a set of managerial, routine practices geared toward safety (beware of tomahawks) and security (the evicted nurse was not allowed back). Deputy Faderman summarized his interpretation of his job, one well represented in muster discourse: "Our role is to make sure that they do their time in accordance with the law. That's it. Our job is to make sure that we maintain the safety of ourselves, the people that are coming in and out of the facility, and the safety of the facility itself. That's it. That's our job." Muster reflected this procedural orientation. The thrice-daily ritual ensured that everything in jail, even potentially shocking things like inmates' weaponry or staff-inmate trysts, was routine. One could get a clear, albeit sterile, sense of what custody officially meant from attending muster.

When deputies left the predictable organization of muster and entered the pods, though, the meaning of custody was made real. This was the moment when pastoral contradictions emerged. Custody was enacted in various ways, from the bureaucratic administration of living space to the management of interpersonal relations, within the carceral space of the jail, in which both physical architecture and discursive formations enabled this form of caregiving. At one level, deputies orchestrated custody through a sense of routine and duty.

For instance, here is a sample of activities from a daytime deputy's shift: arrive in the pod at 7 a.m.; do a quick walk around the cells to check on the women, most of whom went back to sleep after 4:30 a.m. breakfast;[13] answer a 7:15 phone call from the "movement deputies" stationed in the holding area near the clinic, to talk about who was on the clinic list for the day; call out the names and line up the women scheduled to go to clinic; prompt the women going to the in-jail school for a General Educational Development (GED) diploma to wait for their escort on the upper level at 7:55 a.m.; put on a pair of medical gloves and pat down every inmate leaving the pod for clinic or class; inspect every dorm area and ensure there is no contraband; when the kitchen duty inmate workers arrive at 9:30 a.m. with two carts of stacked lunch trays, supervise the pod workers who distribute lunch; at 10 a.m., after the call to inmates announces that lunch is being served, stand guard as inmates receive and eat a tray of food; supervise lunch tray collection; communicate with the clinic for 10:30 a.m. pill call; inspect inmates' open mouths post-medication; supervise one hour of "quiet time" in which inmates must stay on their beds; at 12 p.m., direct a civilian worker to classrooms to conduct classes like violence prevention or group therapy; count the presence of all inmates, who stand beside their beds at 2 p.m.; and, at 3 p.m., be relieved by swing shift deputies. This pattern of activities was, roughly, repeated every day, with minor variations including the content of inmate programming or the distribution of items inmates purchased from commissary.

As part of managing the routine, deputies enacted the custody mission "to maintain a safe and secure jail system and to facilitate an environment in which the various educational and rehabilitation programs can accomplish their missions." When "civilians" (non-inmates and nonuniformed personnel) such as attorneys, community volunteers, or even medical staff entered the pods, deputies took their job of maintaining the safety of these civilians seriously. Implied in the seriousness of this work was a sense that the inmates were dangerous.

On one particular evening, the conflict between safety and care was especially problematic. Eliza, a doula (trained birth support person) with whom I had worked to start a program in jail, was teaching a participatory class to help women understand basic processes in their sexual and repro- ductive health. These weekly sessions had become popular and the women had come to trust Eliza and the other doulas who came with her. Towards the end of the class, a woman collapsed onto the floor and started convuls- ing. She was having a seizure. Eliza, also a registered nurse, immediately tended to the seizing woman to make her safe—she helped her to her side, moved chairs and people away, and asked the deputy to call the jail nurses. Her gestures were met with opposition. "You back off and get away from her immediately!" the deputy yelled. Eliza was confused, taken aback.

The deputy continued by threatening, "I can have your security clear- ance revoked!" By then, the woman's seizure had stopped. She had come to by the time the jail nurses arrived. But Eliza and the inmates who had witnessed the event were still in shock. Many of them, including Eliza, came to me for advice and to express how traumatic this moment was— not only because they witnessed the seizure, but because they watched the deputy thwart Eliza's qualified help. Other deputies, later, shared their perspectives on such instances, saying, "We need to make sure that civil- ians who come in here are safe. She could have been faking that seizure, then done something to anyone trying to help." Here, the custody charge for maintaining safety was geared toward a potential for danger for a non- inmate, rather than the safety and health of an inmate in the potentially dangerous throes of a seizure.

CUSTODY AS SOCIALITY

Amid the highly scheduled structure of jail and the regimented safety focus, there was continual face-to-face proximity between deputies and inmates. This resulted from the "pod" design of the San Francisco jail's housing units, and a custodial strategy called "direct supervision." The "pod" design stands in contrast to the "linear" design with rows of iron bar cells so often depicted in the media and still present in many jails and pris- ons. In the pod system, cells (except those on higher level security) had no doors. The cells in each pod were organized in a circular layout, and opened to a common area where inmates ate and socialized. San Francisco built these pod-style dorms in the early 2000s in a deliberate attempt to create community, make more space for programming, and foster therapeutic transformation, as one administrator relayed to me. Deputies were stationed on a platform located panoptically in the middle of the circular, open pod. The platform was armed with control buttons for the locked cells, computers for documenting, and various supplies. The platform itself was open, which made it easy for inmates to approach, either by looking up from the lower level or by stopping directly at the guard platform in the middle of the staircase connecting the lower and upper levels of the pod. The constant deputy-inmate interaction, which the pod design forced, created tremendous opportunities for custody to operate as a social relationship.

With permission, women constantly approached the deputies to ask for all kinds of things: toilet paper when the stalls were low; permission to use the bathroom; medical care request forms; books from the shelf of old, donated books. So as to not be bothered with requests, many deputies made menstrual products freely available in a plastic bag tied to the handrail at the bottom of the staircase, though women in locked "ad seg" cells could not freely access them. One night I watched as a woman in ad seg pantomimed to Deputy Brody that she needed a tampon. Instead of getting up from her comfortable perch, opening the gate and giving the woman a tampon directly, the deputy asked another non–ad seg inmate to retrieve one from the bag. The woman casually obliged, like she was doing a friend a simple favor, and then tossed the tampon around the gate and into the ad seg area. Deputy Brody then, with the touch of a button at her command tower, "popped" open the menstruating ad seg inmate's cell door, and she retrieved the tampon from the table on which it had landed.

While this might seem like an instance of laziness, Deputy Brody and the inmates laughed together the entire time, cracking jokes about flying tampons. At one level, the inmates' reliance on deputies for something as personal as menstrual supplies is a reminder of how the prisoner's body is considered a collection of biological processes, detached from a social self.[14] But at another level, the dependent relationship enabled spontaneity and sociality through shared humor. Moreover, the amusing episode arose from an inmate's menstruation; the flying tampon was evidence that guards' regulatory involvement in inmates' intimate bodily processes was not strictly controlling. This was not the rote work of custody represented at muster. The intimacy garnered through this constant interface between inmates and custodians, even over what appeared to be the most biologically basic needs, allowed for the punctuation of custody with softness and humor.

Custody was an ongoing practice at the San Francisco jail. It demanded a skilled negotiation between the bureaucratic distance of a carceral regime and the proximity furnished by both pod architecture and inmates' intimate needs. There were many ways in which the jail reaffirmed distance between the deputies and inmates. The most obvious was the power differential that maintained them in a hierarchical configuration. The deputy, a citizen with rights and opportunities in mainstream society, spent time at the jail as a matter of chosen employment; the inmate, stripped through incarceration of many of her citizen rights, spent time there for allegedly committing a crime.[15] The contrast between the deputies' black, armed uniforms and the inmates' baggy orange uniforms reinforced the differences between them.

Moreover, the guarding nature of custody included elements of distance. Deputies were not in charge of deciding a person should be in jail (that role was reserved for police officers and judges). This auxiliary position to the criminal justice system allowed those providing custody a sense of being a neutral bystander. Deputies felt they were there simply to do a job, "to make sure that they do their time in accordance with the law," as one deputy dispassionately stated. Deputies carried out a set of tasks; counting, documenting, and performing other paper duties provided the distance necessary to think of inmates as generic objects of governance.[16] Another deputy explained his detachment from the inmates: "I don't get mad at them. Because to get mad, you have to care. And I don't care." This deputy expressed the ultimate indifference, the profoundly unsentimental sentiment of bureaucracy. The potential for this indifference is endemic to modern prisons and jails—so much so that it provided the basis for the Supreme Court's 1976 mandate that prisons provide medical care.[17]

PROXIMITY AND DISTANCE IN CUSTODY

Rhodes's analysis of physical proximity and distance in a maximum security prison is a useful starting point for considering how care can arise
from this specter of indifference.[18] Rhodes describes how prison guards
and prisoners constantly negotiate the distance imposed by thick concrete
walls and psychological isolation and the physical closeness experienced
in guards' forceful regulation of inmates' behavior. Distance in the presence of bodily proximity is not, she argues, a static geography to be maintained and from which indifference arises. Rather, the management of
distance and proximity afforded by the prison setting is a dynamic, ongoing process that is the very "social fabric" of the place.[19] It was through
such constant negotiation of space in the San Francisco jail that social
connections were cultivated, and this sociality contributed to the ambiguous intimacy of custody as a carcerally prescribed relationship.

The open deputy platform at the San Francisco jail was representative
of this sociality based on managing distance and proximity. Deputies listened to women when they approached their custodians for platform
chats, and sometimes deputies invited them into conversation. I observed
most of the deputies rub hand sanitizer on their hands before and after
interactions, and in many cases, they put on disposable gloves. Even as
they engaged in casual or personal conversation with the women, deputies
were wary of caring too much. As one deputy told me: "They've all got a
story they try to tell you, and you just can't get sucked in." Not getting
sucked in might manifest as a deputy barely listening to a woman's story,
which on the surface appears a lack of engagement. But it does not signal
the absence of human connection, for working not to get sucked into
inmates' stories is an active "accomplishment" of managing ongoing, precarious social relations.[20]

The bodily proximity of inmates and deputies in the San Francisco jail
pods was, as I have already described, significant. Likewise, the bureaucratic features of carceral distance were present. Dealing with this carcerally given reality was indeed a constant and social negotiation, as in
Rhodes's maximum security prison. Pastoral custody in the San Francisco
jail sheds light on how these negotiations wrestle with caregiving—care
that is not so much the flip side of indifference, but that emerges from the

same work of distance and proximity. The same deputies who would bark out orders and arbitrarily revoke "free time," or who would sit at the guard platform playing with their iPhones—all techniques that create distance by affirming hierarchy—would also seek out opportunities for proximity.[21] Deputy Brody, from the flying tampon episode, made one of her periodic inspection walk-arounds one evening. It was close to 9 p.m., but lights were not out yet. Deputy Brody stopped at an ad seg cell. She opened the small latched door embedded in the larger, locked glass door and invited conversation with the inmate. "What book are you reading?" she asked. For the next few minutes, the two talked about literature.

Another afternoon in B-pod, Deputy Bellinson had just carried out her custodial task of inspecting each person's cell for cleanliness and contra-band. While the inspection practices involved rustling through inmates' few belongings and personal space, the roteness of the task was also part of the distancing, rule-based bureaucracy of the institution. The women of B-pod had passed the inspection, and were granted free time. Deputy Bellinson turned the three pod TVs on, and set them to a local channel. On the streets five blocks from jail, there was a parade to welcome home the San Francisco Giants, who had just won the World Series. I sat with several women on the lower level as we cheered the players on. Out of the corner of my eye, I could see upstairs that Deputy Bellinson had paused in her busy work to watch the televised parade. Although she could have chosen other empty places to sit, she casually took a seat next to an inmate. The two sat together on the same level, laughing together at the players' celebratory antics.

CUSTODY AS CHOICE

These were sought-out opportunities within the mundane rhythms of the jail. But even in the closeness of shared entertainment, like watching TV, proximity was not an either / or scenario. Anna, who was six weeks preg-nant in jail, was angered by the way deputies worked through carceral distance and closeness:

> Like, that's how they really—especially as far as deputized staff, that's how they talk to you. You know, that's how they treat you. Like, you're gutter

alligator or something that you can't even see in the gutter. And, they just look at you like "Uh." Like, if they touch you, they could just die. . . . But, you want to still have some type of dealings with me because you're bored. You know, some deputies, they want to play cards with you and they'll put on gloves. But, you asked me to play cards with you. Seriously?

What Anna described was not the familiar trope of deputies' indifference. Rather, she was frustrated by the ambivalent ways in which deputies socially engaged her. A deputy wearing gloves while choosing to play cards with an inmate perfectly encapsulates the tension intrinsic to the work of custody. Anna experienced this not as care but as a demeaning interaction in which deputies exploited her in the service of entertainment.

Evelyn, on the other hand, found card games with deputies therapeutic. During one postpartum incarceration, Evelyn learned that five-month-old baby Carolyn was in the hospital with recurrent seizures. Evelyn felt "frustrated" and "antsy," because she could not contact her aunt caring for her infant to get health updates. One night on her rounds, Deputy Walker could see that Evelyn had not yet fallen asleep. Although lights were out in the pod, the deputy gave Evelyn permission to get out of bed. At the deputy's suggestion, the two played cards in the dim light of the pod, and Evelyn shared her woes—like friends, perhaps like family members, but certainly not like powerful guard and submissive charge. And yet at the same time that they shared this intimacy, the power differential remained, for Deputy Walker had to give permission for Evelyn to get out of bed. Evelyn played at the deputy's whim (which could change at any moment). Custody came with this enmeshing of friendship and power.

Evelyn told me about this late-night game in passing, as part of the larger story about how she was managing her maternal angst. That the deputy would be a comforting part of that process was not exceptional to Evelyn. It was a kindness that did not surprise her after her years in jail. Evelyn had come to care about the deputies too. "Certain deputies and I, we are hella close. I ask how their children are doing. . . . I know Deputy Walker is sick [with an autoimmune disease]. So that's my friend. So, when she came back [to work] I was like 'Where you been?' She was like, 'I'm sick.' I almost cried." Evelyn's emotional response to a deputy's suffering is extraordinary. But it is also not surprising, given the care with which deputies enacted pastoral custody.

These examples demonstrate choices deputies made in cultivating what they deemed an appropriate distance from and proximity to inmates. This perennial topic in corrections magazines and at professional conferences is usually discussed in terms of the dangers of crossing a line—presumed to be static—between inmate and staff. Playing cards to comfort an aching mother, reveling in local sports pride, discussing books—these are not acts of crossing a line or staying behind it. These acts demonstrate the constant play of the line the carceral environment prescribes. That deputies made these choices about how to comport themselves with inmates was clear in the example of Deputy Faderman, who unequivocally believed his custody role was "to make sure that they do their time in accordance with the law, that's it." For after this, he added, "Now anything that we do outside of those parameters can be determined by whoever is making the decisions."

Those choices of engagement were precisely the point of the parameters of custody. In addition to custodial choices inside, jail deputies decided how to interact with the inmates once they were released from jail. Run-ins inevitably occurred, since the corners, alleyways, and daily rent hotels where many enjailed women spent their nonjail time were located just a few blocks from the jail. Some deputies told me they would say no more than hello if they ran into former inmates on the street. Other deputies told me they had gone to bars to have drinks with them.

This kneading of distance between staff and inmates, folding in and stretching out, comprises the fundamental activity of intimacy in the jail. Indeed, the carceral institution must constantly grapple with the intimacy that arises from the totalizing nature of its regimes. Interactions within its walls are fraught with ambivalence—a characteristic Berlant ascribes to everyday intimacy: "Contradictory desires mark the intimacy of daily life: people want both to be overwhelmed and omnipotent, caring and aggressive, known and incognito. These polar energies get played out in the intimate zones of everyday life."[22] Such contradictory desires were at the heart of how deputies and inmates engaged each other. Of course, incarcerated women had less agency than deputies in directing the kneading of distance. Some women yearned for closeness when they approached the platform; other women monosyllabically rejected deputies' erratic invitations to chat. Nevertheless, the consistency of seemingly rigid structures of carcerality, bureaucracy, and punishment were, paradoxically, what freed people in this space to explore the nuances of intimacy and care.

Moreover, while the carceral institution imposed a suprastructure of distance between inmates and staff, the broader realities of mass incarceration folded them closer together. Many of the women were connected to each other in their exclusion from the legal economy and in the poverty that precipitated much of their petty crime and resulted in their incarceration. These same women were connected to the deputies in that their incarceration provided the deputies with jobs, as well as the benefits and security that accompanied those jobs. The deputies depended on these women for their survival as profoundly—though in very different ways— as the women in jail depended on the deputies.

This interdependence was rarely discussed openly, although a few women shared their recognition of the economic role they played in deputies' lives. This connectivity points to another way that distance, intimacy, and care were interconnected in jail. Intimacy, Berlant also writes, "links the instability of individual lives to the trajectories of the collective."[23] This collective impulse emerged in the San Francisco jail, albeit intermittently, as a result of the distance deputies had from "the system" that deemed these women worthy of incarceration in the first place. It was not the deputies, after all, who arrested women and charged them with crimes. This bureaucratically imposed distance creates the potential for indifference toward inmates. But the deputies' removal from the decision also enabled them to generate their own narratives about why the women were in jail.

"WE'RE THE CATCHALL, BUT WE'RE NOT"

Most of the deputies I spent time with disclosed their interpretations of the state of affairs. Many of them offered predictably disparaging comments about the bad choices the women in jail made, which landed them, repeatedly, in jail. Yet there was also surprising consistency in the sympathetic and structurally oriented narratives deputies had cultivated over years of working in this environment. When I briefly described my research project to deputies or to senior administrative staff, they often offered a spontaneous analysis of the criminal justice system that included a deep awareness of the interplay between addiction, poverty, education, mental illness, abandonment, and abuse.

I was perhaps most surprised by Deputy Allston. I had observed her at muster and when she escorted patients to the jail clinic. She moved slowly and awkwardly, and was easily winded when she walked up stairs. Her face's resting expression conveyed annoyance. So I was taken aback, when we sat alone at a table in E-pod, to hear her narrative of "the system." I asked her what had kept her working at this job for thirty years. This was her ten-minute response:

If people get complacent and people just clock in and clock out without seeing the other human aspect of this, I question if they really should be in this profession, jail or custody.

I am very proud to be born and raised in this area. So, I feel that I'm a part of the population, and I don't consider myself necessarily apart. I think I'm lucky I've lived by this, if you're not part of the solution, then you're part of the problem. If you don't partake in this society and be part of it, then you really have no cause to complain. I mean, a lot of people do a lot of complaining, but then they don't actually participate in the communities that they are responsible for. . . . I think that when I'm dealing with this population, I bring a different—even the inmates will tell me, because they go, "Deputy Allston, you're cool. You're a regular person." I told them, "Yeah, I am a regular person, but I'm still professional. I'm still going to do my job. Don't expect me to bend over just because I show you my humanity."

These are the people that are riding the bus next to you. These are the people in the mall. These are the people in the movie theaters with you. These are the people that may go to your place of worship. . . . I mean, they're not absent from the society that you're in. They just don't see them as inmates. When you're in here it's so easy. You think they're locked away, but they're only here in transition. So, they're going to transition right back out.

The criminal is really drugs and alcohol, and domestic abuse. There is so much of it, all of these things. We know what they are, but we're not addressing them. So, consequently, we're just round and round. We're just like hamsters on a wheel with each and every person that comes through the system. I'm like, "But this is the same population. Do you guys not get it?" You can get a whole list of names, and once you start cross-referencing all of these names, then you get it. Oh, okay.

The catchall right now is the criminal system. That's the thing. We're the catchall, but we're not. This is what I've seen happen. We're not truly equipped or the most appropriate way to handle this segment of the population. We're not meant to be a mental ward. We're not meant to be a medical catchall. What happens with these people when they're not getting their needs met? Guess what? Why not commit a crime and at least get something. You get a bed. You get linen. You get food on the regular. You're safer than you would be living on the corner in an alleyway, or being beaten by your lover, pimp, whatever, or pusher, or being stuck in a mental institution or a psychiatric ward. This is where they come. This is where they go. Women that don't have access to just regular prenatal healthcare, dental, all of that stuff, why not commit a crime? They're going to get some of their needs met.

Are they criminals? I don't think so. They do things, and they live a high-risk life, but I don't think that they are. I would say about a good third of the population are just here for psychiatric problems. They do things and they break the law, but they're not really criminals. To me, they don't have the competency. They do what they have to do to survive, but they're not actual criminals.

They get programs here. They don't get this on the outside. At least here they get treated a little bit more human by my perspective.

Deputy Allston's monologue perfectly summarizes one of the main analyses offered in this book: that society's abandonment of people has resulted in jail becoming their safe place; jail is not equipped to care for people in the ways they need, in ways that should happen outside of jail. In her reflection, Deputy Allston was aware of how we are all, including her, complicit in this phenomenon of locking people up as a substitute for providing adequate public services. This critical commentary also maintained a sense of distance from laws and decisions to incarcerate certain people. Because her job was to be a custodian of people whom someone else decided to send to jail, Deputy Allston could retain a sympathetic proximity to the women she guarded.

Shortly after this conversation, I saw Deputy Allston comforting an inmate after bad news from court. Her words of solace, her concerned facial expression, and the basic fact of her attention to the inmate's suffering displayed her care. More broadly, her comprehensive assessment, culled from over thirty years at her job, linked her to the inmates through a shared sense of injustice. Of course, Deputy Allston participated in the injustice, too—her caregiving took place in an unjust arrangement. But nonetheless she could script herself—quietly, as she told me she had never shared these views with anyone—into a collective narrative, one that connected her and the inmates to the inhumanity of the criminal justice system. Deputy Allston's consciousness was part of the intimacy and care that characterized her enactment of custody.

CUSTODY VS. MEDICAL

This distance from systemic and legal operations that facilitated caregiving also arose from deputies' separateness from medical services at the jail. Deputies were necessary mediators between inmates and medical staff. Women relied on deputies to transmit information about their health needs in the pod to nurses and to ensure that they got necessary care. Deputies knew that medical care could be variable in terms of response time and quality. For example, one morning at 1 a.m., Chandra told Deputy Peterson she was having severe abdominal pain. Deputy Peterson called the head night nurse, who told her someone would try to come, but there were only two nurses covering the entire jail. Then they waited.

CHANDRA: You called medical?
DEPUTY PETERSON: Yeah, I called medical. They said you've got to wait.
CHANDRA: But I'm in pain!

Chandra was groaning loudly. Deputy Peterson worried about other people trying to sleep, as well as Chandra's discomfort. But there was nothing more she could do, other than shrug her shoulders and furrow her brow with sympathy; "I'm sorry, I'm sorry, I already called medical." What more could she do? She was not a nurse. Inmate and deputy waited together, aligned.

Eventually the nurse came, performed a cursory exam, and diagnosed the patient with indigestion. Some Tums eased Chandra's pain. As the nurse gathered his things, Deputy Peterson chimed in: "Could you give her a few more for the rest of the night?" He did. I observed similar moments of advocacy, when deputies sat with waiting patients, stroked their shoulders, reassured them verbally, and generally tried their best to comfort them.

Some deputies commiserated with inmates when they felt that their symptoms were disregarded or mismanaged. Deputy Allston got worked up as she shared observations about the provision of medical services in the jail:

> There's some inattentiveness [from the nurses]. There's no real listening sometimes. . . . There are some nurses that I'm looking at what they're doing and I know that it's not right, but I'm not going to step in. I'm not a medical person, but common sense dictates some things. I can't, for liability purposes, circumvent what the medical staff is doing when I know, I know, that it's not right. It puts us within a rock and hard place, because we're not going to tell the medical their job. *It's really gut wrenching sometimes. It's extremely difficult.*

Deputy Allston's frustration involved both sympathy for inmates as well as awareness of her own position in the risk-management scheme of the jail. Despite her authorized power, it was a liability issue to challenge medical staff's expertise. And so in these instances of medical inattentiveness, Deputy Allston would patiently listen to women's complaints. Some deputies even offered tactical suggestions, directing them to nurses they had come to trust as competent, and steering them away from others. Deputies' distance from the medical system in jail, like their distance from the system that sent these women to jail, allowed them to tend medical issues in a nonclinical way. For Deputy Allston, dealing with the shortcomings of the jail medical system was part of her custody mission, especially when, she suggested, nurses did not adequately serve this function: "It's us that are actually watching the inmates, making sure they're safe and secure while they're in custody during the time they're incarcerated." Deputy Allston applied the custody language of "safety and security" to the job she thought the nurses should be doing. This implied both a health and caregiving dimension to her understanding of safety and security. Yet because of the nurses' deficiencies, it was "actually" she who had to do this work. This conflation of expected roles of caregiving and control is representative of the contradictory nature of pastoral custody.

PARENTAL CUSTODY

In addition to the custody of law enforcement, another common usage of "custody" is in terms of parental guardianship. Custody, in this case, means an official certification of who is legally bound to care for a child. Parental custody is called into question in cases of divorce or institutionally defined inability to parent, where the institution is usually CPS. Kima, Evelyn, and women like them frequently discussed gaining custody of their children. It was perhaps a cruel irony that they were themselves "in custody," as they fixated on the custody of their children. The parent-child relationship, too, contains elements of pastoral care, in that it combines the supervision and regulation of behavior that characterizes the shepherd's benevolence. Relationships between parent and child are, of course, variable and contradictory, capable of love, violence, care, indifference. The lens of parental ties is thus apt when considering the custodial role that jail and its staff play in the lives of women cycling through its space. As one deputy remarked about the multiplicity of her role, "Sometimes you're required to act as medical [staff], psychiatrist, *mother, father,* confidante" (emphasis added).

The authoritarian cadence to how prison and jail workers speak to inmates is well known. But it should not be taken for granted simply as part of the process in which prisoners become subjects, or as a paramilitary form of punishment. Seeing the authoritarian parental dimensions in deputies' pastoral custody is important in understanding how jail can be experienced as home for women like Kima and Evelyn. At mealtimes, at pill call, when calling out women to line up for court or clinic, I heard deputies bellow instructions with loud, domineering, and even demeaning tones. At pill call one evening, Deputy Walker barked at the women: "Line up! Like ducks in a row. Remember kindergarten, first grade? Line up! No talking. You don't need to talk to get your pills. One line! You think I'm joking?" Threats to "write you up" for not following instructions were common, as were instructions to "get your lazy ass out of bed." These moments, as revealed by the elementary school reference, were infantilizing. Chandra compared this infantilizing treatment from the deputies to her own childhood experiences. "I was abused as a child. The petty psychological interactions with the deputies, they feel emotionally abusive. I'm being treated like a child."

Others have written about the parental character of carceral custody. In her account of women in prison from the 1970s, sociologist Kathryn Watterson elaborates on Chandra's analogy.[24] Watterson likens the entire prison system to an abusive parent, infantilizing women and creating a situation of forced dependency whereby inmates rely on the total institution for their every need.[25] Rhodes sees, as well, the less-abusive possibilities of parenting in a prison setting. Professionals who work with mentally ill and behaviorally challenging inmates, for instance, can assume a "parental orientation" with inmates to distance themselves from "custodial imperatives" of safety and control. They can then be more attentive to prisoners' emotional states.[26] The San Francisco jail deputies' periodic parental tendencies help us see that custody is itself a form of care which sutures kindness and cruelty together.

Some deputies were conscious of this move to treat adult inmate women like children, but they believed that this was what they needed. "Most of them never had a mother to teach them how to behave," I had several deputies reflect to me after yelling orders like a drill sergeant. Informal decorum lessons were common, with deputies correcting inmates on how to say "please" and "thank you," and on how to talk without being noisy. The parental impulse at these moments, though disciplinary in nature, also came from the parental place of care, of trying to impart wisdom to a developing child.

By virtue of their jobs, deputies were present when women had interpersonal conflicts with other inmates over watching TV in the pod, upsetting phone calls with boyfriends, or, as described in chapter 5, when they had miscarriages. Deputy Harrison possessed a sense of inevitability about the advisory role her presence cultivated. "I mean, at first they have no other choice but to talk to us. When it comes to certain issues, they don't know where to go. They come up—it could be a legal issue, it could be medical, it could be they're having issues with their bunkies, or they're having issues with other deputies." Deputy Harrison was blunt in her translation of this element of necessity, the insistence of presence, into parental guidance.

I almost feel like they're my kids, and I actually say that to them when they're just being pestering. I'll be like, you guys are worse than my kids.

I have to clothe you, feed you, I have to take you to the doctor, I have to answer your questions, and you know. . . . I mean, back then a couple of years ago before I got into the church and stuff like that, my attitude was like, you know, I don't even want to hear it because you're saying the same old thing. Now, I don't say that to them. I do give them the lectures, and I tell them you can go ahead and cry if you want. I don't care. You're going to hear it because you know you did wrong. You know you messed up, this and that. So, I still listen to them, because that's what they want. That's what they need. Maybe this will be the time, or maybe something I say will be enough to make them say, "You know what? She said this, and I'm going to try." You know? So, I still give it a try.

Her attitude was representative of what many other deputies also expressed. It is also suggestive of "tough love"—a classic, though not always effective, parenting approach. Another deputy similarly echoed her view of herself as parental in her job; in her case, she noted its impact on her own desire to have children, for "it's like birth control to work here. . . . I don't need kids with this job!" Clearly, then, many deputies at the San Francisco women's jail experienced their custodial role as parental.

All of this points to the complexity of the relationships involved in custody. The daily work of a custody officer in jail may, officially, consist of maintaining safety and security. But when that job occurs in the collective living space of inmates, where every aspect of the women's lives must be administered, it is impossible to avoid intimacy, even if confronting it means actively rejecting it, such as with hand sanitizer or gloves. Through custody, jail creates a forced and enforced intimacy among jail workers and inmates in collective living spaces, and makes it possible to conceive of the jail as a type of home.

8 At Home in Jail

Sitting in the cold royal blue chair
Reminiscing ten years that loneliness bears.
Inclined to recite an unnatural form.
Stuck in a cell, a fishbowl for a dorm. . . .
Lying flat on a mattress, which felt hard as cement.
Resuscitation of joy, which was bound to ferment.

Excerpt from "Poetry Blues," by Kima

"MY WORST DAY IN JAIL . . ."

Kima and I sat in one of the classrooms in E-pod, where we could have some auditory privacy. The glass walls of the room allowed other inmates and deputies to look in, but Kima was not concerned about this; she was accustomed to the constant surveillance of jail. She was also accustomed to the people who were watching her. She felt at ease in E-pod. Kima, too, looked out through the glass: at who was talking to whom, who was sitting where, what time was displayed on the clock. Kima had just returned to jail, having been on the streets for only a few days since her last incarceration. With the distractedness that I had come to expect in our conversations, Kima looked through the glass, picked at her nails, then looked down at her feet. She wore standard issue flip-flops. On each, a name was etched in blue ballpoint pen: "Dante," on the left, commemorated a pregnancy she lost through miscarriage; "Koia," on the right, recognized her five-month-old baby who was now being cared for by one of Kima's cousins.

I asked Kima whether she thought she would try to go to a drug treatment program again after jail this time. Her ruminations on life in a program quickly led her back to her present situation in jail, and where she had come from off the streets. "I mean, my worst day in jail is way better than my best day on the streets," she said. I had heard Kima say this before, but each time the comparison emerged, I had to pause to digest it. It was a profound statement. Kima continued, "It is hard out there. It's danger-ous. You never know when stealing something from someone's car is going to get you killed."[1]

Kima lived in a constant state of uncertainty and danger. Her survival-ist mode of living included the daily potential for physical and sexual vio-lence from fists, knives, guns, being raped, and taking drugs. "I always get hurt when I'm out of jail," Kima said, and I looked at her right index finger, which was swollen, red, and missing a nail. On the streets, she had burned her index finger with a hot crack pipe, and the wounded skin became infected. Within twenty-four hours of her arrival in jail, she had seen one of the clinicians, David, in the clinic. He lanced open her swollen digit so that the pus could drain out, and prescribed her antibiotics. Kima contin-ued, offering insight into her own recidivism: "I always get hurt when I'm out of jail. I think that's why I keep coming back here; even though I don't like it, at least it's safe."[2]

Kima summarized here a tragic state of affairs, one in which economic insecurity and the frayed safety net, coupled with the expansion of carceral institutions, have made jail a safe and even desirable place for women like her.[3] In contrast to their precarious and sometimes violent lives on the streets, jail provided safety and stability, and thus became a version of home. But this version of home is shaded with the knowledge that safety is predicated on criminality: punishment is the institutional form that safety and security takes. Kima's index finger, injured on the streets and healed in jail, symbolizes the relationship between the violence of the streets and the care of carcerality.

"HI, FAMILY"

In the previous chapter, I discussed how custody relations acquire character-istics of parent-child relationships. The familial metaphor for life inside institutions of incarceration extends to relations among inmates themselves.

Indeed, several scholars have conducted studies of the familial dynamics of daily life in women's prisons. Their analyses reveal that it is common for women who are incarcerated for multiple years to form family groupings. Studies from the 1960s of the social worlds female prisoners created emphasized the importance of kinship structures; they described how women imported traditional male / female gender roles into same-sex yet heteronormative sexual and familial dyads.[4] Later studies explored how crafting a pseudo-family structure, including sexual relationships, which replicated women's familial relationships in the community, was central to how women experienced prison.[5]

Barbara Owen's study of a California prison in the 1990s also affirmed the centrality of family and inmate relationships to women's ways of existing in prison. Relationships with staff were less important and less nuanced than relationships between inmates, she argued. In fact, Owen characterized inmate-staff relations as being either cooperative or conflict relationships.[6] These and other studies present a limited view of prison kinship.[7] While they delve into some emotional and physical intimacies among inmates, they do not incorporate custody staff, presuming them to be static rule enforcers. Furthermore, they rely on stereotyped notions of gender identity and the nuclear family, while hypersexualizing women in prison. Despite the limitations of these studies, they reveal the potential for different types of familial connections within the communal living arrangements of incarceration—even in jail, where different people come and go every day.

This was most evident in D-pod, a designated, in-jail drug treatment program run by the community organization Whitman House.[8] Whitman House also ran community facilities that many incarcerated women had spent time in, either voluntarily or by court mandate. The agenda to impose familial ties was announced by the program's name: SISTERS— "Sisters In Sober Treatment Empowered in Recovery."[9] In fact, the counselors who came to the jail to facilitate the program taught the women to call each other family. During the evening ritual of "sunset circle" in D-pod, the women shared their feelings, and something about their day, beginning their individual testimonials with "Hi, family."

This mantra seeped into the way people talked to each other and to me about the program. Most of the women from D-pod with whom I interacted commented, without prompting, on how special the place was, how it felt like family. This is not to say that D-pod contained a clear family structure, or that, in their parental custody role, deputies headed a D-pod family unit.[10] But it speaks to the possibility of overlap in the institutions of jail and kinship. Nellie, the woman whose miscarriage I discussed in chapter 5, reflected with gratitude on the warmth of D-pod, which she missed when she moved to E-pod: "D-pod was so much better. Over there we all acted different over there. It was just such a loving family over there. It was so great over there, you know? It really was. In D-pod it was my sisters over there. We was all cool, and it was like a family." Nellie proceeded to talk about her miscarriage experience, and how kind and supportive inmates and deputies had been. It had been one month, but she still warmed to the thought of the deputies who helped her. "They have a heart too. You know they do. So that made me feel good to know that they do care."

Notably, the tenor of D-pod appreciated by Nellie and others seemed to evoke family in their nonjail lives. Other studies of family networks in women's prisons also consider inmates' outside families, and show how women try to replicate their outside family life in prison.[11] But Nellie, like Kima, hardly had the predictable nonjail family alluded to in the prison studies. Nellie spent her early childhood with her mother and stepfather. Both were drug addicts, and her stepfather, whom she called Dad, beat her mother often. Beginning at a young age, Nellie helped her mother steal things to finance her dad's heroin addiction, because when he was high, he was not abusive. He only beat Nellie once, an incident she remembered vividly. Still, Nellie thought of him as "a good dad. As far as like he took care of me and made sure I had what I needed and everything." It didn't matter that "what I needed" were items Nellie and her stepfather stole together.

Nellie's mom was in and out of prison much of Nellie's childhood. Eventually, Nellie was placed in foster care. Starting at age 13, she had children of her own. But Nellie remained close with her mom, and wanted to be with her. One way she spent time with her mother was to learn from her:

> Selling sex was something that my mom did. My mom did it, and I'd do what she was doing. I was never encouraged to do it. It was never forced on me. I asked her to teach me. That's what she did, because I asked her to. Me and

my mom was like this [crosses fingers]. My mom, that's my best friend. So, she taught me. I knew it wasn't right for her to show me, or to tell me, but what was she going to do? That's why I love my mom. I miss her so much. . . . We did drugs together and everything. We had a great relationship though. A lot of people didn't understand it, but I had the best mom there was.

Nellie loved her mother deeply. She even stopped using crack for four years to care for her mother, slowly dying from hepatitis C. It was now nine years since her mother's death, and Nellie's eyes still welled up with tears as she told me about her mother.

Nellie's adult family life was similarly disjointed. She had nine children. Though she knew where they were and was in touch, she had only intermittently raised them, due to her struggles with addiction and CPS involvement. It was love for her children, in part, that had led to her current incarceration; she had wanted to make some fast money selling drugs and turning tricks in San Francisco to buy Christmas presents. Nellie's nonjail family experience was based on a combination of consanguinity, co-habitation, separation, shared drug addiction, provision, and care. Nellie's D-pod family, with the exception of biological relatedness, had these elements too.

Similarly, Kima spent her childhood moving between the homes of her drug-addicted mother, aunts, her grandmother, and the streets. She had yet to have a consistent relationship with any of her three children. Kima was angry that a distant, biologically related cousin was currently caring for baby Koia. But her anger was not, she told me, because she had not seen the cousin in fifteen years. Instead, she resented the guardian, and denied her familial ties, because the cousin was not black like Kima and her baby: "Everybody's basically saying, 'Well, she's with family, Kima.' Be okay with it. She's not fuckin' family. If she was family, she wouldn't be white." Kima then considered whether it was love, rather than race, that made a family: "Well, as long as she's being loved. Yeah, okay, as long as she being loved. I don't know that either. She could be with my mama and not be loved, 'cause we were with my grandmother and we had a hard time being loved by my grandmother. So that's just another loophole to me." Family, whether tethered to race, biological relatedness, or love, was not a straightforward relation for Kima.

Indeed, kinship, that classic object of anthropological study, has always incorporated a range of fictive kin relations.[12] Was D-pod sincerely a family environment for Kima and Nellie? Or were they both merely adopting the language of the SISTERS program? Perhaps we can take a cue from Kima's relationship with Deputy Lewis, who had worked at the jail for six years, and whom Kima liked. Kima was relieved when Deputy Lewis came back to work after her own maternity leave, and proudly showed her pictures of baby Koia. They also talked about the supervised visits Kima had with her infant. Kima's familial feelings toward Deputy Lewis were encapsulated by the name she called the deputy: "Titi," an affectionate nickname meaning "auntie." Kima proudly pointed to Deputy Lewis one day and said, "See, there's my titi. She'll help me." Kima was having a skirmish with another inmate and wanted to be moved to a different pod. She trusted that her "titi" Deputy Lewis would try to make it happen. For Kima, this trust was enabled by the custody provided by Deputy Lewis. Both Deputy Lewis—who spoke in chapter 7 about her role including being "mother and father"—and Kima likened their co-presence to fictive kin.

Kinship also involves a diverse set of relations through which people experience "processes of caring and being cared for."[13] Not all relations of care involve kinship, and not all familial relations include caregiving. But relations of care can nonetheless be a foundation for experiences of kinship.[14] Deputies in the San Francisco jail, for the most part, recognized jail as a space where people experienced the need to be cared for. Their recognition may have been demonstrated through the custody mandate, in the simplest sense of tending to functional aspects of living—food, sleep, hygiene. But even some of the gruffest deputies, when I talked with them individually, offered deeply sympathetic analyses of their charges, and expressed desire to help these women break out of their cycles of incarceration and addiction. Kima had come to expect that her Titi would help. Nellie felt nurtured by deputies and inmates comforting her through a miscarriage. These relations of care helped prompt women to use words like family and titi. What's more, the familial dimensions of jail tapped into an ideal of stability and need fulfillment that many of these women had not experienced growing up or in their current lives outside of jail.

HOMECOMING

Familial and caregiving intimacies, ambivalent though they might be, helped to furnish the jail with the trappings of home. Indeed, as one incarcerated woman told me, "Some people, it's just like, when they're in jail, they're home." Kima was even proprietary when I asked her once what she thought about the fact that many deputies treated medical staff like they were guests: "Guests? *They're* [the deputies] the guests. We're here all the time and I don't care how many doubles they work they're not here all the time. We shit here. We go to church here." Inmates continuously inhabited the space of the jail, but deputies left at the end of their shifts and could go elsewhere to eat, pray, and sleep. According to Kima, this ability to leave made deputies guests in the inmates' space, the inmates' home.

Deputies observed a homecoming quality, as well, when women returned to jail. I watched as recently arrested women entered B-pod. Though ragged from the streets, still high or coming down, many of them brightened when they saw familiar faces. They smiled and waved to friends, with what one deputy joked was a "Miss America wave." "Hey girl!! Good to see you! How you been?" Women knew each other from the streets, from previous times in jail, or both. They also knew the deputies. Kima actually kept a few items, such as poems she had handwritten, stored in jail. When released, she entrusted an inmate with a longer sentence with these belongings, which she would retrieve a few weeks later when she returned after a chaotic run on the streets. Administrative reports, of course, would simplify this reality into a recidivism statistic, rather than representing an intimate relationship with the institution.

Upon arriving in B-pod, most women knew the routine, and needed little directing from pod deputies to the bedrolls containing a sheet, a blanket, and a towel, with which they would make their beds on a thin, dark blue, foam mattress in their assigned cell. And then, exhausted from whatever preceded their arrest and from the processing of CJ1, they would plop down on their assigned bed and sleep. Evelyn, as with many others, would sleep for days at a time, catching up from a month of street-life insomnia based on having no safe place to sleep, her body crashing from the adrenaline surge of crack.

Familiarity, routine, rest, safety. These elements are, at a visceral level, evocative of home. A place that is once defined by carcerality and qualities of home begs the question: what is home? Scholars have long been concerned with the concept of home. Government agencies attempt to define the absence of home in census data about homelessness. Hallmark cards and pop songs try to capture the meaning of home with platitudes such as, "Home is where the heart is." Home is at once an imagined ideal and a material structure. Theories of home have explored its relatively recent emergence as a physical place within which property and people are safe.[15] Home is also understood as a site for the maintenance and reproduction of social norms, as well as a consumptive unit.[16] Feminist theorists have long argued that the gendered domesticity of home has naturalized repressive cultural expectations for men and women.[17] Given these varied social, economic, political, and cultural dimensions, home defies a singular definition. Instead, home might be considered a field of experience, a way of being "at home in the world."[18]

The absence of home, or homelessness, is perhaps one way to contextualize Evelyn and Kim's experience of jail as home. By official and common-sense understandings, they were homeless: they lacked permanent addresses; they moved from the corner to daily rent hotel rooms to drug treatment programs to extended kin's houses to jail.[19] Their reality out of jail was not unlike Bourgois and Schonberg's vivid description of the everyday lives and broader political economy of homeless drug addicts, or Knight's account of pregnant women struggling with addiction and marginal housing.[20] The people who Bourgois, Schonberg, and Knight describe live precariously, excluded from the mainstream economy and experiencing, alternately, forced dependency on the state and abandonment by it. Despite being categorized as homeless, these people also build shelters, informal economies, internal racial hierarchies, and systems of care; they have intimate and affinal kin relationships. The category "homeless" here has meaning only as a political and demographic label, for these people find ways of being at home in the world.

DWELLING

The experience of home involves people, sentiments, relationships, inhabiting space, all in ongoing negotiation of ways of being in the world. To inhabit a home is to dwell in it, but to dwell does not necessarily require a particular place. According to Heidegger, dwelling is an essential feature of being in the world; it is what humans do.[21] We dwell in buildings we build and inhabit. "To dwell," he writes, "means to remain at peace within the free sphere that safeguards each thing in its nature. *The fundamental character of dwelling is this sparing and preserving*" (italics in original).[22] Dwelling, therefore, is a process of ensuring safety in order to exist in the world. Relatedly, home is a way of dwelling, and dwelling is a way of being at home. Careful not to romanticize Heidegger's conception of dwelling, Timothy Ingold reminds us that home may not be a pleasant or peaceful place for all, and that its dwelling practices take place within fields of power.[23]

Infusing Heidegger's existential take on dwelling and safety with Ingold's recognition of the relational power aspects of experiences of dwelling provides a useful framework for thinking about how jail is home. Heidegger's idea of "Safeguarding each thing in its nature," which implies that home preserves the sense that it is safe to be oneself, occurs "within the free sphere." Ingold considers unequal power relations. These positions are not mutually exclusive, and facilitate the perspective that people can safely dwell in places laden with hierarchical regimes, like a jail.

To some degree, the notion that people dwell in carceral institutions is not surprising. Ethnographies and personal accounts of life in prison depict how women, confined to the same place for extended periods of time, create semblances of home life.[24] The prison is where their lives unfold—where they eat, sleep, bathe, and socialize—for the duration of their incarceration. Predictably, humans do what they can to build a comforting, familiar space when forced to live in a confined space for an extended period of time.[25] This building is what Heidegger equates with dwelling.

Michael Jackson further explores the existential qualities of home, ones that are untethered from spatiality. While wandering with the Walpiri, a nomadic Aboriginal tribe in Australia, Jackson studies how people "transform givenness into choice so that the world into which they are thrown becomes a world they can call their own." What emerges in this process is a lived relationship, sometimes contradictory, among elements, people, sentiments, imagination, materiality, fixity, and movement. The ongoing transformational processes are what constitute "being at home in the world," Jackson argues.[26]

While this conception of home as making a world that feels one's own is useful, the notion of transforming givenness into choice is problematic. Even for the Walpiri tribe, the experience of being at home in the world is involuntarily shaped by the effects of colonial violence and the dispossession of their land. This is true, too, when it comes to incarcerated women who forge ways to feel at home in their carcerally confined world, where their noncarceral lives are characterized by structural violence and racial subordination, rather than free choice. These writings about home frame the everyday features of prison as a spatial-temporal process in which people "do their time" while "carving out a life" for themselves, processes of building and dwelling.[27]

Jail is different than prison. People come to jail for uncertain durations that last anywhere from a few days to a year, and, as discussed, the constant flux of people gives jail a more dynamic configuration than prison. The short intervals of recidivism—during the time I knew Kima, she returned to jail within anywhere from three days to two months of her release—give jail a paradoxical sense of stability and predictability. That is, because jail is folded into the rhythms of people's lives, it can exist as a source of constancy. Instead of working to make themselves at home in the world of jail, as in the studies of life in prison, these women are already at home. Jail exists as a place of refuge rather than as a place where these women must actively create a sense of refuge. The stability of jail in these women's lives gives rise to a fleeting domesticity, in which the rules and prescribed arrangements of power in this forced collective-living situation enable affective relations and intimacy.[28] The seaming together of domestic intimacy and the rule enforcement of carceral custody is characteristic of jailcare.

REFUELING AT HOME

The majority of the women in the San Francisco jail—73 percent if you go by recent Sheriff's Department's statistics—expected to periodically land in jail. Their lives on the street were heavily policed. Many of them were on probation or parole, both of which entailed a plethora of reporting and behavioral requirements that furnished many "violation" opportunities, which, in turn, could send them back to jail. Furthermore, repeated exposure to the jail made it an unexceptional, normative part of their lives. The metaphor of the "revolving door" was so frequently expressed by inmates and deputies alike (and in criminal justice policy circles) that it is hard to overstate the degree to which it was taken for granted. As one inmate succinctly summarized, "they're like revolving doors here in jail. When I walk out, I'm walking right back in."

When I talked with women in jail about their lives, I usually asked whether they thought they would be coming back. With rare exceptions, most of them said yes, probably. I once asked Evelyn while she was preparing for release if she thought it would be her last time in jail:

> I'm not going to say that. I'm not going to say that. I hate when people say, "I'm never coming back to jail," and then you see them in jail again because that makes you a hypocrite. I don't want to be a hypocrite, so I'm not going to say that. I'm going to say I'm going to try to make this my last time. I'm not going to say this is going to be my last time, because I don't know. Everything I'm planning on doing right now might backfire. I might smell fresh air and everything that I have intentions on doing might go out the door. I think that I won't know until I'm tested with that free air. People say a lot of stuff when they're in here, and then they get out those 7th Street doors, and they smell that free air, and they don't have people in black and yellow telling them what to do, and they have the opportunity to walk up the street to 6th Street and get whatever it is under the sun they possibly might want. So, I'm not going to say it [that I won't be back].

Evelyn had grown accustomed to the presence of jail in her life, either as the place she was or the place she might soon be sent. In articulating her expectations that jail would continue to be a presence in her life, Evelyn identified the contingency of any sense of freedom in her life. The "free air" outside jail offered what she saw as the choice to use drugs, as 6th Street, a few blocks from the jail, teemed with people buying, selling, and using drugs. Evelyn also observed that deputies, "people in black and yellow," kept inmates safe by telling them what to do. In other words, the regimented structure of carcerality kept her safe from the free air on 6th Street that was heavy with drugs and violence. For Evelyn, that supposed freedom was an uncertain realm that reinscribed the likelihood of jail. Home is a place you know you can always return to. And so, for Evelyn, was jail.

Recidivism is more than a statistic of failure. It is a public account of how we as a society care for our most vulnerable and "disposable" individuals. As this and previous chapters have described, cycles of recidivism cultivated ambivalent intimacy among inmates and those who worked in the jail. The flux between jail and not-jail complicates Heidegger's perspective on dwelling, which he introduces as "to remain, to stay in a place."[29] Dwelling in jail adds a temporal conditionality to this sense of permanence.

The lived experience of the revolving door meant that people developed a relationship with the institution itself, and what its space enabled. Women knew to expect regimentation. They were told what to do by deputies, infantilized by requirements that they ask permission to use the bathroom, and served consistently bland food. Yet they had also come to expect the institution would be a place of nurturance or, in the language of both the women and the deputies, a place for "refueling."[30] This metaphor suggests a cycle in which fuel is drained and then refilled. Home, in accordance with its range of meanings, can also be understood as replenishment.

The cyclic aspect of women like Kima and Evelyn's lives included physical depletion during their intervals on the streets. Both of them faced thirty-day stretches in which they did not sleep more than a few hours at a time, rode the catecholamine rhythms of crack, and lived hour to hour to survive. There was immediate danger, too, in the ever present possibility for physical violence, sexual assault, and various complications from drug use, like when Kima burned her finger while lighting a crack pipe. Their bodies, as well as their psyches, were shaped and exhausted by this constant precarity. They knew jail would replenish them through shelter, food, and medical care. During her pregnancy, Evelyn had turned herself in, both to access prenatal care and to remove herself from the draining and danger-filled street environment. Jail was where Evelyn and Kima knew they could rest.[31] I should note, however, that although so many of the women I spoke to identified the relative safety of jail compared to the streets, jail in general remains an unsafe place for many people—from assault by inmates or guards, to the consequences of neglectful medical care rampant at other facilities.

The expectation that jail would serve as a refueling site manifested in many ways—slumber, nutrition, hygiene supplies, pharmaceuticals. Chapter 3 described the document triage practices for Nina, who continuously requested nutritional supplement shakes. Her insistence on these liquid calories was premised on her expectation that jail was where "I gain my weight back."[32] The brand name of these supplements, "Boost," symbolizes Nina's perception of jail as a boost to her nutrition before she returned to the streets.

Deputy Mullins did her part to help the women clean up and refuel when they came to jail. When women entered the pod, fresh off the streets, she strongly encouraged them to shower. "If they won't shower, this is how I get 'em to clean up," she told me on the platform one evening, opening her bag to reveal fragrant bottles of lotions and shower gels from Victoria's Secret, hyperfeminine upgrades from the standard-issue bar soaps. "This is my trick to get the stinky ones to shower!" Her enticements struck me as parental, a parent cajoling her child to clean the mud from her body after playing outside. Additionally, her "trick" combined regulatory governance with tender care in a way that was consistent with the ambiguous kindness women had come to expect from the jail.

Many women equated jail with home because of the opportunities it offered for rest and relaxation. Time in jail and prison is minutely planned, but within the regimentation, some is activity-free. Taken to an extreme, the absence of planned activities (like school or counseling) undermines the rehabilitative quality of incarceration, a widespread critique of many prisons and jails in the age of mass incarceration. But some women at the San Francisco jail appreciated the idle time, which they viewed as a respite from the chaos of life outside of jail. Jayla told me the story of the scar on her hand from a copper pipe heist gone awry. She laughed as she recounted the caper, and then told me she appreciated coming to jail as a break from that kind of turmoil. She bemoaned the excess of activities, reminiscing about the good-old, pre-pod days when jail had fewer daily activities. "Back then, there was time for respite, to relax. But now there's so much going on—class, programming—and they make you go to programming. If you refuse one day, because you are tired, then you can't get the other services they offer, they just take it as a refusal for everything else. You get punished for not going." For Jayla, the activity-filled agenda of rehabilitation at the San Francisco jail interfered with what she desired from jail: a periodic refuge, a place to rest.

One of the most notable ways jail behaved as a home-like site of replenishment was through medical care. Kima's injured index finger is a case in point, for she did not seek medical expertise until she came to jail. Women I spent time with in the pods and women who were my patients in the jail interfaced with the health care system outside of the jail in a range of ways. A few had primary care doctors at one of San Francisco's safety net clinics. Some women took advantage of their eligibility for Medicaid or San Francisco's innovative universal health care coverage plan. Most of them knew of clinics where they could walk in and get free health care services. And yet a sizeable majority of them admitted they only accessed medical care in jail. Ironically, some reported avoiding the county hospital's emergency room if they had outstanding warrants, since Sheriff's Department deputies provided security there and they did not want to get arrested. Nonetheless, people knew from experience that they could rely on jail for medical care. "It's just not a priority for me out there," a number of women admitted guiltily, ashamed to admit to a doctor that tending their addiction was a more immediate concern than medical attention.

Karen was one such woman. I came to know her during her cycles through E-pod, and her visits to the jail clinic. After a few days of rest in jail, her demeanor was friendly and spirited. Karen recounted the restorative role that jail played in her life by first referencing the familiar relationship she had with the medical staff:

> When I first get here they had me go down three days in a row when you're kicking to do vital signs and stuff. I go down there with attitudes and stuff. I give the nurses a hard time. But they're actually used to me. . . . The nurse, she just gave me my medication, right? She said, "Oh, my God, you look so much better. You look alive." I said, "What do you mean?" She goes, "You don't know how bad you look when you come in here." I be like, "Are you serious? Am I that bad?" She goes, "Oh, my God, you're like the dead walking, Karen, I'm not even going to lie."

Far from expressing disbelief over the nurse's assessment, Karen presented this exchange to me as an example of her awareness of jail's role in her well-being. The grammatical structure of Karen's quote is also telling:

"*when* I first *get* here," "*when* you *come* in here." The phrasing implies recurrent events, not a singular past occurrence.

Karen was grateful for jail. This gratitude resulted from her sense that her health was restored as her medical needs were tended in jail.

> This is going to sound dumb for me to say it, but I appreciate when I do get arrested because I get to get my health back together, you know what I'm saying? Most of my medical care is taken care of in the jail because for the last, I'm going to say, ten or thirteen years I've been incarcerated more than I've been outside. So yes, I do get my most care in jail. I be out there and not even caring about myself, which is not good. . . . You know, I kind of like— this is like—I needed a rest, I mean, get some proper food, eat right. I'm able to get my—and my thyroid medication, I take them every day, you know. *I'm able to get my health back in order and be like myself again.*

Jail gave Karen the opportunity to reorganize herself through attention to her physical well-being, like taking her thyroid medication. Health care in jail, then, was more than just the provision of services during the time she was incarcerated. Indeed, it exceeded the temporality and spatiality of jail and represented Karen's embodied being in the world, as she became like herself. And here we come back to dwelling. Recall that "the fundamental character of dwelling is this sparing and preserving."[33] "Sparing," Heidegger explains, "takes place when we leave something beforehand in its own nature, when we return it specifically to its being."[34] Karen's linking of thyroid pills and other medical services to her sense of self reveals that jail was likewise sparing for her. This is not to say that Karen and others who refuel in jail do not dwell outside of jail. Rather, it is to say that dwelling in jail is perversely sustaining for the existence of someone like Karen, regardless of where she is located.

The pervasive sense of jail as a space of refueling implies that the women who stayed there were fortifying themselves for life outside of jail. This was, to some degree, true, as descriptions of Karen's, Kima's, and Evelyn's everyday insomnia suggest. But the reality of recidivism meant that jail's "fuel" also existed for its own sake. That is, jail was the site of normative living for many people. Kima, ever an astute observer of her own situation, summed up the tensions between life inside and outside jail encompassed by the notion of "refueling": "We actually live here and survive out there."

DANCING TO BEYONCÉ

One of the first times I stepped out of the exam room in the jail clinic and into the pods was the day of the "D-pod Talent and Fun Show," which I had learned about from Kima at a prenatal checkup. When I arrived in D-pod, there were about thirty light blue chairs set up in rows on the lower level of the pod, all facing a makeshift stage area. The women of D-pod sat expectantly in the chairs, while a few raced around setting up props. Grace, a counselor from Whitman House who ran the drug treatment program in D-pod, was standing in front of the crowd reviewing ground rules for proper behavior at a performance—at least, a performance in a jail with deputies standing guard: no yelling; keep applause light. "Are we allowed to laugh?" an older inmate asked. "Of course you can!" Grace affirmed, as though it were a silly question; I looked up at the deputies on the platform and knew it was actually a logical question, given the circumstances.

Then the show began—singing, card tricks, humorous skits. One woman named Suzanne read jokes from a letter her grandmother had sent her. Her letter began, "Suzie, read these to the girls, I think they'll like them!" Suzanne lightheartedly editorialized for her podmates before continuing: "I think she thinks I'm at summer camp, not in jail." The other women laughed, and Suzanne had not even started the joke-telling. Kima often took center stage during the show—reciting Maya Angelou and her own poetry, singing a blues song, and dancing seductively to Beyoncé's "Get Me Bodied." During the performances, a few women sat in the back looking bored or doing a Sudoku puzzle. But most of them were engaged, swaying to the music, applauding quietly, and, since permission was granted, laughing. They were having fun. They were relaxed and at ease.

I did not think much of Suzanne's summer camp comment at the time, but it stuck with me. Perhaps because I spent much of my own childhood having fun and formative experiences at summer camp, I was unsettled by Suzanne's sarcastic analogy. But the more time I spent in the pods, the more I saw disconcerting parallels: the daily schedule, hanging out on bunk beds, communal living, fights and alliances, arts and crafts. In jail, too, a range of activities produced a range of emotions. Women had a safe place to have fun, albeit under the watchful eye of a uniformed officer, and with the constant threat of arbitrary degradation and violence.

Of course the relaxed, upbeat mood of the talent show was not present for every woman every day. To be sure, the same women who happily performed at the show, at other times got angry at fellow inmates and deputies. Women complained about being told what to do. I saw Kima lose her temper one day after a skirmish with her bunkie; she dumped the contents of her dinner tray into the garbage as soon as it was handed to her and mumbled, "This is bullshit." There were lockdowns and searches when drug possession in jail was suspected. These events occurred on the same days as movie showings and talent shows, all of them folded into the rhythms of what seemed like a normal life.

Holiday times in jail accentuated the unsettling opportunities to feel at home. On Halloween, Deputy Chang brought bags of candy for the women in the pod, and they joked about how they were already wearing festive orange for the occasion. Birthdays were also cause for women to celebrate. One evening during free time, I saw Kima limping to a narrow room known as the pantry, where there was a microwave for inmate use. "What happened?" I inquired about her limp. "Oh, I was doing some splits yesterday. I'm just sore!" Kima chuckled. I reflected on her ability and freedom to do splits in jail, and thought about the relative difficulty of doing so on the concrete sidewalks outside or the cramped quarters of a daily rent hotel room. Kima was making a batch of confections: Jolly Rancher suckers. She melted the candies in the microwave, stuck plastic spoons in the molten sugar, and waited for them to solidify into lollipops to hand out to a group of women celebrating an inmate's birthday. Included in the celebration were Kima's suckers, some art projects, and a makeshift cake concocted from commissary sweets. It was a traditional birthday party, made possible by the shared space of the jail, scheduled free time, and ingenuity.

At the same time that the holidays accentuated the jail's home-like qualities, they reminded people that they were separated from their families. This was especially true for Thanksgiving and Christmas. Even women who did not celebrate with their families outside of jail felt the punitive isolation from their world outside, and the exacerbation of feelings of disconnection. Perhaps recognizing this potential for holiday-induced despair, the jail hosted several holiday events. There were traditional turkey and stuffing meals, performances by a local gospel choir, and more talent shows. Members of a volunteer church group called "Women Aglow" brought guitars one evening. We all held hands and belted out a loud and spirited rendition of "Jingle Bells."

Kima appreciated this sense of normalcy enabled by the structure of the jail. One day, we sat in a classroom, catching up since her last incarceration, which had been nine days ago. She noticed that I was wearing new boots, and I noticed that her hair was shorter—she always shaved her head when she got to jail, because it was easier to manage. Kima again compared her worst days in jail and on the streets:

> My worst days out there—I would want it to outweigh any good days in here, but the truth is it doesn't. . . . I was tricking. I was selling dope. I was doing this. I was doing that. Right now what I want to do is—I don't want to have to go out there and live in that, and be in that chaos and deal with that struggle, 'cause it's hard. We just don't want to be in jail 'cause we don't want people to tell us what to do. But see, when we have people telling us what to do, that's how we end up living better. That's how we end up living, is 'cause somebody else is controlling it. We have a sense of some kind of normalcy.

Kima acknowledged that the same carceral regimes intended to punish her simultaneously enabled her to live what felt like a normal life. Jail was home; jail permitted Kima, as Heidegger wrote, "to dwell, to be set at peace . . . within the free sphere that safeguards each thing in its nature."[35] Here in jail, Kima could be the performer that her extroverted personality craved, to feel normal as she danced to Beyoncé. Despite the perceived and actual perils of the living environment of jail and the demeaning acts of punishment, women also experienced jail as a safe place—the ultimate safety net.

AT HOME IN JAIL

These thoughts of home, homelessness, refuge, and jail were running through my mind one cool November evening. Evelyn had given birth to baby Carolyn six weeks earlier and was living at Revelation House, a residential drug treatment program for mothers and babies. Despite the fact that Evelyn was doing all the "right" things at the time of Carolyn's birth,

CPS decided that she had not resided at Revelation House long enough to have her baby with her in the program.[36] The subsequent weeks were composed of a series of CPS-organized "TDMs"—team decision-making meetings—court appearances, periods gathering documents from Evelyn's own time in foster care, twice-weekly supervised visits with baby Carolyn, and group-therapy sessions. All the while, she was living with other mothers similarly struggling to make things work. To make things more difficult, this was happening during the immediate postpartum period, a time of hormonal fluctuations and physical and psychic recovery from pregnancy.

Social workers assigned to Evelyn's case switched several times, and every week seemed to bring a new, bureaucratically crafted argument for why she could not have baby Carolyn at Revelation House. Finally, one hopeful day in early November, just after Evelyn and I celebrated President Barack Obama's election to his second term, the judge planned to finalize Evelyn's reunification with baby Carolyn in two days. I picked Evelyn up and we met her sister Jada and Aunt Vera in the hallway outside the courtroom. We were all a bit giddy with excitement. And then Evelyn's lawyer showed up, late and looking worried. It seemed the attorney assigned to represent baby Carolyn had introduced a procedural delay to the reunification. Coincidentally, this was the same attorney who had represented Evelyn's first baby, Jack, ten years earlier. When her baby was one month old, Evelyn left the drug treatment program for mothers and babies where they were living; baby Jack was then quickly swept into the foster care system. Aunt Vera was working on getting custody of him so that she could raise him, which Evelyn supported. But in the midst of the proceedings, Aunt Vera was hospitalized. Rather than finding a temporary arrangement until she got better, baby Jack's attorney fast-tracked him into adoption and terminated Evelyn's parental rights without the family's knowledge or consent. This forced separation was still heavy in Evelyn's and Aunt Vera's memories and hearts.

And now, inside the courtroom for baby Carolyn's placement, the judge expressed disbelief at the baby's attorney's demand for a technically based delay. She rolled her eyes and indicated through her questions that she believed it was time to reunite mother and child. Still, the judge was obligated to grant the child attorney's procedural request. She delayed reunification for another week. We were all angry and upset, but Evelyn took it in stride—she was accustomed to this roller coaster.

Four days later was that cool November evening. My phone rang as I settled onto my couch in front of a roaring fire. It was Evelyn. "Hi Doctor Sufrin. I left the program." Her voice was so matter-of-fact that I did not fully register what she was saying. "Yes, I left the program. I left three hours ago. I'm here on 16th and Mission. I called because I wanted you to hear it from me." The phone then cut out. I was in shock. I felt compelled to find her. So I took my heavy coat from the closet, grabbed an orange wool blanket for Evelyn, and left the warmth of my home. I then briskly walked, through my gentrified neighborhood of artisanal coffee shops, the seven blocks to Evelyn's corner, stopping only when I heard a street performer at a corner singing a beautiful acoustic rendition of the song my husband and I had danced to at our wedding: "Home," by Edward Sharpe and the Magnetic Zeros. "Home is wherever I'm with you" went the refrain. What was home for Evelyn? I wondered. Was it Revelation House? Was it the streets? Was it the hope of being with baby Carolyn?

Then I found her. She was sitting on a concrete bench at the 16th and Mission plaza, a place I used to think of merely as the entrance to a subway stop but now recognized as a hub of the drug economy. Evelyn wore a purple and gray–striped hoodie and wire-rimmed glasses she had borrowed from a woman at Revelation House. Her hair, decorated with golden and black braided extensions, was neatly pulled into a ponytail, and she clutched a Louis Vuitton knock-off purse she had gotten from a church charity event for Revelation House residents a few weeks back. Inside the purse were a few belongings, including photographs of baby Carolyn. She looked ladylike, out of place in this nighttime drug market. She also looked terrified. Her eyes did not blink much, and she seemed to be in a daze, which was how I felt, too.

Evelyn explained that she had left Revelation House because the women there "were irritating me." But we both knew that the real reason was Evelyn's profound disappointment at the court's repeated delay of reunification. I tried to persuade her to return to the program, or to let me take her to her Aunt Vera's house, but she gave reasons for why each suggestion would not work. Eventually, Quiana, a woman she knew from the streets and whom we both knew in jail, offered Evelyn the chance to stay the night in her room at the Travelodge Motel, a few blocks away. Quiana gave us the keycard and told us "Room 321." I escorted Evelyn to the motel and gave her twenty dollars. We hugged and she agreed to return to Revelation House the next day, and to call me. She did neither. Weeks later, I found her high on crack cocaine in another part of town. She wore the same purple hoodie; her glasses rested precariously on her face, missing one of the earpieces. I learned that the Travelodge only had two floors, a detail I had not noticed. There was no room 321.

Evelyn was back in jail two months after the cold November night she absconded from Revelation House. I sat with her at a table in B-pod. She spoke for nearly forty-five minutes about her relapse, her sense of failure, the constant pain of missing baby Carolyn. She paused her monologue only to shout out a warm hello to a woman below, a friend. Evelyn also made jokes and laughed as she told me stories. She looked rested and relaxed, unlike when I found her high on crack, hypervigilant, her clothes dirty, her glasses broken. Evelyn was now at ease. And then I thought of hearing the song "Home" en route to finding her that November night. Here in jail, it seemed, Evelyn was home.

Conclusion

Forever never ending, finding ways to belong

Kima, from "Poetry Blues"

MOTHERS AND BABIES

As I write, baby Koia and baby Carolyn each just turned four years old. Both are being raised in suburban homes by extended family members. Their mothers continue to live in the thoroughfare of drug-infested streets and the San Francisco jail. Since Koia's birth, Kima has been in and out of jail well over a dozen times. I last saw Kima in jail, when Koia was twenty months, a year older than when Kima had last seen her during a jail visit. With the names of all of her children etched into her flip-flops, Kima still spoke angrily about the people raising her children, deriding what she knew of their parenting styles and railing about the fact that her three children were in different homes. At the same time, she conceded that she was not able to live differently right now, even with a range of free housing and other services offered by her family and the city. She had not employed these services because, as she said, she was "still complacent. Still complacent with shit. Like, oh, it'll get better when it get better." Kima's fatalism about her life is complex, and signals the tensions among racial discrimination, discourses of personal responsibility, and the role of the safety net, including the ways she has internalized those narratives.

Baby Carolyn is a beautiful little girl with big brown eyes and a smile to match her mother's. Several times, I visited Aunt Vera's home on a quiet cul-de-sac in a suburb forty-five minutes from the same drug corners, daily rent hotel rooms, and jail where Evelyn still spends her time. I remain in awe of Vera's patience, love, and the sacrifices she makes to raise Evelyn's children. Vera and Evelyn have not been in touch since Vera declined a collect call from Evelyn over a year ago; Evelyn has not called back. During my visits, baby Carolyn and her older brother Adam, Evelyn's second-born son, danced around the living room and played with their piles of toys. It was hard not to notice the family portrait hanging on the wall, taken when Evelyn was about ten years old. In this posed photograph with her siblings and extended kin, Evelyn looks like a happy child— though I knew by that point in her life she had already been molested by her father and uncle. The normative scene in which a young Evelyn in a family photograph smiled down on her own children playing below was a jarring contrast to the precarious street life Evelyn was living in San Francisco.

I still wonder what would have happened to Evelyn and baby Carolyn if CPS had allowed them to live together at Revelation House. Would the immediate, constant (and supervised) presence of baby Carolyn in Evelyn's life and the opportunity to develop as a mother have prevented her departure from the program and her subsequent relapse? These questions can't be answered. What is clear is that Evelyn and Kima's reproductive trajectories both remain enmeshed in state control. This is true both in the state's orchestration of certain moments of lives, specifically in terms of their motherhood, and in the state's unfortunate abandonment of them at other moments.

Other scholars have written insightfully about the management of motherhood through the state's child welfare apparatus.[1] This book has attempted to show how, for certain marginalized women (who are, dispro-portionately, women of color), jail has become part of the experiences of managing their fertility and cultivating maternal identity. For some women, being pregnant in jail meant the intimate involvement of jail staff in making determinations about the conditions of their pregnancy, whether this meant hypermedicalization or breaking jail rules to provide special privileges. Jail also offered numerous opportunities for women to feel like mothers, even if they did not see their children outside of jail—opportunities that included classes, opportunities to commune with other incarcerated mothers, in-person visits with their babies, and Mother's Day celebrations. The versions of motherhood available in jail were deeply contingent and necessarily limited. And yet some women felt energized by these opportunities, even desired this jail-cultivated motherhood. There is, as Berlant would argue, a cruelty at the core of this narrative of motherhood, an attachment to an institution that also harms.[2] For women who had been raising their children outside of jail, jail disrupted their routines of motherhood. And for women who were interested in starting (or continuing) a method of birth control, the jail clinic provided birth control.[3] Whether cultivating a sense of motherhood, disrupting it, or enabling women to choose to prevent pregnancy, jail was deeply involved in how women experienced their reproduction.

Alisha, a woman I discussed in chapter 5, had not, as of the last time I spoke with her, during the winter of 2016, been back to jail since her pregnancy with Deijan in 2012. A statistical account of recidivism would call her a success. But those three and a half years were marked by uncertainty and flux. I saw or spoke to Alisha every few months, and each encounter contrasted with the last. She had had at least four stints in different residential drug treatment programs for mothers (some of the same programs in which Evelyn and Kima had spent time). Kicked out of one program for smoking, she managed to stay in the second program even after she got high on her way back from a court appearance, only to leave because the program was not set up for infants. Then she was happy to get a spot at Revelation House. Along the way, she had graduated levels of contact with Deijan, beginning with two hours twice a week, progressing to occasional overnight stays at Revelation House, and then, finally, living together full time at Revelation House and another program. When they were together, I observed her delight at being able to prepare his meals, dress him, and play with him. At one such live-in program, though, Alisha hinted to me that she thought she might be getting kicked out, "because I'm not following the rules." She was looking for another program for them both so she could complete twelve continuous months in a drug treatment program.

But Alisha relapsed several times. She was forced to leave whatever program she was in, and Deijan was put back in foster care. Judges and

CPS workers created various stipulations and schedules so she could still see him. Alisha married Deijan's father, with whom she rented an apartment, paid for out of her supplemental security income check, but her relapses meant she could not live there with Deijan. Eventually, Alisha's sister took him in. Alisha reported enthusiastically that Deijan was thriving with her sister, who was taking better care of him than Alisha could. Despite not being the primary caregiver to her son, she was more involved with him than she had ever been with her other two children. She was happy to see him every other weekend, and thought this arrangement was best for her and for Deijan.

While Alisha crafted an arrangement with her son that could coexist with her ongoing struggles with addiction, Kima and Evelyn had not seen their babies in years. For all of these women, giving birth does not inevitably lead to motherhood. Rather, motherhood is made through the involvement of state institutions—including jail—in their lives. To paraphrase criminal justice scholar Marie Gottschalk, this involvement is the jail beyond the jail.[4] Motherhood is not imaginary, but remains most vibrant in its imagined states in jail. This disjointed reality of maternity is cultivated by their intermittent stints in jail.

Life in "jail beyond jail" takes perseverance and patience. It requires court appearances, supervision, and the stress of rule-filled communal living in residential drug treatment programs. And yet, while Alisha has had more time with her son than Kima or Evelyn have had with their children, this fact cannot be explained by reductively claiming differences in character. Staying out of jail, Alisha told me, was due to the fact that "I haven't committed a crime!" Although she still used illicit substances, drug courts, family court, and drug treatment programs helped eliminate jail from her reality. Alisha accessed a number of safety net services, from official government welfare programs to community outreach services. Though not currently in jail, Alisha is certainly not free from other forms of carcerality, for her time with her son is intensely regulated by the courts, child welfare system, and behavioral models of drug treatment. Moreover, Alisha's contentment with her most recent arrangement of motherhood reflects similar state-managed forces as Kima's and Evelyn's experience of motherhood cultivated by jail. The maternal realities for all of these women show how jail is integrated into their experiences of motherhood.

JAILCARE

This book has argued that regimes of carcerality, whether in jail or a drug treatment program, cannot be understood solely in terms of the power dynamics of subject production. Rather, relationships within these regimes exceed the hierarchical arrangements that we might expect from a clinic or jail. These relationships are based not on some innate human connection that a carceral institution threatens to dismantle. Neither do these relationships serve as a foil to the dehumanizing forces of imprisonment. Rather, relations of care take form precisely within carceral structures. Jail staff bear witness to the effects of the suffering that people experience on the streets; they bear witness to and participate in producing certain forms of motherhood and the forms of life that are possible inside a jail.

Jailcare is thus a form of care that is fundamentally ambivalent. It arises amid circumstances in which a person's deservingness to be cared for is actively called into question, affirmed, and conditionally defined. Jailcare indexes the mutual coexistence of the violence of punitive discipline with the concern and attention of caregiving. This disturbing coexistence reminds us that vulnerability and care are core dimensions of social life, even in harsh institutional settings.

The incident I described in chapter 8 involving the Travelodge keycard for room 321 is a metaphor for this mutuality. In giving Evelyn a key to her motel room, Quiana was performing a gesture that initially appeared as caring and helpful. Later, when I learned that there was no room 321, I felt conned, as if Quiana had duped us. Perhaps she wanted to show Evelyn and me that she cared, that she wanted to help. A few months later when I saw Quiana in jail, she apologized to me for her error, offering a thin explanation about having given us the wrong keycard. This conning of care is a heuristic through which to think about jailcare.

Duplicity, Diane Nelson has argued, is the space in between the victim and perpetrator, in which the state can dupe: where it "claims to represent all the people, that is simply a cover for its docile service to a small class segment," and is "the carrier of both suffering and benefits . . . perpetrator and succor, it dispenses death *and* life."[5] Anyone can dupe or be duped. The space duplicity inhabits is also the space where the care and violence of jailcare exist. This care and violence are not simply opposite poles on a continuum, but are mutually constituted by duplicity.

The constitutional mandate that prisoners have a right to receive health care is emblematic of the tensions and duplicity involved in the "state's carceral burden": if the state is going to put people in the potentially dangerous environment of a prison or jail, then the state is obligated to protect them from harm.[6] The *Estelle* decision, which codified the carceral burden as a constitutional mandate, is the state-sponsored starting point for jailcare, legally binding care to incarceration. And although the care inside carceral institutions is variable in quality and scale from site to site, the state-declared legal mandate makes it conceivable that people—people who are otherwise failed by the state and marginalized by racial oppression—could desire the strange forms of care available inside, even as many incarcerated people may deeply mistrust medical care inside. While these tensions may be debated in courtrooms or codified in policy manuals, their experiential meaning emerges in relationships between jail workers and inmates who work through these tensions in their daily routines in the jail. The delivery of medical care is a crucial window into how carceral structures give rise to care. I have also shown how the ambiguity cultivated in the jail clinic seeps into the entire institution.

If ambivalence is a key sentiment of this project, then I would be remiss to not mention my own ambivalence in my relationships with these women. I first met Kima, Evelyn, and Alisha as patients when they were pregnant in jail. They told me about their drug use, and I saw Evelyn high on crack cocaine while pregnant. This was hard. Doctors are trained to do our best to suppress judgments of our patients' behaviors, to focus, instead, on helping them change. I, like many of my colleagues, contextualize behaviors understood to be unhealthy within the larger structural forces of inequality that have created conditions for pregnant women's addictions. I hold my concern for the harm that drug use may cause these women and their fetuses along with my understanding of and sympathy for systemic factors. As I got to know these women outside the clinical context, I grew even more invested in their overall trajectories, and so, I was frustrated and angry with Evelyn when she left Revelation House. I was disappointed when I saw her a few weeks later, high and selling crack—and I let her know my feelings. And while I was still disappointed when I talked with her in jail a few months later, I was also happy to see her, especially to see her rested and sober. This ambivalence between anger and concern is not something to be resolved. It is, rather, central to the form of care I have described throughout this book.

This book is not strictly about the institutional violence of incarceration, or about good things happening inside jail. Nor is it about trauma, though Evelyn and Kima's lives are saturated with it at individual and structural levels. To be sure, not everyone experiences jail (or prison) in the ways I have described; in places where medical care and other conditions are egregiously dangerous, jail is less capable of being a safety net. I continue to hear from incarcerated women and advocates around the country about pregnant women being told they do not deserve good prenatal care because they are in prison, about daily indignities and abuses of care against incarcerated pregnant women. Such harsh and substandard conditions require action and ethical attention. I want to be clear in acknowledging that many jails and prisons are more outwardly violent and cruel than what I observed at the San Francisco jail. Simultaneously, the emergence of jailcare signals the nuances of mass incarceration. This is a story about how people work through the inherent violence of the current state of affairs every day; about how they make meaning out of the unequal conditions that created an unjust reality of mass incarceration; and about the mechanics of care which can flourish even inside a punitive institution. It is about what happens to people failed in a myriad of ways by the safety net. These phenomena are deeply racially encoded. While it is troubling to think about care in the midst of the multiple forms of violence endemic to incarceration, any account of jail or prison that does not depict the paradoxes in which people live and work is incomplete.

The jail clinic is a crucible of biomedical caregiving, bureaucracy, socially mediated medical triage, intersecting professionalisms, jail's constitutive outside, punishment, health inequalities, citizenship, race, gender, and rights. Yet far from melting into each other in that crucible, these multiple registers remain in constant engagement, articulated in the social interactions among clinic staff, patients, and deputies. This dynamic environment exposes the tensions between the state's responsibilities to care for its people and its assessments of individuals' deservingness of care. This reality does not take for granted the answer to the questions "whose responsibility is it to care for people behind bars?" and "what care do they deserve?" Indeed, deputies address those questions every time they sneak a burrito to a pregnant woman or yell at someone to stop talking in the pill call line. Clinic staff enact their answers when they triage someone with a bulging abscess in the intake jail, or deny an inmate's request for a lower bunk chrono.

The elements of jailcare, tragically, sustain many people who come in and out of jail on a regular basis. They are what make jail part of the safety net, to catch people from the abandonment they experience on the streets. "Safety net" is an apt metaphor for jailcare, for a net can both rescue and constrain. Jailcare is a symptom of social failure, of abandonment of a group of people that includes poor, predominantly black women, whose reproduction has been vilified in policies and broader cultural narratives. Jailcare illustrates how mass incarceration and the frayed safety net are matters of reproductive justice, for they impair women's abilities to parent their children in stable and safe environments. The safety net's shortcomings are not simply a matter of quantity or funding, although shortages of public mental health care, housing, and addiction treatment absolutely play a role. Safety net inadequacies also emerge from the ways services are delivered, from—as the health department administrator I quoted in chapter 1 noted—the nature of the interpersonal relationships and how people are made to feel when accessing services; I witnessed a child welfare worker's hostile, meticulous gaze as she supervised Evelyn's visit with her newborn, a glare that, Evelyn told me, made her feel unfit to be a mother, even as she lovingly breastfed baby Carolyn. Jailcare reflects the failure of society to provide an adequate safety net and the failure of our social imagination to consider that these women have contributions to make to society.[7]

EXPANDING HEALTH CARE ACCESS, CONTRACTING MASS INCARCERATION

The connections between the deficiencies of the U.S. health care system and the health of incarcerated people have long been recognized by public health advocates. Now that the Affordable Care Act has expanded health

care access for millions of people, policy makers are paying closer attention to the links between systems. Prison officials are recognizing that if
Medicaid-eligible inmates are hospitalized for more than twenty-four
hours, Medicaid, rather than the prison, will cover the cost of the hospitalization. States that have expanded Medicaid eligibility recognize that
many more people cycling through prisons and jails will now, upon
release, be covered by Medicaid instead of remaining uninsured. Some
leaders have even gone so far as to say that this expansion could, by providing much-needed medical and mental health care and drug treatment,
keep people out of prison in the long run.[8] The San Francisco Sheriff's
Department devised a system to enroll inmates in health care plans before
they get released from jail, both because of projected savings in health
care costs for the city and because of a desire to improve health care access
for these individuals. Of course, much of this could change since, at the
time of this writing, Congress and President Trump are intent on dismantling the Affordable Care Act.

San Francisco's jailcare thus can be found not only in the ambivalent
relationships of care inside the jail, but also at the policy level. At the same
time that Sheriff's Department leadership approached me and other JMC
leaders to improve the conditions for pregnant women inside the jail, a
San Francisco multi-agency taskforce published a report promoting
community-based alternatives to jail for women in San Francisco. The
report was designed as a blueprint for how the city should use funds from
the 2011 Realignment law—the Supreme Court mandate to depopulate
California prisons—to benefit women. The taskforce at the time was imple-
menting a plan to prioritize sending pregnant women to halfway houses
instead of jail. These commitments—both to making jail more comfortable
for pregnant women and diverting pregnant women from jail when possible—are signs of San Francisco's progressive spirit. Indeed, this spirit is seen
in the fact that the jail population decreased by 29% in the five and a half
years I spent there. The city's probation department recently opened a large,
one-stop shopping center to connect people on probation with a dizzying
array of programs, benefits, classes, health care, and family services. San
Francisco is certainly trying to support people in the community and to
keep them out of jail. But these efforts do not replace jailcare. Nor do they
mean that jailcare is unique to the San Francisco environment, as opposed

to a jail whose health care is delivered by a private company. Jailcare persists in relationships and institutions that are the source of both suffering and benefits.[9] What's more, amid these efforts to improve criminal justice system services, San Francisco is experiencing an intense exacerbation of income inequality, fueled in part by growth in the technology industry; "tent cities" throughout San Francisco have made its homeless population more visible and thus drawn attention to some contradictions in the city's purported commitments to addressing inequalities.[10]

Conversations about criminal justice system reform have recently taken hold among conservative and liberal policy makers at local, state, and federal levels. Legislators, likewise at every level, are passing laws to change policies such as mandatory minimum sentences and punishments for nonviolent crimes. In San Francisco, a grassroots campaign succeeded in 2015 in halting the city from building a new jail.[11] Recognition is growing that the war on drugs and the building of more prisons are injustices that have deepened racial and economic inequality and remain unsustainable ways to govern. Former president Bill Clinton even apologized for his role in the prison boom. The Black Lives Matter national network of activism continues to draw attention to the connections between racial exploitation, mass incarceration, and the various ways that black lives are systematically destroyed. While these conversations are moving the needle on muchneeded reform, they have largely ignored the specific effects of mass incarceration on women.[12] Even as bipartisan conversations of reform consider alternatives to addressing nonviolent crimes, these discussions fall short when it comes to women, most of whom, like Kima and Evelyn, are behind bars because of the effects of trauma, substance abuse, and mental illness.

I would be remiss not to mention the potential impact that the election of Donald Trump as president of the United States might have on mass incarceration and the safety net. As I write, it is the eve of his inauguration, and much uncertainty prevails regarding his policy plans for the criminal justice system, health care coverage, and other safety net services. Yet his racially charged rhetoric and his nominees to lead key agencies that might help women like Kima and Evelyn—such as Ben Carson to lead Housing and Urban Development, Tom Price at the helm of Health and Human Services, and Jeff Sessions as Attorney General—suggest the reinvigoration of punitive, neoliberal policies that will further fray the safety net. While there is little information to predict whether federal sentencing will be harsher, there is nothing to suggest a proactive criminal justice reform agenda. What's more, Trump and Vice President Mike Pence's intended policies have punitive gendered elements to them, such as punishing women for having abortions; such attitudes could encourage federal and local lawmakers to further criminalize women's reproduction, such as incarcerating pregnant women for drug use instead of providing treatment.

The future implications of Trump's appointees and his divisive rhetoric against vulnerable groups are difficult to predict, especially when many criminal justice system reforms could still come at the state and local levels. But it seems reasonable to expect that education opportunities, health care access, addiction treatment, and affordable housing will be even more difficult for women like Kima and Evelyn. Trump-era policies are likely to further marginalize these women. Between Trump's campaigning as the "law and order candidate" and Sessions' racist, anti–civil rights record, there is certainly the potential for racialized mass incarceration to worsen. If policing strategies and sentencing laws do not change at the local level, it is likely that the modest decline in incarcerated populations we have begun to see could reverse.

In the midst of this critical and uncertain moment in which the characteristics of mass incarceration could be reformed or when they could also worsen, it is imperative to understand the reality of jailcare, and its manifestations in women's experiences of reproduction—for this is a reality produced in part by the abandonment and ineffectiveness of a safety net that has the potential to help people. Additionally, in this important moment, it is imperative to avoid the dangerous mistakes of the 1960s and '70s, in which asylums were closed without the necessary investment in community mental health care that people released from institutions needed. Real criminal justice system reform must come with real changes in social and economic programs to care for those whom the safety net has failed. Safety net services must also nourish possibilities for everyday relations of care, from sufficient resources to prevent service provider burnout, to undermining structural racism in programs, to approaches that balance the difficult tension between individual and structural accountability.

Investments in the safety net and ameliorating structural inequalities are essential. But they are insufficient to fully restructure the far and deep reach of incarceration into the fabric of the social, political, and economic reality of the United States. Gottschalk provides a breathtakingly detailed argument for the multiple components of lasting criminal justice system reform, one that sees prisons and jails only as places to house people who pose a grave threat to public safety.[13] While necessary, it is insufficient, she argues, to focus solely on investing in root causes of poverty and other forms of inequality; to define reform through a lens of racial inequality that ignores other marginalized groups; or to release nonviolent offenders, which would still leave the United States with an astronomically high incarceration rate. The current reach and depth of the carceral state requires all these things in order to contract it, along with sentencing reform to reduce sentences especially for nonviolent charges, improvements to abusive and inhumane conditions inside jails and prisons, restructuring the bail system, and a radical shift in the overall reliance on incarceration as punishment. Making more affordable housing realistically available, changing restrictive laws that prevent formerly imprisoned people from seeking employment, making health care affordable and accessible, devising novel strategies for treating addiction—these are but some of the strategies that could stabilize the precarity of the lives of women such as Kima and Evelyn. These are not quick fixes, and they require policy reforms, deep shifts in trenchantly racist social and economic structures, and improvements in the ways safety net services are provided. Jailcare is but one symptom of the failures of society to care for its most marginalized. Jailcare is a central feature of a society that depends on incarceration for much more than keeping the public safe from dangerous criminals.

FOREVER NEVER ENDING

It is disquieting to think about a liberty-depriving, punitive institution like jail as home. It is disturbing to observe Evelyn turning herself in so that she could be cared for, and to hear that Kima "prayed I went to jail." Yet ethnographic exploration of the tensions of everyday living in jail and the contrasting difficulties of survival outside jail has shown the logic in these apparent contradictions. The very structures of carcerality—such as custodial guardianship, the constant proximity of deputies and inmates, the constitutional mandate for medical care, communal living, and scheduled time for reprieve—gave rise to an environment where women experienced the certainty of care and a safe place to be a version of themselves that felt normal; in short, they experienced jail as being at home in an uncertain world. While I have shed light on the joy, comfort, and care that women can feel in jail, these experiences should not displace the broader unequal and racialized conditions that keep them cycling through jail.

However, naming marginalized women's desire for jail as merely another instantiation of their oppression flattens the human experience of their relationships with jail staff, and with the institution itself, into predictable replications of power dynamics. These women's actions within such an understanding would remain limited to the dichotomy of oppression or resistance. Instead, the everyday texture of jail must be understood for the myriad ways that human relations unfold—most surprisingly, for the intimacy of caregiving. These are real experiences for women in jail, full of comfort after miscarriages and ogling at photos of inmates' babies. Women can inhabit and desire seemingly repressive norms as a way of experiencing freedom.[14]

Furthermore, the women themselves were acutely aware of the irony of wanting to be in jail. They desired it and they hated it. In the same conversation in which Kima told me that she has a better life in jail, that "I prayed I went to jail," I asked how she felt about coming back to jail.

cs: Were you upset that you had to come to jail?

KIMA: Yeah, everybody be upset about coming to jail. I mean, look at these people [motions to deputies]. They're horrible.

Yet she also felt affection for some deputies, like her "Titi," Deputy Lewis. Other women expressed similar ambivalence. They told me they appreciated being able to refuel in jail, and then told me how much they hated being in jail. The coexistence of these sentiments connects us again to the phenomenon of home, for, as Jackson notes, home by its very nature encompasses contradictions: "Home is always lived as a relationship, a tension. Sometimes it is between the place one starts out from and the places one puts down roots. . . . Home may evoke security in one context and seem confining in another."[15]

The notion that jail can be a site of caregiving—home—and a place women sometimes desire might make it seem like some part of the larger system "is working," for these marginalized women do experience caregiving. But to read this depiction of the safety net of jailcare in such a pragmatic and fatalistic way ignores the punitive structures from which caregiving arises; it claims to see a glimmer of hope in a fundamentally flawed system, where intimacy can be appreciated as disruptive of carcerality rather than serving to sustain it. The terms of being cared for should not require living in an institution of incarceration. We should not incarcerate pregnant women who "misbehave," or other pregnant women who need care; nor should we make jails harsher. Let me be clear: jail may be integral to the safety net, but it should not be. Jail comes with a host of individual and collective reproductive and other collateral consequences—punitive abuse and deprivation, disruption of families and parental rights, limiting job opportunities, to name but a few—which make it cruel that it has become woven into the safety net. It is, as Wacquant has noted, perverse that the carceral system has become an agency for delivering human services.[16] As a doctor treating patients inside a jail, I continually felt this struggle between relief that I could provide much-needed care to these women, and shame with my complicity in the inequalities of mass incarceration. Jailcare does not improve their lives; it is not an answer to the larger social, economic, and political failures of our unequal system. It merely sustains them as they navigate the marginality of their lives.

Having explored the fundamental ambivalence of jailcare, I return to one of the last times I saw Kima. She was in jail again. Although she speculated about trying another drug treatment program in order to gain custody of baby Koia, she did not speculate about returning to jail. That was a given. We sat in a classroom in E-pod, on the ubiquitous blue plastic chairs. It was just after Martin Luther King Jr. Day and Kima recited a poem she wrote about him. I was so moved by the poem's composition, Kima's talent, and her performance ability that I begged for another poem. She gladly obliged. She took a deep breath, closed her eyes, announced the poem's title, "Poetry Blues," and rhythmically performed the following:

Sitting in the cold royal blue chair
Reminiscing ten years that loneliness bears.
Inclined to recite an unnatural form.
Stuck in a cell, a fishbowl for a dorm.
Conversed upon ways to mend spiritless tasks.
Uncovering the filth buried deep in my past.
A reckless minstrel struck out through a song.
Forever never ending, finding ways to belong.
Lying flat on a mattress, which felt hard as cement.
Resuscitation of joy, which was bound to ferment.
Soaked dried, a thousand and one tears of a wasted ten years.
Renouncing all claims through my unborn fears.
Locked inside a freezing hot shower,
Grasping anger within a slow-paced hour.
A faithful mindless groupie in a maze of addicted lust,
Never always ending disregards reproachful trust.
Transportations of habits inflicting stilled waters.
Washed out, drowned out, and washed up as the street starts to falter.
A regretful exchange for parts of my soul.
Encourage redemption that resurrection may hold—
I can't even breathe—wrote anthems of loss, grief, and of pain.
Exploitation of guilt without a last name.
A rectifiable beat that ticks to no end.
Ending taking on a newfound beginning
In hopes of becoming a reborn friend.

Kima's performance took my breath away. I felt privileged to witness Kima's talents, and sad that the forces structuring her life made jail her stage. When I later reread the transcription of "Poetry Blues," I realized how perfectly Kima represented the reality of her intimate, ambivalent life of recidivism. Kima's disdain for jail is clear in the images of phrases like "cement mattress," "locked in the freezing hot shower," and "anger within a slow-paced hour." Her despair is clear in the phrase, "addicted lust."

And yet she also felt a temporary "resuscitation of joy" in jail. This contrast comprised the chronic everyday of her life, as she moved between the cement mattress and washing up on the streets. This is the experience of recidivism, where the place of return can be home. She, Evelyn, and other women like them exist in these carceral, caregiving processes that seem "forever never ending."

Notes

1. Throughout this book, when I use the word "carceral," I am referring to the physical structures of institutions that punish and confine: jails and prisons. The adjective also, more abstractly, references the punitive logic and hierarchical power structures that subjugate a prisoner's body, and the disciplinary regimes that structure the daily life of incarceration and through which power subtly operates to control subjugated bodies; all these power dynamics constitute various forms of violence inherent to institutions of incarceration.

2. Foucault 1977.

3. See Coates 2015.

4. Willse 2015.

5. Foucault 1994.

6. See also Garcia (2015) and Stevenson (2014) for explorations of the entanglements between violence and care. Garcia explores this link through "anexos," unregulated drug treatment centers in Mexico City. Here, marginalized people who struggle with addiction, and who do not have access to the limited state-sponsored treatment, are "treated" with a clinical routine that includes physical and emotional violence. Stevenson describes the Canadian state's anonymous care of Inuit who suffered in a tuberculosis epidemic in the mid-twentieth century and a current suicide epidemic.

7. Stevenson 2012: 595.

8. Pat Carlen's (2008) concept of "imaginary penalties" connects the notion of prison's disciplinary regime to society's expectations of prison. That is, prison workers try to satisfy society's demand that prison can make the public safer, but they know that the disciplinary practices of custody cannot achieve this, so imprisonment becomes an imaginary penalty focusing on the processes of incarceration rather than outcomes.

9. Weir 2006; Roth 2003.

10. The court system has been involved in a large number of cases which have sorted through the rights that prisons and jails must maintain despite the liberty-depriving conditions of incarceration. Laws enabling or preventing prisoners from voting vary from state to state, but only two states, Maine and Vermont, allow currently incarcerated felons to vote. I was present at the San Francisco jail during the fall election season in 2012, and saw deputies provide and then collect absentee ballots for the women in jail who were eligible to vote.

11. The number of uninsured persons in the United States was approximately 44 million before the Affordable Care Act (ACA) was enacted, and dropped to 28.5 million in 2015 (see http://kff.org/uninsured/fact-sheet/key-facts-about-the-uninsured-population/). While the ACA has provided coverage for millions of people, many more remain uninsured due to the high cost of purchasing non-employer-based insurance and due to Congressional and state-level efforts to curtail the expansion of coverage. As of November 2016, nineteen states declined the offer of federal funds in order to expand their Medicaid programs (see State Refor(u)m at www.nashp.org/states-stand-medicaid-expansion-decisions/). The alternative ways these states are dealing with the ACA's health care mandate leave millions of people without health insurance, perpetuating the situation the ACA hoped to ameliorate. What's more, as of this writing in January 2017, Congress was actively working to repeal the Affordable Care Act (ACA), which repeal is likely to pass under President Trump, and as yet no details have emerged about what might replace the ACA. If the ACA is repealed without a replacement, millions of people who were previously covered will be without health insurance.

12. Watterson 1996; Goffman 2007; Fleury-Steiner 2008.

13. Nolan 1998.

14. In 2006, California's governor Arnold Schwarzenegger declared that the state's prison system was in a "state of emergency" because severe overcrowding had created risks to the health and safety of prisoners and prison workers (see Simon 2013: 253).

15. "Mass incarceration" is a widely used term to reference the vast rise in the numbers of people imprisoned over the last thirty years. Loïc Wacquant (2010a) offers a revised term, "hyperincarceration," to clarify that the surge in incarceration has not involved the masses. Rather, it disproportionately targets poor, black men. Other critics have noted that the descriptor, "mass," suggests that incarceration is worse if more people are involved; the implication is that the

days of five hundred thousand inmates were better, when poor conditions and unequal justice were also rampant (Lorna Rhodes, personal communication, December 12, 2013).

16. Glaze and Parks 2012; Kaeble and Glaze 2016.

17. ACLU, " The Prison Crisis," available at www.aclu.org/prison-crisis.

18. Goodwin 2015: 374.

19. Carson 2015.

20. Davis 1997; Alexander 2010; Wacquant 2010a.

21. Sentencing Project 2015.

22. Goodwin 2015.

23. Wacquant 2010a: 97. See also Tonry 1995; Davis 1997; Wacquant 2009a. For a stunningly thorough account of the forces behind mass incarceration, how it has reshaped key democratic institutions, and the far reach of the carceral state into every aspect of life in the United States, see Gottschalk 2014.

24. Rich, Wakeman, and Dickman 2011.

25. Wacquant 2002: 388.

26. This subject heading alludes to the title of a 2002 article by Loïc Wacquant, "The Curious Eclipse of Prison Ethnography in the Age of Mass Incarceration." In it, he argues that ethnographies of prison, once common for sociologists to do in the 1950s and 1960s, have become sparse in the radically different age of mass incarceration. Several have pointed out that, even in 2002 when Wacquant penned the article, scholars in other disciplines and countries were conducting ethnographies (see Rhodes 2001). I use this subtitle here to signal both that women are often overlooked in discussions of mass incarceration, and that they have been parts of certain conversations in particular ways.

27. See, among others, Goodwin 2015: 375.

28. Women's Prison Association 2009.

29. Minton and Zeng 2016; Carson and Anderson 2016.

30. Carson 2015.

31. In 2014, the incarceration rate for women in prison was 109 / 100,000 for black women, 64 / 100,000 for Hispanic women, and 53 / 100,000 for white women. For men, those numbers were, respectively: 2,724 / 100,000, 1,091 / 100,000, and 465 / 100,000 (Carson 2015).

32. Carson and Sabol 2012.

33. Glaze and Maruschak 2008. This report from the Bureau of Justice Statistics estimated that from 1991–2007 the number of children with an incarcerated parent went from 860,300 to 1,427,500.

34. Sufrin, Kolbi-Molinas, and Roth 2015.

35. Kruttschnitt 2010.

36. Annie E. Casey Foundation 2016.

37. Arditti 2012; Annie E. Casey Foundation 2016.

38. Harlow 1999; Saar et al. 2015.

39. James and Glaze 2006; Fazel et al. 2006.

40. Willers et al. 2008; Clarke et al. 2006.

41. Covington 2007; Kaeble and Glaze 2016.

42. Rebecca Project 2010; ACLUPA 2012; Kraft-Stoler 2015; Goodman, Dawson, and Burlingame 2016.

43. Britton 2003.

44. Kraft-Stoler 2015.

45. Bloom, Owen, and Covington 2003.

46. For a thorough discussion of the implicit gendering of prison regimes, see Bosworth 2000.

47. Braz 2006. The inherent male gendering of institutions of incarceration has also created problems for transgendered individuals. Research has documented that they, especially male to female transgendered prisoners, are at higher risk of sexual assault and other violence, not to mention emotional abuse (ACLU 2014b). Jails and prisons have responded in a variety of ways, with some, such as the LA County Jail, creating a designated housing unit for transgendered women (Routh et al. 2015).

48. Rayna Rapp (2001) has pointed out how reproduction is a critical lens through which to examine key concepts in social theory.

49. Roberts 1999. Such institutional control of poor and black women's reproduction in the United States is not new, of course. White slave masters raped their slaves, in part to produce offspring who could labor on plantations. Eugenics campaigns of the early twentieth century preferentially suppressed the reproduction of poor and immigrant classes.

50. Reich 2005; Roberts 2002.

51. Ackerman, Riggins, and Black 2010; Roberts 1999. See also Knight (2015) for a thorough discussion of the lingering effects of the crack baby myth on poor, pregnant, addicted women living in the daily rent hotels of San Francisco.

52. Tsing 1992.

53. Tsing 1992; Roberts 1999; Paltrow and Flavin 2013. Pregnant women can be convicted of a crime even if they are not found to be in possession of drugs, if there is other evidence they used drugs in pregnancy, such as a positive toxicology screen on the woman or her newborn. In the summer of 2014, lawmakers in Tennessee passed a law that criminalizes mothers whose newborns were exposed to certain illegal drugs in utero.

54. Crowley-Matoka and True 2012; Knight 2015.

55. Gold 2014.

56. Roberts 1999.

57. Carson and Golinelli 2013.

58. Minton 2013.

59. Human Rights Watch 2009.

60. Davis 1997; Wacquant 2001; Alexander 2010.

61. Davis 1997.

62. Wacquant 2001. It is important to note that the convergence of governance of the poor and racialized strategies in the age of mass incarceration should not be taken to mean that race and class are interchangeable categories of oppression; rather, race and class intersect through a broad range of policies, structures, and historical legacies to perpetuate inequalities through incarceration.

63. See www.blacklivesmatter.com.

64. See www.nytimes.com/2016/12/03/nyregion/new-york-state-prisons-inmates-racial-bias.html?_r=0.

65. Gilmore 2007: 247.

66. California Department of Social Services 2014.

67. Annie E. Casey Foundation 2016.

68. Gottschalk 2014: 7.

69. I received approval from the Committee on Human Research at the University of California, San Francisco (the university's Institutional Review Board) to conduct this research, as well as approval from the San Francisco Sheriff's Department and Jail Health Services. There were flyers posted throughout the jail clinic letting women know that I was conducting observational research. Every incarcerated woman, jail worker, and expert whom I interviewed provided voluntary informed consent, including the women whom I followed longitudinally. Because incarcerated persons and pregnant women are categorized as "vulnerable subjects," I followed the additional regulatory requirements to include such people in the study. There is good reason incarcerated people are considered vulnerable research subjects, because of a long history of exploitative, nonconsensual research performed on prisoners' bodies. In addition to the regulatory requirements, I thus did my best to ensure that my informants knew the nature of the research, why I was doing it, and how I would protect their identities as best as I could. I did not enroll anyone as a research subject if she was actively intoxicated, as some women were in their first few days in jail. I attended staff meetings to notify deputies and medical staff about the study, and when I was present in the pods observing and participating in its activities, I told the staff and the women I was there making observations for research. All of the women and workers I spent time with were aware that I would publish the research, and I was able to reach many of them to let them know that a book was forthcoming.

70. I should note that I did not have formal or extensive access to inmates' social worlds and the connections they had among each other. Although I sat with them during meals, observed daily life unfold in the pods, and attended programming with them, I was not able to appreciate with depth the nature of incarcerated women's ways of relating to one another.

71. Sykes 2007; Clemmer 1958; Ward and Kassebaum 1965; Owen 1998.

72. Rhodes 2004. See also Bandyopadhyay 2010.

73. Comfort 2009; Bandyopadhyay 2010.

74. I considered withdrawing from my doctor duties at the jail while I was doing fieldwork, and I also considered finding a new site where I was not known as a doctor. But both of these seemed like undesirable options. If I stopped working at the jail, I would lose my deeply insider perspective. Moreover, my informants would still see me as a doctor. Additionally, I had established a referral level ob / gyn clinic at the jail that provided important services on site, and at the time I was officially beginning my fieldwork, no one was able to take this over. I was not willing to let this service for women in jail wither. As far as finding a new field site, I could never have had the access, trust, and intimate relationships that I had built over the previous four and a half years at the San Francisco jail.

75. Bandyopadhyay 2010.

76. Haraway 1988.

77. Chang 2008; Barton 2011; Wacquant 2011; Sufrin 2015.

78. For other examples of observant participation, see Michael Oldani's (2004) analysis of the pharmaceutical industry's gift economy, based on his own experience of being a Big Pharma drug rep. Loïc Wacquant (2011) trained at a boxing gym to write about the habitus of prize fighters in Chicago's ghetto; Bernadette Barton (2011) was a lesbian in conservative Kentucky, and wrote about the experiences of being gay in the Bible Belt.

79. I am certainly not the first physician anthropologist to write ethnography in a place where she has practiced medicine. Arthur Kleinman (1981, 1995) has developed many of his theoretical contributions to medical anthropology through his work as a psychiatrist, both in Boston and China. Paul Farmer (1992, 1999) has famously done so in Haiti. Vinh-Kim Nguyen (2010) cared for AIDS patients in the Ivory Coast, where he also wrote about the therapeutic sovereignty exacted by the ways these people had to transform themselves in order to access AIDS care. Clare Wendland (2006) delivered babies as an obstetrician in Malawi where she also wrote about the training of Malawian doctors in an age of "global medicine." See my article (2015) for further exploration of the dual practice of medicine and ethnography.

80. See Clifford and Marcus 1986.

81. Han 2012: 24.

82. Stevenson 2012: 595.

83. See Heidegger 2010.

84. See Borneman (1997) for a discussion of filial care defined primarily by love.

85. *Spicer v. Williamson* 1926; *Estelle v. Gamble* 1976; Dolovich 2009.

86. Ticktin 2011.

87. Butler 2009: 14.

88. Quezada, Hart, and Bourgois 2011.

89. Ibid.

90. Butler 2009: 14.

91. Angela Garcia (2010: 68) takes sociality at the heart of care one step further to acknowledge that we have unshared vulnerabilities which, by their very singularity, necessitate "remaining close to one another." As this book will demonstrate, those who work in the jail and who are incarcerated in its walls have divergent and overlapping vulnerabilities through which they, in Garcia's sense, remain close to each other in a myriad of ways.

92. Kleinman and Hanna 2008; DelVecchio Good 1995.

93. Sandelowski 2000.

94. Foucault 1977, 1994.

95. Foucault (1977: 270) even commented on the figure of the prison doctor as the ideal agent for creating transformation in the prisoner. The doctor, in the intimacy of the medical exam, can gain the trust of prisoners better than any other staff, and therefore wield great influence over the prisoner's transformation.

96. Foucault 2007. This analysis of care as violence is prominent in recent writings about humanitarian interventions, where efforts to provide life-saving services are marked by actions and sentiments that reproduce the conditions of suffering and inequality. See, among others, Ticktin 2006, 2011 and Redfield 2005, 2013. Sameena Mulla (2014) also explores how care can be violent, in her account of forensic nursing practices for women seeking care after being raped.

97. Nancy Stoller (2003) provides a sophisticated spatial analysis of health care in a prison; despite her social and political reading of how clinical spaces are constructed within the prison, health care remains something to be accessed, rather than an emergent process. Stoller's ultimate conclusion is that punitive, disciplinary structures interfere with obtaining health care in prisons and preclude the possibility of relations of care.

98. Gilligan 1982; Kittay 1999.

99. Glenn 2012.

100. Mol 2008.

101. Bourdieu and Wacquant 2007.

102. See also Žižek 2008.

103. Lauren Berlant's (2011a: 24) notion of "cruel optimism" encapsulates these unsettling contradictions of jailcare, "attachment to a compromised set of conditions of possibility" that are structured by affects of desire, but this does not preclude the subject's awareness of the attachment's threat.

104. See the ACLU's (2010) report "In for a Penny," documenting how people are imprisoned for being unable to pay legal debts they are too poor to pay. It also reviews the exorbitant bail system that unequally keeps poor people behind bars.

105. Wacquant 2002.

106. Women's Prison Association 2009.

107. Das, Ellen, and Leonard (2008) describe how cycling between the community and both jail and the prison has shaped experiences of domesticity and familial intimacy for black, urban families. Even as parents cycle between home and carceral institutions, even as violence may pervade their intimate spaces, "itinerant domesticities" circulate with them and children still feel care from them.

108. The uneventfulness of recidivism in jail is exemplary of Gilles Deleuze's (1992: 6) point that we have shifted from a strictly disciplinary society to a more dispersive society of control: "Control is short-term and of rapid rates of turnover, but also continuous and without limit, while discipline was of long duration, infinite, and discontinuous."

109. The integrated nature of jails in communities was obvious in the Progressive Era, when jails would allocate space for nonincarcerated individuals who needed shelter for the night (Willse 2015: 82).

110. Irwin 1985.

111. Bourgois and Schonberg 2009.

112. Knight 2015.

113. In fact, given that Knight and I had temporal overlap in our fieldwork, it is possible that we knew some of the same pregnant women.

114. See www.sfsheriff.com/jail_info.html.

115. Inmates can be placed in "ad seg" for a variety of reasons. They could be sent there as punishment for disobeying or "talking back" to a deputy, for violent or aggressive behavior, or even for their own protection if they are deemed to be at risk for assault from other inmates. In some cases, they might be sent to ad seg simply because that was where they were housed when last in jail. This happened to Evelyn every time she entered jail because she had a history many years ago of being aggressive with deputies. After a few days, she was usually placed into the general population.

116. These numbers for the San Francisco jail were provided to me by the San Francisco Sheriff's Department. The "midyear count" is a metric used by the Department of Justice Bureau of Justice Statistics, with census taken on June 30 every year. Although it is a major urban center, San Francisco has a relatively small jail population. For comparison, the largest system, Los Angeles County, houses an average of 22,000 inmates daily (see www.aclu.org/la-county-jails).

117. Van Derbeken 2010.

118. In 2016, a federal judge found that San Francisco police officers were deliberately targeting black people in an undercover drug operation. For instance, undercover agents refused to buy drugs from an Asian woman and then waited for a black woman to sell them drugs (Coleman 2016).

119. For an excellent discussion of the litigation events culminating in the Supreme Court decision, see Simon 2014. With Realignment, people convicted of nonserious, nonsexual, nonviolent crimes, and people violating parole, now

serve their time in county jails instead of state prisons, regardless of the length of their sentence. This could mean that some people would be in jail for years, despite the fact that these facilities are not set up for long-term incarceration.

120. Grattet 2013.

121. The agency name and acronym have been changed.

122. The jail's mental health services were administered through a community-based nonprofit organization, but, like many safety net services in San Francisco, it received funding from the local government.

123. This is a vast topic which is beyond the scope of this book to address, and hundreds of scholars, researchers, policy makers, and activists have written about the overwhelming number of people in prisons and jails who suffer from mental illness. For a harrowing analysis of the carceral approach to mental illness, see Rhodes 2004.

124. Probation and parole departments are also involved in deciding who should be incarcerated. People who are released from jail or prison are often released under conditions of probation or parole, with rules to follow and appointments to report to. Violations of the terms, even technical violations of traveling only a short distance outside of one's restricted geography, may lead to reincarceration.

125. Knight 2014.

126. I have changed the names of places like drug treatment centers, agencies, and other organizations.

127. Simon 2007.

128. Murdoch 2016.

129. Levi and Waldman 2011.

130. Durkheim 1982.

131. Comaroff and Comaroff 1992: 6.

132. Of course for these millions behind bars, and their families and communities, prisons and jails are all too familiar.

133. This term emerged from a personal communication with Lawrence Cohen on April 24, 2013.

134. See Moynihan (1965) for a definition of the "culture of poverty" concept, which overlooks structural forces of racial and other inequalities in favor of full individual responsibility.

135. The word "inmate" applies to someone confined to living in an institution; it has been used especially to signal people housed in asylums for the mentally ill and in prisons. Robert Clemmer increased the usage of this term to describe those in prison in his influential book *The Prison Community* (1958, first published in 1940), in which he provides ethnographic descriptions of inmates' code of conduct. Erving Goffman (2007 [1961]) highlighted the congruence between mental asylums and prisons by using "inmate" for both of these settings in his call for deinstitutionalization of the mentally ill. Some incarcerated people prefer

"prisoner," as a more political term. No single term is sufficient to represent the person who is incarcerated.

136. Hudson 2015.

137. United States Sentencing Commission 2015.

1. INSTITUTIONAL BURDEN TO CARE

1. Robert Perkinson (2010) offers a detailed account of the plantation-based penal system in Texas, and how its economic, exploitative model set the stage for punitive approaches across the country.

2. *Estelle v. Gamble*, 1976.

3. *Estelle* did not provide a list of conditions that constitute serious medical needs. Court cases since *Estelle* have applied the following logic: "Generally, a medical need is serious if it 'has been diagnosed by a physician as mandating treatment or . . . is so obvious that even a lay person would easily recognize the necessity for a doctor's attention' (see *Duran v. Anaya* 1986; *Ramos v. Lamm* 1980). Conditions are also considered to be serious if they 'cause pain, discomfort, or threat to good health' (see *Dean v. Coughlin* 1985)" (Rold 2008: 16).

4. Dolovich 2009.

5. Willen 2012.

6. Classic representations of "the deserving poor" counter representations of the morally inadequate undeserving poor. See Sargent 2012.

7. Wacquant 2001, 2009a, 2009b, 2010a; Institute for Policy Studies 2015.

8. Simon 2007.

9. Saar et al. 2015.

10. Wacquant 2010a: 97. See also Tonry 1995; Davis 1997; Wacquant 2009a.

11. The origins of the term "safety net" are not clear, but historian Guian McKee's search through newspaper archives determined that the first reference to the term was in a 1966 *New York Times* article quoting Franklin Delano Roosevelt in a campaign speech for his race for New York governor: "public assistance will be envisaged as a safety net on the one hand, and as a transmission belt to productive employment on the other." The phrase "safety net" was not widely used until then president Ronald Reagan used the phrase to reassure the public that his widespread government spending cuts would supposedly not impact the social safety net for those with "true needs." See Clark 2013.

12. The federal entitlement programs established by the 1935 Social Security Act were aimed at ensuring the health of the workforce for the larger goal of national well-being. Social security benefits were extended to support certain wage laborers, but excluded farm laborers and domestic workers, which, many have argued, was the de facto racial encoding of the public safety net, since these were the jobs most likely to be held by African Americans. Public assistance pro-

grams were administered at the local level, and susceptible to racial discrimination in determining who could receive benefits (Willse 2015: 39; see also Gilmore 2007).

13. From the start, Medicaid and Medicare excluded inmates: "Care for inmates within a 'public institution' is explicitly listed as ineligible for federal reimbursement" (Social Security Act Amendments 1965, Sec. 1905(a)(15)(A)).

14. Estroff 1981; Brodwin 2013; Gillon 2000. The 1963 Community Mental Health Act was what mandated the closing of these hospitals, and promised to open about two thousand community mental health centers. However, insufficient resources were directed toward this goal.

15. Ford 2015; Kristof 2014.

16. Simon 2007.

17. Feeley and Simon 1992; Simon 2007.

18. Wacquant 2001. Journalist Ta-Nehisi Coates (2015: 82) has grimly summarized this reality of how the criminalized black body has been reconfigured: "One does not build a safety net for a race of predators. One builds a cage."

19. Wacquant 2009a; Willse 2015.

20. See, among others, Wacquant 2001.

21. See Bourgois and Schonberg (2009) for a rich, ethnographic account of the relationship between shifting market forces, urban poverty, drug addiction, and illegality (2009).

22. Roberts 2002; Padró 2004.

23. Such caps—enacted by twenty-three states—believed that they would provide an incentive to poor women to reduce birth rates and to encourage "personal responsibility," though studies have failed to show an effect on the birth rate of mothers on TANF (see Pew Charitable Trusts 2016).

24. Ehrenreich 2015; Roberts 1999; Roberts 2002.

25. In 2016, California became the seventh state to repeal its TANF child cap. An editorial noted the link between such caps and the stereotype of women reproducing for state benefits, and was aptly titled "California Deposes Its 'Welfare Queen'" (Editorial Board 2016).

26. The expansion of the carceral system means not just a sheer increase in the numbers within its walls. It also increasingly reaches into and has profound repercussions on the communities where incarcerated people come from.

27. The 1994 Violent Crime Control and Law Enforcement Act poured billions of dollars into urban police departments and created fifty new federal offenses.

28. This phenomenon in which certain people profit from the warehousing of criminalized, poor, disproportionately black bodies is commonly summarized by the phrase "prison industrial complex," about which much has been written. The concept signals more than just the corporatization and profit-making of punishment; more broadly it describes the political economy of mass incarceration as the redirection of financial resources from public services for the poor into

prisons, and the enmeshment of forces of global capitalism in mass imprisonment. Despite the tenacity of the notion of a "prison industrial complex," it is not
without its critics, even among those critical of mass incarceration, in part
because it obfuscates the role of the state (Wacquant 2010b: 606).

29. When combined with local expenditures, the United States spent $76 bil-
lion on corrections in 2010 (Kyckelhahn 2012, 2013).

30. The war on drugs was launched with full rhetorical and political force in the
1980s. But New York state led the way earlier in the harsh policies of the drug war
when in 1973 then Governor Nelson Rockefeller signed into law a series of statutes
that would punish people who sold as little as two ounces or possessed four ounces
of drugs with long-term prison sentences. This was an unprecedented punitive turn
to manage nonviolent crimes in a manner similar to violent crimes like murder.

31. Baum 2016.

32. Maurer 2006; Tonry 1995; Wacquant 2009b. See also Gottschalk (2013),
who notes that while it is widely acknowledged that policy changes, not dramatic
increases in criminal behavior, spawned mass incarceration, violent crime is
nonetheless unequally distributed, with higher rates in urban, black neighborhoods. Passed in 1994, the Three Strikes law meant that after being convicted of
two felonies, if a person was then convicted of a third crime, even a minor nonviolent one, she would spend the rest of her life in jail. Similar laws were adopted
in two dozen other states and by the federal government.

33. Wacquant 2010a: 1.

34. This is a reality which Alice Goffman (2014) chronicles in her ethnography among black men in Philadelphia who were constantly "on the run" from law
enforcement. She describes the lives of black men whose everyday lives, work,
relationships, and sense of self are organized by fear of arrest. Her work, however, has come under significant critique for, among other things, its questiona-
ble ethnographic ethics and the one-dimensional portrayals of women. For a
critical analysis of her work, see Goodwin 2015.

35. Irwin 2005.

36. See, among others, Foucault 2007; Simon 2007; Cunha 2014.

37. See ACLU report "In for a Penny" 2010.

38. Comfort 2009. See also Coates 2015.

39. If a prisoner has to be hospitalized while incarcerated and if that hospitalization exceeds twenty-four hours, then Medicaid and Medicare can be rein-
stated to cover those health care costs. Some states continue TANF payments
until a person is convicted of a crime, but to ensure continued payments, the new
caretaker of the child must apply anew for these benefits while the original ben-
eficiary caretaker is in custody. Supplemental Security Income continues until
someone has been incarcerated for a full calendar month. Social Security Disa-
bility Insurance gets suspended thirty-one days after being in custody and being
convicted of a crime (Bazelon Center 2006). Housing is another challenge for

those who lived in public housing before their incarceration, as many women in the San Francisco jail recounted to me, since incarceration interferes with paying rent. Furthermore, once individuals have lived away from their unit for more than ninety days, they have violated the lease and can be evicted.

40. Institute for Policy Studies 2015.

41. Ibid.

42. Gottschalk (2014) argues that we should not conflate the "crime problem" with the problem of the carceral state. Tackling "root causes," like poverty, is a longer term project and will not immediately impact incarceration rates. Instead, she contends, the changes should be in the vast policies that have made policing and incarceration a central part of the democratic and governing institutions in the United States. Even releasing those convicted of non-violent crimes would not solve the problem, because there would still be too many people incarcerated and because those categorizations are sometimes hard to sort out. Despite her important arguments, this distinction between addressing root causes and the carceral state is harder to separate when talking about jails, which are such fluid parts of the urban landscape.

43. St. James Infirmary is a nationally known, innovative clinic for sex workers, and is integrated with the city's health department clinics (see www.stjamesin firmary.org). Glide Memorial Church is a local fixture and a nationally known institution, a social justice–oriented church in one of the city's poorest neighborhoods that has provided food, shelter, jobs, health care, and a spiritual home for thousands of San Francisco residents (www.glide.org).

44. See Knight 2015 for a detailed description of "Ladies Night" and of the delivery of safety net services through the daily rent hotels in San Francisco.

45. See Cook 2011.

46. Katz and Brigham 2011.

47. See www.sfdph.org.

48. See San Francisco Sheriff's Department, www.sfsheriff.com/division_ admin_prog.html.

49. The 5 Keys Charter High School was the first to be embedded inside an adult detention facility.

50. See San Francisco Sheriff's Department, www.sfsheriff.com/division_ admin_prog.html.

51. Ho 2016.

52. Willse 2015.

53. Goffman's (2014) ethnography of black men in Philadelphia constantly running from law enforcement describes some men who were arrested for outstanding warrants while attending the births of their children at the hospital. Others were so intent on avoiding arrest at the hospital that they bled for days at home from bullet wounds, or had broken, exposed bones tended to by nonmedical neighbors who worked at a hospital and could steal supplies.

54. Welfare recipients in some states are required to submit urine samples for drug tests as conditions of receiving benefits. This strategy, stigmatizing and punitive, has proven to be a waste of money and not detected significant drug use among beneficiaries. See Landsbaum 2016.

55. Knight 2015: 187.

56. Knight observed a similar discrepancy in her ethnography of pregnant, addicted women in San Francisco. While there were many services for pregnant, addicted women in the city, women did not access them or only accessed them when ordered to by a court or when in jail. Some of the women she described appreciated the interventions of the criminal justice system that forced them into programs. Instead of offering discrete answers for this complicated phenomenon, Knight (2015: 230–31) urges us to bear witness and to ask what the criminal justice system is standing in for.

57. *Spicer v. Williamson*, 132 S.E. 291, 293 (N.C. 1926).

58. Keramet Reiter (2012) and Margo Schlanger (2003) detail the ways courts have played a role in determining the day-to-day conditions of living in and managing prisons, such as space, food, exercise, and access to daylight.

59. Rold 2008: 13.

60. *Stone et al. v. City and County of San Francisco et al.*, C-78-2774 WHO (1992).

61. *Estelle v. Gamble* was an early phase of a trend in which the courts have become deeply involved in defining the physical conditions of incarceration, prisoners' rights, and the prisons' responsibility to provide for inmates (Schlanger 2003; Reiter 2012).

62. Lisa Stevenson (2014) describes a form of "anonymous care" administered by the colonial Canadian government in managing suicide and tuberculosis among indigenous Inuit. In the state's activities to provide care for the Inuit, the identity of the person receiving care becomes insignificant. Anonymous care is indifferent to its object: "To care anonymously is to say 'I care' without specifying for whom" (83). Stevenson posits indifference as the opposite of concern, and anonymous care is a form that lacks concern for the suffering individual. With the "deliberate indifference" to prisoners' suffering prohibited by *Estelle v. Gamble*, concern is not putatively excluded from indifference—for to be deliberately indifferent requires effort and attention.

63. Herzfeld 1992: 33.

64. Ibid.: 1.

65. *Farmer v. Brennan*, 511 U.S. 825 (1994).

66. Dolovich (2009) has critiqued the *Farmer* decision for its narrow concept of punishment at the individual level, holding a guard who may or may not know about the risks of something, rather than the institution and state, accountable. *Farmer* also creates incentives for officers and institutions not to notice potentially dangerous conditions. Notably, the *Estelle* mandate did not make medical

malpractice alone in prison a constitutional violation; instead, it put medical care (or its absence) in the realm of intentionality.

67. There is no central, or even de-centralized, database of prisoner health litigation cases. This estimate was extrapolated from legal scholar Margo Schlanger's compilation of prior articles tabulating the type of prison litigation brought against the facility. In Schlanger's 2003 article, the estimate was that roughly 15 percent of prison litigation pertained to medical care (see footnote 48, p. 1570), with close to forty thousand federal civil lawsuits filed by inmates in one year.

68. Three basic "rights" have been clarified in these cases: a prisoner's right to access care; a prisoner's right to receive treatment that was ordered; and a prisoner's right to a professional medical judgment (Rold 2008).

69. Joao Biehl, Adriana Petryna, and colleagues (2009, 2012) have documented a similar phenomenon in Brazil, where health care is written into the Constitution as a universal right for all citizens. Yet inadequate pharmaceutical supply chains and high prices have prohibited the actualization of this right for many Brazilians, who have sought the court's assistance to secure access to prescription medications. The proliferation of court cases, what the authors call the "judicialisation of the right to health," reveals state failures and a breakdown in the promise of a biomedical collective.

70. For the medicalization of the prisoner, see Simon 2013. This intersection between health care and institutional enforcement certainly has a long history. Dorothy Porter (1999), among others, has written extensively about police involvement in policing public health behaviors to better the health of the nation and ensure the vitality of its citizens for the labor force.

71. This retroactive juridical claim on clinical care resembles malpractice lawsuits, which define clinical competence by arguing in particular instances for its absence (DelVecchio Good 1995).

72. Claitor and Butler 2014.

73. *Brown v. Plata*, 131 S. Ct. 1910 (2011): 13.

74. Somers and Roberts 2008: 407, 413.

75. The modifier "correctional" derives from the general term "correctional facility," which came out of the rehabilitative era of penology when prisons were rooted in a therapeutic ideology; incarceration hoped to be able to *correct* a criminal into an upstanding citizen. Applying "correctional" to health care should not be taken as a commitment to this therapeutic model, but rather as a convenient adjective for the health care provided in jails and prisons.

76. In eighteenth-century England, the Prison Medical Service was created, largely in response to prison reformer John Howard's report of gruesome health conditions. Howard's activism helped to incite a "modern humanitarian consciousness" around the management of people in prisons, a spirit which would resurface in U.S. courts' involvement in prisoner health care (Simon 2014: 8).

77. American Correctional Association 1870: 33.

78. Conover 2001; Simon 2014: 7.

79. Murton and Hyams 1969.

80. Foucault 1977.

81. American Medical Association 1973. This fifty-one-page report documented that 25% of jails had no medical facilities on site, 31% had no physician available, 66% had first aid supplies as their only medical care, and provided a plethora of other statistics to substantiate the absence of medical care.

82. Starting in October 2013, I became a board member on the NCCHC, which is comprised of representatives from over thirty professional medical and correctional administrative organizations. I was the first Ob/Gyn ever to serve on the board. I am currently an active board member, involved in proposing standards and policies that specifically address health care for incarcerated women. Any information I present here is taken either directly from publicly available NCCHC sources or is my own assessment. I am not writing in any official NCCHC capacity.

83. www.ncchc.org.

84. The certification is voluntary, yet there are many unaccredited prisons and jails that also use the NCCHC standards to help guide their practice. The touted benefits include prestige, decreased liability costs from lawsuits, promotion of a well-managed system, and legitimized budget requests. Accreditation does not, however, putatively mean "good" care, nor does its absence signal "bad" care.

85. On the NCCHC website's overview of accreditation, five paragraphs extol the legal benefits of accreditation, including that court cases have held up NCCHC standards as the benchmark and that compliance with the standards will ultimately save money by avoiding litigation. NCCHC accreditation aspires to ensure the "improved health status" of inmates and to provide a public health model of "reduced risk to the community when inmates are released." NCCHC participated in a landmark report to Congress in 2002 on "The Health of Soon to be Released Inmates." See www.ncchc.org.

86. NCCHC 2014.

87. As of 2012, a board-certified medical specialty in correctional medicine now exists, boarded by the American Osteopathy Association (2012). Some health care professionals are also active in the American Correctional Association (ACA), the largest (and oldest, since 1870) professional organization for people working in any capacity at jails and prisons.

88. Pont et al. 2012.

89. Kyckelhahn 2012.

90. von Zielbauer 2005. In 2016, the Department of Justice (2016a) announced that it would no longer contract to private companies at federal prisons.

91. Segura 2013.

92. Gilroy and Kenny 2012: 14, 20.

93. von Zielbauer 2005; Leonard and May 2013; see also Fleury-Steiner 2008.

94. Christensen 2013.

95. Isaacs 2013.

96. While there are other counties besides San Francisco in which jail health is run through the city's health department, it is more common that jail health care is overseen by the local Sheriff's Department.

97. Dumont et al. 2013.

98. This social justice perspective on prisoner health care has some of its roots in the famous and deadly Attica prison riot of 1971. Motivated by the desire to improve prison conditions, especially medical care, inmates in this New York state prison seized control of the institution and took forty-two of the staff hostage.

99. Drucker 2011.

100. This estimate was obtained from the nonprofit search engine www .guidestar.org.

2. TRIAGING THE EVERYDAY, EVERY DAY

1. Goffman's (2007) classic description of the processes by which a person becomes an inmate at a total institution remains relevant today—mortification where they learn the rules and homogenize their behavior with other inmates, and the stripping of their sense of self and replacement with a new sense that is reorganized around things like the institution's privilege system, the regimented schedule, and the subordinate position to the staff. Irwin (1985) described a similar process that was specific to entry into the San Francisco County Jail. What these descriptions omit is that medical sorting is the first step in the process.

2. From the French verb *trier*, to separate or select, the triage concept emerged on the battlefield to classify wounded soldiers into those who were likely to die regardless of intervention and those who might live—and therefore return to battle—if their wounds were treated (see Nguyen 2010). The military rationale has mutated into many forms, from the routinized triage of hospital emergency rooms, to medical humanitarian relief efforts during war or natural disasters (see Redfield 2005; Fassin and Vasquez 2005; Ticktin 2006) or the distribution of HIV treatment (see Nguyen 2010).

3. The anthropology of triage has exposed it to be a biopolitical strategy, reinforcing and creating anew configurations of power through choices about which lives are worthy recipients of life-sustaining interventions. Redfield (2005, 2013) and Didier Fassin (2010) have deepened our understanding of the politics of life at work in triage through the paradigmatic medical humanitarian organization Médicins Sans Frontières, which actively refuses to take sides in conflict zones, deeming all lives equally deserving of rescue. The paradox of this apolitical

stance, Fassin and Redfield argue, is that it is itself a politics of life, creating a necessary hierarchy in order to equitably distribute resources. Furthermore, there is always an asymmetry between workers and sufferers in their risk of dying (Fassin 2010).

4. There were detailed protocols to guide the care of people withdrawing from alcohol and opiates, recognizing that alcohol withdrawal in particular can be fatal.

5. This medical triage as a condition for entry is not unlike what happens in refugee camps. Redfield (2005) describes how refugee triaging is focused on their basic biological processes. He argues that this survivalist mode of triage masks the broader context of suffering that produced the need for intervention in the first place.

6. Many jails and prisons charge a fee, usually around five dollars, for inmates to see a doctor for a nonurgent complaint that was not initiated by the health care provider. The idea, as Lenny corroborated, is to discourage people from abusing the ready and otherwise free access to medical care which they have; that is, monetizing medical care to regulate behavior. Most inmates have some money "on their books" from family members or friends, to buy things at the commissary. So the assumption is that if they can afford to buy Cheetos, they can afford to pay five dollars for a clinic visit. There was no co-payment for any medical service at the San Francisco jail. The medical director was vehemently opposed to this practice, which he considered unethical and dangerous; the financial burden in this already coercive environment would prevent too many people who needed care from coming to the clinic.

7. Willen 2011: 3.

8. Berlant 2004: 6.

9. I would be remiss here not to acknowledge Freddie Gray, a black man, whose tragic and violent death in 2015 in Baltimore has become another high-profile case of police misconduct against black men and women. During an arrest, cell phone video and witnesses recorded that police officers used significant force to drag him into a transport van to take him to jail. Once inside the van, amid his screaming in pain, the officers did not secure him with a seatbelt. En route, he began experiencing difficulty breathing and requested that the officers take him to a hospital. The police officers initially triaged him as being fine, and decided that he could wait until he got to jail where, presumably, he would be assessed by a nurse, though eventually they called the paramedics. His condition rapidly deteriorated, as he had actually suffered a severe spinal cord injury in the van ride when he was unsecured. He died several days later. Although the medical examiner ruled his death a homicide, all six officers charged in his case have been acquitted, sparking further anger and concerns of racial bias in the criminal justice system. An investigation by the U.S. Department of Justice (2016a) concluded that the Baltimore Police Department uses

excessive force, and unlawfully and disproportionately targets African Americans.

10. Having a receiving screening and intake protocol is required to be accredited by the NCCHC (2014).

11. For instance, tuberculosis is the paradigmatic infectious disease for which jail and prison are reservoirs. See Koch (2013) for an analysis of tuberculosis in prisons in the Republic of Georgia.

12. Those who worked in the jail had employer-based health insurance, with a choice of several plans including California's well-known, comprehensive managed care organization Kaiser Permanente. This is not to say that deputies and jail medical staff all "took care of themselves" in the idealized way our culture represents "good health." Some were overweight, ate high-fat foods at work, rarely exercised, smoked, drank excessive alcohol, and participated in other things characterized as "bad health behaviors."

13. As with many local health departments in the United States, San Francisco's had a special team whose job it was to track down people with positive STI results. Even so, there were still people with untreated STIs who came to jail.

14. Jorg Pont and colleagues (2012: 476) have argued an ethical stance, that the intake medical examination "should not issue certifications that prisoners are fit for imprisonment," for this acquiesces professional duties to prison rules. However, whether or not an official certification is given, the existence of an intake exam is a subtle affirmation that incarceration can continue.

15. The Policy and Procedure for "Receiving Triage and Intake Screening" instructed triage nurses to send patients with the following conditions to the hospital and not to "accept" them into the jail until "medically cleared": "1. Signs, symptoms, or history suspicious for active TB. 2. Lacerations requiring suturing. 3. Unresponsiveness. 4. Injuries which require X-ray evaluation. 5. Serious head injuries. 6. Pregnancy with: signs and symptoms of opiate withdrawal or regular and recent use; history of alcohol addiction and pulse above 100 and hallucinations, tremors, sweating, anxiety or irritability; history of crack / cocaine addiction and pulse above 120 and / or blood pressure above 140 / 90; history of daily benzodiazepine use of 60mg or more of diazepam or equivalent and pulse is above 100 and hallucinations, tremors, sweating, anxiety, or irritability; cramping or vaginal bleeding; pulse above 100; blood pressure above 140 / 90 × 2 and no known history of hypertension. 7. Unstable cardiac chest pain. 8. Severe cellulitis, abscesses requiring I&D, infected human bites. 9. Inability to walk or stand unassisted. 10. Peritoneal dialysis. 11. Respiratory distress of unknown and / or unmanageable etiology. 12. Reporting to have ingested narcotics or cocaine. 13. Reporting to have been raped within the last 72 hours. 14. Requiring life sustaining medical equipment not available in the jail. 15. Imminent danger to self or others. 16. Any other serious medical condition requiring emergent care."

16. Despite the risks, many jails and prisons force pregnant women to withdraw and do not provide methadone or other treatment.

17. See Bourgois and Schonberg (2009) for detailed analyses of the political economy and social life of abscesses among homeless drug addicts in San Francisco.

18. The health department director's comment about jail caring for his patients was invoked at public hearings I attended two years in a row, when the San Francisco city council considered contracting jail health care to a private corporation.

19. Being reliant on jail for HIV medications was problematic if someone could not take them outside of jail. With only sporadic treatment, the HIV virus can mutate and develop resistance to anti-retroviral medications, making the drugs ineffective. Because of this, HIV specialists at San Francisco jail were careful in their decisions about whom to give anti-retrovirals to in jail. The specialists also established a clinic outside the jail where their patients could follow-up upon release.

20. Of course, as Foucault (1977) noted, the prison sets up conditions for further "delinquency" of prisoners upon return to society; likewise, the warehouse prisons of mass incarceration are largely devoid of rehabilitative and reentry services that might help people avoid re-arrest. Drug courts are one attempt to try to divert people arrested on low-level drug charges away from jail and into treatment and social services. As James Nolan (1998) argues, drug courts signal how the state has adopted a therapeutic orientation in its approach to managing people. Notably, the success of drug courts in policy documents is typically measured in recidivism rates.

21. This task of confirming people's medications at pharmacies is not standard at every jail. It took two years for triage nurses to accept this verification task as part of their job, because of the perceived extra work that it would entail.

22. Aas 2005.

23. Berlant 2011b: 264.

24. Berlant 2011a: 189.

25. Ian Whitmarsh (2014) makes a case for seeing institutions as a basis for foundationally ambivalent sociality.

26. It should be noted that despite HIPAA's privacy assurances, medical records are always legally discoverable, especially in medical malpractice cases.

27. Berlant 2000.

3. CULTIVATING AMBIGUITY

1. "Sick call" is used throughout correctional medicine to denote daily clinic sessions; it implies that medical care in jail or prison addresses sickness as it arises, rather than preventing it.

2. Flavin 2009; Paltrow and Flavin 2013. Court-ordered intrusions into pregnant women's ability to make autonomous decisions occur not infrequently in the United States. Physician and legal scholar Julie Cantor (2012) has written about the exceptionalism that the desire to protect the fetus interjects into scenarios of patient-refused care, which otherwise would remain at the bedside and would not invite legal arbitration.

3. Brodwin 2013.

4. Ibid.: 4.

5. Ibid.

6. See Sim 1990.

7. Prout and Ross 1988; Anno 2001; Stoller 2003; Pont, Stover, and Wolff 2012.

8. See Whitmarsh 2008.

9. I write "ostensibly" and "allegedly criminal" because at least half of the people in jail were pretrial and had not been convicted of a crime for their arrests; health care providers typically did not know who was pretrial and who was convicted (though they could often make educated guesses).

10. Quezada, Hart, and Bourgois 2011.

11. Angela Garcia (2010) uses the concept of "patient-prisoner" in her work on addiction and loss in rural New Mexico. For Garcia, the patient-prisoner is the subject who gets produced by juridical, medical, and carceral regimes that govern the drug addict through the dual logics of recovery and punishment. This patient-prisoner also exists in the San Francisco jail. But the patient-prisoner I discuss here, from the perspective of medical providers in the jail, is a figure enmeshed in relationships of care, where the attention to the continuities and contradictions of the patient and the prisoner are part of what care means.

12. Rhodes 2004.

13. Ibid.: 184.

14. Anno 2001: 20.

15. Fassin 2010.

16. Holmes and Ponte 2011.

17. In the prison setting, Katja Franko Aas (2005) has explored how the increasing use of guidelines and computer technology in the contemporary penal system allows people to construe prisoners as disjointed bits of information, making them targets for new forms of technologically justified punishment.

18. See, among others, Riles 2001 and Gordillo 2006. Hannah Arendt (1976) saw the mundane, repetitive nature of bureaucracy as fundamental to the state's potential for violence, for bureaucracy's focus on tasks and not humans could lead to detachment and to appreciating the individual as superfluous; the individual could then be destroyed without any concern. Likewise, bureaucracy and technology, Zygmunt Bauman (1989) argues, create physical distance in social relationships and therefore generate indifference to those others from whom one

is distanced. Anthropologists have examined the "social production of indifference" through processes that decontextualize suffering into sterile bureaucratic tasks (Scheper-Hughes 1992; see also Herzfeld 1992 and Weber 2006).

19. Riles 2001 and Aretxaga 2003; Das 2004 and Gordillo 2006.

20. Dolovich 2009.

21. This function of MCRs as entry points into the everyday triage system of the jail medical apparatus gives them a testimonial quality. Nguyen (2010) has analyzed how resourced entities like medical humanitarian nongovernmental organizations make decisions about anti-retroviral therapy in Côte d'Ivoire based on how HIV positive patients represent themselves as worthy therapeutic citizens in their personally crafted HIV narratives (see also Ticktin 2006).

22. I asked nurses, clinicians, deputies, and patients, but none could tell me the social etymology of "chrono" in the San Francisco jail. It is hard to ignore the potential symbolic meaning that might derive from its Greek root *chron*, meaning time. Perhaps the connection is that the privilege granted on a paper "chrono" interrupts the standard routine.

23. Goffman 2007.

24. Vivian herself initiated this pregnancy privilege years ago as an enticement to get pregnant women to stay hydrated. Ice is now an accepted part of the pregnancy privilege package.

25. NCCHC 2014: 129. The right to refuse medical care in prison has played out in recent hunger strike dramas, especially at California's supermax prison Pelican Bay and at the U.S. military's detention camp Guantanamo Bay. In the latter, the force-feeding of detainees by medical professionals eliminates the right of refusal of medical care, and thereby strips inmates of their only opportunity to resist (see, among others, Anderson 2009 and al Hasan Moqbel 2013).

26. One example of a refusal leading to confrontation and fulfillment of anticipated roles involved a pregnant woman named Tami. She refused to come to clinic for an important prenatal visit. Tami was close to her due date and needed to decide if she wanted a cesarean section (which would require scheduling), like she had in her last pregnancy, or to attempt a vaginal delivery (which carries a small risk of rupture of the uterine scar). Despite her refusal, because she was pregnant and because the deputies overheard me talk about the importance of this visit, the deputies brought her down to the clinic against her will. The coercion, combined with her active psychosis, fueled her further resistance when she was in the exam room. With a deputy standing in the doorway for my protection—the only time in six years that I have had a chaperone—Tami would not engage in the discussion about her preferred mode of delivery. Her anger was palpable. And her continued "refusal" led to continued coercion: the psychiatrists, medical director, and city's attorney decided it was reasonable to send her to the hospital for an involuntary psychiatric commitment, where she would also be close to the labor and delivery suite if she went into labor.

4. THE CLINIC ROUTINE

1. Rhodes 2001: 70.

2. Julie Livingston describes an oncology ward in Botswana as more than just a clinical space where suffering bodies are tended to. Rather, the cancer ward is part of the country's political narrative of participatory democracy and universal health care, for staff and patients seek out opportunities for equality in the care of cancer patients. These moral commitments get enacted in the daily intimacies of cancer care, what Livingston (2012) calls "moral intimacies of care."

3. Making people wait is a well-known power of custody routines in general in prisons and jails.

4. Prout and Ross 1988; Stoller 2003.

5. Brodwin 2013.

6. "Sick call" is common lingo in the correctional health world. It reflects the minimum level of care which *Estelle* mandates—that prisons and jails must tend to inmates when they are sick. At many jails and prisons, this is indeed the goal of the clinic, to see people when they are sick. But even at sites that use the prevalent "sick call" moniker, the clinic may also have more preventive health goals as well.

7. See, among many, Glaser and Greifinger 1993.

8. Although illicit substances were hard to come by in the San Francisco jail, they most certainly were used. Drugs might be smuggled in by visitors, or hidden in one's vagina. People found ways to disrupt the sobriety of jail.

9. Vivian and I both noticed a very high prevalence of bacterial vaginosis (BV), an infection from imbalance of vaginal bacteria, among the women we saw in clinic. Women told us how they commonly stored plastic bags of drugs in their vaginas, and we hypothesized a biological explanation that the high prevalence of BV could be related to this.

10. See Leder (1990) for an analysis of how the body's consciousness of itself recedes when it is functioning normally, and becomes more present at times of dysfunction.

11. Bayer and Wilkinson 1995. Direct administration of pharmaceuticals has also long been used in the psychiatric setting; nurses directly administered psychotropic medications to inpatients in mental institutions.

12. These "stacks" of CHART knowledge, as Rhodes (2007: 555) suggests about prison computer systems, could depict patient-prisoners as "carriers of needs and dangers, each with its own institutional response."

13. See Aas (2005: 85–86) for a discussion of the strategic "stacking" electronic knowledge of prisoners.

14. Linde 1999.

15. Importantly, there is often tremendous distrust among incarcerated patients toward correctional health providers, stemming from concerns about

competence, being treated without dignity, and overall distrust of anything from a carceral institution.

16. As it turned out, Connie was diagnosed with and treated for an ectopic pregnancy.

17. Kleinman and Hanna 2008.

18. Goffman (2007: 78) identified a similar, broader tension in total institutions where there is "constant conflict between humane standards on the one hand and institutional efficiency on the other."

19. Angela Garcia (2010: 68) develops an expansive view of care as being with another even amid incommensurable experience, "in which the parameters of the clinic and of the patient are not so easily defined. Perhaps *we* are the patient, and the clinic—intended as a space for healing—is all around us."

5. GESTATING CARE

1. Opiate withdrawal in pregnancy is not recommended, because of a potentially increased risk of miscarriage or stillbirth, and due to the high risk of relapse with detoxification. So the standard of care for pregnant women addicted to opiates includes substitution therapy with methadone or buprenorphine (ACOG 2012).

2. See Bourgois 2000; Knight 2015.

3. Rebecca Project 2010.

4. Morgan and Roberts (2012: 243) develop this concept with heavy influence from Foucauldian notions of the production of regulated subjects, as well as Didier Fassin's work on the politics of valuing life in general and lives in particular: "Reproductive governance refers to the mechanisms through which different historical configurations of actors—such as state institutions, churches, donor agencies, and non-governmental organisations (NGOs)—use legislative controls, economic inducements, moral injunctions, direct coercion, and ethical incitements to produce, monitor and control reproductive behaviors and practices." Reproductive governance is about the kinds of subjects and effects that are produced when various "moral regimes" of valued reproductive behaviors intersect with political economic forces.

5. Roberts 1999; Silliman and Battacharjee 2002.

6. Roth 2012: 5.

7. Johnson 2013; Roth and Ainsworth 2015.

8. This is a classic instance of "stratified reproduction." See Colen 1986; Ginsburg and Rapp 1995.

9. Knight and Plugge 2005.

10. Paltrow and Flavin 2013.

11. See also Tsing 1992.

12. See Knight 2015: 183–84.

13. ACOG 2011. The estimate of 3–5 percent is over ten years old. The absence of updated and systematic data on pregnancy outcomes for women in custody represents the systematic neglect of the needs of pregnant women in correctional institutions. In 2016, I began a research project in which prisons and jails report pregnancy frequency and pregnancy outcomes to a central database.

14. Rebecca Project 2010; see also Ferszt and Clarke 2012.

15. Maruschak 2008.

16. Levi and Waldman 2011; Roth 2012.

17. Claitor and Butler 2014.

18. Sufrin, Kolbi-Molinas, and Roth 2015.

19. For denial of access, see Sufrin et al. 2009 and Roth 2004, 2012; for legal precedent, see Kasdan 2009. In fact, California is the only state which has a statute actively affirming that women in jail and prison have a right to abortion. Starting in 2014, NCCHC standards require: "Pregnant inmates are given comprehensive counseling and assistance in accordance with their expressed desires regarding their pregnancy, whether they elect to keep the child, use adoption services, or have an abortion." Many sites lack policies or otherwise place barriers on abortion access, which effectively forces women to continue pregnancies they might not want to carry. It makes pregnancy part of their punishment, "a uniquely gendered form of punishment" (Roth 2004: 376).

20. Women's Prison Association 2009; Annie E. Casey Foundation 2016.

21. Watterson 1996; Warner 2010; Levi and Waldman 2011.

22. Roth 2012.

23. In fact, this romanticization of motherhood is a strategy that I myself employ in advocacy work I do to help pregnant incarcerated women. I do so fully aware of the feminist implications and historical context of idealizing and essentializing motherhood.

24. See Roth 2012.

25. Inhorn 2007.

26. Van Gennep 1966 and Turner 1969; Duden 1991 and Weir 2006.

27. Casper 1998; Rapp 2001.

28. Berlant 1997.

29. Weir 2006.

30. Clarke et al. 2010.

31. See Somers and Roberts 2008; Ticktin 2011.

32. Another layer of the constructed vulnerability of the fetal subject has to do with research requirements. Federal research requirements identify fetuses and pregnant women as "vulnerable subjects" (Office for Human Research Protections 1993). Presumably this label is applied because experimental interventions have the potential to harm fetuses. There is also an implication that pregnant women are susceptible to coercion when considering participating. Prisoners,

too, constitute another category of "vulnerable research subjects." In a classic risk management strategy of bureaucracy, I had to complete additional paperwork to obtain Institutional Review Board approval for the research that went into *Jailcare*, since I was dealing with pregnant women who were prisoners.

33. Butler 2009: 14.

34. Butler 2009: xvi; Garcia 2010.

35. Rafter 1990; Kann 2005; Talvi 2007: 12.

36. Knight (2015) asks the same question, "what forms of life are possible?", in the daily rent hotels of San Francisco for addicted pregnant women, where drugs, disease, violence, instability, and infestations make the hotels signifiers for the tacit assumptions of unfit motherhood among these pregnant residents. Knight's analysis focuses on the conflicting discourses of individual responsibility and neglect attributed to the women by experts and the women themselves, and the enticements of hope for transformation.

37. The fetus in jail is a contradictory figure, what Ian Whitmarsh (2008), taking a cue from Mary Douglas's pangolin (1957), would call an anomaly. As people manage the potential threat of an anomaly, it becomes something through which "people both pronounce cultural distinctions and imagine their alternatives. With the plural uses of these anomalies, cultural values are simultaneously experienced, made real, and questioned" (Whitmarsh 2008: 13–14).

38. Whitmarsh 2008.

39. Roth 2012.

40. See Casper 1998; Weir 2006; Flavin 2009.

41. These additives were technically adequate caloric increases for pregnancy, but left many pregnant women still hungry. If women were lucky enough to have money put on their books by a friend, relative, or boyfriend outside of jail, then they could buy food off the commissary once a week. Wednesday was commissary delivery day. One Wednesday I was in D-pod and watched as Tenisha, six weeks pregnant, had a clear plastic garbage bag full of Cheetos, Ramen noodles, potato chips, cookies, and candy handed to her. This sustained her.

42. On a visit to a large Midwestern jail, a doctor told me that many women falsely reported being pregnant, knowing the privileges they would be granted for such status. As a result, this booking jail now runs urine pregnancy tests on all women, in order to avoid the exploitation.

43. Bridges 2011: 83; Davis-Floyd 2003.

44. Bridges 2011.

45. Knight and Plugge 2005; Clarke and Adashi 2011.

46. A debate ensued at the San Francisco jail over what constituted the "community standard" with regard to providing routine screening for genetic abnormalities in pregnancy. The test involves a specialized ultrasound that could not be done at the county hospital where jail patients usually went for care. Going to another site meant both extra logistics for the deputies and extra costs for the health depart-

ment. Ultimately, I argued with enough scientific evidence and conviction that the test was approved. The crux of the argument was that this constituted a "serious medical need" and that care had to match the community standard.

47. One week earlier, I had attended a workshop for physicians where I learned about "Motivational Interviewing" as a technical approach for talking about drug and alcohol use with patients. We were guided to ask questions about what patients enjoyed about drugs as a means to get them talking about their addiction. Carr (2011) has explored the potential benefits of motivational interviewing as a collaborative, less disciplinary therapeutic strategy.

48. See, among others, Bosworth 2000; Britton 2003; McCorkle 2013.

49. ACOG 2011.

50. As of January 2017, those states were: Arizona, California, Colorado, Delaware, Florida, Hawaii, Idaho, Illinois, Louisiana, Maine, Maryland, Massachusetts, Minnesota, New Mexico, Nevada, New York, Pennsylvania, Rhode Island, Texas, Vermont, Washington, and West Virginia. The District of Columbia also has a law. The first state to pass an anti-shackling law for pregnant women was Illinois in 2000. The Federal Bureau of Prisons has banned shackling of pregnant women since 2008, and in 2012 Immigration Detention also instituted a similar policy (ACOG 2016).

51. Quinn 2014; Kraft-Stoler 2015.

52. Das (2004), Taussig (1997), and Aretxaga (2003) have explored the spectral performance of the state in the everyday, as a counter to examining state power in its obvious, central locations like governments and militaries. They describe instances where the power of the state is visible in theatrical performances in everyday life, such as rituals of a border checkpoint (Das 2004). Aretxaga (2003) extends these ideas to explain how the rational technologies of control—such as incarceration—that we so often associate with state power are animated less by rationality and more by fantasy, intimacy, and bodily experiences.

53. Published narratives, media reports, and testimonies from lawsuits attest to the fact that the pregnant women who have been shackled during childbirth feel humiliated, devalued, ashamed, traumatized, and less than human. The image of a woman giving birth in chains is graphic and disturbing to the senses. It is an easy reminder of the violence of the carceral apparatus, restraining a woman in the throes of labor pains, ushering a new and idealized life into the world. The issue has been repeatedly framed through human rights discourse, explicitly denouncing the practice as a human rights violation, and a violation of the Eighth Amendment's prohibition of cruel and unusual punishment. Such framings of the issue implicitly attempt to answer the question of what it means to be human, to be a human with rights, and to be humane.

54. In 2010 and 2011, the bill was proposed and passed unanimously in the state legislature. However, each year it was vetoed by the governor, under pressure from correctional organizations.

55. Incidentally, investigation after this meeting revealed that Alex's claim—that the jail oversight board cannot enforce something that is a statute—was incorrect.

56. Bridges 2011.

6. REPRODUCTION AND CARCERAL DESIRE

1. Knight 2015.

2. Caroline Bledsoe (2002) writes about women in Gambia whose understanding of their own fertility was not structured by a temporal model of fertility declining over time. Rather, their "contingency view" of fertility was based on their traumatic reproductive experiences, like stillbirths or childbirth complications. These women used contraceptives not as a way to limit their ability to get pregnant, but to enhance it in the long run because contraceptives helped them regain their strength after a "reproductive mishap." This contingent view of fertility parallels the contingent view of motherhood that women's experiences in jail conditioned them to have, such as experiencing certain elements of separation and togetherness because of an incarceration.

3. See Foucault (1977) among others. He elaborated the techniques of the penitentiary—whose ideological and etymological roots are in "repentance"—as seeking to transform the soul of the prisoner through the disciplinary regimes of the prison.

4. "House of corrections" was a term that came into usage in the seventeenth century. After the passing of the Elizabethan Poor Law, these houses of corrections were built for vagrants and people who did not want to work (Hansan 2011). It is not entirely clear when, in the modern age of punishment, prisons and jails started to become known as "correctional institutions," but it was likely tied to prison reform movements that sought to correct the moral failings of people who had committed crimes. Nowadays, "correctional institution" is used facilely and unironically throughout criminal justice circles to refer to prison or jail, not to connect the institutions to any aspirations of correction.

5. Irwin 2005.

6. Ibid.

7. Haney 2010.

8. Berlant 2011a.

9. Haney 2010; Murphy and Rosenbaum 1999; Knight 2015.

10. Constructing addicted pregnant women as irresponsible citizens was a key discursive strategy in neoliberal welfare reform policies in the 1990s, which focused heavily on individual autonomy and behavior in restructuring the nature of safety net assistance.

11. Campbell 2000; Knight 2015.

12. Murphy and Rosenbaum 1999: 3.

13. Berlant 1997.

14. Villalobos 2014.

15. Haney 2010; Carr 2011; Knight 2015.

16. Haney 2010: 155.

17. Knight (2015) discusses this term in relation to pregnant addicted women in San Francisco. "Kin of last resort" is the family member who takes care of the child and prevents the child from going into the foster care system.

18. Waldram 2012: 11.

19. Reich 2005; Knight 2015.

20. Knight (2015) offers an analysis of intersecting temporalities for poor, addicted pregnant women in San Francisco's daily rent hotels. Addict time (the need to stave off cravings), pregnancy time, jail time, biomedical time (proving she had submitted to an adequate duration of prenatal and other care), treatment time (time in a treatment program that proved she was committed to recovery), hotel time (time to pay the owner), all of these intersecting temporalities structured these women's lives as they struggled to navigate their pregnancies and impending childbirth.

21. There are a few exceptions to this short-term, inevitability of release in jail. People who are tried while in jail and then sentenced to life in prison have little promise of release. Moreover, some trials and sentencing can take years, depending on the process of appeals, and this may make release from jail seem like an unreality.

22. Such policies were in accord with research demonstrating that increased visitation between mothers and non-newborn children reduces recidivism, though this research has been critiqued for assuming all mothers have similar pre-incarceration connections with their children. Many jails and prisons offer no contact visits even for mothers and newborns. Increasingly, in-person visitations are being replaced by video conferencing, where the visitor still has to come to the institution, but can only interact through a video camera. See Showers 1993; Enos 2001: 14.

23. One program did make it beyond the conversation phase, a community-based alternative house for pregnant women and their children. There was space for eleven mothers and their children. While there was much enthusiasm and hope for this supervised alternative to incarceration, several administrators in San Francisco informed me that mismanagement had led to it not being the supportive and successful program people had hoped. Tenisha, whom I described in chapter 5, was one of the few women to live there with her baby, until she went to a drug treatment program. See Cameo House, www.cjcj.org/Direct-services /Cameo-House.html.

24. Those states, as of 2013, were California, Idaho, Illinois, Indiana, Massachusetts, Nebraska, New York, Ohio, South Dakota, Tennessee, Texas, Washington,

and West Virginia. See Gilad and Gat (2013) for a comprehensive overview and analysis of prison nursery programs.

25. See Isralson and Matta 2003.

26. Goshin, Bryne, and Henninger 2013. Avoiding a carcerally enforced separation between a mother and newborn has its benefits. However, many advocates of mothers in prison argue that the best option is to have community-based alternative sentencing programs for these women, where they serve their time under close supervision—either probation or in a residential, supervised program, not unlike a halfway house (Villanueva 2009; Gilad and Gat 2013).

27. Indeed, researchers who study prison nurseries have hinted at this (Byrne, Goshin, and Blanchard-Lewis 2014).

28. Carr 2011.

29. Ibid.: 191.

30. See McCorkle 2013.

31. Guyer 2007.

32. See Rhodes 1998.

33. Toward the end of my fieldwork, the Sheriff's Department's initiative to improve care for pregnant women involved strengthening this already unique allowance of breastfeeding in jail. We procured an electric pump, which is much easier to use than the manual pumps the jail provided; we educated nursing staff better about breastfeeding; we enlisted a lactation specialist who could visit these women in jail; we created more private spaces for women to pump milk; and we increased the number of contact visits between mothers and newborns.

34. Knight (2015: 146) also describes the trauma some women living in San Francisco's daily rent hotels experienced from CPS removing their children. Some of these women creating memory objects of their children, reimagining their maternal trauma in the present.

35. It was notable that the San Francisco jail had a system for breastfeeding, as most jails and prisons do not. In the mid-2000s, a female lieutenant in CJ2 (who is now in a higher administration position in the Sheriff's Department) and medical services leaders worked hard to craft a breast milk policy. Although it was still hard to do in jail, to pump without the direct connection to one's baby, it was important to have that option.

36. Similarly, Knight (2015: 230) writes that some women in the daily rent hotels credited certain interactions with the criminal justice system with helping them secure child custody in the future.

37. Reich 2005.

38. See www.parentinginsideout.org.

39. Megan Comfort (2009) has similarly explored how a carceral institution can cultivate love in romantic relationships. Her ethnographic study of visits between male prisoners and their nonincarcerated female partners shows how, for some women, prison enhanced their romance, because they did not have to

negotiate things like financial logistics or even abusive elements of their relationships. The limited times to visit enabled couples to have picnics and other interactions that replicated an idealized version of romance.

40. Enos 2001.

41. Owen 1998: 58–59.

42. Ibid.: 121.

43. Shalhoub 2015.

44. Nipphatra Harivatorn (2016) has written about the strategies of drug-addicted Thai mothers who committed themselves to traditional Thai notions of motherhood, and adapted their drug use practices around these expectations, as a means to protect and heal them from the shame they internalized. This is an interesting parallel to consider for the San Francisco jail, that mothers immersing themselves in all the maternal activities the jail had to offer could, through their normative promises, potentially ameliorate feelings of stigma and shame that women might have felt from being incarcerated and mothers or pregnant women.

45. Owen 1998; Enos 2001.

46. Similarly, Nancy Scheper-Hughes (1992) has eloquently described how political-economic circumstances characterized by limited resources in a Brazilian shantytown shaped maternal sentiments. Due to malnutrition, diarrheal illnesses, and the government's indifference, mothers expected that only some of their children would survive. They pragmatically calibrated their maternal sentiments and actions to optimize the lives of those whom they sensed would live.

47. Owen 1998; Enos 2001.

48. See Fleetwood (2015) for an analysis of the emotional labor involved in creating and displaying family photographs in prison.

49. Although there are also pregnant, white women who are incarcerated, including at the San Francisco jail, black women were disproportionately represented as the pregnant ones in this jail. Of the twenty pregnant women whom I followed in my research or provided prenatal care to during my fieldwork year, all but two were women of color. These racial pregnancy proportions may be different in other locales, including in prisons, although there are no data on the demographics of pregnant incarcerated women.

50. Reproductive justice is a framework of understanding and a strategy for change that values the rights of all people to have children, to not have children, and to parent their children in safe and healthy environments. It emerged from grassroots groups of women of color who critiqued the narrow focus of white feminists on individualized reproductive choice, in favor of a broader, intersectional understanding of the range of social, political, and economic structures that disproportionately prevent women of color from raising children, and choosing not to have children, in safe environments (see Sistersong, www.sistersong .net). Mass incarceration interferes on many levels with the goals of reproductive

justice by, among many means, incarcerating men and women during their prime reproductive years, separating parents from their children, denying women access to abortion and contraception, and siphoning public funds into prisons instead of schools (Sufrin, Kolbi-Molinas, and Roth 2015).

7. CUSTODY AS FORCED AND ENFORCED INTIMACY

1. See especially Malcolm Feeley and Jonathan Simon's seminal essay "The New Penology" (1992).

2. See San Francisco Sheriff's Department, www.sfsheriff.com/division_custody.html.

3. Foucault 2007: 127.

4. Pastoral care also has strong religious connotations. There is a long tradition of religious leaders, pastors, caring for their constituents, usually through emotional and spiritual guidance. Pastoral care is often the formal name of chaplaincy support services provided to patients in hospitals or the military. In talking about the role of pastoral care in carceral settings, I am not talking about this religious context.

5. Garcia (2010: 131), in her account of intergenerational heroin addiction and treatment programs in bucolic New Mexico, pushes the notion of pastoral care beyond the control of the subject: "far from excluding the possibility of pursuing ethical ideals of caring, pastoral power might actually instantiate such an ideal."

6. *Dreams from the Monster Factory* describes the brutal, sometimes violent conditions in the San Francisco men's jail in the 1990s, based on the observations of a social worker who worked inside (Schwartz 2009).

7. Boredom and the tedium of unscheduled time are other classic techniques of punishment in contemporary U.S. "warehouse prisons" (Irwin 2005). Having nothing to do, day and night, repetitively, can be a form of punishment, and especially in solitary confinement units, can worsen mental illness (see, among others, Rhodes 2004). However, the San Francisco jail was notable for having a very busy schedule of activities—so busy that the programming coordinator sometimes had trouble accommodating all of the volunteers.

8. Irwin 2005.

9. Irwin 1985: 67.

10. Ibid.: 76.

11. Contrary to popular representations, the deputies inside the jail did not carry guns.

12. Even my research made it onto the muster board. Once my ethnographic presence was approved by the sheriff and all of the watch commanders at CJ2, it was ensconced in a memo for the muster board, which was read aloud one day at each shift's muster.

13. Such an early morning wake-up is common at jails and prisons. When I asked the pod deputies, they gave me a logistical explanation. In the morning, they had to distribute women to a variety of places—such as court or the hospital for specialist appointments. These happened early, so breakfast had to happen before then, deputies told me. There are other reasons we could speculate that the jail day started so early in the morning—perhaps so that each of the three work shifts had one meal to coordinate. Perhaps to instill a Protestant ethic of "early to bed, early to rise." Perhaps it was punishment.

14. Rhodes 2009: 205.

15. The professional choice to be a deputy inside a jail is not so simple. For some, it might be a dead-end job. Others see it as opportunities for advancement through the ranks. Indeed, I met many employees of the Sheriff's Department who had started as pod deputies and were now in senior administrative positions at City Hall. Another perspective on the "choice" of this profession is that offered by Ruth Wilson Gilmore (2007). Her meticulous political-economic account of the expansion of California's prison system discusses how the building of prisons in rural outposts creates jobs for the previously unemployed locals.

16. Arendt 1976; Rhodes 2009: 205.

17. Rhodes 2009: 205.

18. Ibid.

19. Ibid.: 207.

20. Rhodes 2009.

21. Cell phones of any kind were prohibited in the pods because of concerns that an inmate could steal it or that deputies would be distracted from their duties. This rule was posted on flyers at the entrance to the jail and in the elevators. Nonetheless, it was still quite common for deputies to have their phones with them. Civilians, too, were not allowed to bring phones into the jail, but I usually did since there was a room in the clinic for my belongings. When my bag was cursorily searched, my phone was rarely discovered. If it was, I explained that it had medical software on it.

22. Berlant 2000: 5.

23. Ibid.: 3.

24. Watterson 1996.

25. Ibid.: 73-83.

26. Rhodes 2004: 123-24.

8. AT HOME IN JAIL

1. When Kima made this reference to breaking into a car, an image from a few months earlier flashed through my mind of my own car with a smashed passenger side window and an absent radio. Though I knew Kima had not broken into

my car (among other reasons, she had been in jail at the time of the break-in), the image reminded me of other ways that Kima and I were connected. The relationship we had was cultivated through our shared experiences of her pregnancy as patient and doctor, of spending time together in the jail as informant and anthropologist. Kima's criminal activities had always seemed petty and peripheral in my mind. Our respective break-in stories reminded me that, despite the intimacy we might have cultivated, we remained in very different places in society.

2. Some of the women Knight (2015: 66) encountered in the daily rent hotels of San Francisco expressed a similar sense of comparative safety. Being on the streets was more dangerous for many women than anything that might happen in a hotel.

3. Bourgois and Schonberg 2009; Wacquant 2001, 2009a, 2009b, 2010a.

4. Ward and Kassebaum 1965; Giallombardo 1966.

5. Propper 1982; Larson 1984; Leger 1987.

6. Owen 1998: 160.

7. See also Kruttschnitt and Gartner 2005.

8. Jill McCorkle describes one such "in custody" drug treatment program for women in a state prison in her 2013 ethnography, *Breaking Women*. The program's stated goal was to provide a healing alternative to traditional incarceration, so that women could leave prison transformed and ready to start a new life. However, the program used coercive and confrontational tactics to "break women down" and make them realize that they were diseased. The treatment model the women were subjected to emphasized individual choice, and was steeped in racial stereotypes that further pathologized women's behaviors as somehow separate from larger forces in society. McCorkle argues this program was more damaging for women than if they had served their time in a traditional prison. What's more, this program was run by a private company, and thus shows how treating women in prison opens up new markets for profit.

9. This program was started by innovative, dedicated Sheriff's Department leaders in 1992. The model was to have a therapeutic community designed for women and by women inside a jail, with a focus on sisterhood and not hierarchy. A full daily schedule included various activities like recovery groups, individual therapy, acupuncture, journal writing, and group reflection.

10. Unfortunately for many inmates, D-pod closed in early 2013. It was a consequence of a positive change in San Francisco's criminal justice system, whereby fewer people were being sent to jail in the first place, diverted to community-based alternatives to incarceration including drug treatment programs. With many empty cells throughout the jail, it was not cost-effective to keep D-pod open. So these women were moved to E-pod, and integrated with other enjailed women who were not enrolled in the drug treatment program SISTERS. Most of the SISTERS women bemoaned the move after it happened. They could no

longer cultivate the exclusive, intimate family feel to the pod, for they were dispersed into the general population.

11. Heffernan 1972; Propper 1982; Larson 1984; Leger 1987.

12. See, among many others, Stack 1975 and Weston 1991.

13. Borneman 1997: 574.

14. Borneman (1997) provides an illuminating analysis of how care can be at the core of kin affiliations, even apparently contradictory kinship arrangements. He describes a court case in Germany in which an older man tries to legally adopt an adult man as his son. The two men are in a committed romantic relationship, but the younger man could not get benefits after the older man's death because marriage between two men was not recognized. So they put forth a parent-child relationship, made evident by the care the younger provided to the older.

15. Jackson 1995: 86.

16. Foucault 2007; Marx 1978; Engels 1978.

17. Ortner 1974; Ehrenreich and English 2005.

18. Jackson 1995: 122.

19. Willse (2015) provides a nuanced analysis of the production of the category "homeless" by a social services industry and neoliberal economy that relies on people being deprived of housing in order to maintain the forces of the market (2015). Interventions aimed at helping people with housing deprivation are constructed as economic programs, rather than social programs. He argues that this approach reproduces the same conditions that produced housing insecurity in the first place.

20. Bourgois and Schonberg 2010; Knight 2015.

21. Heidegger 1971.

22. Ibid.: 147.

23. Ingold 2005: 503.

24. Owen 1998.

25. Robert Desjarlais's (1997) ethnography of people living in a homeless shelter chronicles a similar sense of "settling in" to an institutional space. The communal aspects of shelter living, along with the lack of viable alternatives, allowed people to cultivate a sense of daily routine in a space, like jail, intended to be temporary.

26. Jackson 1995: 123.

27. Kruttschnitt and Gartner 2005; Owen 1998: 81.

28. Valeria Procupez (2008) describes a group of people in Buenos Aires who live collectively while also working politically to change housing policies. She shows the ways people craft domesticity not as a specific space or set of relationships, but as a process through which experiences of space and relations are articulated. Spaces and relations can be at once domestic and nondomestic, meaning that the sense of domesticity infusing a place can be fleeting. This is apt

for the jail, too, where the domestic mode in the pods arises from the carceral modes.

29. Heidegger 1971: 144.

30. See Comfort (2009) for further examples of how the carceral institution itself is woven into intimate relationships.

31. Bledsoe's (2002) analysis of Gambian women's contingent view of their reproductive bodies as depleted by traumatic births, with contraception replenishing their future fertility, shares elements with the respite and sustaining qualities some women experienced in the San Francisco jail, and how they envisioned their embodied sense of well-being. Unlike the women Bledsoe describes, for women in jail, jail was not the central lens through which they viewed their fertility.

32. Weight gain in jail is a complicated issue. The availability of any food nourishes those who are underweight when they enter jail. But there are also people for whom their poverty manifests in obesity, and they come to jail overweight. While incarcerated, many people gain an excessive amount of weight, due in part to the combination of being sedentary and eating tasteless meals that inmates supplement with junk food from the commissary (Clarke and Waring 2012). At the San Francisco women's jail, there was a treadmill in each pod, though I rarely saw it used. Some women danced to exercise videos during free time. But most women were sedentary. Excessive weight gain while incarcerated remains an underexplored area of the harmful effects of incarceration.

33. Heidegger 1971: 147.

34. Ibid.

35. Ibid.: 147.

36. Knight (2015: 83) describes this as "treatment time." CPS uses the time a woman has spent in a drug treatment program as a benchmark for her worthy motherhood.

CONCLUSION

1. See among others Reich 2005; Roberts 2002.

2. Berlant 2011b.

3. I helped to spearhead efforts to expand women's access to family planning services while in jail. While survey research has documented that many incarcerated women want to start a method while still in custody (Clarke et al. 2006; LaRochelle et al. 2012), I was mindful of the coercive environment of jail and of histories of institutionally suppressing the reproduction of poor women of color. Our family planning protocols incorporated this awareness by focusing on a woman's desires about pregnancy, rather than just on birth control. We offered pre-conception counseling for women who wanted to be pregnant, and if a

woman chose a long-acting birth control method that a doctor had to insert, like an intrauterine device, she had at least two separate clinic visits to be sure she wanted this method (Sufrin, Oxnard, et al. 2015).

4. See Gottschalk 2014, chapter 11.

5. Nelson 2010: 23.

6. Dolovich 2009: 891.

7. I thank Michele Goodwin for helping to articulate this sense of failure of our collective imagination to value these women.

8. Beiser 2014.

9. See Nelson 2010: 23.

10. See www.nytimes.com/2016/12/17/opinion/sunday/the-tent-cities-of-san-francisco.html?_r=0.

11. The proposal to build a new jail was motivated by the closure of an existing jail because it was seismically unsafe (Green 2015).

12. Goodwin 2015.

13. Gottschalk 2015.

14. Mahmood 2005.

15. Jackson 1995: 122.

16. Wacquant 2002: 388.

Bibliography

Aas, Katja Franko. 2005. *Sentencing in the Age of Information: From Faust to Macintosh*. Coogee, NSW: Glass House Press.

Ackerman, John P., Tracy Riggins, and Maureen Black. 2010. "A Review of the Effects of Prenatal Cocaine Exposure among School-aged Children." *Pediatrics* 125(3): 554–65.

Alexander, Michelle. 2010. *The New Jim Crow: Mass Incarceration in the Age of Colorblindness*. New York: New Press.

al Hasan Moqbel, Samir Naji. 2013. "Gitmo Is Killing Me." *New York Times*, April 14. www.nytimes.com/2013/04/15/opinion/hunger-striking-at-guantanamo-bay.html. Accessed January 24, 2017.

American Civil Liberties Union (ACLU). 2010. "In for a Penny: The Rise of America's New Debtors' Prisons." www.aclu.org/files/assets/InForAPenny_web.pdf. Accessed January 24, 2017.

———. 2014a. "LA County Jails." www.aclu.org/la-county-jails. Accessed January 19, 2017.

———. 2014b. "End the Abuse: Protecting LGBTI Prisoners from Sexual Assault." www.aclu.org/other/prison-rape-elimination-act-prea-toolkit-end-abuse-protecting-lgbti-prisoners-sexual-assault. Accessed January 24, 2017.

———. "The Prison Crisis." www.aclu.org/prison-crisis. Accessed January 24, 2017.

American Civil Liberties Union of Pennsylvania (ACLUPA). 2012. "Reproductive Health Locked Up: An Examination of Pennsylvania Jail Policies." www .aclupa.org/download_file/view_inline/756/484/. Accessed January 24, 2017.
American College of Obstetricians and Gynecologists (ACOG). 2011. "Health Care for Pregnant and Postpartum Incarcerated Women and Adolescent Females." Committee Opinion no. 511. *Obstetrics and Gynecology* 118: 1198–202.
———. 2012. "Opioid Abuse, Dependence, and Addiction in Pregnancy." Committee Opinion no. 524. *Obstetrics and Gynecology* 119: 1070–76.
———. 2016. "Incarcerated Pregnant Women: Limiting Use of Restraints." 2016 ACOG State Legislation Tally. www.acog.org/About-ACOG/ACOG-Departments/State-Legislative-Activities/Shackling-of-Incarcerated-Pregnant-Inmates. Accessed January 24, 2017.
American Correctional Association. 1870. *Declaration of Principles Adopted and Promulgated by the 1870 Congress of the National Prison Association.* www.aca.org/aca_prod_imis/docs/Exec/1870Declaration_of_Principles .pdf. Accessed January 24, 2017.
American Medical Association. 1973. *Medical Care in U.S. Jails, 1972 AMA Survey.* Chicago: American Medical Association.
American Osteopathic Association. 2012. "Approval of Certification of Added Qualifications (CAQ) Jurisdiction in Correctional Medicine / Conjoint Exam Process." www.osteopathic.org/inside-aoa/events/midyear-meeting /Documents/2012-midyear-meeting-documents/B-16-Correctional-Medicine-BOS.pdf. Accessed January 24, 2017.
Anderson, Patrick. 2009. "There Will Be No Bobby Sands in Guantánamo Bay." *PMLA* 124(5): 1729–36.
Annie E. Casey Foundation. 2016. "A Shared Sentence: The Devastating Toll of Parental Incarceration on Kids, Families, and Communities." www.aecf.org /resources/a-shared-sentence/. Accessed January 24, 2017.
Anno, B. Jaye. 2001. *Correctional Health Care: Guidelines for the Management of an Adequate Delivery System.* Chicago: National Commission on Correctional Health Care.
Arditti, Joyce A. 2012. *Parental Incarceration and the Family: Psychological and Social Effects of Imprisonment on Children, Parents, and Caregivers.* New York: New York University Press.
Arendt, Hannah. 1976. *The Origins of Totalitarianism.* New York: Harcourt.
Aretxaga, Begoña. 2003. "Maddening States." *Annual Review of Anthropology* 32: 393–410.
Bandyopadhyay, Mahuya. 2010. *Everyday Life in a Prison: Confinement, Surveillance, Resistance.* New Delhi: Orient Black Swan.
Barton, Bernadette. 2011. "My Auto / Ethnographic Dilemma: Who Owns the Story?" *Qualitative Sociology* 34: 431–45.

Baum, Dan. 2016. "Legalize It All: How to Win the War on Drugs." *Harpers Magazine,* April. http://harpers.org/archive/2016/04/legalize-it-all/. Accessed January 24, 2017.

Bauman, Zygmunt. 1989. *Modernity and the Holocaust.* Ithaca, NY: Cornell University Press.

Bayer, Ronald, and David Wilkinson. 1995. "Directly Observed Therapy for Tuberculosis: History of an Idea." *Lancet* 345(8964): 1545–48.

Bazelon Center for Mental Health Law. 2006. *Arrested? What Happens to Your Benefits If You Go to Jail or Prison? A Guide to Federal Rules on SSI, SSDI, Medicaid, Medicare, and Veterans Benefits for Adults with Disabilities.* Written by Chris Koyanagi. Edited by Lee Carty. Judge David L. Bazelon Center for Mental Health Law. www.kitsapgov.com/pubdef/Forms /LinkClick.Benefits.pdf/. Accessed January 24, 2017.

Beiser, Vince. 2014. "Obamacare Is a Powerful New Crime-Fighting Tool." *Atlantic,* January 14. www.theatlantic.com/national/archive/2014/01 /obamacare-is-a-powerful-new-crime-fighting-tool/283058/. Accessed January 24, 2017.

Berlant, Lauren. 1997. *The Queen of America Goes to Washington City: Essays on Sex and Citizenship.* Durham, NC: Duke University Press.

———. 2000. *Intimacy.* Chicago: University of Chicago Press.

———. 2004. "Introduction: Compassion (and Withholding)." In *Compassion: The Culture and Politics of an Emotion,* ed. Lauren Berlant, 1–14. New York: Routledge.

———. 2011a. *Cruel Optimism.* Durham, NC: Duke University Press.

———. 2011b. "A Properly Political Concept of Love: Three Approaches in Ten Pages." *Cultural Anthropology* 26(4): 683–91.

Biehl, Joao, Joseph Amon, Mariana Socal, and Adriana Petryna. 2012. "Between the Court and the Clinic: Lawsuits for Medicines and the Right to Health in Brazil." *Health and Human Rights* 14(1): 36–52.

Biehl, Joao, Adriana Petryna, Alex Gertner, Joseph Amon, and Paulo D. Picon. 2009. "Judicialisation of the Right to Health in Brazil." *Lancet* 373(9682): 2182–84.

Black Lives Matter. 2016. www.blacklivesmatter.com. Accessed January 24, 2017.

Bledsoe, Caroline H. 2002. *Contingent Lives: Fertility, Time, and Aging in West Africa.* Chicago: University of Chicago Press.

Bloom, Barbara, Barbara Owen, and Stephanie Covington. 2003. *Gender Responsive Strategies: Research, Practice and Guiding Principles for Women Offenders.* National Institute of Corrections, U.S. Department of Justice. Accession No. 018017.

Borneman, John. 1997. "Caring and Being Cared For: Displacing Marriage, Kinship, Gender and Sexuality." *International Social Science Journal* 49(154): 573–84.

Bosworth, Mary. 2000. "Confining Femininity: A History of Gender, Power, and Imprisonment." *Theoretical Criminology* 4: 265–85.

Bourdieu, Pierre, and Loïc Wacquant. 2007. "Symbolic Violence." In *Violence in War and Peace: An Anthology*, ed. Nancy Scheper-Hughes and Philippe Bourgois, 272–74. Malden, MA: Blackwell.

Bourgois, Philippe. 2000. "Disciplining Addictions: The Bio-politics of Methadone and Heroin in the United States." *Culture, Medicine, and Psychiatry* 24: 165–95.

——, and Jeff Schonberg. 2009. *Righteous Dopefiend.* Berkeley: University of California Press.

Braz, Rose. 2006. "Kinder, Gentler Gender Responsive Cages: Prison Expansion Is Not Prison Reform." *Women, Girls and Criminal Justice* (October/November): 87–88, 91.

Bridges, Khiara. 2011. *Reproducing Race: An Ethnography of Pregnancy as a Site of Racialization.* Berkeley: University of California Press.

Britton, Dana. 2003. *At Work in the Iron Cage: The Prison as Gendered Organization.* New York: New York University Press.

Brodwin, Paul. 2013. *Everyday Ethics: Voices from the Front Line of Community Psychiatry.* Berkeley: University of California Press.

Butler, Judith. 2009. *Frames of War: When Is Life Grievable?* New York: Verso.

Byrne, Mary W., Lorie Goshin, and Barbara Blanchard-Lewis. 2012. "Maternal Separations during the Reentry Years for 100 Infants Raised in a Prison Nursery." *Family Court Review* 50(1): 77–90.

California Department of Social Services. 2014. *California—Child and Family Services Review: City and County of San Francisco Self Assessment.* www .sfhsa.org/asset/ReportsDataResources/2014_SF_CSA_Master__FINAL_ APPROVED.pdf. Accessed January 24, 2017.

Cameo House, Center on Juvenile and Criminal Justice. www.cjcj.org /Direct-services/Cameo-House.html. Accessed January 19, 2017.

Campbell, Nancy. 2000. *Using Women: Gender, Drug Policy, and Social Justice.* Routledge: New York.

Cantor, Julie. 2012. "Court-Ordered Care: A Complication of Pregnancy to Avoid." *New England Journal of Medicine* 366(24): 2237–40.

Carlen, Pat. 2008. "Imaginary Penalties and Risk-Crazed Governance." In *Imaginary Penalties*, ed. Pat Carlen. Portland, OR: Willan.

Carr, E. Summerson. 2011. *Scripting Addiction: The Politics of Therapeutic Talk and American Sobriety.* Princeton, NJ: Princeton University Press.

Carson, E. Ann, and Elizabeth Anderson. 2016. *Prisoners in 2015.* Bureau of Justice Statistics. Washington, DC: U.S. Department of Justice. NCJ 250229.

Carson, E. Ann, and Daniela Golinelli. 2013. *Prisoners in 2012: Advance Counts.* Bureau of Justice Statistics. Washington, DC: U.S. Department of Justice. NCJ 242467.

Carson, E. Ann, and William J. Sabol. 2012. "Prisoners in 2011." Bureau of Justice Statistics. Washington, DC: U.S. Department of Justice. NCJ 239808.

Casper, Monica J. 1998. *The Making of the Unborn Patient: A Social Anatomy of Fetal Surgery.* New Brunswick, NJ: Rutgers University Press.

Chang, Heewon. 2008. *Autoethnography as Method.* Walnut Creek, CA: Left Coast Press.

Christensen, Dan. 2013. "Florida Prison Healthcare Providers Sued Hundreds of Times." *Miami Herald,* October 2. www.miamiherald.com/news/state /article1955813.html. Accessed January 24, 2017.

Claitor, D., and B. Butler. 2014. "Pregnant Women in Texas County Jails Deserve Better Than This." *Dallas Morning News,* June 27. www.dallasnews .com/opinion/latest-columns/20140626-pregnant-women-in-texas-county-jails-deserve-better-than-this.ece. Accessed January 24, 2017.

Clark, Krissy. 2013. "How Did the Social Safety Net Get Its Name?" *Marketplace,* April 2. www.marketplace.org/topics/wealth-poverty/show-your-safety-net /how-did-social-safety-net-get-its-name. Accessed January 24, 2017.

Clarke, Adele, Janet K. Shim, Laura Mamo, Jennifer Ruth Fosket, and Jennifer R. Fishman, eds. 2010. *Biomedicalization: Technoscientific Transformations of Health, Illness, and U.S. Biomedicine.* Durham, NC: Duke University Press.

Clarke, Jennifer, and Eli Adashi. 2011. "Perinatal Care for Incarcerated Patients: A 25-Year-Old Woman Pregnant in Jail." *Journal of the American Medical Association* 305(9): 923–29.

Clarke, Jennifer, Megan Hebert, Cynthia Rosengard, Jennifer Rose, Kristen DaSilva, and Michael Stein. 2006. "Reproductive Health Care and Family Planning Needs among Incarcerated Women." *American Journal of Public Health* 96(5): 834–39.

Clarke, Jennifer, and Molly E. Waring. 2012. "Overweight, Obesity, and Weight Change among Incarcerated Women." *Journal of Correctional Health Care* 18(4): 285–92.

Clemmer, Donald. 1958. *The Prison Community.* New York: Holt, Rinehart and Winston.

Clifford, James, and George Marcus. 1986. *Writing Culture: The Poetics and Politics of Ethnography.* Berkeley: University of California Press.

Coates, Ta-Nehisi. 2015. "The Black Family in the Age of Mass Incarceration." *Atlantic,* October. www.theatlantic.com/magazine/archive/2015/10/the-black-family-in-the-age-of-mass-incarceration/403246/.

Coleman, Novella. 2016. "Federal Judge Confirms that San Francisco Police Target Black People in Drug Law Enforcement." *American Civil Liberties Union of Northern California,* July 1. www.aclunc.org/blog/federal-judge-confirms-san-francisco-police-target-black-people-drug-law-enforcement. Accessed January 24, 2017.

Colen, Shellee. 1986. "'With Respect and Feelings': Voices of West Indian Childcare and Domestic Workers in New York City." In *All American Women: Lines that Divide, Ties that Bind*, ed. Johnnetta B. Cole. New York: Free Press.

Comaroff, John, and Jean Comaroff. 1992. *Ethnography and the Historical Imagination*. Boulder, CO: Westview Press.

Comfort, Megan. 2009. *Doing Time Together: Love and Family in the Shadow of the Prison*. Chicago: University of Chicago Press.

Conover, Ted. 2001. *Newjack: Guarding Sing Sing*. New York: Vintage Books.

Cook, Tristan. 2011. "SFGH's Ward 86: Pioneering HIV/AIDS Care for 30 Years." *UCSF News Center*, June 7. www.ucsf.edu/news/2011/06/9988/sfghs-ward-86-pioneering-hiv-aids-care-30-years. Accessed January 24, 2017.

Covington, Stephanie. 2007. "Women and the Criminal Justice System." *Women's Health Issues* 17: 180–82.

Crowley-Matoka, Megan, and Gala True. 2012. "'No One Wants to Be the Candy Man': Ambivalent Medicalization and Clinician Subjectivity in Pain Management." *Cultural Anthropology* 27(4): 689–712.

Cunha, Manuela. 2014. "The Ethnography of Prisons and Penal Confinement." *Annual Review of Anthropology* 43: 217–33.

Das, Veena. 2004. "The Signature of the State: The Paradox of Illegibility." In *Anthropology in the Margins of the State*, ed. Veena Das and Deborah Poole. Santa Fe: School of American Research Press.

———, Jonathan Ellen, and Laurie Leonard. 2008. "On the Modalities of the Domestic." *Home Cultures* 5(3): 349–72.

Davis, Angela. 1997. *Race and Criminalization: Black Americans and the Punishment Industry*. New York: Pantheon Books.

Davis-Floyd, Robbie. 2003. *Birth as an American Rite of Passage*. Berkeley: University of California Press.

Deleuze, Gilles. 1992. "Postscript on the Societies of Control." *October* 59: 3–7.

DelVecchio Good, Mary-Jo. 1995. *American Medicine: The Quest for Competence*. Berkeley: University of California Press.

Desjarlais, Robert. 1997. *Shelter Blues: Sanity and Selfhood among the Homeless*. Philadelphia: University of Pennsylvania Press.

Dolovich, Sharon. 2009. "Cruelty, Prison Conditions, and the Eighth Amendment." *New York University Law Review* 84(4): 881–979.

Douglas, Mary. 1957. "Animals in Lélé Religious Symbolism." *Africa: Journal of the International African Institute* 27(1): 46–58.

Drucker, Ernest. 2011. *A Plague of Prisons: The Epidemiology of Mass Incarceration in America*. New York: New Press.

Duane, Daniel. 2016. "The Tent Cities of San Francisco." *New York Times*, December 17. www.nytimes.com/2016/12/17/opinion/sunday/the-tent-cities-of-san-francisco.html?_r=0. Accessed January 19, 2017.

Duden, Barbara. 1991. *The Woman beneath the Skin: A Doctor's Patients in Eighteenth-Century Germany.* Translated by Thomas Dunlap. Cambridge, MA: Harvard University Press.

Dumont, Dora, Brad Brockmann, Samuel Dickman, Nicole Alexander, and Josiah D. Rich. 2013. "Public Health and the Epidemic of Incarceration." *Annual Review of Public Health* 33: 325–39.

Durkheim, Emile. 1982. *The Rules of Sociological Method: New York and Selected Texts on Sociology and Its Methods.* New York: Macmillan.

Editorial Board. 2016. "California Deposes Its 'Welfare Queen.'" *New York Times,* July 23. www.nytimes.com/2016/07/24/opinion/sunday/california-deposes-its-welfare-queen.html?_r = 0. Accessed January 24, 2017.

Ehrenreich, Barbara. 2015. "It Is Expensive to Be Poor." *Atlantic,* January 13. www.theatlantic.com/business/archive/2014/01/it-is-expensive-to-be-poor/282979/. Accessed January 24, 2017.

———, and Deirdre English. 2005. *For Her Own Good: Two Centuries of the Experts' Advice to Women.* New York: Random House.

Engels, Frederick. 1978. "The Origin of the Family, Private Property, and the State." In *The Marx-Engels Reader,* ed. Robert C. Tucker. New York: W. W. Norton.

Enos, Sandra. 2001. *Mothering from the Inside: Parenting in a Women's Prison.* Albany: State University of New York Press.

Estroff, Sue E. 1981. *Making It Crazy: An Ethnography of Psychiatric Clients in an American Community.* Berkeley: University of California Press.

Farmer, Paul. 1992. *AIDS and Accusation: Haiti and the Geography of Blame.* Berkeley: University of California Press.

———. 1999. *Infections and Inequalities: The Modern Plagues.* Berkeley: University of California Press.

Fassin, Didier. 2010. "Inequality of Lives, Hierarchies of Humanity: Moral Commitments and Ethical Dilemmas of Humanitarianism." In *In the Name of Humanity: The Government of Threat and Care,* ed. Ilana Feldman and Miriam Ticktin, 238–55. Durham, NC: Duke University Press.

———, and Paula Vasquez. 2005. "Humanitarian Exception as the Rule." *American Ethnologist* 32(3): 389–405.

Fazel, Seena, Parveen Bains, and Helen Doll. 2006. "Substance Abuse and Dependence in Prisoners: A Systematic Review." *Addiction* 101(2): 181–91.

Feeley, Malcolm, and Jonathan Simon. 1992. "The New Penology: Notes on the Emerging Strategy of Corrections and Its Implications." *Criminology* 30(4): 449–74.

Ferszt, G. G., and J. G. Clarke. 2012. "Health Care of Pregnant Women in U. S. State Prisons." *Journal of Health Care for the Poor and Underserved* 23(2): 557–69.

Flavin, Jeanne. 2009. *Our Bodies, Our Crimes: The Policing of Women's Reproduction in America*. New York: New York University Press.

Fleetwood, Nicole R. 2015. "Posing in Prison: Family Photographs, Emotional Labor, and Carceral Intimacy." *Public Culture* 27(3): 487–511.

Fleury-Steiner, Benjamin. 2008. *Dying Inside: The HIV/AIDS Ward at Limestone Prison*. Ann Arbor: University of Michigan Press.

Ford, Matt. 2015. "America's Largest Mental Hospital Is a Jail." *Atlantic*, June 18. www.theatlantic.com/politics/archive/2015/06/americas-largest-mental-hospital-is-a-jail/395012/. Accessed January 24, 2017.

Foucault, Michel. 1977. *Discipline and Punish: The Birth of the Prison*. Translated by Alan Sheridan. New York: Vintage Books.

———. 1994. "Politics of Health in the Eighteenth Century." In *The Essential Foucault: Selections from the Essential Works of Foucault 1954–1984*, ed. Paul Rabinow and Nikolas Rose, 338–50. New York: New Press.

———. 2007. *Security, Territory, Population: Lectures at the College de France, 1978–1979*. Translated by Graham Burchell. New York: Picador.

Garcia, Angela. 2010. *The Pastoral Clinic: Addiction and Depression along the Rio Grande*. Berkeley: University of California Press.

———. 2015. "Serenity: Violence, Inequality, and Recovery on the Edge of Mexico City." *Medical Anthropology Quarterly* 29(4): 455–72.

Giallombardo, Rose. 1966. *Society of Women: A Study of a Women's Prison*. New York: Wiley.

Gilad, Michal, and Tal Gat. 2013. "*U.S. v. My Mommy:* Evaluation of Prison Nurseries as a Solution for Children of Incarcerated Women." *New York University Review of Law and Social Change* 36: 372–402.

Gilligan, Carol. 1982. *In a Different Voice: Psychological Theory and Women's Development*. Cambridge, MA: Harvard University Press.

Gillon, Steven M. 2000. "Politics of Deinstitutionalization." In *That's Not What We Meant To Do: Reform and Its Unintended Consequences in Twentieth-Century America*. New York: W. W. Norton.

Gilmore, Ruth Wilson. 2007. *Golden Gulag: Prisons, Surplus, Crisis and Opposition in Globalizing California*. Berkeley: University of California Press.

Gilroy, Leonard, and Harris Kenny. 2012. "Texas, Other States Exploring Prison Health Care Privatization." *Corrections Forum* 21(3): 14–20.

Ginsburg, Faye, and Rayna Rapp, eds. 1995. *Conceiving the New World Order: The Global Politics of Reproduction*. Berkeley: University of California Press.

Glaser, Jordan B., and Robert B. Greifinger. 1993. "Correctional Health Care: A Public Health Opportunity." *Annals of Internal Medicine* 118(2): 139–45.

Glaze, Lauren E., and Laura Maruschak. 2008. *Parents in Prison and Their Minor Children*. Washington, DC: Bureau of Justice Statistics. NCJ 222984.

Glaze, Lauren E., and Erica Parks. 2012. *Correctional Populations in the United States, 2011.* Washington, DC: Bureau of Justice Statistics. NCJ 239972.

Glenn, Evelyn Nakano. 2012. *Forced to Care: Coercion and Caregiving in America.* Cambridge, MA: Harvard University Press.

Goffman, Alice. 2014. *On the Run: Fugitive Life in an American City.* Chicago: University of Chicago Press.

Goffman, Erving. 2007 [1961]. *Asylums: Essays on the Social Situation of Mental Patients and Other Inmates.* New Brunswick, NJ: Transaction.

Gold, Rachel Benson. 2014. "Guarding against Coercion While Ensuring Access: A Delicate Balance." *Guttmacher Policy Review* 17(3): 8–14.

Goodman, Melissa, Ruth Dawson, and Phyllida Burlingame. 2016. "Reproductive Health behind Bars in California." American Civil Liberties Union of California. www.aclunc.org/ReproductiveHealthBehindBars_Report. Accessed January 24, 2017.

Goodwin, Michele. 2015. "Invisible Women: Mass Incarceration's Forgotten Casualties." *Texas Law Review* 94(2): 353–86.

Gordillo, Gastón. 2006. "The Crucible of Citizenship: ID-paper Fetishism in the Argentinean Chaco." *American Ethnologist* 33(2): 162–76.

Goshin, Lorie S., Mary W. Byrne, and Barbara Blanchard-Lewis. 2014. "Preschool Outcomes of Children Who Lived as Infants in a Prison Nursery." *Prison Journal* 94(2): 139–58.

Goshin, Lorie S., Mary W. Byrne, and Alana M. Henninger. 2013. "Recidivism after Release from a Prison Nursery Program." *Public Health Nursing* 31(2): 109–17.

Gottschalk, Marie. 2013. "Caught: Race, Neoliberalism, and the Future of Penal Reform and American Politics." Conference abstract for Prison Scholarship Roundtable, University of Michigan, January 31–February 1. www.law.umich .edu/workshopsandsymposia/Pages/prisonroundtable.aspx. Accessed January 24, 2017.

———. 2014. *Caught: The Prison State and the Lockdown of American Politics.* Princeton, NJ: Princeton University Press.

Grattet, Ryken. 2013. "Realignment in California: The Story So Far." *Crime Report,* July 22. www.ppic.org/main/commentary.asp?i=1379. Accessed January 24, 2017.

Green, Emily. 2015. "No New Jail after S. F. Supervisors Refuse to Allocate Funds." *San Francisco Chronicle,* December 16. www.sfgate.com/bayarea /article/No-new-jail-S-F-supervisors-refuse-to-6700835.php. Accessed January 24, 2017.

Guidestar. www.guidestar.org. Accessed January 24, 2017.

Guyer, Jane. 2007. "Prophecy and the Near Future: Thoughts on Macroeconomic, Evangelical, and Punctuated Time." *Cultural Anthropology* 34(3): 409–21.

Han, Clara. 2012. *Life in Debt: Times of Care and Violence in Neoliberal Chile.* Berkeley: University of California Press.

Haney, Lynn. 2010. *Offending Women: Power, Punishment, and the Regulation of Desire.* Berkeley: University of California Press.

Hansan, J. E. 2011. "English Poor Laws: Historical Precedents of Tax-supported Relief for the Poor." www.socialwelfarehistory.com/programs/poor-laws/. Accessed January 24, 2017.

Haraway, Donna. 1988 "Situated Knowledges: The Science Question in Feminism and the Privilege of Partial Perspective." *Feminist Studies* 14(3): 575–99.

Haritavorn, Niphattra. 2016. "I Am Just a 'Maae' (Mother): Experiences of Mothers Injecting Drugs in Thailand." *Sociology of Health and Illness* 38(7): 1167–79.

Harlow, Caroline Wolf. 1999. *Prior Abuse Reported by Inmates and Probationers.* Bureau of Justice Statistics. Washington, DC: U.S. Department of Justice. NCJ 172879.

Heffernan, Esther. 1972. *Making It in Prison: The Square, the Cool and the Life.* New York: Wiley and Sons.

Heidegger, Martin. 1971. "Building Dwelling Thinking." In *Poetry, Language, Thought,* trans. Albert Hofstadter, 143–59. New York: Harper Colophon Books.

———. 2010. *Being and Time.* Translated by Joan Stambaugh. Albany: State University of New York Press.

Herzfeld, Michael. 1992. *The Social Production of Indifference: Exploring the Symbolic Roots of Western Bureaucracy.* New York: Berg.

Ho, Vivian. 2016. "SF Pilot Program Looks to Help Drug Users, Not Arrest Them." *San Francisco Chronicle,* May 8. www.sfchronicle.com/crime/article/SF-pilot-program-looks-to-help-drug-users-not-7421843.php. Accessed January 24, 2017.

Holmes, Seth, and Maya Ponte. 2011. "En-case-ing the Patient: Disciplining Uncertainty in Medical Student Patient Presentations." *Culture, Medicine, and Psychiatry* 35: 163–82.

Hudson, David. 2015. "President Obama: 'Our Criminal Justice System Isn't as Smart as It Should Be.'" *White House Blog.* www.whitehouse.gov/blog/2015/07/15/president-obama-our-criminal-justice-system-isnt-smart-it-should-be. Accessed January 24, 2017.

Human Rights Watch. 2009. "Decades of Disparity: Drug Arrests and Race in the United States." www.hrw.org/report/2009/03/02/decades-disparity/drug-arrests-and-race-united-states. Accessed January 24, 2017.

Ingold, Tim. 2005. "Towards a Politics of Dwelling." *Conservation and Society* 3(2): 501–8.

Inhorn, Marcia. 2007. "Introduction: Defining Health: A Dozen Messages from More Than 150 Ethnographies." In *Reproductive Disruptions: Gender,*

Technology, and Biopolitics in the New Millennium, ed. Marcia Inhorn, 1–41. New York: Berghahn Books.

Institute for Policy Studies. 2015. *The Poor Get Prison.* Karen Dolan and Jodi L. Carr, co-authors. Washington, DC: Institute for Policy Studies.

Irwin, John. 1985. *The Jail: Managing the Underclass in American Society.* Berkeley: University of California Press.

———. 2005. *The Warehouse Prison: Disposal of the New Dangerous Class.* Los Angeles: Roxbury.

Isaacs, Caroline. 2013. "Death Yards: Continuing Problems with Arizona's Correctional Health Care." Tuscon: American Friends Service Committee. http://afsc.org/sites/afsc.civicactions.net/files/documents/DeathYards FINAL.pdf. Accessed January 24, 2017.

Isralson, Odile, and Lina Matta. 2003. *Prison Lullabies.* Brown Hats Production. www.prisonlullabies.com/. Accessed January 24, 2017.

Jackson, Michael. 1995. *At Home in the World.* Durham, NC: Duke University Press.

James, Doris J., and Lauren E. Glaze. 2006. *Mental Health Problems of Prison and Jail Inmates.* Bureau of Justice Statistics. Washington, DC: U.S. Department of Justice. NCJ 213600.

Johnson, Corey. 2013. "Female Inmates Sterilized in California Prisons without Approval." *Center for Investigative Reporting,* July 7. www.cironline.org /reports/female-inmates-sterilized-california-prisons-without-approval-4917. Accessed January 24, 2017.

Kaeble, Danielle, and Lauren Glaze. 2016. "Correctional Populations in the United States, 2015." Bureau of Justice Statistics. Washington, DC: U.S. Department of Justice. NCJ 250374.

Kaiser Family Foundation. 2016. "Key Facts about the Uninsured Population." September 29. www.kff.org/uninsured/fact-sheet/key-facts-about-the-uninsured-population/. Accessed January 24, 2017.

Kann, Mark. 2005. *Punishment, Prisons, and Patriarchy: Liberty and Power in the Early American Republic.* New York: New York University Press.

Kasdan, Diana. 2009. "Abortion Access for Incarcerated Women: Are Correctional Health Practices in Conflict with Constitutional Standards?" *Perspectives in Sexual and Reproductive Health* 41(1): 59–62.

Katz, Mitchell H., and Tangerine M. Brigham. 2011. "Transforming a Traditional Safety Net into a Coordinated Care System: Lessons from Healthy San Francisco." *HealthAffairs* 30(2): 237–45.

Kittay, Eva Feder. 1999. *Love's Labor: Essays on Women, Equality, and Dependency.* New York: Routledge.

Kleinman, Arthur. 1981. *Patients and Healers in the Context of Culture: An Exploration of the Borderland between Anthropology, Medicine, and Psychiatry.* Berkeley: University of California Press.

———. 1995. *Writing at the Margin: Discourse between Anthropology and Medicine.* Berkeley: University of California Press.

———, and Bridget Hanna. 2008. "Catastrophe, Caregiving and Today's Biomedicine." *Biosocieties* 3: 287–301.

Knight, Heather. 2014. "Income Inequality on Par with Developing Nations." *San Francisco Chronicle,* June 25. www.sfgate.com/bayarea/article/Income-inequality-on-par-with-developing-nations-5486434.php. Accessed January 24, 2017.

Knight, Kelly. 2015. *addicted.pregnant.poor.* Durham, NC: Duke University Press.

Knight, Marian, and Emma Plugge. 2005. "The Outcomes of Pregnancy among Imprisoned Women: A Systematic Review." *British Journal of Obstetrics and Gynecology* 112: 1467–74.

Koch, Erin. 2013. *Free Market Tuberculosis: Managing Epidemics in Post-Soviet Georgia.* Nashville: Vanderbilt University Press.

Kraft-Stoler, Tamar. 2015. "Reproductive Injustice: The State of Reproductive Health Care for Women in New York State Prisons." Correctional Association of New York. www.correctionalassociation.org/wp-content/uploads/2015/03/Reproductive-Injustice-FULL-REPORT-FINAL-2-11-15.pdf.

Kristof, Nicholas. 2014. "Inside a Mental Hospital Called Jail." *New York Times,* February 8. www.nytimes.com/2014/02/09/opinion/sunday/inside-a-mental-hospital-called-jail.html?_r=0. Accessed January 24, 2017.

Kruttschnitt, Candace. 2010. "The Paradox of Women's Imprisonment." *Daedalus* 139(3): 32–42.

———, and Rosemary Gartner. 2005. *Marking Time in the Golden State: Women's Imprisonment in California.* Cambridge: Cambridge University Press.

Kyckelhahn, Tracey. 2012. *State Corrections Expenditures, FY 1982–2010.* Bureau of Justice Statistics. Washington, DC: U.S. Department of Justice. NCJ 239672.

———. 2013. *Local Government Corrections Expenditures, FY 2005–2011.* Bureau of Justice Statistics. Washington, DC: U.S. Department of Justice. NCJ 243527.

Landsbaum, Claire. 2016. "North Carolina Releases Results of Welfare-Applicant Drug Tests, and Barely Any Came Back Positive." *New York Magazine,* February 10. www.nymag.com/daily/intelligencer/2016/02/ncs-welfare-drug-tests-find-minimal-drug-use.html. Accessed January 24, 2017.

LaRochelle, Flynn, Cynthia Castro, Joe Goldenson, Jacqueline P. Tulsky, Deborah L. Cohan, Paul Blumenthal, and Carolyn B. Sufrin. 2012. "Contraception Use and Barriers to Access among Newly Arrested Women." *Journal of Correctional Health Care* 18(2): 111–19.

Larson, James H. 1984. "Women, Friendship, and Adaptation to Prison." *Journal of Criminal Justice* 12(6): 601–15.

Leder, Drew. 1990. *The Absent Body*. Chicago: University of Chicago Press.

Leger, Robert. 1987. "Lesbianism among Women Prisoners: Participants and Nonparticipants." *Criminal Justice and Behavior* 14(4): 448–67.

Leonard, Abigail, and Adam May. 2013. "Arizona's Privatized Prison Health Care under Fire after Deaths." *Aljazeera America,* December 2. http://america.aljazeera.com/watch/shows/america-tonight/america-tonight-blog/2013/12/2/arizona-s-privatizedprisonhealthcareunderfireafterdeaths.html. Accessed January 24, 2017.

Levi, Robin, and Ayelet Waldman, eds. 2011. *Inside This Place, Not of It: Narratives from Women's Prisons*. San Francisco: McSweeney's Books.

Linde, Charlotte. 1999. "The Transformation of Narrative Syntax into Institutional Memory." *Narrative Inquiry* 9(1): 139–74.

Livingston, Julie. 2012. *Improvising Medicine: An African Oncology Ward in an Emerging Cancer Epidemic*. Durham, NC: Duke University Press.

Mahmood, Saba. 2005. *Politics of Piety: The Islamic Revival and the Feminist Subject*. Princeton, NJ: Princeton University Press.

Maruschak, Lauren M. 2008. *Medical Problems of Prisoners*. Bureau of Justice Statistics. Washington, DC: U. S. Department of Justice. NCJ 221740.

Marx, Karl. 1978. "Manifesto of the Communist Party." *The Marx-Engels Reader,* ed. Robert C. Tucker. New York: W. W. Norton.

Maurer, Marc. 2006. *Race to Incarcerate*. New York: New Press.

McCorkle, Jill A. 2013. *Breaking Women: Gender, Race, and the New Politics of Imprisonment*. New York: New York University Press.

Minton, Todd D. 2013. *Jail Inmates at Midyear 2012: Statistical Tables*. Bureau of Justice Statistics. Washington, DC: U. S. Department of Justice. NCJ 241264.

———, and Zhen Zeng. 2016. *Jail Inmates in 2015*. Bureau of Justice Statistics. Washington, DC: U. S. Department of Justice. NCJ 250394.

Mol, Annemarie. 2008. *The Logic of Care: Health and the Problem of Patient Choice*. London: Routledge.

Morgan, Lynn M., and Elizabeth F. S. Roberts. 2012. "Reproductive Governance in Latin America." *Anthropology and Medicine* 19(2): 241–54.

Moynihan, Daniel Patrick. 1965. *The Negro Family: The Case for National Action* (The Moynihan Report). Washington, DC: Office of Policy Planning and Research, U. S. Department of Labor.

Mulla, Sameena. 2014. *The Violence of Care: Rape Victims, Forensic Nurses, and Sexual Assault Intervention*. New York: New York University Press.

Murdoch, Sebastian. 2016. "Kentucky Jail Sends Black Woman to Court with No Pants. This Judge Won't Have It." *Huffington Post,* July 30. www.huffingtonpost.com/entry/kentucky-jail-woman-no-pants_us_579cf681e4b0e2e15eb61eec. Accessed January 24, 2017.

Murphy, Sheigla, and Marsha Rosenbaum. 1999. *Pregnant Women on Drugs: Combating Stereotypes and Stigma.* New Brunswick, NJ: Rutgers University Press.

Murton, Tom, and Joe Hyams. 1969. *Accomplices to the Crime.* New York: Grove Press.

National Commission on Correctional Health Care (NCCHC). 2002. *The Health of Soon-to-be-Released Inmates: A Report to Congress.* Washington, DC: U.S. Department of Justice.

———. 2014. *Standards for Health Care in Jails.* Chicago: NCCHC.

———. 2016. Website. www.ncchc.org. Accessed January 24, 2017.

Nelson, Diane. 2010. *Reckoning: The Ends of War in Guatemala.* Durham, NC: Duke University Press.

Nguyen, Vinh-Kim. 2010. *The Republic of Therapy: Triage and Sovereignty in West Africa's Time of AIDS.* Durham, NC: Duke University Press.

Nolan, James L. 1998. *The Therapeutic State: Justifying Government at Century's End.* New York: New York University Press.

North Carolina Supreme Court. 1926. *Spicer v. Williamson.* 132 S.E. 291, 293.

Office for Human Research Protections (OHRP). 1993. "Special Classes of Subjects." *Institutional Review Board Guidebook.* https://archive.hhs.gov /ohrp/irb/irb_chapter6.htm. Accessed January 24, 2017.

Oldani, Michael. 2004. "Thick Prescriptions: Toward an Interpretation of Pharmaceutical Sales Practices." *Medical Anthropology Quarterly* 18(3): 325–56.

Ortner, Sherry B. 1974. "Is Female to Male as Nature Is to Culture?" *Woman, Culture, and Society,* ed. Michelle Zimbalist Rosaldo and Louise Lamphere, 67–88. Stanford, CA: Stanford University Press.

Owen, Barbara. 1998. *"In the Mix": Struggle and Survival in a Women's Prison.* Albany: State University of New York Press.

Padró, Fernando F. 2004. *Statistical Handbook on the Social Safety Net.* Santa Barbara: ABC-CLIO Greenwood.

Paltrow, Lynn, and Jeanne Flavin. 2013. "Arrests of and Forced Interventions on Pregnant Women in the United States, 1973–2005: Implications for Women's Legal Status and Public Health." *Journal of Health Politics, Policy and Law* 38(2): 299–343.

Parenting Inside Out. 2016. www.parentinginsideout.org. Accessed January 24, 2017.

Perkinson, Robert. 2010. *Texas Tough: The Rise of America's Prison Empire.* New York: Metropolitan Books.

Pew Charitable Trusts. 2016. "Do Limits on Family Assets Affect Participation in, Costs of TANF?" www.pewtrusts.org/en/research-and-analysis/issue-briefs /2016/07/do-limits-on-family-assets-affect-participation-in-costs-of-tanf. Accessed January 24, 2017.

Pont, Jörg, Heino Stover, and Hans Wolff. 2012. "Dual Loyalty in Prison Health Care." *American Journal of Public Health* 102(3): 475–80.

Porter, Dorothy. 1999. *Health, Civilization and the State: A History of Public Health from Ancient to Modern Times.* London: Routledge.

Procupez, Valeria. 2008. "Beyond Home: Forging the Domestic in Shared Housing." *Home Cultures: Journal of Architecture, Design and Domestic Space* 5(3): 327–48.

Propper, Alice M. 1982. "Make-believe Families and Homosexuality among Imprisoned Girls." *Criminology* 20(1): 127–38.

Prout, Curtis, and Robert N. Ross. 1988. *Care and Punishment: The Dilemmas of Prison Medicine.* Pittsburgh: University of Pittsburgh Press.

Quezada, James, Laurie K. Hart, and Philippe Bourgois. 2011. "Structural Vulnerability and Health: Latino Migrant Laborers in the United States." *Medical Anthropology* 30(4): 339–62.

Quinn, Audrey. 2014. "In Labor, in Chains: The Outrageous Shackling of Pregnant Inmates." *New York Times,* July 26. www.nytimes.com/2014/07 /27/opinion/sunday/the-outrageous-shackling-of-pregnant-inmates .html?module = Search&mabReward = relbias%3Ar&_r = 1. Accessed January 24, 2017.

Rafter, Nicole H. 1990. *Partial Justice: Women, Prisons and Social Control.* New Brunswick, NJ: Transaction.

Rapp, Rayna. 2001. "Gender, Body, Biomedicine: How Some Feminist Concerns Dragged Reproduction to the Center of Social Theory." *Medical Anthropology Quarterly* 15(4): 466–77.

Rebecca Project for Human Rights. 2010. *Mothers behind Bars: A State-by-State Report Card and Analysis of Federal Policies on Conditions of Confinement for Pregnant and Parenting Women and the Effect on Their Children.* Washington, DC: National Women's Law Center.

Redfield, Peter. 2005. "Doctors, Borders, and Life in Crisis." *Cultural Anthropology* 20(3): 328–61.

———. 2013. *Life in Crisis: The Ethical Journey of Doctors without Borders.* Berkeley: University of California Press.

Reich, Jennifer. 2005. *Fixing Families: Parents, Power, and the Child Welfare System.* New York: Routledge.

Reiter, Keramet. 2012. "The Most Restrictive Alternative: A Litigation History of Solitary Confinement in U. S. Prisons, 1960–2006." *Studies in Law, Politics and Society* 57: 69–123.

Rhodes, Lorna. 1998. "Panoptical Intimacies." *Public Culture* 10(2): 285–311.

———. 2001. "Toward an Anthropology of Prisons." *Annual Review of Anthropology* 30: 65–83.

———. 2004. *Total Confinement: Madness and Reason in the Maximum Security Prison.* Berkeley: University of California Press.

———. 2007. "Supermax as a Technology of Punishment." *Social Research* 74(2): 547–66.

———. 2009. "Supermax Prisons and the Trajectory of Exception." Special issue, New Perspectives on Crime and Criminal Justice. *Studies in Law, Politics and Society* 47: 193–218.

Rich, Josiah D., Sarah E. Wakeman, and Samuel L. Dickman. 2011. "Medicine and the Epidemic of Incarceration in the United States." *New England Journal of Medicine* 364(22): 2081–83.

Riles, Annalise, ed. 2001. *Documents: Artifacts of Modern Knowledge*. Ann Arbor: University of Michigan Press.

Roberts, Dorothy. 1999. *Killing the Black Body: Race, Reproduction, and the Meaning of Liberty*. New York: Vintage Books.

———. 2002. *Shattered Bonds: The Color of Child Welfare*. New York: Basic Civitas Books.

Rold, William. 2008. "Thirty Years after *Estelle v. Gamble:* A Legal Retrospective." *Journal of Correctional Health Care* 14: 11–20.

Roth, Rachel. 2003. *Making Women Pay: The Hidden Costs of Fetal Rights*. New York: Cornell University Press.

———. 2004. "Do Prisoners Have Abortion Rights?" *Feminist Studies* 30(2): 353–81.

———. 2012. " 'She doesn't deserve to be treated like this': Prisons as Sites of Reproductive Injustice." Reproductive Laws for the 21st Century papers. Washington, DC: Center for Women Policy Studies.

———, and Sara L. Ainsworth. 2015. " 'If They Hand You a Paper, You Sign It': A Call to End the Sterilization of Women in Prison." *Hastings Women's Law Journal* 26(1): 7–50.

Routh, D., G. Abess, D. Makin, M. K. Storh, C. Hemmens, and J. Yoo. 2015. "Transgender Inmates in Prisons: A Review of Applicable Statutes and Policies." *International Journal of Offender Therapy and Comparative Criminology* (September 14): Epub ahead of print.

Saar, Malkida Saada, Rebecca Epstein, Lindsay Rosenthal, and Yasmin Vafa. 2015. "The Sexual Abuse to Prison Pipeline: The Girls' Story." Washington, DC: Center for Poverty and Inequality, Georgetown University Law Center.

Sandelowski, Margarete. 2000. *Devices and Desires: Gender, Technology, and American Nursing*. Chapel Hill: University of North Carolina Press.

San Francisco Department of Public Health. www.sfdph.org. Accessed January 24, 2017.

San Francisco Sheriff's Department. 2016. "Sheriff's Administration and Programs Division." www.sfsheriff.com/division_admin_prog.html. Accessed January 24, 2017.

———. 2016. "Sheriff's Custody Division." www.sfsheriff.com/division_custody .html. Accessed January 24, 2017.

Sargent, Carolyn. 2012. "'Deservingness' and the Politics of Health Care." *Social Science and Medicine* 74: 855–57.

Scheper-Hughes, Nancy. 1992. *Death without Weeping: The Violence of Everyday Life in Brazil.* Berkeley: University of California Press.

Schlanger, Margo. 2003. "Inmate Litigation." *Harvard Law Review* 116(6): 1555–706.

Schwartz, Sunny. 2009. *Dreams from the Monster Factory: A Tale of Prison, Redemption, and One Woman's Fight to Restore Justice to All.* New York: Simon and Schuster.

Schwirtz, Michael, Michael Winerip, and Robert Gebeloff. 2016. "The Scourge of Racial Bias in New York's State Prisons." *New York Times.* December 3. www.nytimes.com/2016/12/03/nyregion/new-york-state-prisons-inmates-racial-bias.html?_r=0. Accessed January 19, 2017.

Segura, Liliana. 2013. "With 2.3 Million People Incarcerated in the US, Prisons Are Big Business." *Nation,* October 1. www.thenation.com/prison-profiteers. Accessed January 24, 2017.

Sentencing Project. 2015. "Incarcerated Women: Fact Sheet." Washington, DC: Sentencing Project. www.sentencingproject.org/wp-content/uploads/2016/02/Incarcerated-Women-and-Girls.pdf. Accessed January 24, 2017.

Shalhoub, Naima. 2015. "Live in San Francisco County Jail." Recorded May 5, 2015.

Showers, Jacy. 1993. "Assessing and Remedying Parenting Knowledge among Women Inmates." *Journal of Offender Rehabilitation* 20: 35–46.

Silliman, Jael, and Anannya Bhattacharjee, eds. 2002. *Policing the National Body: Race, Gender and Criminalization in the United States.* Boston: South End Press.

Sim, Joe. 1990. *Medical Power in Prisons: The Prison Medical Service in England, 1774–1989.* Buckingham: Open University Press.

Simon, Jonathan. 2007. *Governing through Crime: How the War on Crime Transformed American Democracy and Created a Culture of Fear.* Oxford: Oxford University Press.

———. 2013. "Courts and the Penal State: Lessons from California's Decades of Prison Litigation and Expansion." *California Journal of Politics and Policy* 5(2): 252–65.

———. 2014. *Mass Incarceration on Trial: A Remarkable Court Decision and the Future of Prisons in America.* New York: New Press.

Sistersong: Women of Color Reproductive Justice Collective. www.sistersong.net. Accessed January 24, 2017.

Somers, Margaret, and Christopher N.J. Roberts. 2008. "Toward a New Sociology of Rights: A Genealogy of 'Buried Bodies' of Citizenship and Human Rights." *Annual Review of Law in Social Science* 4: 385–425.

Stack, Carol. 1975. *All Our Kin: Strategies for Survival in a Black Community.* New York: Harper and Row.

State Refor(u)m. 2016. *Where States Stand on Medicaid Expansion Decisions.* Produced by Anita Cardwell and Caitlin Sheedy. www.nashp.org/states-stand-medicaid-expansion-decisions/. Accessed January 19, 2017.

Stevenson, Lisa. 2012. "The Psychic Life of Biopolitics: Survival, Cooperation, and Inuit Community." *American Ethnologist* 39(3): 592–613.

———. 2014. *Life beside Itself: Imagining Care in the Canadian Arctic.* Oakland: University of California Press.

Stoller, Nancy. 2003. "Space, Place and Movement as Aspects of Health Care in Three Women's Prisons." *Social Science and Medicine* 56: 2263–75.

Stone et al. v. City and County of San Francisco et al. 1992. U.S. District Court. C-78-2774 WHO.

Sufrin, Carolyn. 2015. "'Doctor, Why Didn't You Adopt *My* Baby?': Observant Participation, Care, and the Simultaneous Practice of Medicine and Anthropology." *Culture, Medicine, and Psychiatry* 39(4): 614–33.

Sufrin, Carolyn, Mitchell D. Creinin, and Judy C. Chang. 2009. "Incarcerated Women and Abortion Provision: A Survey of Correctional Health Providers." *Perspectives on Sexual and Reproductive Health* 41(1): 6–11.

Sufrin, Carolyn, Alexa Kolbi-Molinas, and Rachel Roth. 2015. "Reproductive Justice, Health Disparities, and Incarcerated Women in the United States." *Perspectives in Sexual and Reproductive Health* 47(4): 213–19.

Sufrin, Carolyn, Tianyi Oxnard, Joe Goldenson, Kristin Simonson, and Andrea Jackson. 2015. "Long-Acting, Reversible Contraceptives for Incarcerated Women: Feasibility and Safety of On-site Provision." *Perspectives in Sexual and Reproductive Health* 47(4): 203–11.

Sykes, Gresham. 2007. *The Society of Captives: A Study of a Maximum Security Prison.* Princeton, NJ: Princeton University Press.

Talvi, Silja J.A. 2007. *Women behind Bars: The Crisis of Women in the U.S. Prison System.* Emeryville, CA: Seal Press.

Taussig, Michael. 1997. *The Magic of the State.* New York: Routledge.

Ticktin, Miriam. 2006. "Where Ethics and Politics Meet: The Violence of Humanitarianism in France." *American Ethnologist* 33(1): 33–49.

———. 2011. *Casualties of Care: Immigration and the Politics of Humanitarianism in France.* Berkeley: University of California Press.

Tonry, Michael. 1995. *Malign Neglect: Race, Crime and Punishment in America.* New York: Oxford University Press.

Tsing, Anna Lowenhaupt. 1992. "Monster Stories: Women Charged with Perinatal Endangerment." In *Uncertain Terms: Negotiating Gender in American Culture,* ed. Faye Ginsburg and Anna Lowenhaupt Tsing, 284–99. Boston: Beacon Press.

Turner, Victor. 1969. *The Ritual Process: Structure and Anti-Structure*. Chicago: Aldine.

United States Department of Justice. 2016a. "Phasing Out Our Use of Private Prisons." www.justice.gov/opa/blog/phasing-out-our-use-private-prisons. Accessed January 24, 2017.

———. 2016b. "Investigation of the Baltimore City Police Department." www.justice.gov/opa/file/883366/download. Accessed January 24, 2017.

United States Sentencing Commission. 2015. "Statement on Bipartisan Sentencing Reform Legislation." www.ussc.gov/about/news/press-releases/november-18–2015. Accessed January 24, 2017.

United States Supreme Court. 1976. *Estelle v. Gamble*. 429 U.S. 97.

———. 1994. *Farmer v. Brennan*, 511 U.S. 825.

———. 2011. *Brown v. Plata*, 09–1233, 563 U.S. 493.

Van Derbeken, Jaxon. 2010. "Drug Lab Scandal Jeopardizes Hundreds of Cases." *SF Gate*, March 28. www.sfgate.com/news/article/Drug-lab-scandal-jeopardizes-hundreds-of-cases-3269092.php. Accessed January 24, 2017.

Van Gennep, Arnold. 1966. *The Rites of Passage*. Chicago: University of Chicago Press.

Villalobos, Ana. 2014. *Motherload: Making It All Better in Insecure Times*. Oakland: University of California Press.

Villanueva, Chandra Kring. 2009. *Mothers, Infants, and Imprisonment: A National Look at Prison Nurseries and Community-Based Alternatives*. New York: Institute on Women and Criminal Justice, Women's Prison Association.

von Zielbauer, Paul. 2005. "As Health Care in Jails Goes Private, 10 Days Can Be a Death Sentence." *New York Times*, February 27.

Wacquant, Loïc. 2001. "Deadly Symbiosis: When Ghetto and Prison Meet and Mesh." In *Mass Imprisonment: Social Causes and Consequences*, ed. David Garland. London: Sage.

———. 2002. "The Curious Eclipse of Prison Ethnography in the Age of Mass Incarceration." *Ethnography* 3(4): 371–97.

———. 2009a. *Punishing the Poor: The Neoliberal Government of Social Insecurity*. Durham, NC: Duke University Press.

———. 2009b. *Prisons of Poverty*. Minneapolis: University of Minnesota Press.

———. 2010a. "Class, Race and Hyperincarceration in Revanchist America." *Daedalus* 140(3): 70–90.

———. 2010b. "Prisoner Re-entry as Myth and Ceremony." *Dialectical Anthropology* 34(4): 605–20.

———. 2011. "Habitus as Topic and Tool: Reflections on Becoming a Prizefighter." *Qualitative Research in Psychology* 8: 81–92.

Waldram, James. 2012. *Hound Pound Narrative: Sexual Offender Habilitation and the Anthropology of Therapeutic Intervention*. Berkeley: University of California Press.

Ward, David, and Gene Kassebaum. 1965. *Women's Prison: Sex and Social Structure*. New York: Aldine.

Warner, Kebby. 2010. "Pregnancy, Motherhood, and Loss in Prison: A Personal Story." In *Interrupted Life: Experiences of Incarcerated Women in the United States*, ed. Rickie Solinger, Paula C. Johnson, Martha L. Raimon, Tina Reynolds, and Ruby C. Tapia. Berkeley: University of California Press.

Watterson, Kathryn. 1996. *Women in Prison: Inside the Concrete Womb*. Boston: Northeastern Press.

Weber, Max. 2006. "Bureaucracy." In *The Anthropology of the State: A Reader*, ed. Aradhana Sharma and Akhil Gupta, 49–70. Malden, MA: Blackwell.

Weir, Lorna. 2006. *Pregnancy, Risk and Biopolitics: On the Threshold of the Living Subject*. New York: Routledge.

Wendland, Clare. 2006. "The Vanishing Mother: Cesarean Section and 'Evidence-Based Obstetrics.'" *Medical Anthropology Quarterly* 21(2): 218–33.

Weston, Kath. 1991. *Families We Choose: Lesbians, Gays, Kinship*. New York: Columbia University Press.

Whitmarsh, Ian. 2008. *Biomedical Ambiguities: Race, Asthma, and the Contested Meaning of Genetic Research in the Caribbean*. Ithaca, NY: Cornell University Press.

———. 2014. "The No / Name of the Institution." *Anthropological Quarterly* 87(3): 855–81.

Willen, Sarah. 2011. "Do 'Illegal' Im / migrants Have a Right to Health? Engaging Ethical Theory as Social Practice at a Tel Aviv Open Clinic." *Medical Anthropology Quarterly* 25(3): 303–30.

———. 2012. "How Is Health-related 'Deservingness' Reckoned? Perspectives from Unauthorized Im / migrants in Tel Aviv." *Social Science in Medicine* 74(6): 812–21.

Willers, Denise M., Jeffrey F. Peipert, Jenifer E. Allsworth, Michael D. Stein, Jennifer S. Rose, and Jennifer G. Clarke. 2008. "Prevalence and Predictors of Sexually Transmitted Infection among Newly Incarcerated Females." *Sexually Transmitted Diseases* 35(1): 68–72.

Willse, Craig. 2015. *The Value of Homelessness*. Minneapolis: University of Minnesota Press.

Women's Prison Association. 2009. "Quick Facts: Women and Criminal Justice." New York: Institute on Women and Criminal Justice. www .wpaonline.org/resources/quick-facts. Accessed January 24, 2017.

Žižek, Slavoj. 2008. *Violence: Six Sideways Reflections*. New York: Picador.

Index

Page numbers in italic refer to illustrations.

304 INDEX

266n26; low birth weight, 125; preterm
birth, 125, 141; in shackles, 148, 149, 152,
174; stillbirth, 125, 126, 134
birth control. *See* contraception (birth
control)
Black Lives Matter, 13, 238
black women, 22, 36, 236; hypermedicalized
model of pregnancy and, 140–41; incarceration rate of, 9, 124, 247n31; perceived
epidemic of "crack babies" and, 11–12;
stereotyping of poor black mothers, 12, 14,
45, 278n8; welfare reform and, 45
Bledsoe, Caroline, 272n2, 280n31
bleeding, vaginal, 31, 87, 135, 143, 145
BMI (body mass index), 93
boredom, 107, 113, 276n7
Borneman, John, 279n14
Bourgois, Philippe, 26, 215
B-pod housing unit, 109, 127, 182, 189, 197,
214, 228
breastfeeding, 171, 172–73, 183, 274n33,
274n35
Bridges, Khiara, 140, 142
Brodwin, Paul, 82–83
Brown v. Plata, 29, 53
bureaucracy, 90, 99–100, 116, 197, 200,
265n18; enactment of custody and, 191;
lack of sentiment in, 52, 195
Butler, Judith, 22

California, 31, 246n14, 255n25; depopulation
of overcrowded prisons, 36, 53, 237;
Kaiser Permanente care organization,
263n12; law against shackling of pregnant women, 149–50; Pelican Bay supermax prison, 266n25; "Three Strikes" law,
46, 256n32; unlawful sterilizations in,
124–25
California Coalition for Women Prisoners, 60
Cantor, Julie, 265n2
capitalism, 169, 256n28
"carceral burden," 41–42, 51, 53, 58, 90, 101,
234
carcerality, 6, 15, 61, 200, 214, 240–41;
caregiving and, 35; degrading elements
of, 190; entry into carceral institutions,
16–17; gendered dimension of, 9; incoherence of, 83; motherhood co-produced
with, 183; regimentation structure of, 218
care: assumptions of, 21–24; custody as form
of, 186; equivalence of, 88–89; feminist
theories of, 23; jail clinic staff approach

to, 106–7; labors of, 23; MCRs as social
scaffolding of, 89–94, *92;* pastoral, 186,
190, 205, 276n4; patient-refused, 82;
protective gestures and, 88; recidivism
and, 74; relational aspects of, 14, 22, 63,
67, 70, 142; refusal of, *96–97, 98,* 99,
265n2, 266nn25–26; routines of, 101–2,
115–16. *See also* "correctional health care"
caregiving, 33, 35, 78, 80, 100, 179; biomedical, 235; complications of, 102; familial
relations and, 213; intimacy of, 21, 22,
241; primary caregiver, 232
Carlen, Pat, 246n8
Carr, E. Summerson, 168, 169
Carson, Ben, 238
case management, 30
CHART (Correctional Health Assessment
Record and Tracking), 75, 78, 113,
267n12; MCRs and, 89, 90, 105; tedium
of, 111–13; triage questionnaire, 65–66
"cheeking," 109
childbirth. *See* birth
childcare, 45, 107
child custody, 4, 121, 156, 160, 176, 274n36
Child Protective Services (CPS), 6, 133, 152,
165, 205, 230; "One Family" program
and, 166, 175–76; "police hold" on newborns, 20, 171–73; removal of children
from mothers, 26, 274n34; scripts
rehearsed and performed for CPS workers, 169; TDMs (team decision-making
meetings), 226; time spent in drug
treatment programs and, 280n36
children, 21, 229–32; abandonment of, 81;
parental incarceration and, 9, 10, 247n33;
separated from mothers at birth, 126;
supervised visits with babies, 179
child welfare system, 11, 45, 143, 172, 232;
motherhood managed through, 230;
supervised visits with newborns and, 236
"chronos" (special privilege forms), 90,
94–96, *95,* 99, 266n22
civil rights activism, 44
Clemmer, Robert, 253n135
Clinton, Bill, 45, 238
Coates, Ta-Nehisi, 255n18
Comfort, Megan, 46, 274n39
Community Mental Health Act (1963),
255n14
compassion, 30, 58; care and, 21, 24; deservingness and, 68–69; triage and, 67
consent decree, in San Francisco County
Jail, 51

Constitution, U.S., 7, 52

constitutional rights, 7, 56, 241; *Estelle* mandate and, 53, 94, 258–59n66; state's carceral burden and, 234

contraception (birth control), 10, 133, 231, 280–81n3; IUDs, 89, 179; Norplant birth control implants, 12

Corizon, 57–58

"correctional health care," 42, 54–58, 88, 259n75

County Jail 1 (CJ1), 91, 127, 154, 156, 160; "angry chair" in, 63–64; as "booking jail," 27, 214; inmate release from, 102; medical clearance from, 72–73; patient privacy in, 78; triage in, 62–63, 65, 66, 68, 69

County Jail 2 (CJ2), 27, 28, 65, 72, 274n35; "count time" of inmates in, 113; 2 South clinic area, 102

"crack babies," myth of, 11, 248n51

crack cocaine, 1, 70, 93, 107, 157, 214; crack pipes, 2; use during pregnancy, 234

crime/criminality, 43, 46, 147, 277–78n1; criminal identity, 87; as dangerous life, 209; drugs and, 4; fear of, 44; felonies, 25; nonviolent, 9, 28, 29; violent, 8, 256n30, 256n32; women's pathways to, 11

criminal justice system, 5, 7, 25, 122, 143; inhumanity of, 203; juvenile detention, 10; mother-infant bonding and, 166; racial bias in, 14; racial dispossession and, 46; racist policies, 8; reform of, 20, 34, 239; in San Francisco, 48

"cruel optimism," 36, 159, 251n103

custody, 6, 36, 88; birth in, 124, 133, 145; care and, 60–61; as choice, 197–200; as everyday work of jail, 30, 185–87; medical routines and, 83; medical services separated from, 203–4; parental role of deputies, 205–7; pastoral, 187, 196, 198, 204; proximity and distance in, 196–97; routines of, 102; as safety, 190–93; as sociality, 193–95; triage and, 62, 71; ubiquity of punishment, 187–190. *See also* child custody

custody card, 71

Das, Veena, 271n52

"deliberate indifference," 41–42, 52–53, 56, 60, 70, 142, 258n62

deputies, 30, 77, 85, 113; choice of employment, 195, 277n15; dependency on, 188; enactment of custody by, 192; favoritism toward some inmates, 127–29; interpretations of carceral environment, 200–203;

jail care and, 83, 84; jail clinic routine and, 101; as mediators, 203–204; parental custody and, 205–7; "pod deputy," 134; pregnant, 134, 137, 146; privilege system and, 95–96; refusal of care and, 97, 99; views of pregnant inmates, 121, 133

deservingness, of care, 16, 35, 43, 61, 83, 99, 235; carceral burden and, 41–42; maternal ideal and, 140; MCRs (medical care request forms) and, 93; moral judgment and, 85; obligation to care and, 51; routines of care and, 116; triage and, 66–69

Desjarlais, Robert, 279n25

diabetes, 62–63, 65, 66; blood sugar checks and, 107, 113; as "high risk" medical condition, 77

"direct supervision," in pods, 193

disease prevention, 59

doctors, 33, 55, 56, 251n95; doctor-patient relationship, 18; "dual loyalty problem" and, 57; inmates shamed by, 126

documents, relational character of, 99–100

Dolovich, Sharon, 42, 51, 258n66

DOT (directly observed therapy), 109, 111

Douglas, Mary, 270n37

doulas, 4, 193

D-pod housing unit, 138, 139; closure of, 278n10; drug treatment program in, 168, 210, 223; "sunset circle" in, 211; talent show in, 3, 137, 223–24

drug addiction, 1, 4, 5, 8, 18, 141; abandonment of children and, 81; criminal stories and, 86; factors in interplay with, 201; heroin, 95, 107, 157, 167; marginalization and, 84; medicalization of, 12; neoliberal ideology of personal responsibility and, 161, 272n10; opiate withdrawal, 10, 268n1; of pregnant women inmates, 34; reproduction shaped by, 181; sexual abuse and, 143; withdrawal from, 32

drug courts, 7, 232, 264n20

drug laws, 36, 37, 46

drug treatment programs, 28, 48, 49, 50, 168, 183, 242; communal living in residential programs, 232; CPS and, 176; homelessness and, 215; inmates' ruminations on life in, 208–9; for mothers, 231; women broken down by, 278n8. *See also* Revelation House

dwelling, in carceral institutions, 215–17, 219

Eighth Amendment (prohibition of "cruel and unusual punishment"), 7, 41, 52, 271n53